DISCARD

CHICAGO PUBLIC LIBRARY
WRIGHTWOOD - ASHBURN BRANCH
8530 S. KEDZIE 60652

African Americans in the Media Today

African Americans in the Media Today

An Encyclopedia

Volume 1

A–L

SAM G. RILEY

GREENWOOD PRESS
Westport, Connecticut • London

Library of Congress Cataloging-in-Publication Data

Riley, Sam G.
    African Americans in the media today : an encyclopedia / Sam G. Riley.
      p. cm.
    Includes bibliographical references and index.
    ISBN: 978–0–313–33679–9 (set : alk. paper)—ISBN: 978–0–313–33680–5
    (vol. 1 : alk. paper)—ISBN: 978–0–313–33681–2 (vol. 2: alk. paper)
    1. African Americans in the mass media industry—Encyclopedias.
    2. Mass media—United States—Encyclopedias. I. Title.
    P94.5.A372U568   2007
    302.23089'96073—dc22   2007008192

British Library Cataloguing in Publication Data is available.

Copyright © 2007 by Sam G. Riley

All rights reserved. No portion of this book may be
reproduced, by any process or technique, without the
express written consent of the publisher.

Library of Congress Catalog Card Number: 2007008192
ISBN-13: 978–0–313–33679–9 (Set)   ISBN-10: 0–313–33679–2 (Set)
        978–0–313–33680–5 (Vol. 1)   0–313–33680–6 (Vol. 1)
        978–0–313–33681–2 (Vol. 2)   0–313–33681–4 (Vol. 2)

First published in 2007

Greenwood Press, 88 Post Road West, Westport, CT 06881
An imprint of Greenwood Publishing Group, Inc.
www.greenwood.com

Printed in the United States of America

∞

The paper used in this book complies with the
Permanent Paper Standard issued by the National
Information Standards Organization (Z39.48–1984).

10 9 8 7 6 5 4 3 2 1

This reference work is dedicated to the countless individuals who, due to racial prejudice, were unable to find success of the kind showcased in these two volumes of biographical career sketches.

Contents

List of Entries	ix
Entries of People by Field or Endeavor	xv
Acknowledgments	xxi
Introduction	xxiii
Timeline	xxix
The Encyclopedia	1
Selected Bibliography	547
Index	561

List of Entries

Mumia Abu-Jamal: imprisoned former syndicated columnist
Norma Adams-Wade: *Dallas Morning News*
Ronnie Agnew: executive editor, columnist, the *Clarion-Ledger* (Jackson, MS)
Tina Alexander-Sellers: news director, KTRE (Lufkin, TX)
Ron Allen: NBC news correspondent
Monroe Anderson: editor, *Savoy* magazine
Caesar Andrews: executive editor, *Detroit Free Press*
Jabari Asim: The Washington Post Writers Group columnist
Mervin Raymond Aubespin: artist/reporter/administrator, *Louisville Courier-Journal*

Isaac J. Bailey: *Knight Ridder* columnist
Dean P. Baquet: Executive vice president and editor, *Los Angeles Times*
Betty Winston Bayé: Gannett Newspapers columnist
Lerone Bennett: executive editor, *Ebony* magazine
Kevin B. Blackistone: sports columnist, *Dallas Morning News*
Gerald M. Boyd: deceased managing editor, the *New York Times*
Edward "Ed" R. Bradley: deceased correspondent, *60 Minutes* (deceased)
Donna Britt: The Washington Post Writers Group columnist
William A. Brower: deceased columnist, the *Blade of Toledo*
James Brown: cohost, "NFL Sunday," Fox
William Anthony "Tony" Brown: former host, "Tony Brown's Journal," PBS

Kenneth F. Bunting: executive editor, *Seattle Post-Intelligencer*
Maureen Bunyon: anchor, ABC 7 (Washington, DC)
Earl Caldwell: ex-reporter, columnist, the *New York Times*
Jonathan Capehart: former editorial writer, columnist, *N.Y. Daily News*
Farai Chideya: TV political analyst, radio host; ex-columnist, *N.Y. Daily News*
Barbara Ciara: managing editor/anchor, WTKR News (Norfolk, VA)
Ron Claiborne: correspondent, ABC News
Keith T. Clinkscales: president, *Vibe* magazine
Errol A. Cockfield Jr.: *Newsday* bureau chief
Desiree Cooper: *Detroit Free Press* columnist
Cheryl Corley: senior reporter, Chicago Bureau, NPR
Stanley Crouch: *N.Y. Daily News* columnist
James N. Crutchfield: president and publisher, the *Beacon Journal* (Akron, OH)
George E. Curry: editor and columnist, BlackPress USA.com
Mary Cecelia Curtis: *Knight Ridder* columnist

Leon DeCosta Dash Jr.: ex-the *Washington Post* reporter
Joe Davidson: reporter, *Philadelphia Bulletin*
Allison J. Davis: CBS vice president, helped launch MSNBC Online
Belva Davis: pioneering West Coast broadcaster
Merlene Davis: *Lexington Herald*-Leader

List of Entries

Wayne J. Dawkins: contributing editor, BlackJournalists.com
Michael Days: *Philadelphia Daily News* editor
Eric Deggans: media critic, *St. Petersburg Times*
Paul Delaney: reporter, the *New York Times*
Lewis Walter Diuguid: *Kansas City Star* columnist
Kyle Donovan: publisher, *NV* magazine
William Douglas: White House Correspondent, *Knight Ridder*
Harold Dow: correspondent, *48 Hours* (CBS)
Joel P. Dreyfuss: editor-in-chief, Red Herring Web site, ex-editor, *Fortune*
Karen Brown Dunlap: president, Poynter Institute

Alfred Adam Edmond Jr.: editor-in-chief, *Black Enterprise Magazine*
Tamala Edwards: ABC-TV anchor and correspondent
Laurence (Larry) A. Elder: Creators Syndicate columnist
Lolis Eric Elie: *Times Picayune* (New Orleans) columnist
E. David Ellington: founder, NetNoir online media service
Sidmel Karen Estes-Sumpter: executive editor, Fox 5 (Atlanta, GA)

Faith Fancher: reporter, KTVU-TV (Oakland, CA)
Harris Faulkner: FOX announcer
Arthur Fennell: anchor/managing editor, Comcast Network (Philadelphia, PA)
Renee Ferguson: investigative reporter, NBC News
Michael Fields: southern bureau chief for NPR News
Albert E. Fitzpatrick: retired executive/editor, *Akron Beacon Journal*, *Knight Ridder*
Michael A. Fletcher: reporter, the *Washington Post*
Charles Gerald Fraser Jr.: ex-reporter, the *New York Times*, now with *Earth Times*
Sam Fulwood III: columnist, the *Plain Dealer* (Cleveland, OH)

Dorothy Pearl Butler Gilliam: just-retired columnist, the *Washington Post*
Wendell Goler: White House correspondent, FOX News Channel
Sean Gonsalves: *Cape Cod Times* columnist

Malvin "Mal" Russell Goode: deceased ABC news reporter
Ed Gordon: host of "News & Notes with Ed Gordon" on NPR
Earl Gilbert Graves: founder, publisher, *Black Enterpris*
Lauren Green: news update anchor, FOX News Channel
Vertamae Grosvenor: cultural correspondent, NPR
Bryant Gumbel: "Real Sports with Bryant Gumbel," HBO
Greg Gumbel: sportscaster, CBS

Princell Hair: executive vice president and general manager, CNN/US
Arsenio Hall: former host, "The Arsenio Hall Show"
Charlotte H. Hall: editor, vice president, *Orlando Sentinel*
Ken Hamblin: former columnist, radio commentator
C.B. Hanif: *Palm Beach Post* ombudsman
Jay T. Harris: ex-publisher, *San Jose Mercury*
Leon M. Harris Jr.: WJLA-TV, Washington, DC
Karla Garrett Harshaw: editor, Springfield (OH) *News-Sun*
Hermene Demaris Hartman: founder, *N'DIGO*
Wil Haygood: Style Section writer, the *Washington Post*
Angelo B. Henderson: reporter, the *Wall Street Journal*, *Detroit News*
Bob Herbert: the *New York Times* News Service columnist
Fred Hickman: sportscaster, ESPN
Steven A. Holmes: reporter, the *New York Times*
Lester Holt: MSNBC news anchor
Alan J. Hughes: features editor, *Black Enterprise Magazine*
Catherine "Cathy" Liggins Hughes: founder, Black News Talk Radio: WOL-AM
Karen Hunter: *NY Daily News* columnist
Charlayne Hunter-Gault: former national correspondent, the *NewsHour*

Gwen Ifill: moderator of Washington Week, on public television
Bennie Ivory: ex-editor, *Louisville Courier-Journal*

Derrick Z. Jackson: *Boston Globe* columnist
Robert L. Jamieson Jr.: *Seattle Post-Intelligencer* columnist

List of Entries

Vernon D. Jarrett: *Chicago Tribune, Sun-Times* (deceased)

Stebbins Jefferson: *Palm Beach Post* columnist

John Harold Johnson: deceased founder, publisher, Johnson Publishing Company

Robert L. Johnson: founder of Black Entertainment Television

Roy S. Johnson: online columnist, AOL BlackVoices

Starlet Marie Jones: TV host, "The View," ABC

Thomas Joyner: host, *The Tom Joyner Show* on radio

Eugene A. Kane: columnist, *Milwaukee Journal Sentinel*

Tonnya Kennedy: managing editor, the *State* (Columbia, SC)

Allison Keyes: reporter, "The Travis Smiley Show," NPR

Colbert (Colby) I. King: *Washington Post* columnist

Emery King: anchor, WDIV-TV (Detroit, MI)

Beverly Kirk: newscaster, PBS /NPR Newsbrief

Sam Harold Lacy: deceased sportswriter, *Baltimore Afro-American*

Don Lemon: coanchor, NBC5 News

Dwight Lewis: columnist, *The Tennessean* (Nashville, TN)

Edward T. Lewis: CEO, Essence Communications

Norman Alton Lockman: Gannett News Service columnist (deceased)

Errol T. Louis: *New York Sun*, the *Daily News* columnist

Herbert Lowe: staff writer, *Newsday*

Vicki Mabrey: ABC *Nightline* correspondent

Marcus Mabry: chief of correspondents, *Newsweek*

Joseph Edward Madison: radio host

Paula Walker Madison: president and general manager, KNBC4 (Los Angeles, CA)

Julianne Marie Malveaux: CEO, Last Word Productions, columnist

Suzanne Malveaux: CNN anchor

Pluria W. Marshall Sr.: chairman, National Black Media Coalition

Sherrie Marshall: executive editor of Georgia's *Macon Telegraph*

Michel McQueen Martin: Nightline correspondent and guest anchor, ABC News

Roland S. Martin: Creators Syndicate columnist, news editor, *Savoy* magazine

Paul S. Mason: senior vice president, ABC News

Deborah Mathis: Gannett News Service columnist; TV commentator

Bill Maxwell: former the *New York Times* News Service columnist

Nancy Hicks Maynard: first black mainstream newswoman in New York City. Now retired

Sheryl McCarthy: *Newsday* columnist

Angela McGlowan: Fox News analyst

Robert G. McGruder: deceased executive editor, the *Detroit Free Press*

Kevin Merida: reporter, the *Washington Post*

John Xavier Miller: public editor and columnist, *Detroit Free Press*

Courtland Milloy: The Washington Post Writers Group columnist

Everett J. Mitchell II: editor, the *Tennessean* (Nashville, TN)

Mary A. Mitchell: *Chicago Sun-Times* columnist

Russ Mitchell: coanchor, CBS News Saturday Morning

Bryan K. Monroe: assistant vice president, news, *Knight Ridder*

Acel Moore: *Philadelphia Inquirer* columnist

Gregory L. Moore: editor, *Denver Post*

Thomas Morgan III: reporter, the *New York Times*, *Washington Post*

Valerie Coleman Morris: finance news anchor, CNN

Jill Nelson: freelance journalist, MSNBC.com commentator

Vickie Newton: anchor, DMOV-TV (St. Louis, MO)

Art Norman: coanchor, NBC5 News

Tony Norman: *Pittsburgh Post-Gazette* columnist

Michele Norris: host of NPR's "All Things Considered"

Maria de la Soledad O'Brien: anchor, CNN

Clarence Eugene Page: Tribune Media Services columnist

Lutrelle F. Palmer: deceased Chicago columnist, radio commentator, newspaper publisher

Richard D. Parsons: CEO, Time Warner

Leslie (Les) Payne: Tribune Media Services columnist, associate managing editor, *Newsday*

List of Entries

Brenda Payton: *Oakland Tribune* columnist
Joseph Perkins: Newspaper Enterprise Association columnist
David Person: *Huntsville Times* columnist
Peggy Mitchell Peterman: *St. Petersburg Times* columnist (deceased)
Julian Martin Phillips: FOX News anchor, "Fox and Friends Weekend"
Ponchitta Marie Anne Vincent Pierce: TV host, producer; magazine writer/editor
Byron Pitts: national correspondent, CBS News
Leonard Pitts Jr.: *Knight Ridder* columnist
Alexander Ceasar Poinsett: an editor at *Ebony* magazine
Marquita Pool-Eckert: retired producer, CBS News
Renee Francine Poussaint: former CBS network correspondent
Adam Clayton Powell III: former broadcast executive, new-media proponent
Shaun Powell: sports columnist, *Newsday*
Condace Pressley: WSB Radio, Atlanta, assistant program director
Richard E. Prince: Gannett Newspapers columnist
Glenn Proctor: vice president and executive editor, *Richmond Times-Dispatch*

Norma R. Quarles: news anchor, reporter, CNN, NBC

James Ragland: *Dallas Morning News* columnist
Toni Randolph: reporter, Minnesota Public Radio
Ahmad Rashad: sportscaster, NBC producer
William James Raspberry: former The Washington Post Writers Group columnist
Bob Reid: production head, Discovery Channel Primetime
William C. Rhoden: sports columnist, the *New York Times*
Linda Johnson Rice: publisher, Johnson Publishing Company
Clem Richardson: *NY Daily News* columnist
W. Curtis Riddle: president and publisher, the *News Journal* (Wilmington, DE)
Wilbert Rideau: former editor the *Angolite Magazine*
Jason L. Riley: senior editorial writer, *The Wall Street Journal*

Rochelle Riley: Columnist *Detroit Free Press*
Deborah Roberts: reporter, ABC News
Osborne "Ozzie" Sinclaire Roberts Jr.: *San Diego Union-Tribune* columnist
Robin Roberts: sportscaster, ABC, ESPN
Troy Roberts: *48 Hours* correspondent, CBS News
Eugene Robinson: WPWG columnist
Maxie (Max) Cleveland Robinson Jr.: deceased cohost, *ABC World News Tonight*
Johnathan A. Rodgers: CBS executive, CEO of TV-One
Albert Lincoln Roker: NBC weatherman, *Today Show* host
Carl Thomas Rowan: King Features Syndicate, deceased
Mark E. Russell: managing editor, *Orlando Sentinel*

Terence Samuel: ex-chief correspondent, *U.S. News & World Report*
Otis L. Sanford: managing editor, *Commercial Appeal* (Memphis, TN)
Barry Saunders: *News and Observer* (Raleigh, NC) columnist
Warner Saunders: coanchor, NBC5 News
Neal T. Scarbrough: vice president, editor-in-chief, ESPN.com
Stuart Scott: ESPN anchor, "Sports Center"
Bernard Shaw: retired anchor, CNN News
E.R. Shipp: *NY Daily News* columnist
Debra Adams Simmons: editor, *Akron Beacon Journal*
Carole Simpson: former ABC, NBC news anchor
Michelle Singletary: The Washington Post Writers Group columnist
Tavis Smiley: host, "The Tavis Smiley Show," NPR
Clarence O. Smith: cofounder, Essence Communications
Elmer Smith: *Philadelphia Daily News* columnist
Thomas Sowell: Creators Syndicate columnist
Collins Spencer: news anchor, "CNN Headline News"
Brent A. Staples: the *New York Times* editorial writer
Shay Stevens: overnight editor, NPR News
Pearl Stewart: founder, Black College Wire
Charles (Chuck) Sumner Stone Jr.: former Universal Press Syndicate columnist
Rene Syler: anchor, "The Early Show," CBS

List of Entries

Susan L. Taylor: former editor-in-chief, *Essence* magazine
Pierre Thomas: Justice Department correspondent, ABC News
Wendi C. Thomas: columnist, *Commercial Appeal* (Memphis, TN)
Pamela Thomas-Graham: former CEO, CNBC
Melba Tolliver: retired anchor, reporter for News 12 (Long Island, NY)
Hollis Towns: managing editor of the *Cincinnati Enquirer*
Cynthia Anne Tucker: Universal Press Syndicate columnist
Lisa Tutman: reporter, NBC5 News

Adaora Udoji: news correspondent, CNN News Worldwide

Adrian Walker: *Boston Globe* columnist
Hal Walker: deceased CBS News correspondent
Liz Walker: newsmagazine show host, WBZ (Boston, MA)
Carlos Watson: political analyst, CNN News
Diane Marie Weathers: former editor-in-chief, *Essence* magazine
Tonyaa Weathersbee: *Florida Times-Union* columnist

Mark Whitaker: editor, *Newsweek*
Jack E. White: retired columnist, correspondent *Time* magazine
Fredricka Whitfield: news anchor, CNN/US (Atlanta, GA)
Jason Whitlock: sports columnist, *Kansas City Star*
DeWayne Wickham: Gannett Newspapers columnist
Michael Wilbon: sports columnist, *Washington Post*
Ralph Wiley: deceased sports columnist, *Oakland Tribune*, *Sports Illustrated*
Roger Wood Wilkins: publisher, *The Crisis*
Armstrong Williams: former TMS columnist, TV host
Byron Williams: *Oakland Tribune* columnist
Juan Williams: correspondent, "Morning Edition," NPR, Fox anchor/reporter
Michael Paul Williams: columnist, *Richmond Times-Dispatch*
Montel Brian Williams: television show host
Walter Edward Williams: Creators Syndicate coloumnist
Brenda Wilson: senior correspondent, editor, NPR
Oprah Gail Winfrey: television show host
N. Don Wycliff: *Chicago Tribune* columnist

Entries of People by Field or Endeavor

Syndicated Columnists

Mumia Abu-Jamal: imprisoned syndicated columnist
Jabari Asim: The Washington Post Writers Group
Isaac J. Bailey: *Knight Ridder*
Betty Winston Bayé: Gannett Newspapers
Donna Britt: The Washington Post Writers Group
Mary Cecelia Curtis: *Knight Ridder*
Laurence (Larry) A. Elder: Creators Syndicate
Bob A. Herbert: *New York Times* News Service
Norman Alton Lockman: Gannett News Service
Roland S. Martin: Creators Syndicate, News Editor for *Savoy* Magazine, radio host
Deborah Mathis: Gannett News Service, TV commentator
Bill Maxwell: *New York Times* News Service
Courtland Milloy: The Washington Post Writers Group
Clarence Eugene Page: Tribune Media Services
Leslie (Les) Payne: Tribune Media Services, Associate managing editor and investigative reporter, Newsday
Joseph Perkins: Newspaper Enterprise Association
Leonard Pitts Jr.: *Knight Ridder*
Richard E. Prince: Gannett Newspapers
William James Raspberry: The Washington Post Writers Group
Eugene Robinson: The Washington Post Writers Group
Carl Thomas Rowan: King Features Syndicate. Deceased.
Michelle Singletary: The Washington Post Writers Group
Thomas Sowell: Creators Sydicate
Charles (Chuck) Sumner Stone Jr.: Universal Press Syndicate
Cynthia Anne Tucker: Universal Press Syndicate
DeWayne Wickham: Gannett Newspapers
Armstrong Williams: TMS, TV host
Walter Edward Williams: Creators Syndicate

Local Columnists

Norma Adams-Wade: *Dallas Morning News*
William A. Brower: the *Blade of Toledo*
Desiree Cooper: *Detroit Free Press*
Stanley Crouch: *New York Daily News*
Merlene Davis: *Lexington Herald-Leader*
Lewis Walter Diuguid: *Kansas City Star*

Entries of People by Field or Endeavor

Lolis Eric Elie: *Times Picayune* (New Orleans)
Sam Fulwood III: the *Plain Dealer* (Cleveland)
Dorothy Pearl Butler Gilliam: retired, *Washington Post*
C.B. Hanif: *Palm Beach Post* ombudsman
Karen Hunter: *New York Daily News*
Derrick Z. Jackson: Boston Globe
Robert L. Jamieson Jr.: *Seattle Post-Intelligencer*
Vernon D. Jarrett: *Chicago Tribune, Sun-Times* (deceased)
Stebbins Jefferson: *Palm Beach Post*
Eugene A. Kane: *Milwaukee Journal-Sentinel*
Colbert (Colby) I. King: *Washington Post*
Dwight Lewis: *Tennessean* (Nashville)
Errol T. Louis: *New York Sun*, then *Daily News*
Sheryl McCarthy: *Newsday*
John Xavier Miller: public editor and columnist, *Detroit Free Press*
Mary A. Mitchell: *Chicago Sun-Times*
Acel Moore: *Philadelphia Inquirer*
Tony Norman: *Pittsburgh Post-Gazette*
Brenda Payton: *Oakland Tribune*
David Person: *Huntsville Times*
Peggy Mitchell Peterman: *St. Petersburg Times* (retired)
James Ragland: *Dallas Morning News*
Clem Richardson: *New York Daily News*
Rochelle Riley: *Detroit Free Press*
Osborne "Ozzie" Sinclaire Roberts Jr.: *San Diego Union-Tribune*
Barry Saunders: *News and Observer* (Raleigh, NL)
E.R. Shipp: *New York Daily News*
Elmer Smith: *Philadelphia Daily News*
Wendi C. Thomas: *Commercial Appeal* (Memphis, TN)
Adrian Walker: *Boston Globe*
Tonyaa Weathersbee: *Florida Times-Union*
Byron Williams: West Coast column writer
Michael Paul Williams: *Richmond Times-Dispatch*
N. Don Wycliff: *Chicago Tribune*

Broadcast News Figures

Tina Alexander-Sellers: news director, KTRE Lufkin, TX
Ron Allen: news correspondent, NBC
Edward "Ed" R. Bradley: deceased correspondent, 60 Minutes
William Anthony "Tony" Brown: former host, Tony Brown's Journal on PBS
Maureen Bunyon: anchor, ABC 7, Washington, DC
Barbara Ciara: managing editor/anchor, WTKR News, Norfolk, VA
Ron Claiborne: correspondent, ABC News
Cheryl Corley: senior reporter, Chicago Bureau, NPR
Belva Davis: pioneering West Coast broadcaster
Harold Dow: correspondent, 48 Hours (CBS)
Tamala Edwards: ABC-TV anchor and correspondent
Sidmel Karen Estes-Sumpter: executive editor, FOX 5 Atlanta
Faith Fancher: reporter, KTVU-TV Oakland, CA
Harris Faulkner: FOX anchor
Arthur Fennell: anchor/managing editor, Comcast Network, Philadelphia
Renee Ferguson: investigative reporter, NBC News
Michael Fields: southern bureau chief for NPR News
Wendell Goler: White House correspondent, FOX News Channel
Malvin "Mal" Russell Goode: deceased ABC news reporter
Ed Gordon: host of News & Notes with Ed Gordon on NPR
Lauren Green: news update anchor, FOX News Channel
Vertamae Grosvenor: cultural correspondent, NPR
Princell Hair: executive vice president and general manager, CNN/US
Ken Hamblin: former columnist, radio commentator
Leon M. Harris Jr.: WJLA-TV, Washington, DC
Lester Holt: MSNBC news anchor
Catherine "Cathy" Liggins Hughes: founder, Black News Talk Radio: WOL-AM
Charlayne Hunter-Gault: former national correspondent, the NewsHour

Entries of People by Field or Endeavor

Gwen Ifill: moderator of Washington Week, on public television
Robert L. Johnson: founder of Black Entertainment Television
Starlet Marie Jones: TV host, "The View," ABC
Thomas Joyner: host, "The Tom Joyner Show" on radio
Allison Keyes: reporter, "The Travis Smiley Show," NPR
Emery King: anchor/producer, WDIV-TV, Detroit
Beverly Kirk: newscaster, PBS /NPR Newsbrief
Don Lemon: coanchor, NBC5 News
Vicki Mabrey: ABC Nightline correspondent
Joseph Edward Madison: radio host
Paula Walker Madison: president and general manager, KNBC4, Los Angeles
Suzanne Malveaux: CNN anchor
Michel McQueen Martin: Nightline correspondent and guest anchor, ABC News
Paul S. Mason: senior vice president, ABC News
Angela McGlowan: FOX News analyst
Russ Mitchell: coanchor, CBS News Saturday Morning
Valerie Coleman Morris: finance news anchor, CNN
Jill Nelson: freelance journalist, MSNBC.com commentator
Vickie Newton: anchor, KMOV-TV, St. Louis, MO
Art Norman: coanchor, NBC5 News
Michele Norris: host of NPR's "All Things Considered"
Maria de la Soledad O'Brien: anchor, CNN
Julian Martin Phillips: FOX News anchor, "FOX and Friends Weekend"
Ponchitta Marie Anne Vincent Pierce: TV host, producer; magazine writer/editor
Byron Pitts: national correspondent, CBS News
Marquita Pool-Eckert: just-retired producer, CBS News
Renee Francine Poussaint: former CBS network correspondent
Adam Clayton Powell III: former broadcast exec, new media proponent
Condace Pressley: WSB Radio, Atlanta, assistant program director
Norma R. Quarles: news anchor, reporter for CNN, NBC

Toni Randolph: reporter, Minnesota Public Radio
Bob Reid: production head, Discovery Channel Primetime
Deborah Roberts: reporter, ABC News
Troy Roberts: 48 Hours correspondent, CBS News
Maxie (Max) Cleveland Robinson Jr.: cohost of ABC World News Tonight, first black network anchor in America. Deceased, 1988.
Johnathan A. Rodgers: CBS executive, CEO of TV-One
Albert Lincoln Roker: NBC weatherman, host of the Today Show
Warner Saunders: coanchor, NBC5 News
Bernard Shaw: retired anchor, CNN News
Carole Simpson: former ABC, NBC news anchor
Tavis Smiley: host, "The Travis Smiley Show," NPR
Collins Spencer: news anchor, CNN Headline News
Shay Stevens: overnight editor, NPR News
Rene Syler: anchor, "The Early Show," CBS
Pierre Thomas: Justice Department correspondent, ABC News
Pamela Thomas-Graham: former CEO, CNBC
Melba Tolliver: retired anchor, reporter for News 12 (Long Island, NY)
Lisa Tutman: general assignment reporter, NBC5 News
Adaora Udoji: news correspondent, CNN News Worldwide
Hal Walker: deceased in 2003. The first black correspondent for CBS News
Liz Walker: WBZ, Boston
Carlos Watson: political analyst, CNN News
Fredricka Whitfield: news anchor, CNN/US, Atlanta
Juan Williams: senior correspondent, Morning Edition, NPR; FOX News anchor/reporter
Montel Brian Williams: television show host
Brenda Wilson: senior correspondent, editor, NPR
Oprah Gail Winfrey: television show host

xvii

Entries of People by Field or Endeavor

Magazine Figures

Monroe Anderson: editor, *Savoy*
Lerone Bennett: executive editor, *Ebony* Magazine
Keith T. Clinkscales: president, *Vibe* magazine
Kyle Donovan: publisher, *NV* magazine
Alfred Adam Edmond Jr.: editor-in-chief, *Black Enterprise* Magazine
Earl Gilbert Graves: founder and publisher, *Black Enterprise* Magazine
Hermene Demaris Hartman: founder, *N'DIGO*
Alan J. Hughes: features editor, *Black Enterprise* Magazine
John Harold Johnson: deceased founder and publisher, Johnson Publishing Company
Edward T. Lewis: CEO, Essence Communications
Marcus Mabry: chief of correspondents, *Newsweek*
Alexander Ceasar Poinsett: an editor for 26 years at *Ebony* Magazine
Linda Johnson Rice: publisher, Johnson Publishing Company
Wilbert Rideau: former editor, the *Angolite*
Terence Samuel: ex-chief congressional correspondent, U.S. News & World Report
Clarence O. Smith: cofounder, Essence Communications
Susan L. Taylor: former editor-in-chief, *Essence*
Diane Marie Weathers: former editor-in-chief, *Essence*
Mark Whitaker: editor, *Newsweek*
Jack E. White: retired columnist, correspondent, *Time*
Roger Wood Wilkins: publisher, the *Crisis*

Sports

SPORTS COLUMNISTS
Kevin B. Blackistone: *Dallas Morning News*
Roy S. Johnson: columnist, SI.com and AOL Black Voices
Sam Harold Lacy: *Baltimore Afro-American*. Deceased in 2003
Shaun Powell: *Newsday*
William C. Rhoden: *New York Times*
Jason Whitlock: *Kansas City Star*, ESPN
Michael Wilbon: *Washington Post*
Ralph Wiley: *Oakland Tribune* and *Sports Illustrated*

SPORTSCASTERS
James Brown: cohost, FOX's NFL Sunday
Bryant Gumbel: HBO, "Real Sports" with Bryant Gumbel
Greg Gumbel: CBS sports
Fred Hickman: ESPN
Ahmad Rashad: ex-host, now executive producer, "Inside Stuff" on NBC
Robin Roberts: ABC, ESPN
Neal T. Scarbrough: vice president, editor-in-chief, ESPN.com
Stuart Scott: ESPN Anchor, Sports Center

Other

Ronnie Agnew: executive editor, columnist, the *Clarion-Ledger* (Jackson, MS)
Caesar Andrews: executive editor, *Detroit Free Press*
Mervin Raymond Aubespin: retired artist/reporter/administrator, *Louisville Courier-Journal*
Dean P. Baquet: executive vice president and editor, *Los Angeles Times*

Entries of People by Field or Endeavor

Gerald M. Boyd: former managing editor, *New York Times*

Kenneth Bunting: Executive editor, *Seattle Post-Intelligencer*

Earl Caldwell: ex-reporter, columnist, *New York Times*

Jonathan Capehart: former editorial writer, columnist, *New York Daily News*

Farai Chideya: TV political analyst and radio host, ex-columnist with *New York Daily News*

Errol A. Cockfield Jr.: bureau chief, *Newsday*

James N. Crutchfield: president, the *Journal Beacon* (Akron)

George E. Curry: editor and columnist, BlackPressUSA.com

Leon Decosta Dash Jr.: former *Washington Post* reporter

Joe Davidson: reporter, *Philadelphia Bulletin*

Allison J. Davis: CBS vice president, helped launch MSNBC Online

Wayne J. Dawkins: contributory editor, BlackJournalists.com; CEO, Augusta Press

Michael Days: editor, *Philadelphia Daily News*

Eric Deggans: media critic, *St. Petersburg Times*

Paul Delaney: former *New York Times* reporter

William Douglas: Knight Ridder correspondent

Joel P. Dreyfuss: editor in chief, Red Herring Web Site. (Former) senior editor, *Fortune*

Karen Brown Dunlap: president, The Poynter Institute

E. David Ellington: founder of NetNoir online media service

Albert E. Fitzpatrick: retired executive/editor, *Akron Beacon Journal*, *Knight Ridder*

Michael A. Fletcher: reporter, *Washington Post*

Charles Gerald Fraser Jr.: ex-reporter, *New York Times*, now with *Earth Times*

Arsenio Hall: former host, "The Arsenio Hall Show"

Charlotte H. Hall: editor, vice president, *Orlando Sentinel*

Jay T. Harris: ex-publisher, *San Jose Mercury*

Karla Garrett Harshaw: editor, Springfield (OH) *News-Sun*

Wil Haygood: Style section writer, *Washington Post*

Angelo B. Henderson: reporter, *Wall Street Journal*, *Detroit News*

Steven A. Holmes: reporter, *New York Times*

Bennie Ivory: executive editor, *The Courier-Journal* (Louisville)

Starlet Jones: TV host, "The View," ABC

Tonnya Kennedy: managing editor, the State (Columbia, SC)

Herbert Lowe: staff writer, *Newsday*

Julianne Marie Malveaux: CEO, Last Word Productions, columnist

Pluria W. Marshall Sr.: chairman, National Black Media Coalition

Sherrie Marshall: executive editor, *Macon Telegraph*

Nancy Hicks Maynard: first black mainstream newswoman in New York City. Now retired

Robert G. McGruder: former executive editor, the *Detroit Free Press*

Kevin Merida: reporter, *Washington Post*

Everett J. Mitchell II: editor, the *Tennessean* (Nashville)

Bryan K. Monroe: assistant vice president, news, *Knight Ridder*

Gregory L. Moore: editor, the Denver Post

Thomas Morgan III: reporter, *New York Times*, *Washington Post*

Jill Nelson: freelance journalist, MSNBC.com commentator

Lutrelle F. Palmer: deceased Chicago columnist, radio commentator, newspaper publisher

Richard D. Parsons: Time Warner CEO

Glenn Proctor: executive editor, *Richmond Times-Dispatch*

W. Curtis Riddle: president and publisher, the *News Journal*, Wilmington, DE

Jason L. Riley: senior editorial writer, the *Wall Street Journal*

Mark E. Russell—managing editor, Orlando Sentinel

Otis L. Sanford: managing editor, the Commercial Appeal (Memphis, TN)

Debra Adams Simmons: former editor, *Akron Beacon Journal*

Brent A. Staples: *New York Times* editorial writer

Pearl Stewart: ex-editor, *Oakland Tribune*; founder, *Black College Wire*

Hollis Towns: managing editor, the *Cincinnati Enquirer*

Montel Brian Williams: television show host

Oprah Gail Winfrey: television show host

xix

Acknowledgments

The author would like to acknowledge the help of four individuals in the early stages of this book project. Reviewing the proposed contents list were former Philadelphia columnist and now retired University of North Carolina at Chapel Hill journalism professor Chuck Stone, who added a number of names of people I had missed, as did ex-Florida columnist and now Stillman College journalism faculty member Bill Maxwell and my former Virginia Tech student Pierre Thomas, now a correspondent with ABC News. Also, my Virginia Tech journalism colleague Roland Lazenby made valuable suggestions about which sports journalists I might include. Finally, I acknowledge the patience and forbearance of my wife Becky for putting up with the stiff time demands this project made of me.

Introduction

Much has been written about the failure of the U.S. news media to achieve racial population parity in their hiring practices, and their failure is undeniably true. African Americans, the focus of this biographical reference work, make up around 26 percent of our nation's population but only perhaps 11 percent of newspaper newsroom employees. Many a U.S. newspaper has no black or other minority employees at all. More effort needs to be expended in order to move toward parity, especially inasmuch as the part of the population referred to as "people of color" is rapidly growing. That having been said, the racial makeup of newsrooms, broadcast stations and the like is vastly different today from the segregated situation that existed in 1971, when I was a shiny new assistant professor in the Journalism Department of Temple University in Philadelphia.

In those bygone days, to turn on one's television and see a dark-complected anchor or reporter was about as likely as seeing a broadcaster from Mars. I was aware that although most African-American journalists still worked for the historically black press, a handful had managed to find jobs in mainstream papers. I learned more about this situation than I otherwise would have by virtue of the fact that until an office of my own became available, I shared an office with Armistead Pride, historian of the black press and a real gentleman. At that time, I was a regular reader of the nationally syndicated columns of Carl Rowan and William Raspberry. To a lesser degree, I was familiar with the *Philadelphia Bulletin*'s Claude Lewis, the *Chicago Tribune*'s Vernon Jarrett and the *New York Times*' Earl Caldwell. Most of all, I was soon filled with admiring delight at the audacity and skill of Philadelphia columnist Chuck Stone of the *Daily News*. Not only did he write a fascinating column that made readers sit up and ponder things they had not previously taken much notice of, but he boldly stood up to the threat and swagger of the Rizzo years in Philadelphia, a time in which the official line while Frank Rizzo was police chief (later mayor) could hardly have been described as friendly to people of color. Black fugitives from the law, afraid to surrender to Philadelphia police for fear of beatings or

Introduction

worse, would instead turn themselves in to columnist Stone, who would escort them to police headquarters. He was also called in to mediate prison riots and in the 1970s was one of the city's most renowned journalists and a heroic figure to myself and most of my colleagues.

Of the journalists just named, Rowan began his column in 1965, Raspberry in 1966, Lewis and Caldwell in 1969, Jarrett in 1970 and Stone in 1972. These pioneering figures were joined in the 1970s by Walter Williams, Bob Hayes, Ozzie Roberts, Susan Watson, William A. Brower, Dorothy Gilliam, Juan Williams and a few others. In the late 1970s, a quite good column by Robert C. Maynard acquainted me with this talented individual who later, in 1983, would become the first African American to own and publish a mainstream newspaper, California's *Oakland Tribune*. Two other early column voices that ought not to go without mention here are George Schuyler, who wrote a syndicated column from 1953 until the late 1970s, and NAACP Executive Secretary Roy Wilkins, whose syndicated column ran from 1969 to 1980.

Moving to broadcasting, the first African American to appear on television was an entertainer, Ethel Waters, who sang on an NBC variety show in 1939. A decade later, the earliest African-American television show, also on NBC, featured the singing of a trio called The Three Flames. Much later, in 1962, appeared the first black network newscaster, Mel Goode, on ABC. A pioneering news anchor who is a woman of color is Charlayne Hunter-Gault, who in 1983, joined the PBS show "The MacNeil/Lehrer News Hour"; and Arsenio Hall, in 1988, became the earliest African-American host of a national television talk show, "The Arsenio Hall Show." Many African-American "firsts" are noted in these pages, but as someone else once observed, the trouble that arises when anyone writing history—ancient or modern—identifies an individual as having been first at something, a later historian may very well locate someone else who was even "firster."

The decade in which black journalists began to move into mainstream media jobs, then, was the 1970s. Prior to that time, African Americans working for the predominantly white media were few and far between. The first black editor of a U.S. mainstream paper appears to have been Henry O. Flipper, also the first African-American graduate of West Point; Flipper edited the Arizona *Sunday Herald* in 1889. Decades later, after the subsiding of the dramatic civil rights demonstrations that shook most of white America out of complacent acceptance of the status quo, the hiring of African-American news people slowed for a time, then accelerated more rapidly in the 1980s and still more rapidly in the 1990s. By the dawning of the new millennium, even though parity remained a distant goal, African Americans in news media jobs nevertheless had achieved a sort of critical mass. Broadcasting had outpaced print media in hiring minority people, mainly due to FCC regulations, now rescinded. In the absence of such regulation, it is possible that the television industry's 20 percent minority employment figure could suffer a decline.

Introduction

In 1993, Bob Herbert became the first black columnist at the *New York Times*, where he had worked as early as 1985 as that paper's first black city editor, investigative reporter and editorial writer. In 1998, Mark Whitaker became the first black to edit one of America's three major newsweeklies, *Newsweek*. Of all the media, magazines have had the worst record of minority hiring. A pioneer in this medium was Earl Brown, who in 1940 was the first African American to write for *Life* magazine. Since that time, few African Americans have risen to positions of prominence in U.S. mainstream magazines.

The many, many journalists of the historically black newspaper press have received substantial earlier attention from scholars, as have some of the very first African Americans to work for the various mainstream media. For that reason they do not appear in these pages. This reference work's purpose is to add to those earlier scholarly contributions by describing the careers of a selection of 246 African Americans currently working in the news media. Also included in that number are a few individuals who are recently deceased, have recently retired and/or have left working journalism to teach their craft to students. These individuals, then, work or very recently worked in news or news-related jobs at or with newspapers, syndicates, magazines, radio and television, and online media.

The author's hope is that this compilation of information about contemporary and near-contemporary African-American news media figures will provide a convenient source of information primarily for journalism students and scholars as well as those in African-American studies curricula, and secondarily, for anyone else looking for information about one or more of these 246 media figures. Following this introduction and before the 246 entries appears a timeline that shows in capsule form how the accomplishments of the individuals featured in this work unfolded over time. The biographical entries in the two volumes of this work are arranged alphabetically by news figures' last names. A bibliography of other recent work on African-American journalism and related matters and a general index follow the entries.

The author's intent was to include today's most accomplished African-American journalists, with an eye to geographic spread, and to include a few younger individuals of special promise. In a handful of cases, requests for biographical information were met with no response, or sufficient material for an entry could not be found; hence, those individuals did not "make the book."

Some entries are more complete than others as to such details as one's date of birth. Due to the specter of identity theft, some of the individuals profiled in this reference work did not want that information made public. Also, in on-camera television work, the need to be (or at least appear) forever young also might have been a factor in reluctance to reveal one's age. The Internet was an invaluable source of information for writing these entries, and whenever possible, e-mail was used to contact these journalists to learn more about them. Because of the heavy volume of dishonest messages with which all

Introduction

present-day e-mail users must cope, there were times when some journalists were understandably dubious about requests for personal information they received from a stranger via this convenient and economical, yet tainted medium.

In each biographical entry, the author attempted to give date and place of birth, date of death for the small number of recently deceased individuals included, educational background and a career summary. For writers, a brief description of typical topics addressed and positions taken on those topics also was included. At the end of each entry, the author has placed a list of all books written or edited by that individual—and there are many—plus a section of "Further Readings." Preceding those two sections, for as many entries as possible, appears a column or story written by the person profiled. These stories serve as examples of these African-American journalists' work and also reveal issues important to the writers profiled. Most of these original documents were written by columnists and reporters, as opposed to editors, publishers, broadcasters or others whose primary job is something other than writing. Even though they are not news people per se, such television talk show hosts as Oprah Winfrey, Arsenio Hall, Montel Williams and Star Jones have been included, inasmuch as news events and issues are often discussed on their programs. New-media people, such as Allison Davis, Joel Dreyfuss and E. David Ellington also are represented.

In selecting the columns and stories to reprint beneath the biographical entries of as many of these writers as possible, my aim was not to produce a partisan screed. All save a few of the individuals profiled in this reference work were of liberal, hence Democratic political leanings, especially insofar as the current war in Iraq is concerned. My own view of this war, and of the George W. Bush administration, is as dim as that of most of the journalists whose remarks are reprinted here, although the expression of that view in this reference work was a byproduct rather than an original motivation for doing the project.

Why, then, did a white journalism professor of late middle age—and a Southerner at that—choose to write this reference work? Two of the journalists contacted for information about themselves asked me this question directly, albeit very politely; and the same question was implied in the tone of quite a few others who apparently were not comfortable coming right out and asking.

First, I chose this project because, as best I could determine, no one else was doing it. Second, the considerable strides made by people of color working in our nation's news media have largely coincided with the years I have been teaching and writing about journalism. To my way of thinking, the success stories of the 246 individuals profiled in these pages are, viewed collectively, a very important larger story of positive change in our society. It is a story that needs telling—to record recent history and, I hope, to inspire minority youngsters who might be interested in media careers. Third, without wishing to sound sanctimonious, I did this project out of profound respect for the talent and accomplishment of people who, compared to myself, have had extra obstacles to overcome in their careers—people whose forebears had to suffer our nation's greatest shame: more than 240 years of slavery followed by another century of rampant discrimination. The matter of race remains an issue of raw-nerve sensitivity in our nation, yet conditions today are so very much better than they were prior to the 1970s. I feel honored to have had the opportunity to contribute, if only in a modest way, to celebrating and chronicling this important change in American society.

Timeline

1964   Carl Rowan becomes director of the United States Information Agency.
1965   Congress passes the Voting Rights Act.
       Activist Malcolm X (Malcolm Little) is killed.
       Peggy Peterman is hired to write for the *St. Petersburg Times* in Florida.
1966   Belva Davis becomes the first black television news anchor on the West Coast.
       Nancy Hicks Maynard becomes a *New York Post* reporter and is at that time the only black newswoman in the city's mainstream press.
       William Raspberry begins writing his *Washington Post* column, which later is widely syndicated.
1967   Earl Caldwell becomes a *New York Times* reporter.
       Merv Aubespin becomes the first black staffer on the *Courier-Journal* in Louisville, Kentucky.
       Jonathan Rodgers becomes the first black writer at *Sports Illustrated Magazine*.
       Edward Brook of Massachusette became the first African-American elected to the U.S. Senate.
1968   Martin Luther King Jr. is assassinated.
       Ponchitta Pierce becomes a "CBS Evening News" correspondent.
       Warner Saunders' television show "For Blacks Only" premiers on WSL-TV in Chicago.
       Clarence O. Smith and Edward T. Lewis found Essence Communications.
       Melba Tolliver becomes one of the early black television news anchors in New York City.
       Shirley Chisholm becomes the first African-American women elected to Congress (for New York)
1969   Norman Lockman becomes the first black reporter for the *News Journal* in Wilmington, Delaware.
       Les Payne begins a succession of jobs at *Newsday* that culminate in his syndicated column.
       Clarence Page becomes a reporter for the *Chicago* Tribune.
       Max Robinson is the first African American to work as a television news anchor in Washington, D.C.
       Roy Wilkins' column "Along the Way" is distributed by the Register and Tribune Syndicate.
1970   Earl Graves founds *Black Enterprise* magazine.
       Edward T. Lewis and Clarence O. Smith cofound *Essence* magazine.
1971   Tony Brown becomes founding dean of the Howard University School of Journalism.
       Lu Palmer launches his talk radio show "Lu's Notebook" in Chicago.
1972   William Dilday becomes the nation's first African American to work as station manager of a mainstream television station, WLBT in Jackson, Mississippi.
       Chuck Stone launches his *Philadelphia Daily News* column.
       Jack E. White becomes a staff writer at *Time* magazine.
       Roger Wilkins joins the editorial department of the *Washington Post*.
1973   Faith Fancher becomes the first black television reporter in Knoxville, Tennessee.
       Photographer Pluria Marshall founds the National Black Media Coalition.
       Chuck Stone, Acel Moore and Claude Lewis cofound the Philadelphia Association of Black Journalists.

Timeline

1974   Ozzie Roberts joins the staff of the *San Diego Union-Tribune*, for which he later becomes a columnist.
Susan Watson begins her column at the *Detroit Free Press*.
Roger Wilkins is hired by the *New York Times* and becomes the first black member of its editorial board.
Juan Williams begins writing for the *Washington Post*.

1975   The National Association of Black Journalists is founded in Washington, D.C., by 44 journalists, with Chuck Stone as its first president.

1976   Convicted bank robber and murderer Wilbert Rideau becomes editor of the prison magazine the *Angolite*.
Hal Walker becomes the first black correspondent for CBS News.
Robert Maynard becomes the first black panelist to participate in a presidential campaign debate.

1977   The Institute for Journalism Education is founded in Oakland, California.
The first year for "Tony Brown's Journal," the nation's longest-running African-American public affairs show.

1978   Charlayne Hunter-Gault is the first black woman anchor of a national television news show, "The MacNeil/Lehrer Report."
Max Robinson is the first black network television anchor, at ABC-TV.
Sam Fulwood begins his career as a *Charlotte Observer* reporter in North Carolina.

1979   Jim Vance and Sue Simmons are the first black national television coanchors, at WRC-TV in Washington, D.C.
Stanley Crouch begins writing for the *Village Voice* in New York City.
Bob Reid becomes the first broadcaster elected president of NABJ.
Brenda Wilson is hired by National Public Radio.

1980   Fred Hickson is one of CNN's original sports show hosts.
Cathy Hughes founds Radio One network.
Bernard Shaw becomes principal Washington anchor for Cable News Network.
E.R. Shipp becomes a correspondent for the *New York Times*.
Eugene Robinson joins the *Washington Post*.
Liz Walker begins a long run as news anchor at Boston's CBS4 and is that station's first black anchor.
Michael Wilbon becomes a *Washington Post* sportswriter.

1981   Brenda Payton begins her column at the *Oakland Tribune*.
Susan Taylor becomes editor-in-chief of *Essence* magazine.
Walter Williams' conservative column is distributed by Heritage Features, later by Creators Syndicate.
Pam McAllister Johnson becomes the first black woman publisher of a mainstream newspaper, New York's *Ithaca Journal*.

1982   Thomas Greer becomes the first black sports editor at a mainstream metropolitan daily, the *Plain Dealer* of Cleveland, Ohio.
Bryant Gumbel becomes cohost of NBC's "Today Show."
Elmer Smith begins as a *Philadelphia Daily News* sportswriter.
Michael Paul Williams begins writing for the *Richmond Times-Dispatch* in Virginia.
Ralph Wiley becomes a sports writer at *Sports Illustrated*.

Timeline

1983 Betty Anne Williams of the Associated Press is the first black president of the Washington Press Club.
Vernon Jarrett becomes a Chicago *Sun-Times* columnist.
Courtland Milloy begins writing his first *Washington Post* column.
Robert Maynard becomes the first black owner of a mainstream metropolitan newspaper, the *Oakland Tribune*.
Cynthia Tucker becomes an *Atlanta Constitution* columnist and editorial writer.

1984 Wil Haygood becomes a writer for the *Boston Globe*.
Claude Lewis writes editorials and begins a column at the *Philadelphia Inquirer*.
Thomas Sowell's column appears in nearly 150 newspapers via Creators Syndicate.
Norma Quarles is a panelist in the vice-presidential campaign debate.

1985 Bob Herbert begins writing the first of his two *New York Times* columns.
Eugene Kane begins writing his *Milwaukee Journal Sentinel* column.
Tonyaa Weathersbee joins the *Florida Times-Union* and becomes a columnist.
DeWayne Wickham becomes a Gannett News Service columnist.
Tony Brown founds the Council for the Economic Development of Black Americans.

1986 Jill Nelson becomes the first black woman writer for the *Washington Post's* Sunday magazine.
Oprah Winfrey's hour-long program "The Oprah Winfrey Show" premiers.

1987 Adam Clayton Powell III becomes the first black vice president of National Public Radio.
Al Roker joins NBC's "Today Show."
Alfred Edmond becomes editor of *Black Enterprise* magazine.

1988 Derrick Jackson becomes a *Boston Globe* columnist.
Deborah Mathis begins writing a column for the *Arkansas Gazette*.
Bill Maxwell begins writing a *Tampa Tribune* column that is distributed to other papers by the New York Times Regional Newspaper Group.
Carole Simpson begins as weekend anchor of ABC's "World News Tonight."

1989 Arsenio Hall begins hosting the first black late-night television talk show, "The Arsenio Hall Show."
Hermene Hartman founds the Chicago "magpaper" *N'Digo*.

1990 Shay Stevens becomes overnight editor for National Public Radio.
Colbert King becomes a *Washington Post* columnist.
Brent Staples becomes a *New York Times* editorial writer.
Ken Hamblin begins writing his conservative *Denver Post* column, which is carried by the New York Times Syndicate.
Marquita Pool-Eckert becomes senior producer of "CBS Sunday Morning."
Robin Roberts becomes ESPN's first black on-air personality, working as an anchor and host for "Sports Center."
Ralph Wiley becomes a sports commentator for ESPN.
Douglas Wilder and Virginia becomes the first African-American governor in the United States.

1991 Montel Williams becomes the first African-American man to host a daytime television talk show, "The Montel Williams Show."
Sidmel Estes-Sumpter is the first woman elected president of NABJ.

1992 Ron Allen becomes the first black broadcaster to have worked for CBS, ABC and NBC.

Timeline

	Pearl Stewart becomes the first black woman editor of a major mainstream metropolitan daily, the *Oakland Tribune*.
	Carol Moseley Braun becomes the first African-American woman in the U.S. Senate.
1993	Bob Herbert is the first black columnist at the *New York Times*.
	Oakland's Institute for Journalism Education is renamed the Robert C. Maynard Institute for Journalism Education.
	Wayne Dawkins publishes the *NABJ Story* a year after founding his own book publishing firm, the August Press.
	Stuart Scott begins anchoring and cohosting sports shows for ESPN2.
1994	Tom Joyner's "The Tom Joyner Show" premiers and is syndicated to 29 radio stations.
	Leonard Pitts begins his column at the *Miami Herald*.
	Curtis Riddle becomes president and publisher of the *News Journal* in New Castle, Delaware.
	Jason Whitlock becomes a syndicated *Kansas City Star* sports columnist.
	The first Unity conference is held in Atlanta, with representation for the NABJ and the associations of Asian-American, Hispanic and Native-American journalists.
1996	William Kennard becomes the first black chairman of the Federal Communications Commission.
	Tony Norman begins his *Pittsburgh Post-Gazette* column.
	William Rhoden begins his "Sports of the Times" column in the *New York Times*.
	Al Roker replaces Willard Scott as NBC's "Today Show" weatherman.
1997	Bennie Ivory becomes executive editor and vice president of the *Courier-Journal* in Louisville, Kentucky.
	Bob Reid becomes executive producer of the Discovery Channel.
	Michelle Singletary begins her syndicated personal finance column at the *Washington Post*.
	Investigative reporter Pierre Thomas leaves the *Washington Post* for CNN.
1998	Mark Whitaker is the earliest African American to edit one of the three leading newsweeklies, *Newsweek*.
	Adrian Walker begins his *Boston Globe* column.
1999	Kyle Donovan founds Envy Publishing Group and launches *NV* magazine.
	Michael Fields becomes the first Southern bureau chief for National Public Radio.
	John X. Miller becomes ombudsman of the *Detroit Free Press*.
2000	The *New York Times* publishes the Pulitzer Prize-winning series "How Race Is Lived in America," with Gerald Boyd as co-senior editor.
	Don Wycliff becomes public editor and columnist for the *Chicago Tribune*.
	Kenneth Bunting becomes executive editor of the Seattle, Washington, *Post-Intelligencer*.
	Joel Dreyfuss becomes editor-in-chief of the Web site Urban Box Office.
	George Curry is elected the first black president of the American Society of Magazine Editors.
	Roy Johnson leaves *Sports Illustrated* to become founding editor of *Savoy* magazine.

Timeline

        Paula Madison becomes the first African-American woman to serve as general manager of a network-owned television station in a top-five market, at KNBC in Los Angeles.

        Gregory Moore becomes editor of the *Denver Post*.

        Jason Riley becomes a senior editorial page writer at the *Wall Street Journal*.

        Terence Samuel becomes chief congressional correspondent for *U.S. News & World Report* magazine.

2001   Gerald Boyd becomes managing editor of the *New York Times*.

        James Crutchfield becomes president and publisher of the *Beacon Journal* in Akron, Ohio.

        Jay T. Harris makes a strong statement about the bottom-line mentality of the newspaper industry by resigning as publisher and chairman of the *San Jose Mercury*, a position he had assumed in 1994.

        Robert Jamieson becomes a *Seattle Post-Intelligencer* columnist.

        Marcus Mabry becomes chief of correspondents for *Newsweek* magazine.

        Sherrie Marshall becomes executive editor of Georgia's *Macon Telegraph*.

        Renee Poussaint and Camille Cosby launch the National Visionary Leadership Project.

        Tavis Smiley begins hosting "The Tavis Smiley Show," the first NPR show targeted at a black audience.

        Pamela Thomas-Graham becomes president and CEO of CNBC.

        Diane Weathers becomes editor-in-chief of *Essence* magazine.

2002   Bryan Monroe becomes the Knight Ridder newspaper group's assistant vice president for news.

        Gregory Moore becomes editor of the *Denver Post*.

        Michele Norris joins the staff of National Public Radio.

        Richard Parsons becomes chairman and CEO of Time Warner.

        Richard Prince begins his "Richard Prince's Journal-isms" online feature.

        Otis Sanford becomes managing editor of the *Commercial Appeal* in Memphis, Tennessee.

        Pearl Stewart founds the Black College Wire news service.

        Rene Syler becomes the first black woman to anchor a morning television news show, "The Early Show," on CBS.

2003   Ronnie Agnew becomes the first black executive editor of *The Clarion Ledger*, Mississippi's largest newspaper.

        Jonathan Rodgers becomes CEO of cable television network TV-One.

        Debra Simmons becomes the first black editor of the *Beacon Journal* in Akron, Ohio.

        Wendi Thomas begins her metro column in the *Commercial Appeal* of Memphis, Tennessee.

2004   Karla Harshaw is elected as the first African-American woman president of the American Society of Newspaper Editors.

        Charlotte Hall becomes editor and vice president of Florida's *Orlando Sentinel*.

        Gwen Ifill becomes the first black moderator of a vice presidential debate.

        Mark Russell becomes managing editor of Florida's *Orlando Sentinel*.

        Hollis Towns becomes managing editor of the *Cincinnati Enquirer*.

2005   Eugene Robinson begins writing his *Washington Post* column.

Timeline

Dean Baquet becomes editor of the *Los Angeles Times*, the largest newspaper on the West Coast.

Michael Days is the first African American to serve as editor and executive vice president of the *Philadelphia Daily News*.

Eric Deggans becomes the first black media critic at Florida's *St. Petersburg Times*.

Ed Gordon premiers the NPR show "News & Notes with Ed Gordon."

Linda Johnson Rice takes over as publisher of Johnson Publishing Company after her father's death.

Robin Roberts becomes a coanchor of ABC's "Good Morning America."

2006 Neal Scarbrough becomes general manager and editor of sports for America Online.

A

Abu-Jamal, Mumia (23 April 1954–)

A columnist very different from the norm is Mumia Abu-Jamal (born Wesley Cook), who has been on death row from his 1982 conviction for the murder of a Philadelphia police officer until 2007. In December 2001, a federal district judge overturned his death sentence, but the district attorney immediately appealed, thereby leaving the prisoner on death row. Prior to his arrest, he had become minister of information for the Philadelphia Black Panther Party, had been a print and radio journalist and was president of the Philadelphia Society of Black Journalists. During his incarceration, he has published five books, written a column that was carried by various historically black newspapers and that was syndicated to a wider audience in 2000 by CLM Global News Group, freelanced for a few magazines, written for his own Website and arranged to air a series of commentaries on National Public Radio, which were cancelled after pressure was brought to bear by Sen. Robert Dole, the Philadelphia police and others. At this writing in January 2006, the United States Court of Appeals for the Third Circuit has ordered a review of several issues that Abu-Jamal's lawyers claim prevented him from getting a fair trial. He remains in his cell, writing his commentaries by hand with the insert from a ballpoint pen, the only writing implement allowed him by prison officials. Since the 2005 execution of Clarence "Tookie" Williams, Abu-Jamal is very likely the nation's most famous African-American inmate.

He was born in Philadelphia as Wesley Cook and changed his name when, as a teenager, he joined the Black Panther Party. His supporters now assert that he was under police surveillance since he was 15, at which age he was writing for the party's national *Black Panther* newspaper and had been named the Panthers' Minister of Information. Those were especially rough times in

Philadelphia, a city whose brotherly love was very little evident between its large black population and its blustering, showboating police chief, then mayor, Frank Rizzo. Abu-Jamal moved into radio at Philadelphia's black-oriented station WDAS-FM, where he did commentaries and interviews. He won a Peabody Award in his early twenties for his reporting on a visit by the Pope; and in 1981, a year before the murder case that brought about his imprisonment, he became president of the city's Association of Black Journalists. Prior to his arrest, he had no criminal record, but his support of the city's militant MOVE organization resulted in some stations dropping his airtime, and he began moonlighting as a taxi driver to support his family. According to Abu-Jamal, on the night of 9 December 1981, while driving his taxi on Locust Street, he saw a white policeman beating his brother, William (Wesley) Cook, with a flashlight. Abu-Jamal stopped to intervene, and in the resulting struggle, both he and the officer, Daniel Faulkner, were shot. The officer died; Abu-Jamal recovered and claimed that another man had shot the officer and had fled the scene. What actually happened is extremely difficult to decipher. Abu-Jamal's critics point out that he was arrested wearing a holster for his legally registered .38-caliber handgun and that bullets removed from the dead officer's brain matched the shells remaining in the gun. They cite five eyewitnesses who identified him as the shooter, and claim that several other people later heard him confess to the crime. The most extensive published account that paints Abu-Jamal as guilty has been Daniel J. Flynn's monograph *Cop Killer: How Mumia Abu-Jamal Conned Millions Into Believing He Was Framed*. His supporters, on the other hand, claim that neither police tested Abu-Jamal's gun to confirm that it had been fired, nor did they test his hands for gunpowder residue. These critics complain that the judge assigned to the trial, Albert F. Sabo, had a close connection to the Philadelphia police and that he had a long record of guilty verdicts and capital punishment sentences, mainly for African-American defendants. They claim that all but one black juror were removed from the jury. They also argue that two of the witnesses against Abu-Jamal were prostitutes and one a convicted arsonist, that some witnesses offered conflicting accounts of what they observed at the scene of the crime and that some witnesses confirmed the presence of another man who fled before police arrived. They charge police intimidation of witnesses, especially the prostitutes and the arsonist, and complain that the lawyer appointed for the defense was incompetent and was later disbarred. When Abu-Jamal asked the court to allow him to defend himself, they claim, he was taken from the courtroom and was given no access to what was going on in court. In short, his supporters paint Abu-Jamal as a political prisoner and have compared his jailing to the incarceration of South Africa's Nelson Mandela. Still others think that Abu-Jamal was probably guilty but that he failed to receive a fair trial. In that camp was the ABC news show "20/20," which featured the results of its four-month investigation on the 9 December 1998 program. They concluded that he had not received a fair trial but hinted that he was probably guilty of the shooting. Another book, David Lindorff's *Killing Time: An Investigation Into the Death Row Case of Mumia Abu-Jamal*, pictures Abu-Jamal as the victim of a frame-up. Yet another book, by one of Abu-Jamal's former lawyers, Daniel R. Williams, was *Executing Justice: An Inside Account of the Case of Mumia Abu-Jamal*; Williams' conclusion is that Abu-Jamal was not guilty.

In 1995, Abu-Jamal collected a number of his essays and published them as a book: *Live From Death Row*. Prison authorities responded by placing him in disciplinary confinement, saying that he had violated a state law against operating a business or profession while in prison. The Philadelphia Fraternal Order of Police tried unsuccessfully to prevent the book's publication. A second book of his essays appeared in 1997: *Death Blossom: Reflections from a Prisoner of Conscience*. His third book, *All Things Censored* (2000), was sold with a compact disc containing selections from his radio commentaries. His fourth book, *Faith of Our Fathers: An Examination of the Spiritual Life of African and African-American People*, came out in 2003, and *We Want Freedom: A Life in the Black Panther Party*, appeared in 2004. Each book was done with a different publisher; his work is held in many U.S. libraries and reportedly has been translated in seven other languages. Also while in custody, Abu-Jamal has taken advantage of distance learning to complete a B.A. from Goddard College and an M.A. from California State University, Dominiguez Hills. He also writes for his own Website, The Mumia Abu-Jamal Freedom Journal (www.mumia.org) and for a second site: the Mobilization to Free Mumia Abu-Jamal (www.freemumia.org).

Not only has he plead his own case of justice denied, but Abu-Jamal has gained a substantial amount of high-profile support. In October 2003, he was made an honorary citizen of Paris, and he was presented that honor by Mayor Bertrand Delanoe; this recognition was largely in protest of the death penalty, which had been abolished in France in 1981. French President Jacques Chirac and South Africa's Nelson Mandela have also spoken for Abu-Jamal. The Japanese Diet and the European Parliament have expressed concern or support, as have Amnesty International, Human Rights Watch, the NAACP and several U.S. labor organizations. Hollywood has entered the ranks of his supporters, in the persons of actors and directors Paul Newman, Whoopi Goldberg, Oliver Stone and Susan Sarandon; and the popular music groups Rage Against the Machine, The Beastie Boys and Public Enemy have expressed support. One celebrity who initially supported him, maverick filmmaker Michael Moore, reversed his position in his book *Dude, Where's My Country*, joining the ranks of observers who do not support the death penalty and do not think Abu-Jamal got a fair trial, yet conclude that he probably did the crime.

In 1989, the Pennsylvania Supreme Court reviewed Abu-Jamal's case but found no judicial improprieties in the way the trial had been conducted. Then in December 2001, a federal district judge overturned his death sentence because of problems with the trial judge's instructions to the jury. The people appealed, leaving Abu-Jamal on death row, but in December 2005, the U.S. Court of Appeals for the Third Circuit ordered another review of several issues stemming from the way the prosecution and trial were conducted. Opening briefs were to be filed in mid-January 2006. Another unexpected event had been a May 2001 confession by an African-American man named Arnold Beverly, who claimed that he, not Abu-Jamal, had been the killer. Authorities do not appear to have found his confession credible.

Abu-Jamal's commentaries and columns have ranged widely in subject matter. In June 2000, he, from his prison cell, deplored the recent actions of young black and Puerto Rican men who had grabbed and stripped women in New York's Central Park. The writer criticized their actions as a hateful attempt to terrorize and dominate women. In August of that year, his topic was the sad sameness of the Republican and Democratic parties, which he characterized as one evil party having two names. In January 2003, Abu-Jamal gave his take on why the United States went into Iraq: oil. In one part of that commentary, he adroitly mocked George W. Bush and the variety of "reasons" the president has cited for his decision to invade that country. An October 2003 commentary followed up on that theme, saying that such wars serve not the people's interests, but those of big business; and in November 2005, after Rep. John Murtha (D-Pa.) called for withdrawal of U.S. troops from Iraq, Abu-Jamal wrote in support of Murtha's position, saying that the bloom was finally off the war. Not all of his writing has been aimed at criticism of government or social ills. A May 2003 commentary, for example, was a tribute to singer Nina Simone and a plea for a return to a better quality of popular music than that of recent years. Guilty or innocent, the man has a good deal of talent as a writer.

Books by Mumia Abu-Jamal: *Live from Death Row* (Reading, Mass.: Addison-Wesley, 1995); *Death Blossoms: Reflections from a Prisoner of Conscience* (Farmington, Pa.: Plough, 1997); *All Things Censored* (New York: Seven Stories Press, 2000); *Faith of Our Fathers: An Examination of the Spiritual Life of African and African-American People* (Trenton, N.J.: Africa World Press, 2003); *We Want Freedom: A Life in the Black Panther Party* (Cambridge, Mass.: South End Press, 2004).

Further Readings: Bisson, Terry. *On a Move: The Story of Mumia Abu-Jamal.* Farmington, Pa.: Litmus Books, 2000; Flynn, Dan. *Cop Killer: How Mumia Abu-Jamal Conned Millions into Believing He Was Framed.* Washington, D.C.: Accuracy in Academia, 1999; Lindorff, Dave. *Killing Time: An Investigation into the Death Row Case of Mumia Abu-Jamal.* Monroe, Me.: Common Courage Press, 2003; Weinglass, Leonard. *Race for Justice: Mumia Abu-Jamal's Fight Against the Death Penalty.* Monroe, Me.: Common Courage Press, 1995; Williams, Daniel R. *Executing Justice: An Inside Account of the Case of Mumia Abu-Jamal.* New York: St. Martin's Press, 2001.

Adams-Wade, Norma (?–)

Norma Adams-Wade retired in December 2002 after three decades with the *Dallas Morning News*, where she was hired in 1974 as the first full-time black reporter for a mainstream Dallas newspaper. She had earned her bachelors in journalism at the University of Texas in Austin and had considered becoming a singer before deciding on a career in journalism. In retirement, she continues to write a weekly column for the paper. Adams-Wade was a founding member of the National Association of Black Journalists and started that organization's five-state Southwestern regional chapter, which she directed for two years. Upon her retirement, she was honored by the House of Representatives of the 78th Texas Legislature in a resolution passed on 23 April 2003. She was accorded the Lifetime Achievement Award given by the Dallas-Fort Worth Association of Black Communicators and the Juanita Craft Award for community service in journalism from the Dallas chapter of the NAACP. Her *Morning News* mentor was the late Julia Scott Reid, who, without benefit of a college degree, became the first black columnist for the paper, and one of the earliest African Americans to work in a mainstream newsroom in the South. Reid suffered a debilitating stroke in 1978 and died in June 2005.

Adams-Wade's weekly column, which appeared on Tuesdays, was sometimes on a single topic, such as the example below that describes an unusual libel suit, but on most Tuesdays, she gave her readers what is usually called an "items column"—one that relates two or more separate events or items of interest for Dallas' black community. She alerted her readers to events such as the Texas Black Invitational Rodeo, sponsored by the city's African American Museum, and cultural events, such as a collection of black-and-white photos taken by local schoolchildren and exhibited as "Through the Eyes of Our Children," or the play "Bridges," a look at homelessness, protest and politics that was a tribute to a local homeless advocate who had been shot to death in 1994. Another of her columns praised a Dallas couple, Terry and Dalphine Hogg, who operate a vocational training academy to provide job skills for released prisoners and other people with troubled pasts.

"Note-taker Faces Libel Lawsuit" by Norma Adams-Wade

Paul Clark of Dallas has always prided himself on his ability to take thorough notes.

But the former federal employee and volunteer civil rights advocate says his thoroughness got him sued. He and a Dallas-based nonprofit group are defendants in an upcoming libel and defamation trial in Athens, Texas.

Gladys Elaine Jenkins, an Athens City Council member, sued Mr. Clark and Black Citizens for Justice, Law and Order, a Dallas-based organization that helps people with employment and civil-rights discrimination complaints.

Daisy Joe of Dallas, the founder and volunteer executive director of Black Citizens, is named in the suit as the nonprofit group's responsible party.

Ms. Jenkins says Mr. Clark's notes—taken during a public meeting in which some of Athens' black residents complained about unfair treatment by the city and police—defamed her and are malicious and libelous. Mr. Clark and Mrs. Joe said they were shocked to learn they had been sued because they say the dispute does not involve them.

"All I did was take notes," Mr. Clark said, referring to the November 2002 gathering. "I never said a word the entire meeting."

Mrs. Joe, who has been recovering from cancer in recent years, said she was ill and was not in Athens when the event occurred. She said the stress of the suit and the coming trial are exacerbating her condition.

"This is an insane nightmare," Mrs. Joe said, adding that neither she nor Mr. Clark knows the council member.

Ms. Jenkins could not be reached for comment. But Dan Moore, the Athens city attorney who is representing her, said a jury would determine whether Mr. Clark's notes are malicious.

The conflict "is unfortunate but serious," Mr. Moore said.

He said the notes record false and unsubstantiated claims that Ms. Jenkins "was a convicted felon and had served time in prison."

"The truth is she's never even had a ticket," he said. "She's never been arrested or charged... [with] any felony."

Kent Starr, the Dallas attorney for Mr. Clark and Mrs. Joe, says the case is significant because his clients are defending an individual's right to record a public conversation without malice, even though the speakers may make unsubstantiated remarks about a public figure.

Mr. Clark said he went to Athens because the North Athens Black Citizens of Concern asked him to come and help them prepare for a meeting with the City Council.

He took the notes while the residents met at a location away from City Hall, he said.

The Dallas nonprofit group sent the information to U.S. Rep. Pete Sessions, R-Dallas, asking for help. The congressman used to represent the Athens area and had some background about the issues.

He said he attempted to get both sides to resolve the community tensions and Ms. Jenkins' dispute without a trial.

"We have attempted to work on this for years," Mr. Sessions said.

Mickey Williams, president of the North American citizens group, and Barbara Bowman, a member, said they asked various organizations to help them enforce an earlier agreement with the city, which the residents contend is ineffective.

"We were searching for anybody that would help us," said Ms. Bowman, an Athens bail bondswoman.

The suit is set for trial at 9 A.M. July 6 in the 173rd District Court in Athens. But Mr. Starr requested a July 1 hearing on his motion to dismiss the suit.

He contends there is no evidence to prove that the notes are malicious, and, he added, the notes are protected under a legal privilege.

Source: Reprinted with permission of *The Dallas Morning News*. This column appeared on 15 June 2004.

Further Readings: Prince, Richard. "Norma Adams-Wade Retiring from Dallas Morning News." [Online, 1 January 2003]. Richard Prince's Journal-isms Web site www.maynardije.org; "Resolution." [Online, 23 April 2003]. Texas State Capitol Web site www.capitol.state.tx.us.

Agnew, Ronnie (c.1963?–)

Born poor in Lee County, Mississippi, Ronnie Agnew overcame adversity to succeed in journalism and become the first African-American executive editor of the *Clarion-Ledger* in Jackson, Mississippi, the state's largest-circulation newspaper. He also writes a Sunday column for this paper. He was the seventh of nine children born to a father who at the time worked as a sharecropper and a mother who worked at a chicken processing plant. Of the nine siblings, eight went to college thanks to their parents' emphasis on education as the path to a better life. Part of Agnew's upbringing was in Tupelo, and after his father found a factory job, the remainder of his youth was spent in nearby Saltillo, Mississippi. Agnew graduated from Saltillo High School and went to the University of Mississippi. There, he majored in broadcast journalism and English and dreamed of being an on-air broadcaster, but a professor encouraged him to make use of his writing talent. After his 1984 graduation, Agnew moved to Biloxi and to a reporting job at the *Sun Herald*. He was a backup sports reporter as well and recalls covering football at Mississippi Valley State University, a small school in the Delta. There, he reported on the exploits of a standout player, receiver Jerry Rice, who went on to remarkable fame in the NFL. Agnew now uses that experience as an object lesson for his new reporters: never forget the people you cover. Another lesson from his upbringing and early reporting experience is the need for newspapers to speak for people who lack the forum to speak for themselves. Agnew's next job was at the *Cincinnati Enquirer*; there, he became assistant city editor in 1988 and began his march up the editorial ranks. In 1993, he was named managing editor of the *Hattiesburg American*, which like the *Enquirer*, is part of the Gannett group. In 1997, he moved up again, this time to be editor of the *Dothan Eagle* in Alabama. He joined the *Clarion-Ledger* as its managing editor in February 2001 and in August 2003, became executive editor, succeeding Shawn McIntosh, who left for a new position at the *Atlanta Journal and Constitution*. Agnew's promotion was hailed by many as a remarkable success story, inasmuch as the *Clarion-Ledger* had been a fierce proponent of racial segregation during the civil rights struggle of the 1950s and 1960s.

Since becoming executive editor, Agnew's main battles have been for access to public records. While Agnew was the managing editor, the paper sued because its reporters had been denied access to a meeting of the Jackson City Council that officials characterized as "a private, informal gathering." The Mississippi Supreme Court ruled in the paper's favor in February 2004. Less successful was the *Clarion-Ledger*'s suit to gain access to information about dealings involving a state-subsidized Nissan plant in Madison County, Mississippi. In December 2004, a judge ruled that these records were private financial information and could remain confidential.

As editor, Agnew enjoys the reputation of being an approachable, reasonable boss who has a genuine concern for his staffers. As Sunday columnist, he has communicated with his paper's readers on many topics. He has urged more police action to bring order to Jackson's remaining pockets of poverty, where, he wrote, some people act as if they are part of a "Gunsmoke" episode. Agnew attributes this tendency toward violence to poverty and a feeling of hopelessness on the part of some residents. Another column served as his forum for saying goodbye to two longtime sportswriters who were leaving the paper. His 4 July 2004 column, written after a visit to New York, reflected on that city as the ultimate melting pot, containing people of more diverse ethnicity that perhaps anywhere else. It is, he wrote, a place where old assumptions die and new insights can be gained. A later column that year examined the ethical considerations behind the paper's decision to publish a photograph of a father who had just learned of his daughter's murder. In October 2004, he wrote about how his newspaper suddenly found itself in possession of an exclusive story out of Iraq, where soldiers with a Quartermaster company had refused to deliver fuel due to inadequate armor on their vehicles. Some of the troops were from

Mississippi and had e-mailed their wives, asking them to get the story told in the United States. When Edgar Ray Killen was finally jailed for his hate-crime murder of three civil rights workers in 1964, Agnew used the occasion to tell the story of another victim, Mississippi store owner Vernon Dahmer, who had helped African Americans register to vote and who was beaten to death in 1966. In a January 2005 column, Agnew described his disappointment with the recent efforts of the national NAACP but his admiration of the multiracial social agenda being advocated by that organization's Mississippi president, Derrick Johnson.

"New York City Illustrates Why America Works—Its People" by Ronnie Agnew

Times Square was up to its old tricks on this sunny New York City weekend.

If there were tangible signs that terrorists had scared off tourists to this vibrant city, it surely wasn't evident on my recent trip.

The mass of humanity and the insanity of New York City cab drivers made an afternoon walk rise to the level of going through an obstacle course at Camp Shelby. Bodies unavoidably banged in the streets without the intimidating gaze of impending conflict. Sounds absolutely miserable, right? Not for me. Every minute gave me new revelation.

The throng of people scurrying about served as an example of the strength of this country. It served as a not-so-subtle lesson that terrorists didn't win that day on 9-11. Freedom and independence did.

As we celebrate our nation's independence today, it is important to remember that we are emboldened because of the collection of people that we are. Sometimes eclectic. Sometimes divided. Sometimes combative. Always American.

Melting Pot

New York is easily our ultimate melting pot. It is not for the faint of heart, but it is our best example of why America works.

It is a city where political ideologies collide. There are more ethnic groups here than perhaps anywhere in the world.

This is a place where assumptions quickly die.

A person with skin as dark as my own may claim France as her place of origin. A person with a Caucasian hue may just as likely be German or Hispanic. Gay people walk through the street hand-in-hand without meriting a notice. Different people for sure. But they have one thing in common: They are all American and many risked everything to get here.

This is a town where a Cuban pitcher paid millions to throw a ball couldn't find the strike zone until his wife escaped the clutches of an oppressive Castro.

It's a town where millions of people of all races lined city streets to celebrate Mexican heritage, an ethnicity far removed from their own.

Different Faces

It's a place where thousands of Mississippians now living in New York gathered in Central Park to eat catfish, drink sweet tea and swap stories about their part of America. It's a city where thousands packed an efficient but dirty subway train headed to Yankee Stadium to watch people with names like Jeter, Rodriguez, Giambi, Matsui—themselves a collection of America's different faces.

People all over the world are willing to leave all that they have behind just to experience a little of the freedom that we have by birthright.

We are not a perfect country. How could we be when we have so many differences?

But praise the Lord, we are free.

Source: The column reprinted above originally appeared in *The Clarion-Ledger* on 4 July 2004 and appears here by permission of Mr. Agnew.

Further Readings: "Clarion-Ledger Names New Editor." [Online, 23 August 2002]. Editor & Publisher Web site www.editorandpublisher.com; Metz, Sylvain. "Agnew Named Executive Editor." [Online, 23 August 2002]. The Clarion-Ledger site http://orig.clarionledger.com/news; "My First Job." [Online, 24 February 2005]. Chips Quinn Scholars Web site www.chipsquinn.org/jobs/first; Wenner, Kathryn S. "Jackson Action." [Online, October 2002]. American Journalism Review Web site www.ajr.org.

Alexander-Sellers, Tina (?–)

Tina Alexander-Sellers, a native of Lufkin, Texas, is vice president and news director of station KTRE-TV in Lufkin, Texas. She was born Tina Alexander. She graduated from Lufkin High School and went on for a communications degree from Stephen F. Austin State University in nearby Nacogdoches, Texas. She first worked for two Texas radio stations and then returned home by securing a job at KTRE-TV, where over the years, she has been a reporter, news anchor, producer and news director. In addition to her present duties as news director, she produces a weekly segment titled "Somebody's Got To Do It," about jobs necessary to life in the station's market area, and a monthly public affairs program, "Inside East Texas." Sister station to KLTV Tyler, Texas, KTRE, a Raycom Media station and ABC affiliate, covers the Lufkin-Nacogdoches Piney Woods area of the state.

A pillar of her community, Alexander-Sellers is on the boards of the Angelina County Chamber of Commerce, of which she was chair in 2001; Angelina Beautiful Clean, which she chaired in 2000; the Woodland Heights Medical Center; the Woman's Shelter of East Texas; the Lufkin High School Alumni Association; and the Texas State Crimestoppers. She belongs to the Chamber Coalition for a Better Community and the Lufkin Junior League and is a mentor with H.O.S.T.S., Helping One Student to Succeed. At the professional level, she is a member of the National Association of Black Journalists and the Radio-Television News Directors Association. She has taken training courses with Leadership Lufkin and with the development program of the National Association of Broadcasting Management, and in 2003 was a McCormick Fellow and participated in the seminar for television executives at Northwestern University in Evanston, Illinois. Alexander-Sellers has been recognized by the organization Young Women in America, Special Olympics, the American Cancer Society and the Angelina County United Way. She has received a chamber of commerce Pinnacle Award, the Outstanding Woman in Broadcasting award given by the American Association of University Women and the Outstanding Community Service award of the group Top Ladies of Distinction. She was also named Woman of the Year by the Eta Epsilon chapter of Alpha Kappa Alpha, and Gov. Rick Perry named her to the Black Republican Council of Texas.

Further Readings: "Tina Alexander." [Online]. KTRE Web site www.ktre.com; "Tina Alexander Sellers, WHMC Board Member." [Online]. Woodland Heights Medical Center site, http://63.151.5.93/sellers.

Allen, Ron (1957–)

Broadcast journalist Ron Allen can claim the distinction of having worked for each of the three principal U.S. networks: CBS, ABC, and now, NBC. He is currently a news correspondent for NBC in New York. Allen's father worked for United Airlines in Newark, and his mother was an elementary school secretary. He holds both the B.A. and M.A. in political science from the University of Pennsylvania and has done some additional work at the doctoral level. While a student, he was president of the Onyx Honor Society and received the University of Pennsylvania Trustees Award for his scholarly research. His career began in 1980 as a desk assistant for CBS radio news in New York City. In 1983, he became bureau chief at one of that network's affiliate stations, WFSB-TV in Hartford, Connecticut; and in 1984, he was hired as a general assignment reporter by another CBS affiliate, station WCVB-TV in Boston. He became host of a weekly public issues program on this station and at times was called upon to anchor newscasts as well. He changed jobs again in 1988 and became a correspondent for CBS News, worked for three years out of Washington, D.C., and for three more years out of Los Angeles. During the former three years, he was assigned to cover the White House and the Pentagon and also reported on the devastation caused by Hurricane Hugo; and in Los Angeles he reported on the beating of Rodney King by city police and the unrest that followed. He also reported from abroad, out of Asia and Central America. He remained with CBS until 1992, when he joined NBC as a London-based news correspondent. Some of his biggest stories include the 1993 U.S.-led United Nations attempt to provide humanitarian intervention in Somalia and in 1994, reported on Rwandan genocide, famine in Sudan and the elections in South Africa. Later in 1994 and early 1995, he was in Los Angeles reporting on the O.J. Simpson murder trial. In 1996, he again switched networks, this time working for NBC as a correspondent for "NBC Nightly News," "Today" and MSNBC. He continued in his role as a foreign correspondent, reporting from a variety of trouble spots: Afghanistan, Pakistan, Kosovo during the anti-Milosevic bombing, Baghdad, Israel, Gaza, the West Bank, Zaire when longtime president Mobutu was overthrown in 1997 by Tutsi forces in the First Congo War and Mozambique during the 2000 flooding there. In 2005, he returned to the United States and now works for NBC News and MSNBC in New York.

The longtime correspondent has received considerable recognition for his work. He won Associated Press awards for his part in team news coverage in 1983 and 1984. His reporting in 1987 on poor conditions at a mental health facility in Massachusetts won him the George Foster Peabody Award, a Robert F. Kennedy award, a National Headliner award and a UPI award. In 1989, he and CBS News colleagues won an Emmy for reporting on Hurricane Hugo, and in 1994 he received another Emmy and a Robert F. Kennedy award for his reporting for ABC News on famine in the Sudan. His 1995 reporting from Rwanda earned him 1995 National Headliner, Overseas Press Club, National Association of Black Journalists and U.S. International Film and Video Festival awards. A second Overseas Press Club award came his way in 1996 for his writing on ethnic violence in Rwanda, and in 1997, he won yet another

Overseas Press Club award for coverage of the ouster of Zaire's president Mobutu by Tutsi forces in the First Congo War. In 1999, he was selected as the NABJ journalist of the year. Allen received a third Overseas Press Club award in that same year for his reporting on Kosovo plus the Edward R. Murrow Award for Best Network Newscast for his "NBC Nightly News" reports from Belgrade during the NATO attacks in June of that year.

In early 2006, Allen took part in the Woodrow Wilson Visiting Fellows Program, in which nonacademic professionals spend a week on the campuses of liberal arts colleges and universities. At the Seattle meeting of the NABJ in 1999, Allen met fellow broadcast journalist Adaora Udoji; they were married in 2005 following a coincidence that had resulted in both of them being posted to Islamabad, Pakistan, at roughly the same time. Udoji, formerly with ABC Television, is now a general news correspondent for CNN. The couple made *New York Magazine* in 2006 for their purchase of a $2 million apartment in a new Upper West Side highrise.

Further Readings: "Adaora Udoji and Ron Allen." [Online, 6 October 2002]. New York Times Web site www.nytimes.com; Robledo, S. Jhoanna. "The $35,000-a-Month Rental." [Online, January 2005]. New York Magazine Web site www.nymetro.com; "Ron Allen, NBC Correspondent." [Online, 26 July 2005]. MSNBC Web site www.msnbc.msn.com.

Anderson, Monroe (6 April 1947–)

Former Chicago broadcasting executive Monroe Anderson is currently editor of the national magazine *Savoy*, which was relaunched in February 2005. A native of Gary, Indiana, he received a B.A. in 1970 at Indiana University. He worked briefly in 1968 for *Newsweek* and in 1969 for the *Post-Tribune* in Indianapolis. From 1970 to 1972, he was a writer for the *National Observer*, then from 1972 to 1974, was assistant editor of *Ebony Magazine*, after which he was a reporter for the *Chicago Tribune*. He later worked for Viacom and in 1988 and 1989, was press secretary for Eugene Sawyer, mayor of Chicago. Thereafter, he was director of station services and community affairs for WBBM-TV, a CBS station in Chicago. Anderson retired from broadcasting in 2002 and came out of retirement to take the editorial helm of slick, sophisticated *Savoy* upon its reappearance in mid-February 2005. The magazine had first appeared in 2001 under the ownership of Vanguarde Media, headed by Keith Clinkscales. Due to insufficient capitalization, the magazine went into Chapter 11 bankruptcy in 2003 and was bought at bankruptcy auction by Jungle Media, Inc. In June 2004, this company in turn sold *Savoy* to Hermene Hartman, publisher of the successful Chicago weekly *N'Digo*. The relaunched magazine, now owned by Hartman's Hartman Publishing Group subsidiary Jazzy Communications, is quite similar to its original in appearance and content. Anderson contributes a monthly column of his own, "Monroe's Doctrine," which addresses social and political issues. Anderson won several awards for outstanding investigative journalism while at the *Chicago Tribune* and later received UPI's best community service award (1980) and the New York State Bar Association Media Award in 1986. He contributed a chapter, "Why Evans Lost," to *Restoration 1989: Chicago Elects a New Mayor*, edited by Paul Michael Green and Melvin G. Holli (Chicago: Lyceum Books, 1991).

Further Readings: Cottman, Michael H. "Savoy Magazine Gears Up For Its Long-Awaited Relaunch." [Online, 28 January 2005]. Black America.com Web site www.blackamericaweb.com; "Savoy Magazine Is Black!" [Online, 8 February 2005]. PR Newswire site http://sev.prnewswire.com/magazines.

Andrews, Caesar (5 December 1958–)

Mobile, Alabama-born Caesar Andrews is executive editor of the *Detroit Free Press*; prior to taking that position in 2005, he had been editor of Gannett News Service. He is a 1979 journalism graduate of Grambling State University, and following commencement, he became a staff writer for *Florida Today* in Melbourne, Florida. Andrews has remarked that he was initially attracted to a career in journalism by a combination of his love of reading, his appreciation of the written word and a desire to do something that would benefit the public. He became fully committed to newspaper journalism, he has said, after covering Hurricane Frederick, which hit the Mobile Bay area in September 1979 with 140 mph winds and also did considerable damage in Meridian and Biloxi, Mississippi. Andrews left *Today* to become managing editor of the *Tribune*, a Brevard County, Florida, weekly paper, and held that job until 1982, when he became one of the initial staffers for *USA Today*, Gannett's national newspaper. He worked there as a states editor, assistant national editor and deputy managing editor for bonus sections, after which he returned to *Florida Today* to resume working as its managing editor. His next job with Gannett was as executive editor of the *Reporter* in Lansdale, Pennsylvania. In 1991 he took a year off as a practicing newspaperman to work for one year as journalist-in-residence at Grambling State University. In 1992, he moved farther north to work in New York as executive editor of the *Rockland Journal-News* in West Nyack. He was senior managing editor of the Gannett Suburban Newspapers during 1996, and in 1997 became editor of Gannett News Service, which produces and distributes news stories for the Gannett Group's 101 papers.

Andrews, a bachelor, has been active in a variety of journalism organizations. His most prominent post thus far was president of the Associated Press Managing Editors in 2002; he is now the APME representative on the Accrediting Council on Education in Journalism and Mass Communications and is on the Committee on Recognition for the Council for Higher Education

Accreditation. Andrews also chairs the Education for Journalism Committee of the American Society of Newspaper Editors. He is a board member of the National Press Foundation and is a member of the National Association of Black Journalists and the National Association of Minority Media Executives. Andrews has lectured at the American Press Institute and the Maynard Institute for Journalism Education at Northwestern University. In 1995, he was a Pulitzer Prize juror for the explanatory journalism category and was on the steering committee for the John S. and James I. Knight Foundation's Sunshine Week in 2006. He has taken part in other education-oriented activities as a participant of the media leaders forum at Louisiana State University's Manship School of Mass Communication and as a speaker at Winthrop University's Mass Communication Week. Andrews points out that leadership is not mainly about being popular, yet he has remarked that the part of management he likes least is when people's jobs are in jeopardy. He distinguishes between management and leadership in that the manager must apply policy and process to keep the work flowing, whereas the leader must think ahead and must encourage and inspire.

Further Readings: "Caesar Andrews Moves to Detroit Free Press." [Online, 2005]. Gannett News Watch Web site www.gannett.com/go/newswatch; "Journalism, Blogging & Diversity: Caesar Andrews Responds." [Online, 14 February 2005]. Poynter Institute Web site www.poynter.org; Morgan, Arlene Notoro. "A Love of Words Leads Caesar Andrews to a Career in Journalism, Where He Puts the Emphasis on the Individual." [Online, 1 July 2001]. American Society of Newspaper Editors Web site www.asne.org; "My First Job: Caesar Andrews." [Online]. Chips Quinn Web site www.chipsquinn.org/jobs/first.

Asim, Jabari (?–)

Jabari Asim writes a weekly op-ed column syndicated since 2003 by the Washington Post Writer's Group. He is also senior editor of *Washington Post Book World*, assistant editor of the journal *Drumvoices Revue* published at Southern Illinois University, and founding editor of the literary journal *Eyeball*. In addition, he is a reviewer, book author and editor, poet and playwright.

Prior to joining the *Post*, Asim worked at the St. Louis *Post-Dispatch*, copy editing for the editorial section, editing the weekend section and serving as book editor. His commentaries had appeared in the *Phoenix Gazette*, BlackElectorate.com and Salon.com, and his work as a literary essayist appeared in *The Furious Flowering of African-American Poetry* (1999). His criticism has been published in the *Detroit News*, the *Village Voice*, the *International Herald Tribune*, *Emerge*, *Code* and *Hungry Mind Review*.

Joining the *Washington Post* in 1996, Asim assigned reviews and directed coverage of literary topics. During 2001 and 2002, he wrote a book review column that ran on Tuesdays in the Style section, then began his op-ed column in 2003. He uses his column to explore what he terms the ways in which politics, social issues and the popular culture intersect. Such intersections were plentiful in the 2004 presidential elections. Asim wondered whether John Kerry's enormous lead among black voters might result in complacency on the part of the Democrats. After the election, Asim wrote about the 89 percent of black voters mourning the result with turned stomachs, likening the feeling to the characters on the popular television drama "Lost." In the face of the success of what he called Bush's right-wing wrecking crew and the whirlpool of the Democrats' clueless, indifferent performance, Asim appeared to agree with Harvard professor Michael Dawson that increasing numbers of African-Americans might be more attracted to third-party candidates in future elections. His assessment was that the election left blacks with very little political leverage, the hot demographic having become arch-conservative white evangelicals. He was pleased, however, with the sensational success in the Illinois senatorial race of Democrat Barack Obama and the embarrassment suffered by the Republicans as their original candidate, Jack Ryan, who withdrew due to marital troubles, and the subsequent scramble to replace him with anyone having name recognition.

In a highly personal column headlined "Higher Education, Lower Enthusiasm," he took his own son to task for the boy's failing to appreciate the opportunities now available to high-performing black high school students, who are being actively courted by universities, a situation that differs greatly from that of the not so long ago days when most college-bound African-Americans went to historically black colleges.

In a column that was a sort of microcosm of U.S. race relations, Asim reflected on the accomplishments of Althea Gibson, the first black to win the U.S. Open tennis tournament, and how she had paved the way for Serena and Venus Williams. He was impressed by the courtesy officials showed Serena Williams following a 2004 U.S. Open match she lost, in part attributable to a series of egregiously bad calls by an umpire.

Reproduced below is Asim's take on a little-discussed corner of race relations: white discomfort over the work of black cartoonists.

Asim's poetry has appeared in such venues as *Painted Bride Quarterly, Shooting Star Review, Catalyst, Obsidian II* and *Black American Literature Forum* as well as in *Soulfires: Young Black Men on Love and Violence* (New York: Penguin Books, 1996) and *Role Call: A Generational Anthology of Social & Political Black Literature & Art* (Chicago: Third World Press, 2002). He was the sole contributor to have both poetry and short fiction anthologized in *In the Tradition: An Anthology of Young Black Writers* (New York: Writers & Readers Pub., 1992). His own books have been a novel for young readers and an edited book on justice and the law.

"Why Are There Still Too Few Nonwhite Cartoonists" by Jabari Asim

The University of Michigan is spending $100,000 on a bunch of jokes.

For three years, some of the university's finest minds will get together and pursue what promises to be a thorny question: Why do people laugh at cartoons?

Scholars at Michigan hope to find out by studying cartoons published in The New Yorker, beginning with those that appeared in the magazine's first issues in 1925. The announcement of the study coincides with the release of a mammoth book containing 2,500 cartoons from The New Yorker archives. (It comes with a pair of CD-ROMs containing all 68,647 cartoons published up to last February.) As perhaps the nation's most consistent source of stellar one-panel gags, The New Yorker seems a logical place to start. I wouldn't stop there, however.

I'm a fan of New Yorker cartoons. In addition to being funny they are also oddly reassuring. Featuring neurotic and often wealthy white folks, they provide some comfort in showing that the privileged may be different from you and me, but they are just as screwed up. I even own collections of several of the artists who made names as New Yorker cartoonists, including Charles Addams, Charles Barsotti and George Booth. But when I cracked open the new book I looked in vain for the work of one artist in particular: Robb Armstrong.

Armstrong's panel appeared in The New Yorker's much-discussed "Black in America" issue, published in April 1996. It showed a graying, pinstripe-bedecked black professional looking on attentively as his white boss, a bow-tied, well-fed sort, prepares to fire him. "Gosh, it kills me to do this to you, Worthington," the boss says, "but you're not turning out to be as black as we had hoped."

Like many of the cartoons in that issue, the gag successfully addressed the tricky identity issues surrounding race in an increasingly multicultural society. Armstrong tapped into the concerns of black professionals who, in books such as Ellis Cose's "Rage of a Privileged Class," often expressed fears about being perceived as too black or not black enough. But what distinguished Armstrong's gag was its creator's racial background. Best known as the artist behind "Jump Start," a warmhearted strip about a young married couple, Armstrong was the sole black cartoonist to have his work included in an issue devoted to black culture.

The discrepancy was especially curious in light of the editors' apparent success at locating and including the work of black illustrators and writers in the issue. Could black cartoonists be that hard to find? Lee Lorenz, who was cartoon editor at the time, told the Village Voice that the magazine had purchased eight drawings from black cartoonists but ultimately decided to include only the contribution from Armstrong. "The black cartoons were more difficult for people to handle than had been anticipated," Lorenz said.

Eight years later, the impressive diversity that has begun to creep into the pages of The New Yorker—with maddening slowness, to be sure—has yet to show up much in the cartoons. Minus Addams' undeniably racist minstrel-faced cannibals of yesteryear, there are even fewer dark faces showing up in the panels. Evidently the magazine decided that the easiest way to avoid stepping on racial sensitivities is to leave blacks and other minorities out of the cartoons altogether.

The New Yorker is not alone in its inability to grapple efficiently with this issue. In September, The Washington Post quietly declined to run a week's worth of "The Boondocks" strips. The cartoon is the brainchild of Aaron McGruder, a talented and fearless African-American artist whose work often provokes strong reactions—negative and positive. Rather than risk rubbing readers the wrong way, the Post and a handful of other major papers—unwisely—opted for the timid route and printed reruns instead.

Editors' confusion about racial commentary in cartoons demonstrates the enduring power of these tiny drawings to perplex and infuriate as well as amuse. At the same time, one wonders why publications have failed to learn from the rise of comedians such as Dave Chappelle, Margaret Cho and Chris Rock (and before them, Richard Pryor and Eddie Murphy). Their popularity suggests that audiences have less difficulty "handling" racial humor than is often supposed.

Why, then, are there still so few nonwhite cartoonists working in mainstream forums? And why are those few still greeted with trepidation and concern?

These, too, are $100,000 questions.

Source: © 2005, *The Washington Post*. Reprinted with permission. This column originally appeared on 4 October 2004.

Books by Jabari Asim: *The Road to Freedom* (Lincolnwood, Ill.: Jamestown, 2000); editor, *Not Guilty: Twelve Black Men Speak Out on Law, Justice, and Life* (New York: Amistad Press, 2001).
Further Readings: "Jabari Asim." [Online]. California Newsreel Web site www.newsreel.org; "Jabari Asim." [Online]. The Washington Post Writers Group Web site www.postwritersgroup.com.

Aubespin, Mervin Raymond (30 June 1937–)

Merv Aubespin retired in 2002 after a 34-year career at the *Louisville Courier-Journal* in Kentucky; his nickname, "Uncle Merv," stems from his avuncular appearance and his reputation as a mentor for aspiring young journalists. He was born in Cajun country at Opelousas, Louisiana, and finished high school by age 15. He attended Tuskegee Institute, where he studied industrial arts with the intention of a career teaching that subject but instead fell under the influence of a social studies professor. This influence, added to the interest in newspapers and magazines fostered earlier by his mother and a favorite aunt, began to aim him in a different direction. Also, while Aubespin was visiting Montgomery with his college roommate, one of his friend's aunts, scolding the boys for their callow college-boy interests, took them to church to meet her new minister, Martin Luther King. Aubespin and his friend began working with the Rev. King, helping organize civil rights boycotts and demonstrations, which got the young Aubespin arrested roughly 30 times. He spent his college summers in Mississippi, Alabama, Georgia and Louisiana, keeping a step ahead of the Ku Klux Klan, and marched with King from Selma to Montgomery. Aubespin graduated in 1958, taught school in Louisville, where one of his students was Cassius Clay, future boxing great. Aubespin left teaching for a higher-paying job with B.F. Goodrich. After six months, however, he was drafted and spent the next two years as an Army enlisted man at Fort Knox and Fort Hood, studying art in his spare time. He returned to B.F. Goodrich and helped found a black art workshop. In 1967, he learned about an opening in the *Courier-Journal* art department and offered the paper his services on a two-week trial basis. He was the first African American on the department's staff and was hired on his second day there. The times were rife with racial conflict, and during a 1968 Louisville rally, which turned into a riot, an editor asked Aubespin if he would accompany a white reporter to cover the action—essentially to protect the man. When the riot became dangerous, Aubespin suggested that the reporter might want to leave. Aubespin remained on the scene, then phoned in what he had observed. The paper dispatched its best photographer by cab to join him, but when his taxi was overturned by rioters, the photographer returned to the safety of the newspaper. Aubespin arranged by phone for a friend who did photography in black nightclubs and his own younger brother to handle the photography for the paper. Executive editor Norman Isaacs called Aubespin in to thank him, asking what the paper could do for him. He asked that the photographer and his brother be hired, which was done. Soon management decided to make a reporter out of Aubespin, and in 1971, he was sent to a minority journalism workshop at Columbia University in New York. In the following year, he also did some postgraduate study at the University of Louisville, where he concentrated on the psychology of poverty. He worked as a reporter until 1984, then became director of minority recruitment and an assistant to the executive editor, and finally associate editor for development. He has seen the newspaper's human complexion change considerably since 1967, when, as the only black on the staff, he often felt, in his words, like a fly in a bowl of milk or a pebble in the newspaper's shoe.

Aubespin has been active in the National Association of Black Journalists, serving as its president from 1983 to 1985. He designed the NABJ logo and provided the organization its first office in the *Courier-Journal* building. During this time, he led a group of African-American journalists to West Africa to report on drought conditions and two years thereafter, led a second such trip to the same region. He made outreach to the mainstream media one of his missions and in 1979, founded the Louisville Association of Black Communicators of which he was the first president; he later served a second term as president. Before becoming president of NABJ, he had served from 1979 to 1981 as a regional director of that organization. He also was chairman of the American Society of Newspaper Editors' Human Resources Committee and, although he himself never worked as a copy editor, he considered these men and women the unsung heroes of journalism and championed their cause for greater recognition. In Chapel Hill in 1997, he helped organize a Freedom Forum–funded national conference for copy editors, during which the American Copy Editors Society was founded. The conference was repeated several times at other universities until the funding ran out. Today, this society continues to grow and annually awards a $2,500 Aubespin Scholarship to students who plan to become copy editors. In 1997, he traveled with a group of U.S. journalists to Guatemala to observe conditions at the end of its long civil war. At the end of 1997, he traveled to Senegal to report on poverty in that nation, and he spoke at a seminar in Timbuktu, Mali, in 2000.

Aubespin has been a popular campus speaker and has advised journalism programs at the University of Kentucky, Western Kentucky University, Franklin College, Howard University and Jackson State University. He has been a media consultant for the United Nations Development Programs and in this capacity has traveled to the Ivory Coast, South Africa, Mozambique, Mali, Mauritania, Senegal, Niger and Burkina Faso. His role as mentor has earned him many recognitions, such as the 1991 Distinguished Service to Journalism Award of the Association of Schools of Journalism and Mass Communications and in the same year, the Black College Communication Association award, which now bears his own name. He was inducted into the NABJ Hall of Fame in 1994 and the Kentucky Journalism Hall of Fame in 1995.

In 1990, he received the Ida B. Wells Award for leadership in securing journalism employment for minorities. In November 1997, he traveled to Guatemala with an international group of journalists to observe peacekeeping efforts following the end of that nation's 36-year civil war, and in December 1997, he spoke in Senegal on poverty issue reporting. In December 2000, he spoke at a seminar in Timbuktu, Mali, on Africa's negative image in the media. Probably even more satisfying to him than his awards and travel is the fact that his daughter, Eleska Aubespin, followed his journalistic footsteps and is a reporter for *Florida Today* in the city of Melbourne. In retirement, he consults for the *Courier-Journal*, paints and collects African art.

"Comment" by Mervin Aubespin

For many west Africans, Goree Island in Senegal is an escape from the hot bush country or from the teeming metropolitan areas—a tropical retreat.

There are no asphalt roads, no bicycles, scooters or automobiles. Instead, a visitor to Goree Island finds lanes, ankle-deep with sand, and weather-beaten houses, with cool courtyards shaded by flowering trees. On warm days its small beach is crowded with beautiful women and lean young men who amuse themselves by diving off the seawall into bluish-green clear water.

But to many black American tourists, this small island, about two miles west of Senegal's capital, Dakar, is a memorial to the millions of Africans transported to Europe and America as slaves.

I visited the island in 1986 while reporting on Senegal's effort to combat the devastation of drought and the encroachment of the desert.

Like most first-time visitors, I had been enchanted by the island's charm and its smiling mystery.

At the infamous House of Slaves, I listened with journalistic detachment to curator Joseph Ndiaye recount the atrocities committed on my luckless forefathers.

The history lesson he related would haunt me for two years. Upon my return to the United States, I wrote about the human suffering brought on by the drought. But I couldn't think of the words to write about Goree.

Last December, I visited Senegal and Goree Island again. I was invited to the country by government and UNICEF officials to participate in a "Ceremony of Remembrance" and ground breaking for a memorial on Goree to the millions of people who died and suffered during the middle passage to slavery.

I felt a powerful sense of urgency upon my arrival in Dakar, the country's largest city. There was almost uncontrollable anticipation and excitement when my host, Djibril Diallo, a UNICEF aide, and my journalist colleagues agreed to visit Goree the next morning—three days before the scheduled ceremonies.

Though tired from a nine-hour flight across the Atlantic, I spent an almost sleepless night, like a youngster waiting for Christmas or a birthday.

For centuries, Goree's strategic location at the westernmost part of Africa made it an important port in the slave trade between that continent and America and the Caribbean.

American colonies received their first shipload of slaves in 1619 from Goree Island, then a Dutch trading post. Historians estimate that from 1536 through 1848, when the French abolished slavery on Goree, more than 40 million Africans were shipped from West Africa. About half came through Goree.

As we approached the boomerang-shaped island by ferryboat, the black cliffs in the distance and the red roofs of the sun-bleached pastel-colored buildings that edge the small beach were the most distinct features.

Our ferry swung around the tip of the island and docked at a narrow jetty. I recognized Fort d'Estrees, now a prison. And I remembered why the attractive buildings and public square originally were built. The former slave auction site didn't seem so attractive anymore.

We were ushered into the courtyard of the slave house, a structure that once stood on the island to serve the same purpose.

As many as 400 slaves at a time were kept at the house and sometimes had to wait months before being shipped to Europe, America or other ports.

Curator Ndiaye, who has made the house and its history his life's work, explained that dozens of slaves were manacled and forced into dark, 30-by-20-foot dungeons. There was a cell for the men, a cell for the women and cells for boys and girls. There was a cell for breeding and another for pregnant women.

There was a room for weighing and cells where slaves were fattened in preparation for their long sea journey.

The curator explained that the stronger stayed alive by fighting others for food and that the weaker died there on en route to America.

There also was a very special cell reserved for the more recalcitrant. "Problem slaves" were chained to the wall of this closet-sized room, and sea water was piped in to keep them almost submerged.

Ndiaye talked about how slave traders lived a floor above the cells in cool, comfortable quarters, while down below unruly captives were manacled with heavy chains and iron balls.

He demonstrated the special treatment reserved for those who resisted their captors. He showed the iron spikes that were driven through the feet of those who might try to escape and the iron hooks that were used to seal the lips of those who might plot or lead.

As Ndiaye talked, I drifted away from the group. I had heard the story before.

I was on an emotional rollercoaster. I felt a tremendous sadness, and an anger that frightened even me.

I entered one of the dark, damp cells and sat alone on the stone floor for minutes that seemed like hours. And then it happened.

Sensations vastly different from the journalistic detachment of my previous visit surged through me. Inside my head, I heard the screams. I heard the moaning, the cries of frightened little children snatched from their mothers' arms. I heard the voices, the crack of the leather whips.

I closed my eyes and ran my hands along the damp, flaking walls of the cell; the walls told me their secrets—of the time my forefathers huddled, terrified, in this unholy place.

I could feel the heat of the branding irons and smell the burning flesh.

Stepping outside the cell, I looked down the long corridor that passes beneath the breeze-filled quarters of the slave traders upstairs.

At the end of the corridor, I saw the door that opens to the sea and, at another time, to the ships waiting for their human cargo.

A sign above said "The Doorway of No Return."

Indeed it was, for African slaves who passed through that door and others like it never again set foot on the soil of their homeland.

Staring at the sea through the open door at the end of the corridor, I heard the sounds again: the muffled clanging of chains as very distant relatives were loaded on ships, the moaning, the crying.

I could hear the frenzy of sharks being fed those captives who hadn't survived the wait in the cells or were too sick or too difficult to handle for the long ocean voyage.

Still on the emotional rollercoaster, I felt hatred. I felt anger at man's cruelty to man. And, for a moment, I wondered at the ironic possibility that the ancestors of the curator and the ancestors of my other new African friends could well have been among those who captured and sold my forefathers into slavery.

I also felt a respect for the strength that has helped my people endure. Truly, only the strongest would survive the capture, the cells, the chains, the voyage across the Atlantic and the treatment upon their arrival in a new land.

And, I felt love, a most profound love for what I had come from.

Then I cried.

Now I know why I returned to this haunting but charming island, with its atmosphere of smiling mystery. I am at peace with myself. I've gone home. I, too, have found my roots.

Source: © *The Courier-Journal*. The above story appeared in the 17 April 1988 issue of *The Courier-Journal Magazine* and appears here with the paper's permission.

Further Readings: "ACES Banquet Salutes Merv Aubespin." [Online, 2002]. American Copy Editors Society Web site www.copydesk.org; Marriott, Michel. "A Salute to NABJ's Presidents: Merv Aubespin." [Online]. National Association of Black Journalists site http://members.nabj.org.

B

Bailey, Isaac J. (25 November 1972–)

Isaac Bailey of the Myrtle Beach, S.C., *Sun News* is a talented young columnist. Bailey grew up as one of 11 children in the tiny South Carolina town of St. Stephen. He majored in psychology at Davidson College, where he graduated in 1995, after which he spent a year freelancing for the *Charlotte Observer*, writing features for the front page, the local section, and the Neighbors feature. In 1997, he joined the Myrtle Beach paper and for the following three years worked the city council beat and was at various times a community news reporter, general assignment reporter, designer and feature writer. He became a columnist in 2000; his first column appears below. From 2000 to 2003, he wrote the column only monthly and devoted most of his time to the business beat, reporting on real estate trends and other business topics. His column mainly dealt with race relations but more recently has been broadened greatly in its scope. From 2003 to early 2005, Bailey was business editor of the *Sun News*, then gave up that position to concentrate on his column, which now appears thrice weekly and is distributed nationally on the Knight Ridder wire.

Now enjoying free rein to write about whatever he wishes, Bailey uses his column to tackle many issues. He takes Detroit to task for its apparent death wish in offering the American consumer ever heavier, less gas-efficient trucks and "muscle cars" in the face of certain increases in gas prices, yet he admits to being attracted by the macho image of such vehicles. He cautions against depending on the coastal condo market as a quick way to make money, noting that a boom market can suddenly nosedive and leave both developers and buyers financially stranded. He examines both sides of the capital punishment debate—hard to do for someone whose own older brother is serving a life sentence for murder. He, at 6 feet tall and 228 pounds, grumbles about the federal government's overly simplistic body mass index as its measure of obesity, pointing out, tongue in cheek, that the popular image of Uncle Sam looks as if he has not eaten in 230 years. He demands that men hold each other more accountable for rape and other forms of abuse against women. Just prior to the presidential election, he lays bare the various clichés of "being counted," letting one's voice be heard and other such arguments used in urging people to get out and vote, yet he admits that he usually feels that in voting, he is selecting the lesser of two evils in an age when politicians know they can not get into office unless they tell us what we want to hear rather than what we need to hear. He presses one of his state's representatives in Congress for that gentleman's stance on same-sex marriage but can not get a straight answer and in another column, chides television evangelists for suggesting that our nation was attacked on September 11, 2001, because of our growing acceptance of gays. And he admits to being tired of having to defend his home state, where part of the population seems stuck in the past.

In 1998, Bailey won the News Story of the Year award from the *Sun News* for a story he wrote on the homeless in Myrtle Beach, S.C. He took first place in 1999 in the South Carolina Press Association competition; in 2000, he won two first-place awards: in column writing and spot news reporting. In 2003, he again took two first place awards: column writing and in-depth reporting.

"The Hardest Piece I've Ever Written" by Isaac J. Bailey

When you have finished this, you would have read the hardest piece I've ever written. Many times, fear has forced my fingers away from the keyboard.

For I, too, have felt that certain fear we rarely talk about and almost never admit feeling: the fear of black men. Yes, despite my 6'0" 220 pound frame. Despite my college football background.

Despite my growing up with eight brothers—black brothers—and attending an almost all-black high school.

I've felt myself brace, tense up, when walking down a sidewalk toward a group of folks that look like me.

I've heard myself think, heard myself say, things that suggest those vile, racist stereotypes reside in me.

In me, despite my God-fearing foundation.

When I watch the evening news and see a black man accused of a crime, I cringe. But there is no surprise in my eyes.

For when I close them and think of criminal, I see black, and male.

Someone who looks just like me.

I've learned racism springs from somewhere other than our rational mind. When you have finished this, you would have read the hardest piece I've ever written, for it's hard to admit one's shortcomings, hard to stand up on a stage and tell you that I'm just like you.

Hard to accept the irony of the images that haunt me and chase me, knowing others have crossed the road to avoid my dark presence, followed my every move in and out of stores, looked straight through me, never noticing I was—I am.

But I must tell you, for it's the only way I know to get your attention. The only way to help you move past the fear that has kept so many mired in a cloud of confusion and irrational thought.

For I know where the irrational has been birthed. Right there in the percentages—almost 70 percent of South Carolina inmates are black, about 50 percent nationwide—and the images.

Seldom, though, do we question how the image of me affects those who must judge me.

I know of what I speak. My oldest brother is a convicted murderer. A high school friend is blind from a gunshot wound to the head, shot by others who look like us. Other high school friends are in prison for armed robbery and car jacking.

A student I once tutored is dead from the bullet of a police officer, an officer he shot and killed a split second earlier.

All black. All male. Every one.

I've seen the ugliness that can make us forget there is so much beauty. The beauty of my brothers proudly raising their sons and daughters and respecting their wives. The beauty of the many black males who work in ties and three-piece suits or aprons and McDonald's hats to provide for families they love.

When you have finished reading this, you would have read the hardest piece I've ever written, for there's no logical way to explain away fact. Facts we've grown accustomed to citing, too lazy to examine.

For what do they say about me, and the nine out of 10 black males who never commit violent crimes or the more than seven out of 10 who never see the inside of a courtroom as a defendant.

What do they say about the studies that show that when income and educational levels are factored in, there is no statistical difference in violence levels between blacks and whites.

What do they say about the man you—I—greeted last night with suspicion, when all he was ready to return was a smile. A gentle glance.

What does it say about us, all of us, who dare demand justice and equality and fairness, but dare not examine subconscious forces that stand in the way for fear of being labeled something that we are: flawed human beings who sometimes make irrational, snap judgments.

It says absolutely nothing.

Yet, all too much.

Source: The above column is reproduced here with the permission of *The Sun News*.

Baquet, Dean P. (1957–)

Affable Dean Baquet, whose last name is pronounced "BA-kay," became editor of the West Coast's largest newspaper, the *Los Angeles Times*, in August 2005. He was born in New Orleans to a family that owned and operated Eddie's restaurant and is of Creole heritage, descended from Haitians. Baquet attended the well-regarded Roman Catholic St. Augustine High School in New Orleans and was an English major at Columbia University. But after doing an internship at the now-defunct New Orleans *States-Item*, he left school without graduating to become a police reporter at the paper. He and Jim Amoss, who later became editor of the *Times-Picayune*, worked as a team, and Baquet is godfather to Amoss's son. Next, Baquet reported for the *Times Picayune* in New Orleans. He worked as a journalist in his hometown for around seven years. From 1984 to 1990, he was on the staff of the *Chicago Tribune*, where he was chief investigative reporter and associate metropolitan editor for investigations. In 1988, he, Ann Marie Lipinski and William Gaines were a reporting team that won a Pulitzer Prize for investigating corruption involving Chicago's City Council. In 1990, he was hired away by the *New York Times* to work as a metropolitan reporter. His investigative work was widened to national scope, and in 1992, he became special projects editor for business. He was the *Times'* national editor for a little more than five years, 1995–2000, and was not only well liked, but regarded as a good prospect for the executive editor position at that paper. With another reporter, he was a Pulitzer finalist for investigative work on the level of care in New York hospitals. In 2000, Baquet was enticed to Los Angeles by the highly regarded John S. Carroll, who had taken over as editor of the *Los Angeles Times*. As managing editor, Baquet worked closely with

Carroll to raise the paper's national reputation. In five years, despite circulation losses and having had to cut roughly 10 percent of the editorial staff, the two editors increased the investigative focus of the *Times*, winning 13 Pulitzer prizes. Editor Carroll finally tired of battling with the Chicago corporate headquarters of the Tribune Company, the *Times*' owner, due to the parent company's unrelenting focus on the bottom line. Carroll retired, at least temporarily, and in August 2005, Baquet, then age 48, became the first editor of color to head the Los Angeles paper. A man known as a reporter's editor, Baquet is described by his coworkers as invigorating, smart, classy, dynamic, fun to work with and driven, yet caring and engaging. When he assumed the position of editor, Baquet was also named the *Times*' executive vice president. At this time, the *Times*' publisher accentuated the line between news and opinion by deciding that the editorial section editor, Michael Kinsley, would henceforth report not to the editor, but to the publisher. It has been reported that the top management of Tribune Company assured Baquet that he would be allowed to keep the resources to maintain journalistic quality and to hold onto the *Times*' position as the state and region's largest and most prestigious newspaper.

In October 2005, the investigative-minded Baquet revealed that he was considering adding a Hollywood gossip column to increase coverage of motion picture celebrities. He also came out in favor of using briefer stories to appeal to readers having short attention spans. He split his former managing editor duties among three individuals and appointed entertainment reporter and editor Joel Sappell to a new position as executive editor, interactive. Sappell was part of a major controversy while Baquet was managing editor: the paper's decision in 2003 to run page-one stories revealing that gubernatorial candidate Arnold Schwarzenegger had been accused of groping six women. These stories appeared just prior to the recall election that unseated Gov. Gray Davis and put Schwarzenegger in office. To complaints from the new governor's supporters that both Gov. Davis and fellow candidate Cruz Bustamonte got front-page treatment in the *Times*, while items about Schwarzenegger usually were buried inside the paper, Baquet reportedly responded archly that inside the paper, after all, is where movie ads usually run. Conservatives were furious, and subscriptions to the paper were cancelled, although the cancellation numbers reported have varied considerably. As editor, Baquet has taken pains to ensure the paper's coverage of the war in Iraq is of superior quality. Heavy coverage was also given to the Hurricane Katrina story, and the paper's magazine section was retooled. In November 2005, however, Baquet announced that his news staff had to be cut by another 85 people by the end of year, by attrition, voluntary separations or layoffs. Although he was still left with the second largest newsroom in the nation, deep cuts for two years running must have hurt his hopes for the paper. Baquet, who has chosen not to join the National Association of Black Journalists and does not appear to be much of a joiner in general, has been a Pulitzer jury member and is on the National Advisory

Board of the Poynter Institute. He is also on the board of directors of the Committee to Protect Journalists, and even though he did not graduate, Columbia College of Columbia University has honored him as an outstanding alumnus with its John Jay Award. Baquet has a younger brother, Terry Baquet, who is page one editor for the *Times-Picayune* in New Orleans.

Further Readings: "Baquet Era Begins." [Online, 20 July 2005]. LA Observed Web site www.laobserved.com; Darman, Jonathan. "Tough Times at the Times." Newsweek, 1 August 2005, p. 48; Kurtz, Howard. "L.A. Times Names Dean Baquet as Top Editor." [Online, 21 July 2005]. Washington Post Web site www.washingtonpost.cpm; Lewis, Monica. "L.A. Times' Dean Baquet Joins Growing Ranks of Black Newspaper Editors." [Online, 24 July 2005]. Black America Web site www.blackamericaweb.com; Roderick, Kevin. "The Hot Seat." [Online, November 005]. Kevin Roderick Web site www.kevinroderick.com; Shah, Diane K. "The New Los Angeles Times." [Online, May/June 2002]. Columbia Journalism Review Web site www.djr.org/issues/2002; Smolkin, Rachel. "Nothing But Fans." [Online, 3 August 2005]. American Journalism Review Web site www.ajr.org.

Bayé, Betty Winston (12 April 1946–)

Betty Bayé is an editorial writer and columnist for the Louisville *Courier-Journal* in Kentucky. A native of Brooklyn, N.Y., she graduated in communications from Hunter College of the City University of New York in 1979 and received the M.S. from Columbia University's School of Journalism in 1980. From that same year through 1984 she was a reporter for the *Daily Argus* in Mount Vernon, N.Y., after which she joined the *Courier-Journal*, working first as a reporter, then from 1986–1988 as assistant city editor. From 1988–1990 she was assistant editor for the neighborhoods section, and in 1990 and 1991 she was a Nieman Fellow at Harvard University. She has written her general column, which appears on Thursdays and is distributed nationally by the Gannett News Service, since 1991. Her column usually deals with various aspects of the African-American experience.

The example of Bayé's work that appears below was written upon the death of longtime South Carolina Sen. Strom Thurmond, long an opponent of civil rights for blacks. The irony of the situation came to light only after his death: that he had fathered a child in 1925 with Essie Mae Williams, African American. Responding to comedian Bill Cosby's now famous criticisms of poor blacks, Bayé agreed with most of his remarks but pointed out that what he said applied not just to U.S. blacks, but to poor Americans in general. His complaints also apply, she wrote, to middle- and upper-class people, who can afford a psychiatrist, whereas poor people have to go crazy in public. She also pointed out that the phenomenon of a high-achieving black person publicly criticizing his low-achieving brothers and sisters was hardly original to Cosby, citing earlier lambasting by such diverse individuals as W.E.B. Du Bois, Zora Neale Hurston, Jesse Jackson, Martin Luther King, Jr., Louis Farrakhan, musician Wynton Marsalis and comedian Chris Rock. After filling out her census form, she reflected in a 2001 column about the imprecise nature of the term "black," inasmuch as so many of us have some racial variety in our ancestry. She offered herself as an example, citing both Caucasian and Native American ancestors, yet she simply checked the box for "black" on her census form, saying that when she looks in the mirror, the reflection looks black to her and adding that black is also what security personnel see when they look at her suspiciously in department stores. And in another column, she laments that so many Americans, black and white, appear to have given up on the idea of integration and instead have drawn back into their separate camps.

Another Bayé lament is that our nation imprisons more of its citizens than any other country, that we have turned the building and running of prisons into a form of private enterprise, and that we had been guilty of prisoner abuse long before the infamous revelations at Abu Ghraib prison in Iraq. A very special column was her tribute to veteran Delaware columnist Norm Lockman of the *Wilmington News Journal* upon his retirement due to the complications of Lou Gehrig's disease.

Bayé has published two books—the first a novel, the second a collection of her columns.

"Yesterday's Hypocritical Silence Yields to Today's Selective Outrage" by Betty Bayé

On the occasion of Strom Thurmond's death on June 26, 2003, South Carolina Congressman Joe Wilson misspoke when he said, "We are just so grateful that he has seen the birth of his first grandchild."

The fact is that Thurmond's first grandchild and three others had been born many years prior to the "first" grandchild that Wilson had in mind.

And Thurmond was aware of those grandchildren. In fact, he had met them, though he never publicly acknowledged their existence.

The again, how could he? For 78 years, the longest-serving member of the U.S. Senate never publicly acknowledged their mother, his own and oldest child.

Essie Mae Washington Williams was born in 1925 to Thurmond, who was 22, and Carrie Cutler, a 16-year-old African American employed by Thurmond's family. The child's existence wasn't all that remarkable; many white sons of the South fathered children with black women.

What was and is remarkable, though, is that so many leading Americans and their biographers, who couldn't have avoided being aware of such relationships, opted to ignore all those elephants sitting in America's living room, not just as the nation bloodied and disgraced itself during slavery and the Civil War but also during the 20th Century's battles over segregation and civil rights.

Thurmond spent a significant chunk of his long public life, both as governor of South Carolina and in the Senate, advocating white supremacy and opposing civil rights legislation.

The hypocrite railed in public against "race-mixing" even though he engaged in private in the most intimate sort.

Rumors swirled around him, to be sure, but his daughter kept her peace until after he died at the age of 100 in 2003.

"I didn't want to ruin his career," the gracious retired schoolteacher told Dan Rather in a "60 Minutes" interview in December 2003.

Williams might have carried the secret to her won grave had not her children encouraged her to claim her birthright and to, finally, unburden herself of the cross she'd carried all her life.

Her autobiography, *Dear Senator: A Memoir by the Daughter of Strom Thurmond*, will be published next month. It may paint a more sympathetic portrait of Thurmond, who was never a hero of anybody where I come from.

Williams told Rather, for example, that she didn't learn that her father was white until she was 16 years old. It was 1941 when her mother announced, "I want to take you to meet your father."

"I knew I had a dad somewhere, but I had never met him, and nobody ever talked about him," Williams said.

As for Thurmond's race, Williams said, "I didn't give it a great deal of thought... I was very happy to meet him."

The two met many times over the years, usually at Thurmond's request. He provided financial assistance, and he visited her fairly often when he was governor and she was studying at the all-black college in South Carolina that Thurmond recommended she attend.

Nevertheless, Williams' early lack of curiosity about her father and the lack of candor by her mother, and the aunt and uncle who raised her, probably seem odd these days, when people rush onto TV to bare the most intimate details of their lives.

Hard to believe, maybe, but there really were times, even when I was growing up, that children didn't dare ask adults penetrating questions. The rule was that children should be seen and not heard. So a lot of stuff, some of it bad, some contradictory and some simply explanatory, got swept under the rug and stayed there.

The press also was pretty good at keeping quiet about the scandalous, embarrassing and hypocritical behavior of American heroes, who preached one thing in public, but practiced another behind closed doors.

In earlier times, the Watergate scandal may not have cut short Richard Nixon's political career. Bill Clinton may not have been impeached, and former New York City Police Commissioner Bernard Kerik's adultery and reputed mob ties may not have disqualified him to replace Tom Ridge as director of homeland security.

Still, I can't decide which is better and which worse.

Is it the deafening silence of generations past that left so many in the dark, not only about their heroes, but also their own family trees? Or is it the selective moral outrage of these times?

Today, some people's skuzzy behavior renders them morally unfit to serve, while others guilty of far worse, and often neither as talented or prepared to lead, are allowed to keep on keeping on.

And woe to any who dare expose their leaden feet.

Source: This column appeared in the *Courier-Journal* on 23 December 2004, and appears here by permission of Ms. Bayé and the Louisville *Courier-Journal*.

Books by Betty Winston: As Betty Winston, *The Africans* (Wayne, Pa.: Banbury, 1983); *Blackbird* (Newport News, Va.: August Press, 2000).

Further Readings: Acosta, Alan. "The Wrong Background: Issues of Newsroom Employment." [Online]. Center for Media Literacy Web site www.medialit.org; "Betty Baye: Columnist for 'The Courier Journal,' a Gannett Publication." [Online]. The Howland Group Web site www.howlandgroup.com/workplacetrends; "Columnist Visits UK in Commemoration of African American History Month." [Online, 1 February 2006]. University of Kentucky site http://news.uky.edu/news.

Bennett, Lerone (17 October 1928–)

Recently retired executive editor of *Ebony Magazine*, the nation's largest-circulation magazine published by and for African Americans, Lerone Bennett has been editor, journalist and a prolific social historian. His central message is that black Americans need to know their own history in order to realize their strengths. He was born in Clarksdale, Mississippi, the son of a chauffeur and a restaurant cook. The family moved to Jackson, and although

Jackson was as segregated as any U.S. city could be, it was nevertheless the home of three historically black colleges—Jackson State, Tugaloo and Campbell—and hence offered inspiration to bright young African Americans such as Bennett. He also worked as a newsboy and copy boy for two historically black Jackson papers, the *Mississippi Enterprise* and the *Jackson Advocate*. He attended Morehouse College in Atlanta, was inducted into Phi Beta Kappa and graduated in 1949 with the A.B. He continued his schooling for a short time at Atlanta University and considered pursuing a career in law before instead deciding upon journalism, beginning as a reporter at the historically black *Atlanta Daily World*, where he worked in 1949 and 1950. He served as an Army enlisted man in 1951 and 1952. He returned to the *Daily World* and was promoted to city editor in 1952; and during 1952 and in 1953, became associate editor of *Jet* magazine in Chicago. In 1954, he became associate editor of *Ebony*, a magazine that had been launched in 1945 to publicize black success stories not covered in America's mainstream magazines. He was made senior editor in 1958 and executive editor in 1987. His publisher, John H. Johnson, suggested that he write about black history, and his *Ebony* articles on the subject led to his first book, *Before the Mayflower*, which appeared in 1962. The book described black society and accomplishment in Egypt and the Sudan long before the Pilgrims arrived at Plymouth Rock, moved to the enslavement of blacks in America and concluded with the protests of the early Civil Rights movement. The book eventually sold very well and provided Bennett encouragement to further exercise his interest in history, which he attributes to the influence of a favorite high school teacher and to historian Benjamin Mays, who was president of Morehouse during Bennett's student years. Since the early 1960s, he has published several more books, some on the recent history of U.S. civil rights, others about earlier accomplishments by blacks. In 1964, Bennett produced *What Manner of Man*, a biography of Martin Luther King, Jr., whom he had known in college and with whom he had protested against racial bigotry. His accomplishments as a popular historian were recognized in 1968 when he taught at Northwestern University as a visiting professor of history.

Bennett's most controversial book appeared in 2000; it was *Forced Into Glory: Abraham Lincoln's White Dream*, in which he deconstructs the usual image of the president, arguing the Lincoln was a white supremacist whose real desire was to send African Americans back to Africa. Bennett argues that Lincoln was forced by circumstances into becoming The Great Emancipator, the role for which he is remembered by most Americans—black and white—as America's greatest president. In answer to the attacks of his critics, Bennett has said that his book simply takes the unusual approach of examining a white leader from the viewpoint of the people who were being oppressed. Certainly Bennett is not afraid of controversy and is a forceful advocate of financial reparations for Americans whose ancestors were slaves, a movement that appears to be on hold in the midst of the war on terror and the nation's uncertain, off-again-on-again economy. He also predicts the likelihood of another wave of U.S. civil rights protests at some time in the present century.

Throughout his long career, Bennett has received many honors, among which are the Literature Award of the American Academy of Arts and Letters in 1978, the Salute to Greatness Award from the King Center for Non-Violent Social Change in 1996, the Lamplighter Award for Corporate Leadership given by the Black Leadership Forum in 2001, the American Book Awards' Lifetime Achievement Award given by the Before Columbus Foundation in 2002 and the Carter G. Woodson Lifetime Achievement Award from the Association for the Study of African American Literature and History in 2003. He has served on the boards of trustees of the Chicago Historical Society and Columbia College in Chicago and on President Bill Clinton's Committee on the Arts and Humanities and the National Advisory Commission on Civil Disorders. He was a delegate in 1974 to the Sixth Pan-African Congress in Tanzania and a representative at the Second World Festival of Black and African Art in Nigeria in 1977. He has been the recipient of at least 10 honorary degrees, beginning in 1966 when his alma mater made him an honorary doctor of humane letters. Bennett has been a frequent guest speaker at U.S. colleges and universities and was a consultant for the movie "Amistad."

Bennett had intended to retire in October 2003 when he turned 75, but publisher John Johnson and his daughter and successor Linda Johnson Rice persuaded him to remain a bit longer. Bennett finally retired in February 2005, planning to continue to write occasionally for *Ebony* and to publish several more books in his retirement years. He contends that the field of black history has only had its surface scratched and wishes to make a few more contributions of his own to it. He is also sure to take every opportunity to stress to black Americans that if they use their economic clout, they can strongly influence their own future. He has pointed out that if the economic resources of African Americans were separated from those of the nation as a whole, they would represent the world's ninth richest economy. From the start of his career Bennett wanted to reach a mass audience of black Americans, an opportunity that his position at *Ebony* afforded him. He has also connected with that audience with his books published by the Johnson Publishing Company and by contributing poetry, short stories and articles to the books of others.

Books by Lerone Bennett: *Before the Mayflower: History of Black America* (Chicago: Johnson Publishing Co., 1962); *The Negro Mood, and Other Essays* (Chicago: Johnson Publishing Co., 1964); *What Manner of Man: A Biography of Martin Luther King, Jr.* (Chicago: Johnson Publishing Co., 1964); *Confrontation: Black and White* (Chicago: Johnson Publishing Co., 1965); *Black Power U.S.A.: The Human Side of Reconstruction, 1867–1877* (Chicago: Johnson Publishing Co., 1967); *Pioneers in Protest* (Baltimore, Penguin Books, 1968); ed., *Ebony Pictorial History of Black America* (Chicago: Johnson Publishing Co., 1971); *The Challenge of Blackness* (Chicago: Johnson Publishing Co., 1972); *IBW and Education for Liberation* (Chicago: Third World Press, 1973); *The Shaping of Black America* (Chicago: Johnson Publishing Co., 1975); *Wade in the Water: Great Moments in Black History* (Chicago: Johnson Publishing Co., 1979); with John H. Johnson, *Succeeding Against the Odds* (New York: Warner Books, 1989); *Forced Into Glory: Abraham Lincoln's White Dream* (Chicago: Johnson Publishing Co., 2000).

Further Readings: "Bennett, Lerone." *Current Biography Yearbook 2001.* (New York: H.W. Wilson, 2001), pp. 20–24; Davis, Nancy. "Ebony Editor Spotlights Black America's Economic Clout." [Online, 19 January 2005]. University of Michigan Ross School of Business Web site www.bus.umich.edu; Golphin, Vincent F.A. "A Distinguished Gentleman." [Online, 2000]. About...Time Magazine Web site www.abouttimemag.com; Hackbarth, Paul. "Ebony Editor Lerone Bennett Gets a Rousing Start." [Online, 14 February 2005]. The Current Online Web site www.thecurrentonline.com/news; "Lerone Bennett Retires From Ebony." [Online, 15 February 2005]. The *Scaramento Observer* Web site www.sacobserver.com/business, Meeks, Nia Ngina. "Publisher Marks 50 Years and Isn't Retiring." [Online, 24 September 2004]. The Sacramento Observer Web site www.sacobserver.com/news.

Blackistone, Kevin B. (c.1961–)

One of America's most talented sportswriters is Kevin Blackistone, who has been a SportsDay columnist for the *Dallas Morning News* since 1991 and a member of that paper's staff since 1986. He was born in Washington, D.C., and grew up mainly in Hyattsville, Maryland. He earned a bachelor's degree from Northwestern University in 1981 and went to work as a *Boston Globe* reporter. His second job was with the *Chicago Reporter*, a monthly investigative magazine, where he wrote on race and other social issues from 1983 until he came to the Dallas paper in 1986. He worked in Dallas as a city desk reporter at first, then began reporting on business and economic news. He was assigned to cover Nelson Mandela's visit to the United States in 1990, after which he moved to sportswriting. He became a full-time columnist in 1991. In a biographical blurb on the paper's Web site, Blackistone is quoted as saying that his most memorable assignment was traveling to Europe and spending a month there writing about its sports scene. He also remarked that the most memorable sports event he had covered was the boxing match in which Mike Tyson bit off part of one of his opponent's ears.

Whereas some sportswriters do little more than drivel on about how the Mighty Bears beat the Mighty Lions, repeating one sports cliché after another, Blackistone gives his readers the unexpected. His sports columns, therefore, have a longer than average shelf life. An example is a September 1999 column he wrote poking fun at the generally uppity game of golf, a sport in which winners are expected not to exult after their victories, but to restrain themselves with Victorian decorum. Seizing on America's tradition of forgiving athletes for any crime short of murder—if they play well enough—he wrote in 2001 about a rookie lineman for the Dallas Cowboys who had wrecked his truck, and then covered by telling police the truck had been stolen. In 2003, without taking sides on whether baseball slugger Barry Bonds had used performance-enhancing steroids, Blackistone suggested that Bonds submit to testing to settle the matter. Later that year, when basketball great Alonzo Mourning announced his retirement due to his need for a kidney transplant,

Blackistone recalled earlier athletes who had needed transplants and reflected on the visibility that celebrities bring to the need for organ donations. Around the same time, he began a 10-part examination of college athletics in America, beginning with a discussion of the first televised college football game, which was between Fordham and Waynesburg College in 1939, back when sports were sports, not big business. In that column, he introduced the theme of the series: that modern-day college sports had become virtually divorced from the avowed purpose of college. The next column in the series asserted that university administrations and faculties needed to reassert a reasonable level of control over their campus athletic programs. Subsequent columns in the series suggested that student athletes should be treated more like students than employees of the university; that in the off-season, athletes should be allowed to do something apart from their sport; that spending on campus athletic facilities should be brought under control; and that summer sports camps should be owned and operated by universities, not by their coaches.

Another sports column of the unexpected appeared in January 2004 and contained his reflections on what he called the first rule of press box behavior: no cheering. A few days later he wrote about one of the National Collegiate Athletic Association (NCAA)'s dubious rules that had prevented a Northwestern University football player who was a drama major from appearing in a play—until the player sued and won court permission. A column in July 2005 named Roger Federer as the most dominant athlete in any sport and cyclist Lance Armstrong as the most dominant in any one sporting event. A month later, Blackistone wrote about Armstrong's seven consecutive wins in the Tour de France, which the columnist labeled the Bore de France, but a later column lauded the famous cyclist's Lance Armstrong Foundation for its success in increasing awareness about cancer and promoting earlier detection. In August 2005, Blackistone weighed in on the matter of American Indian team or mascot names, this time agreeing with the NCAA for its recommendation that such names be changed so as not to cause ethnic offense.

"Blame '39 TV Game for Crisis: Before Fordham vs. Waynesburg, Athletics and Academics Balanced" by Kevin B. Blackistone

Fordham vs. Waynesburg College. It was supposed to be just another college football season opener in 1939 when they met in a horseshoe-shaped cement stadium on an islet here beneath the Triborough Bridge. There wasn't even much mention of it in the local newspapers. Fordham was a powerhouse. Waynesburg was a cream puff. Fordham romped, 34–7, in front of 9,000 fans.

But there hasn't been a college game in any sport played since that was, as we like to say in sports, bigger. Not a bowl game. Not a Final Four matchup.

For in a corner of the Triborough Stadium that day was what observers recalled looked like a boxcar. On top of it was a tripod. Attached to the tripod was a TV camera.

This was the first college football game televised, or the beginning of the end of college sports as a mere recreational complement to academic life.

There were in the 1880s so-called "tramp" athletes, non-students colleges paid just to suit up for their schools. Stanford and Michigan got $3,500 each to put on the first Rose Bowl in 1902. But those were blips in history.

Blackistone, Kevin B.

Triborough Stadium 1939 was where the ties in the track on which college athletics once chugged came loose. This was where that train started to barrel off the tracks and run over everything in its way, especially integrity and the mission of higher education.

It was a mere experiment. No money was exchanged. No more than a couple hundred TV sets in New York could've picked up the telecast on W2XBS, which went on to become WNBC in New York. Maybe 500 people viewed it.

But college sports and NBC saw the future.

"It wasn't the start of broadcasting games," said North Callahan, who uncovered this game's history while he was NBC's marketing director during the 1980s. "There used to be radio contracts. But there weren't big bucks in radio contracts. Television developed into big money."

The money attracted double-dealers. Cheating and corner-cutting became vogue. The pendulum of importance swung from the student to the athlete in the student-athlete phrase.

Coaches became the highest paid and recognized figures on campuses ostensibly created to educate minds rather than train bodies. Students with athletic talent became commodities of flesh swapped and traded in an open market.

Ironically, the two schools that played in the game that paved the way for the big money, the big TV contracts and the big problems no longer play Division I football.

In other words, they're out of the money, or the mad race for it.

Lucky them. They aren't spending gazillions of public and private money on stadiums and arenas and weight-lifting rooms and losing countless more money on sports that they are bringing in, which is the case for most colleges and universities in the country. They aren't doing class work for kids just so they can plow over others on the football field. They aren't admitting high schoolers because their four-point-something averages are in the 40-yard dash.

Fordham and Waynesburg still exist, undoubtedly, for the real purpose of higher education. Their bosses can sleep at night. William Swan could not.

A good man by all accounts, Swan took his life earlier this year after having to clean up a recruiting scandal he possibly could've thwarted at St. Bonaventure, the school he graduated from, presided over as board chair and loved. He struggled to believe that even he could've lost sight of what college is supposed to be about just to give the basketball team a better chance at one more win, maybe the win that would catapult it into NCAA Tournament riches.

That is how bad things have become in college athletics. Lives aren't just getting wasted; they're being lost. College sports nowadays are all but divorced from the purpose of college.

"Athletics is not like another department [on campus]," said Jim Earl, Oregon professor and co-chair of the Coalition for Intercollegiate Athletics. "It's not a part of the mission [of higher education]."

The question is: What, if anything, can be done to make athletics so, even if remotely?

Not everyone is so certain the situation can be salvaged, or that college sports, as they've grown like some wild monster in a crazed scientist's laboratory, should even have a place on the college campus. Theirs is a minority opinion, however.

The good news is that I was comforted over the last several weeks by college presidents, athletic directors, academics and coaches who believe there are remedies that can be applied, some of which I'll spell out over the next couple of weeks. Like me, they, of course, have vested interests in the multi-billion-dollar industry of college athletics and don't want to see this proverbial baby tossed out with the bath water.

That explains in part why the phrase "college athletic reform" has rolled off more lips in recent days, weeks and months than ever before. As an emissary from NCAA president Myles Brand's office, Wally Renfro, admitted in writing to the nation's sports editors a few weeks ago: "The past six months have been especially turbulent for university administrations that are striving to better integrate their athletics programs into the academic missions of their institutions...Why are coaches being paid so much? How will the arms race be brought under control? Why are student-athletes not getting a greater share of the revenue pie in college sports? Can higher education resolve the problems in intercollegiate athletics, or is governmental intervention the answer?"

The least of college athletics' worries are the personal behavior problems that made for embarrassing headlines earlier this year. Former Iowa State basketball coach Larry Eustachy was caught cavorting in the wee hours with female students on rival campuses, and former Alabama football coach Mike Price left his hotel room in the hands of strippers. For the record, those schools handled those isolated situations properly. Both men were dismissed.

What really plagues college athletics are the issues being discussed regularly now by groups such as the National Institute for Sports Reform. Bookshelves are buckling under the weight of more new tomes on the topic, including one by a former Princeton president that argues Ivy League schools also have their priorities out of line when it comes to academics and athletics. New position papers are everywhere. Even coaches are admitting that something must be done, as evidenced by the basketball coaches' emergency summit in October.

Whatever can be done, however, will require chutzpah, which isn't as strong of a trait off the field for people involved in college sports. They haven't been willing to toss out their modus operandi as easily as they have a sophomore shooting guard who can't shoot, or a conference contract that doesn't look as lucrative as another one the fax machine just spit out. But it's time to do things differently.

"I believe we're beginning to build a critical mass that is raising the right questions," said John Gerdy, an ex-college athlete and college athletics administrator. "None of these groups is going to do it on their own. Trustees. Faculty. Student-athletes. It [college athletics] needs to be hit on all levels. If it doesn't happen within the next five or 10 years, economics will drive us out of business, or the courts will. So we really need to do something."

I'm going to tell you what needs to be done and how.

Source: The above column appeared on 2 December 2003. Reprinted with permission of *The Dallas Morning News*.

Further Readings: "Kevin B. Blackistone." [Online]. The Dallas Morning News Web site www.dallasnews.com.

Boyd, Gerald M. (c.1950–24 November 2006)

Experienced print journalist Gerald Boyd took office as managing editor of the *New York Times* on 5 September 2001, just days before the World Trade Center attacks of 11 September. He was forced out of that position in June 2003 primarily due to the Jason Blair plagiarism affair and secondarily because of the unattributed use of copy written material by freelance reporters in stories bylined by *Times* national correspondent Rick Bragg. In January 2004, Columbia University's Graduate School of Journalism hired Boyd as director of case studies; his assignment was to develop materials that will help faculty members employ the case method of teaching, which has been used more extensively by business and law schools than by journalism programs. Boyd was born in St. Louis, Missouri, and took a journalism and political science degree at the University of Missouri. After his 1973 graduation, he took a job as copyboy, which was not unusual in those days, at the *St. Louis Post-Dispatch*. He soon became a reporter and later in his 10-year stay at that paper, became its White House correspondent. Boyd helped found the St. Louis Association of Black Journalists in 1977 and was its first president. In 1983, he joined the *New York Times* as a political reporter. He became a White House correspondent for the *Times* in 1984, and in 1991, senior editor and special assistant to the managing editor. In 1993, he was promoted to assistant managing editor and, in 1997, to deputy managing editor. In early September 2001, Boyd became the first African American to serve as the paper's managing editor, second in command to executive editor Howell Raines. In this position, he directed coverage of the biggest story of the new century, the terrorist attacks on the World Trade Center. For its coverage of this tragedy, the paper was awarded seven Pulitzer Prizes. Boyd's new job was demanding but initially was marred only by minor controversies, such as the November 2002 spiking of two sports columns regarding the men-only policy of the Augusta Golf Club because the position advocated in these columns did not coincide with the paper's editorial stance on the matter. Then came the forced resignation of reporter Jason Blair, who had been found culpable in multiple incidents of plagiarism and fabrication of direct quotations. Because both Boyd and Blair are African American, many onlookers jumped to the conclusion that Blair had been an affirmative action hire and that Boyd had been his mentor, neither of which appear to have been the case. Rival news media seemed to enjoy taking a few potshots at the nation's "newspaper of record," and the situation worsened a few weeks later when Rick Bragg, a *Times* national correspondent, said to be close to Raines, was found to have used material contributed by freelancers without giving them credit. Bragg, like Blair, had to resign; and five weeks after the Blair affair, on 5 June 2003, Raines and Boyd announced their resignations, which reportedly had been demanded by publisher Arthur Sulzberger Jr. On 9 June, a commentary written by Boyd's old friend George E. Curry appeared on the *Sacramento Observer*'s African-American online site www.sacobserver.com criticizing Raines as having had an imperial management style but supporting Boyd and picturing him as a scapegoat. Boyd, on the other hand, continued to be complimentary of Raines after the two men had to resign—until the appearance of a May 2003 article Raines wrote for *Atlantic Monthly*. Thereafter the two former editors disagreed about who knew what, when. Another statement of regret was written by Errol Cockfield, president of the National Association of Black Journalists. Publisher Sulzberger issued an announcement that former *Times* executive editor Joseph Lelyveld would replace both Raines and Boyd on an interim basis, and in mid-July, former *Times* columnist Bill Keller was named the paper's new executive editor. Boyd was replaced as managing editor by Jill Abramson. The paper's troubles continued with the Valerie Plame-Lewis Libby CIA leak affair in 2005; the *Times*' reaction to this controversy prompted charges not only of arrogance, but of bogus transparency. Criticism of the *Times* continued, and the late-night television comics had a field day. Jay Leno quipped that the *Times* had placed itself on its own bestseller list for fiction.

By this time, Boyd was working with Dean Nicholas Lemann at Columbia's journalism school to develop case studies to help students better understand the often difficult intersection of reporting and management. Boyd was also working on his memoirs, to be published by HarperCollins. He made frequent appearances as a speaker. At the 2002 National Writers Workshop in St. Louis, he spoke on "Journalism in a World Turned Upside Down by 9/11." In this speech, he remarked on the continued relevance of solid journalism, noting that journalists must keep high standards to deserve the public's interest and respect. In October 2003, he gave the Greg Freeman Legacy Lecture at Washington University in St. Louis; the series honors the late *Post-Dispatch* columnist, who had been a student at that university and who died in 2002 at age 46. In March 2004, Boyd gave the keynote address at the awards night program for the School of Journalism and Mass Communications at the University of South Carolina. In this speech, Boyd remarked on the symbolic nature of President George W. Bush's famous statement that he liked to get his news not from journalists but from people he trusts. In the present times, Boyd said, the public needs good journalism but lacks trust in the press. Boyd has received a variety of honors for his work. He shared a Pulitzer Prize in 2000 for national reporting for a *Times* series, "How Race is Lived in America." He was chosen as the NABJ Journalist of the Year in 2001. This organization has also created the Gerald Boyd/Robin Stone Scholarship. In 2002, the University of Missouri awarded Boyd its Honor Medal for Distinguished Service in Journalism. He died of complication from lung cancer in November 2006.

Further Readings: Curry, George E. "Times Lost More Than a Managing Editor." [Online, 9 June 2003]. Sacramento Obsever Web site www.sacobserver.com; Kurtz, Howard. "N.Y. Times' Golf Handicap: Columns on Augusta Killed for Being Out of Line with Paper's Editorials." [Online, 5 December 2002]. Washington Post Web site www.washingtonpost.com; Morgan, Arlene Notoro. "Gerald Boyd: The Art of Leadership." [Online, 30 January 2003]. American Society of Newspaper Editors Web site www.asne.org; Steinberg, Jacques. "Times' 2 Top Editors Resign after Furor on Writer's Fraud." [Online, 6 June 2003]. Free Republic Web site www.freerepublic.com.

Bradley, Edward "Ed" R. (22 January 1941–9 November 2006)

With CBS since 1971, Ed Bradley held many jobs for this network but will be best remembered as a "60 Minutes" correspondent, a job he held since 1981. He was born in Philadelphia and in 1964, received the B.S. in education at Cheney State College. A year before graduating from college, he began his media career reporting news covering baseball and hosting a jazz show as a volunteer on Philadelphia radio station WDAS. He put in one year, 1964, as a sixth grade school teacher, continuing his work at WDAS—in a paid capacity after his 1965 coverage of civil rights-connected riots in Philadelphia—and worked for this station for three more years after turning down a job as an interim principal and leaving teaching. In 1967, he moved to New York City, where he had a four-year run on WCBS radio. At that time, he was the only black journalist at CBS and the only African American on the air in New York City radio. He moved on to television work in 1971, working for that year as a Paris bureau stringer. Seeing something of Europe was a fine experience, but the need to make a better living brought him back to CBS, where he covered the Paris Peace Talks and in 1972, became a war correspondent working out of Saigon.

Bradley, Edward "Ed" R.

He covered the war in Vietnam and Cambodia, returning to the United States after being wounded in the back and arm by mortar fire. He was stationed in Washington, D.C., and in 1974, was assigned to cover the presidential campaign of Jimmy Carter. He also returned to Vietnam in 1975 to cover the fall of Saigon. He did anchor duty for the "CBS Sunday Night News" and was the network's White House correspondent from 1976 to 1981. From 1978 to 1981, he was the main correspondent for "CBS Reports." Then in 1981, Dan Rather left the Sunday night magazine-format show "60 Minutes" to replace Walter Cronkite as anchor of the "CBS Evening News," and Bradley stepped into Rather's old position. He remained in this job for many years, became coeditor of the show in 1981 and became one of the most recognizable of all television journalists. The 2004–2005 season was his twenty-fourth with the program, which has won 77 Emmy awards—more any other television news show. During his first year on "60 Minutes," Bradley won his first Emmy for an interview he did with singer Lena Horne. In his interviewing and delivery, he somehow managed to be both dignified and hip at the same time. In 2005, only three other newscasters have been with "60 Minutes" longer than Bradley: Mike Wallace, there from the show's founding in 1968; Morley Safer, on staff since 1970; and Andy Rooney, who joined the program in 1978. Bradley, a longtime jazz enthusiast, also became host in 1991 of the CBS series "Jazz from Lincoln Center" and in 1992, of the CBS news show "Street Stories." He worked as a floor correspondent at the Republican and Democratic national conventions from 1976 to 1996 and also was active in election night–coverage.

Bradley's honors were many. In 1975, he was recipient of the New York chapter of the National Association of Media Women's Distinguished Commentator Award and was recognized by the National Association of Black Journalists in 1977. He won the George Foster Peabody Broadcasting Award in 1979, the NCAA Anniversary Award in 1989, the Sol Taischoff Award in 1993 and the Robert F. Kennedy Journalism Award in 1996 for a "CBS Reports" story titled "In the Killing Fields of America." He received Alfred I. DuPont-Columbia University awards in 1991 for his "60 Minutes" story on forced labor in China and in 1997 for his "CBS Reports" report on the jury process. In 1994, he won the Overseas Press Club Award for two stories on "60 Minutes" about military facilities in the United States and Russia, and in 1996, he received the Pioneers in Broadcasting Award from the National Association of Black Owned Broadcasters. In 1997, a "60 Minutes" report on a German singer's success despite birth defects won him a George Foster Peabody Award; the Paul White Award of the Radio-Television News Directors Association followed in 2000; and in the same year, a story on AIDS deaths in Africa won him another Peabody Award. Bradley was inducted in 2000 by the New York chapter of the Society of Professional Journalists into the Deadline Club Hall of Fame. Bradley won 18 Emmys, including a Lifetime Achievement Emmy in 2002. In addition, the Radio-Television News Directors Association and Foundation created and endowed the Ed Bradley Scholarship, which each year provides $10,000 to a deserving minority student who wishes to study broadcasting.

During his long career, Bradley often managed to secure hard-to-get interviews. His March 2000 interview with convicted Oklahoma City Federal Building bomber Timothy McVeigh was the lone interview McVeigh granted before his execution. Bradley interviewed Michael Jackson regarding charges of child molestation brought against the entertainer; conducted a much happier interview with English actor Michael Caine, who has appeared in at least 80 films, on the occasion of the star's being knighted as Sir Maurice Micklewhite; and did another tough report about a heart and lung transplant at Duke University Medical Center that failed, amazingly and tragically, because the patient had been given blood of the wrong type. In 1995, Bradley was sued for libel over a "60 Minutes" story he had done about low-cost housing projects known as "colonias" located along the Texas-Mexico border. A woman builder of these structures brought suit, claiming the story had harmed her reputation, but Bradley won the case. In a February 2004 "Larry King Live" interview on CNN, Bradley appeared in the role of interviewee, and on this show, he discussed his experience with severe chest pains and the quintuple bypass operation he had undergone. On this same program, Bradley credited some of his success as an interviewer to advice given to him decades earlier by Mike Wallace: be a good listener, as opposed to trying to dominate an interview. Bradley died in November 2006 of complication from lymphocytic leukemia.

Further Readings: "CNN Larry King Live Interview with Ed Bradley." [Online, 4 February 2004]. CNN site http://edition.cnn.com; "Ed Bradley." [Online]. CNS News Web site www.cbsnews.com; "Ed Bradley: His Dream of Becoming a Radio DJ Led Him to News." [Online]. Maynard Institute Web site www.maynardije.org; "Jackson Interview Transcript." [Online, 28 December 2003]. CBS News Web site www.cbsnews.com; Whelan, Elizabeth M. "Ed Bradley's Mountain vs. John Stossel's Molehill." [Online, 15 August 2000]. American Council on Science and Health Web site www.acsh.org/health issues/news.

Britt, Donna (?–)

Twice each week, Donna Britt's lively, hard-to-categorize Metro column appears in the *Washington Post*. Britt was born in Gary, Indiana. She graduated with a B.A. in mass media arts from Hampton University and in 1979 earned a masters in journalism at the University of Michigan. In the same year, she became a city desk reporter and wrote about lifestyles and fashion for the *Detroit Free Press*, where she worked until joining *USA Today* as its Los Angeles bureau chief. She joined the *Post* in 1989, at first writing for the Style section, than launching her column in March 1992. From 1993 until 2003, she was distributed to other newspapers as part of the Washington Post Writers Group.

She took a hiatus from the column from May 2000 until early 2001, and some time after, Britt married the associate editor of *Post* and political reporter Kevin Merida in 1993; the couple began writing the column together. It was discontinued in 2003 so that Merida could work on a book about Supreme Court justice Clarence Thomas. The Writers Group accurately promoted Britt's column as a pleasant break from the Muzak-like style of a lot of syndicated columns, and at peak syndication, she appeared in a reported 55 newspapers. Her column voice tends to chat rather than pontificate, and she has the knack for making unusual connections, as in a 2004 column that reflected, in fine essay style—going from the particular to the general—after she had read a story in the *New York Times* about the soaring price of rice in Haiti, a country where rice is a very large part of the daily diet. This story about extremely poor people being able to afford even less food appeared on the same page in the *Times*, she wrote, with ads for luxury products ranging from a $325 razor to a $32,330 watch. This stark contrast of haves and have-nots, she reported, moved her to tears, and to the writing of a powerful column that reflected on our polarized nation, and world.

No admirer of the George W. Bush administration, Britt used another column to examine how politicians manipulate the two most basic human emotions, love and fear, to mold voters to their wishes at election time. Her column describes with chilling clarity how a candidate can be portrayed as the loving defender of mother, God and country to gain voter affection. Then comes the application of fear—fear that unless the candidate is elected or reelected, the nation will not be secure. Her sobering conclusion is that playing upon people's fears has been a long-standing American political tradition. Another column that is less than flattering to our leaders and to the body politic concerns the cynical use of religiosity to win or hold office, as voters are instructed that God believes this or that. Spiritually attuned Americans, she writes, have watched with alarm as God was molded into whatever the politicians in charge wanted—currently an Almighty who appears to be mainly upset about human sexual preferences. It would seem in hindsight, however, that the public often watches such political accomplishments with more approval than alarm. Another column on a related topic examined how God has "suffered" in the modern age due to our inability to quantify him.

Britt's column tries to shake readers from complacency, no mean feat in our comfortable and well-entertained society. Instead of attacking windmills, she tilts at sacred cows, such as the Oscars, which she derides as a celebration of expensive clothing. She writes, too, of celebrity and how ordinary Americans tend to lose perspective in the face of it. The springboard for that column was Martha Stewart and how we react differently to her indiscretions than we would to those of someone less famous. The celebrity's surface, she writes, resonates with us more than his or her actions. Britt adds that she has long thought all human beings are essentially nutty, but that the wealthy find it easier to hide their nuttiness, inasmuch as money masks a host of sins. One way to remain happily married, Britt once said on the Oprah Winfrey Show, is to take "marriage sabbaticals" from time to time. Her recommended retreat was Rancho la Puerta in Tecate, Baja California. It is likely, however, that many of Oprah's viewers might find it hard to afford that spa's $2,000–$3,000 a week tariff. In 1995, Britt won the American Society of Newspaper Editors Distinguished Writing Award for column writing.

"Seeing Strength in the Face of Unity" by Donna Britt

I'm unsure exactly what made my eyes moisten, suddenly and unexpectedly, at the National Association of Black Journalists convention in Detroit back in 1982. I was so new in the business, so unsure of my talents, that any colleague's "You can make it!" speech could have dissolved me.

I couldn't explain to the co-worker who found me near tears. But now I have a theory: My fellow journalists' faces did me in.

They were so alive. So comfortable. So animated as their owners discussed new ways of piercing the industry attitudes that challenged them, and that had kept their forebears out of mainstream journalism.

Although most of the faces would have been considered "black," they were amazingly diverse.

I felt similarly Wednesday at the Unity convention, the consortium of four journalism associations that has drawn more than 7,000 journalists "of color" to downtown Washington. The Convention Center's hallways and ballrooms were filled with faces: student-fresh and elder-noble faces. Gold and brown and honey and sand and ivory and chocolate-colored faces. Faces that are different—and yet surprisingly similar.

"It's just a great experience," Julissa Marenco, a general manager at Telemundo in Washington, told me. Marenco's news director persuaded her to attend her first Unity conference.

"It's powerful to come together," Marenco continued. "The name fits perfectly—we're very much united."

Studying the throng, one might naturally ask: Who knew there were so many? So many newspaper, TV, radio, magazine and interactive journalists united by a word that, considering their numbers, suddenly seems absurd: "Minority."

There's nothing minor about the energy generated by conventioneers rubbing elbows, swapping war stories, trumpeting their resumes, giving and seeking advice. More than 1,050 participants represented the Asian Journalists Association; about 2,700 are from NABJ; some 1,200 represent the National Association of Hispanic Journalists; and about 200 are from the Native American Journalists Association.

Also attending are hundreds of freelancers, job-seekers, recruiters and working press members drawn to election-year appearances by President George W. ("I'm not making the NAACP mistake again") Bush, John Kerry and Colin Powell.

Where else can journalists find workshops about how to cover international athletes or Native American life without resorting to stereotype, and about the future of ethnic radio? What other conventions' seminar participants boast such lyrical surnames as Red Horse, Sreenivasan, Hiroyuki and Ofori?

Still, Unity's palpable "We Are the World" vibe doesn't obscure some attendees' concerns. Beneath the camaraderie, note-comparing and cross-ethnic flirting some uncomfortable questions: How many minority journalists will mainstream media embrace? What's this year's color du jour? If your group advances, must mine fall behind?

Such questions seemed validated by a survey released Wednesday by the Unite consortium that showed that 90 percent of the journalists working in the nation's Washington news bureaus are white—in an America whose citizenry is fewer than 70 percent white. Minority journalists make up less than 12 percent of bureau reporters, while minorities represent more than 30 percent of the U.S. population.

Clearly, too few minority journalists are covering the nation's most news-producing city. So the ethnicities of the small percentage who have these coveted positions seem important.

Which hardly fosters Unity.

"I wasn't a big fan of the first two Unity conferences," admitted NABJ President Herbert Lowe, a reporter at *Newsday* in New York. "The [traditional]

NABJ convention means so much to me—it's like a family reunion." Seeing so many strangers from unfamiliar groups at "his" convention felt odd.

But working closely with the presidents of the other minority journalist associations this year helped Lowe realize that "we're all definitely going through the same things."

At Unity, minority journalists' voices and power "are multiplied—you don't get Kerry and Bush and Powell to just NABJ," Lowe continued. Visiting politicos "probably didn't know there were this many journalists of color—they don't see that many at press conferences or on their campaign planes," he continued. "So they're not getting asked questions that matter to our constituents, our communities."

No wonder many attendees feel how I did back in Detroit—surprisingly moved. Pablo Bello, a writer for the Spanish-language newspaper *El Informador* in Fort Worth, came to Unity looking for a job.

He found inspiration.

"The speakers are very passionate," said Bello, 36, who was a reporter in his native Mexico City 14 years ago when he decided to "give myself one year to learn English and get a journalism job." When he couldn't achieve his goal, Bello decided to work on his English and reporting skills 'rather than go back home defeated."

So he feels motivated by photos shown to him by NAHJ's president of the overwhelmingly white White House press corps. He feels "very emotional" when Unity speakers, "some of them immigrants like me, really tell us to go for it."

Unity helped him realize that as minority journalists, "we have strengths, we have qualifications, we have numbers," Bello said.

"We just need a chance to show the mainstream media that we can succeed."

I appreciate Bello's feelings. Yet in the more than two decades since the sight of hundreds of minority journalists moved me to tears, thousands of them *have* succeeded—some brilliantly.

Enough have done well that editors and news directors shouldn't have to be reminded—year after year at conventions such as this one—why it's so important for the journalists who report the news to be as varied as the population they cover. At some point, it seems, diversity shouldn't be a goal.

It should be a reality.

Source: Copyright © 2004, *The Washington Post*. Reprinted with permission. This column appeared on 6 August 2004.

Further Readings: "Syndication for Britt of Washington Post." *Editor & Publisher*. 27 November 1993, p. 33.

Brower, William A. (8 October 1916–28 May 2004)

When William Brower was hired in 1945 by the *Blade of Toledo*, Ohio, he was not only the paper's first black reporter, but one of the only African-American journalists working for a mainstream newspaper. He was born in McColl, South Carolina, but spent most of his youth in High Point, North Carolina. His father was a barber and a Methodist Episcopal circuit preacher. Brower graduated from William Penn High School in High Point, then worked his way through college, earning his 1930 B.A. in journalism at Wilberforce University near Dayton, Ohio. Following graduation, he taught adult education in High Point and Camp Davis, North Carolina, and did some writing for the *Norwalk Journal & Guide* until going to work as a reporter in 1942 at the historically black weekly the *Washington Tribune*. There, his compensation was $20 a week, plus a $1.25 bus pass. Three months later, in January 1943, he switched jobs to the Afro-American newspaper chain's Baltimore, Maryland, paper. He was initially a reporter, but in 1944, moved to Richmond, Virginia, to become the *Richmond Afro-American*'s editor. In July 1945, he moved yet again to take over as editor of the *Philadelphia Afro-American*. Then in late 1945, the year World War II ended, he was hired by the *Blade*. Brower later remarked that unlike so many of the first black reporters hired by the mainstream press, who were given a specifically black beat, he was treated exactly like everyone else in the newsroom and was assigned the usual wide variety of stories. He has remarked that during his long tenure at the *Blade*, he covered virtually every beat with the exception of music, art or cultural affairs, although he occasionally wrote movie reviews. He first worked as a general assignment reporter, then moved to the police beat and after that, the federal courts beat. He was reassigned to city desk rewrite in 1957 and was given the title of assistant city editor. In 1968, he was promoted to news editor and took charge of the Saturday and Sunday editions of the paper. In 1971, he moved up to assistant managing editor of the *Blade* and in 1976, to associate editor. At that time he was also given a column that appeared in the editorial section three times a week. Brower continued in this dual role until his retirement in 1996.

Brower took time off in 1979 and 1980 to teach journalism at Temple University in Philadelphia and also taught at Defiance College in 1974 and 1975 and at Central State University in 1978 and 1979. In 1995, his alma mater, Wilberforce, inducted him into its alumni hall of fame, and in the same year, Toledo officials named a new bridge across the Ottawa River The William A. Brower Bridge, and the National Association of Black Journalists accorded him its Lifetime Achievement Award. Earlier, in 1993, the Ohio General Assembly had honored Brower by establishing a scholarship in his name. A still earlier honor was North Carolina's Order of the Longleaf Pine.

Among the highlights in his long career were his coverage in New York in 1949 of the trial of 11 communists accused of sedition and a major series he wrote in 1951, "Fifteen Million Americans," about black America and racial progress. To allow him to gather material for this series, the *Blade* paid for his travels to 27 states. The 16-part series was reprinted in other newspapers and was nominated for a Pulitzer Prize. Brower reprised this feat in 1971, producing a news series of stories, "Black America—20 Years Later," for which he was recognized with a citation from the Robert F. Kennedy Memorial Foundation. In his final year with the *Blade*, at age 79, Brower and younger colleague Eddie B. Allen, Jr., made yet another trip around the nation; the resulting series, "America in Black & White," detailed great changes and improvements in race relations, yet also observed that a substantial gulf still exists between whites and blacks. Allen later remarked that traveling with Brower had been like a living history lesson. Brower served in 1978 and 1979 as a Pulitzer Prize juror and was a member of the Ohio Humanities Council. As his health declined during his final years, he suffered several small strokes and apparently developed Alzheimer's disease. He died at age 87 in hospice care at an assisted-living center in Toledo. In the early 1990s, when this writer last spoke with

Brower, he believed that he had more years of service in mainstream daily newspaper journalism than any other living African American. He was a modest, gracious individual but proud of the part he played in the integration of American journalism. His good humor shines through in the following column about his "most expensive lunch."

"Incredible Tale of $350 Lunch Tab" by William A. Brower

Somebody called me—I suspect derisively—the last of the big spenders. This is a myth, of course, belonging to the same class as the notion that flag-pole sitters are smart people. But somehow the word—about me—must have migrated to Washington.

During a recent visit to the nation's capital, where big spenders and freeloaders (maybe flag-pole sitters as well) are endemic, I opted for lunch in a Connecticut Avenue bistro a few blocks from the White House.

Perched on a bar seat, I ordered a hot crab sandwich and an inevitable martini. The plate was embroidered with a small cup of potato salad, lettuce and tomato and a couple of orange wedges.

Pretty soon I was to receive the shock of my life as a traveler. After a second libation I asked, in parlance familiar to the ambience, to be cashed out. The barmaid handed me a tab that totaled $350.52.

I knew I was eating in a high-rent district, even by Washington's high-cost-of-living standards, but $350 for a couple of drinks and a sandwich—that was something the least skeptical expense-account auditor would raise his eyebrows about.

In the midst of the sudden trauma I could not help but recall an incident that was a close relative of the crisis. A year earlier I had had dinner with a group of state legislators.

Everybody had dined sumptuously, as they say, and had washed down steaks and seafood with liquor, wine and beer. All had no doubt been accustomed to lavish hospitality from lobbyists and other representatives of the favor-currying interests. They had, in fact, regaled each other with tales about such sybaritic experiences in places such as Paris and New Delhi.

I was just another grape on the vine. Soon the lawmakers began to leave quietly. The waitress became concerned about who was going to pick up the check. Finally I overheard one say: "See the guy who had the Beefeater."

I cannot say that I minded being the host in line of duty. I had become acquainted with 12 news sources that would have taken days had I tried to do it on an individual basis.

Knowing that there might be blank stares had I dared submit an expense account showing what seemed to be outright extortion in Washington, I thought about one of the most convincing expense-account stories I had heard. I had no idea that it would have rescued me if my circumstances had to be explained to disbelieving eyes.

But anyway, one of the largest metropolitan dailies once had a regional correspondent who was a stickler for details in covering a story as well as itemizing expenses. He traveled throughout the South bulldogging stories.

After weeks on one assignment he submitted an expense account that befuddled the organization's auditors. They demanded that the correspondent justify the expense statement.

In one of the most painstaking documents of its kind the correspondent listed item by item, cent by cent, down to the last candy bar or pencil and to the last penny. It was so complete that the paper's managing editor had it published in a professional magazine as a model for expense-account reporting.

I have admitted to momentary panic when I was handed the extravagant check in Washington. I told the barmaid that I was afraid to order another drink—which was a joke in itself since I impose a voluntary limit of two martinis. Obviously she asked what my problem was. I showed her the check.

She appeared dumbfounded just as I had been. The mystery was soon solved, tension abated and everybody had a laugh. It was an error by a computer. The amount actually was $13.45.

A twist of fate had sent me to the posh restaurant environment in the first place. I had mislaid travelers' checks representing a tidy sum. My efforts to get them redeemed were not as easy as the man says on television.

As luck would have it in my case, I found the checks shortly after I had reported them lost. By then they had been invalidated, and I had to go to a redemption office to get them replaced.

Therein was the beginning of what looked for a moment to be the highest-priced meal I ever encountered.

Source: Reprinted with permission of *The Blade of Toledo*, Ohio, July 5, 1984.

Further Readings: "Groundbreaking Journalist Found Voice with Blade." [Online, 31 May 2004]. Toledo Blade Web site www.toledoblade.com; "William Brower, Veteran Newspaper Writer, Editor." *The Atlanta Journal-Constitution*, 2 June 2004, D6.

Brown, James (25 February 1951–)

A big man with a big smile, James Brown is host of "The James Brown Show" and cohost of Fox's "NFL Sunday," the nation's favorite pre-game professional football program. He was born in Washington, D.C., and attended DeMatha High School, where he was a 1968–1969 All-American athlete, senior class president and accomplished scholar. He received a reported 250 college scholarship offers and chose Harvard, where he earned a 1973 B.A. in U.S. government. He also played basketball and was a fourth-round draft pick by the Atlanta Hawks, but was released prior to the start of the season. Disappointed, he tried out for the Boston Celtics but was not selected, after which he took a job with Xerox Corporation. In 1978, after six years with Xerox, Brown auditioned for and landed a game-by-game sports commentator job for Washington Bullets games. When more freelance offers were made by CBS and NBC, he left Xerox to see if he could make a full-time career in broadcasting. He found a job in 1984 with Washington television station WJLA-TV, was host of a radio talk program on Washington's WTEM and took a flexible job with Eastman Kodak to help pay the bills. From 1984 to 1990, he worked for WUSA-TV. He gave this approach five years to work out, and just two weeks before his self-imposed deadline, he was hired as a feature reporter and weekend sports anchor by ABC station WJLA in Washington, D.C. Half a year later, he moved to a CBS affiliate station as an analyst, first for the National Collegiate Athletic Association, then for the National Basketball Association. Reasoning that a play-by-play announcer might have a longer television future than an analyst, Brown convinced CBS Sports to allow him to pair with ex-NFL football player Dan Jiggetts; the combination was the first time a network had used two African Americans to call games. Brown next did play-by-play for college games and in 1992, worked as midday host for the Winter Olympics at Albertville, France. At the next Winter Olympics, in 1994 at Lillehammer, Norway, he was assigned coverage of freestyle skiing. He also hosted "CBS Sports Saturday/Sunday," the Heisman Trophy award show and a special titled "Let Me Be Brave: a Special Climb of Mt. Kilimanjaro."

Toward the end of 1994, Brown moved to Fox to cover NFL games but was first assigned to that network's pregame show for the National Hockey League.

Ever versatile, he has also hosted a variety of boxing programs for Time Warner Sports' pay-per-view division, the issues show "America's Black Forum," and Fox's "World's Funniest." Other assignments have been as a contributor to the HBO show "Real Sports with Bryant Gumbel," "Hoop Dreams: A Reunion" and in 1997, a syndicated radio show, "Coast to Coast with James Brown." From 1998 to 2000, he was host of "James Brown's Pro Football Preview." In 2002, he hosted the "James Brown Show" for Sports News Radio. Other recent specials he has hosted were the History Channel's "Basketball: The Dream Teams", "Michael Jordan and Tiger Woods: Architects of Excellence" in 2000 and "Kobe Bryant: Destiny's Child" in 2001. His "Unsung Heroes" series for Fox Sports also began in 2001. In 2003, he hosted the National Geographic Channel's "Animals of the NFL," which took a look at fierce, powerful animals used as NFL mascots. Also in 2003, he did Fox Sports' "Best Western $10 Million Challenge," a sports reality/competition show cohosted by himself and Jillian Barberie, and for Discovery Travel Channel, "Sports Fan's Road Trip," which involves visits to important sports-related destinations.

The genial, well-liked Brown, known as J.B., has often been recognized for his work. He got the Sportscaster of the Year award in 1996 from Washington's Quarterback Club and the Glenn Brenner Award for excellence in sportscasting in 1998. The Black Broadcasters Alliance awarded him its Golden Mike Award in 1998; in 1999, the American Sportscaster Association named him Studio Host Sportscaster of the Year and in 2002, he received the Excellence Award of the International Black Broadcasters Association. He has been supportive of such organizations as the Marrow Foundation, the Fellowship of Christian Athletes and Darrell Green's Youth Life Foundation, and he works when he can, as a motivational speaker.

Further Readings: "James Brown, Sports Anchor." *The African American Almanac*, 9th ed. Edited by Jeffrey Lehman. Detroit: Gale Group, 2003, pp. 860–61; "James Brown." [Online]. Online Sports Web site www.onlinesports.com.

Brown, William Anthony "Tony" (11 April 1933–)

Seasoned civil rights advocate, journalist and journalism educator Tony Brown is best known as host of the nation's longest-running African-American public affairs show, "Tony Brown's Journal." He was born in Charleston, West Virginia, served as an Army enlisted man from 1953 to 1955 and holds two academic degrees: the B.A. in sociology from Wayne State University in 1959 and the MSW in psychiatric social work from Wayne State in 1961. He worked briefly as a social worker, then landed a job as drama critic for the historically black *Detroit Courier*, where he was later promoted to city editor. He left the newspaper for television and a job with Detroit public television station WTVS. Here, he produced his first show, "C.P.T.," which stood for "Colored People's Time," and also produced and hosted "Free Play," a community-issues program. He relocated to New York City in 1970 to produce "Black Journal," an African-American issues program that had been introduced in 1968 on WNET-TV and that received funding from the Corporation for Public Broadcasting (CPB) and the Ford Foundation. Brown's views about black Americans' need to be self-sufficient and his attempt to establish a bureau in Ethiopia caused the Ford Foundation to withdraw its support and almost alienated the CPB, as well. The loss of funding caused the show a cutback in its programming, but meanwhile, Brown had, in 1971, become the founding dean of the Howard University School of Journalism in the nation's capital, a job he held for three years concurrent with his television work. In 1977, the name of his show was changed to "Tony Brown's Journal." Brown left public television for a five-year period, founding Tony Brown Productions and obtaining the sponsorship of Pepsi for his "Journal" show. Thereafter, he returned to PBS. The show continues to be produced with Brown in charge and is now the longest-running national Public affairs show on public television. On the program, Brown has interviewed a wide variety of leaders, mainly black—from politics, sports, music, entertainment, civil rights and the law. He spoke out in 1991 in favor of conservative judge Clarence Thomas' elevation to the U.S. Supreme Court and around the same time, became a Republican. Since then, Brown's central message has been that well-meaning social programs do more harm than good and that African Americans must stress individual responsibility to empower themselves—in education, family life and business. He criticizes the decline of moral values in contemporary America, sees social programs as contributing to the nation's crushing economic deficit and argues that affirmative action should be based on need, not race.

In 1985, Brown founded the Council for the Economic Development of Black Americans and began a public campaign that he called "Buy Freedom," which urged black Americans to trade with and buy from black-owned businesses. In 1990, he premiered a movie he had written and produced: "The White Girl," street slang for cocaine, the story of an African-American college student who turns to cocaine due to societal pressures. He has often appeared on the National Public Radio (NPR) program "All Things Considered" and in 1995, started his own NPR call-in show, called "Tony Brown," at New York station WLIB-AM. In that same year, he published the first of his three books: *Black Lies, White Lies*, which addressed racial relations in America. In 1996, he turned to new-media technology by founding his own Internet access network, Tony Brown Online, which offered its subscribers information on black-owned businesses plus an African-American dating service aimed at finding suitable spouses to build stable homes. In 1998 and 2003, he authored two more books on the subjects of values and empowerment, and in 2004, Brown was named dean of Hampton

University's Scripps Howard School of Journalism and Communications, which had benefited from a $10 million gift from the media corporation for which it was named. The school, with around 13 faculty and 300 student majors, is housed in an enviable new building, and Scripps Howard included money not only for equipment, but also for providing scholarships and bringing in media professionals as teachers. The new facility was dedicated in autumn 2002.

The hard-working Brown has also founded the National Association of Black Media Producers and is a member of the National Communications Council and the National Association of Black TV and Film Producers. He has worked in the interest of America's historically black colleges and universities and has been honorary chair of the National Organization of Black College Alumni, a board member of the Association for the Study of Afro-American Life and History, the National Business League and the Shaw University Divinity School in Raleigh, North Carolina. He has served on the boards of the Republican Mainstream Committee and the National American Slavery Memorial Advisory Board and has worked with the Harvard Foundation for Intercultural and Race Relations and is committee head on scholarships for African-American students who wish to study at the American University of Paris. He has also been on the boards of the National Black United Fund and the National Center of Afro-American Artists and has served on the communications committee of the National Institute of Mental Health.

Brown's recognitions have been many. In 1973, he was accorded the Operation PUSH Communicator for Freedom Award of the National Newspaper Publishers, and in 1974, *Ebony Magazine* placed him on its list of the Top 50 Black Newsmakers of the Year. In 1977, he received the National Urban League Public Service Award and the International Key Women of America Award. In 1988, he was awarded the Black Psychologists' Community Service Award, and he was recipient of both the Frederick Douglass Liberation Award and the American Psychiatrists Association's Solomon Fuller Award in 1989. He won other honors from the Institute for American Business in 1993, and the Sales and Marketing Executives International Academy of Achievement named him Communicator of the Year in 1994 and Educator of the Year in 1995.

Books by William Anthony "Tony" Brown: *Black Lies, White Lies: The Truth According to Tony Brown* (New York: William Morrow, 1995); *Empower the People: A 7-Step Plan to Overthrow the Conspiracy That Is Stealing Your Money and Freedom* (New York: W. Morrow & Co., 1998); *What Mama Taught Me: The Seven Core Values of Life* (New York: William Morrow, 2003).

Further Readings: "Brown, Tony." In Schnick, Elizabeth A., ed. *1997 Current Biography Yearbook*. New York: H.W. Wilson, pp. 51–54; Prince, Richard. "Tony Brown Named Hampton J-School Dean: Veteran Broadcaster, 71, Opened Howard U School." [Online, 20 July 2004]. Richard Prince's Journal-isms. Maynard Institute Web site www.maynardije.org; Prince, Richard. "Tony Brown Talks of Conciliation." [Online, 21 July 2004]. Richard Prince's Journalisms, Maynard Institute Web site www.maynardije.org; "Tony Brown." In Lehman, Jeffrey, ed. *The African-American Almanac*, 9th ed. Detroit, Mich.: Gale Group, 2003, pp. 862–863.

Bunting, Kenneth F. (c.1949–)

In August 2005, Kenneth Bunting became associate publisher of the *Seattle Post-Intelligencer*; for the five years previous, he had been the paper's executive editor. He was born in Houston, Texas, and holds the bachelor's in journalism and history from Texas Christian University. Bunting has taken other course work at the University of Missouri, Lee College and the University of Kentucky's Salmon P. Chase College of Law. He has also gone through the Advanced Executive Program in the School of Business at Northwestern University. His career began at the *Corpus Christi Caller-Times* in Texas, and he thereafter worked for the *San Antonio Express-News, Cincinnati Post, Sacramento Bee* and *Los Angeles Times*. At the latter paper, he was a reporter and later an assistant city editor, spending nine years. Next, he joined the *Fort Worth Star-Telegram* as state capital bureau head and over the next seven years, served as that paper's city editor, assistant managing editor, deputy managing editor and senior editor. His years with the *Post-Intelligencer* in Seattle began in 1993; he was initially managing editor. After seven years, in January 2000, he was named executive editor and, after five more years, was reassigned as associate publisher, with responsibility for ethics, strategic planning, reader relations and community affairs. He was replaced as editor by the paper's former managing editor, David McCumber. In his new role, Bunting was to write a column that would help readers understand how the newspaper operates. He is on both the paper's executive committee and editorial board. In his column of 4 November 2005, Bunting predicted criticism directed at the news media over their handling of the controversial nomination of Judge Samuel Alito for a place on the U.S. Supreme Court. Media bashing, he wrote, is often more a matter of complainers not wanting to hear views that differ from their own than about lack of media fairness or accuracy. A few days later, Bunting reflected in his column about the CBS "60 Minutes" story that resulted in the end of anchorman Dan Rather's career and about Mary Mapes' book, *Truth and Duty: The Press, the President, and the Privilege of Power* (New York: St. Martin's Press, 2005), in which she tells her side of her own involvement in reporting on President George W. Bush's experiences with the Texas National Guard. Bunting's column made it clear that he had a good deal of sympathy with Rather and had misgivings about the concerted campaign launched against him. In February 2006, Bunting wrote about an appearance by Secretary of Defense Donald Rumsfeld before the Council on Foreign Relations in which the secretary had to eat a small quantity of crow about his earlier statements regarding the administration's practice of paying Iraqi editors to run stories saying things the Bush White House wanted to have said.

Bunting has long been active in the American Society of Newspaper Editors. In 1999, he stood for election to the organization's board and won a coin flip after having tied in the voting with the *Los Angeles Times*' Narda C. Zacchino. At the 2004 ASNE convention, Bunting made a presentation that was later published on www.poynter.org discussing community complaints over his newspaper's coverage of a Seattle area tragedy. The police chief of Tacoma, Washington, had been charged with violent conduct directed at his wife and finally shot her to death, then committed suicide in a shopping center parking lot. Bunting's remarks were made mainly in support of Ruth Teichroeb, the reporter who had handled the story. Bunting spoke again at the 2006 ASNE convention, welcoming members to Seattle. In 2004, presidential candidate John Kerry formed a team of lawyers and others to head off voting irregularities similar to those that had affected the results in Florida four years earlier. Bunting was one of a team of Hearst Corporation representatives who interviewed Kerry in July of that year about this effort. Bunting has been a member of the advisory committee for the Alfred Friendly Press Fellowships program that benefits mid-career reporters and editors and a governor-at-large of Seattle's City Club. He is on the board of the Alliance for Education in Seattle and is a board of directors member of the city's Woodland Park Zoological Society. He participates in the Newspaper Association of America's James K. Batten Leadership Program, in which experienced senior-level minority executives mentor mid-level managers. He has also been a Pulitzer juror, a board member of the National Freedom of Information Coalition, an advisory board member for the Robert C. Maynard Institute for Journalistic Education and a member of the American Red Cross Leadership Council.

"Story of Bush, National Guard Compelling" by Kenneth F. Bunting

Until last week, I had not placed Mary Mapes' new book, "Truth and Duty," on my holiday gift-giving or short-term reading lists.

But the book, scheduled to go on sale this week, is high on both now, since I got an advance read of an annotated excerpt to be published in the December issue of Vanity Fair.

The magazine's excerpt, which ought to be compelling reading for students of politics, journalism and history, deals with the "60 Minutes" segment that got Mapes fired and ended Dan Rather's career on a sour and embarrassing note.

No, the article does not offer any significant new insights or revelations regarding President Bush's National Guard service. Yes, it is a tad defensive.

And Mapes does a great deal of finger pointing—at sources, at network managers and executives, at members of the independent commission appointed by the network to examine what went wrong and especially at those who she said were part of an organized campaign to discredit her work.

Much of Mapes' version and interpretation of what really happened is disputed in parenthetical responses that the magazine, to its credit, bracketed within the narrative.

Still, the image that emerges is not that of a zealot hellbent on a sensational election-year scoop to hurt Bush, but rather that of a journalist who worked hard to get an important story right and is still not convinced she blew it as badly as her critics and popular sentiment would have us believe.

While it is certainly told from her own perspective—the network calls it "revisionist history"—Mapes gives the first detailed accounting to date of what went on inside CBS, beginning the day after the segment aired. As documents supposedly written by Bush's now-deceased Guard commander, Lt. Col. Jerry Killian, were questioned, then denounced as probable forgeries.

Mapes, who grew up in farm country in northwestern Washington and worked for KIRO-TV before going to the network in 1989, tells the story in language that is sometimes earthy, often tinged with anger and at times funny and sarcastic.

Readers of the piece will certainly get a chuckle from her recollections of being cross-examined by former Attorney General Dick Thornburgh on the use and meaning of a reference to horse manure when taking issue with something or someone. If that passage doesn't bring at least a smile, you either have no sense of humor or I ruined it for you by giving away the surprise.

But there is serious history there, too.

On the reporting, Mapes recounts how she got the documents and had them examined by two expert analysts who, she says, "saw nothing to indicate that the memos had been doctored or had not been produced in the early 1970s."

She recalled having them seemingly corroborated by Killian's commander and even, unintentionally one presumes, by White House Communications Director Dan Bartlett. According to Mapes, Maj. Gen. Bobby Hodge said in a telephone interview that the content of the memos matched his recollections of how Killian had "handled Bush's departure from the Guard" three decades earlier. She says that Bartlett, who was actually shown the documents, "claimed that the documents supported their version of events: that then-Lieutenant Bush had asked for permission to leave the unit."

And she dramatically recounts how the mood at CBS deteriorated in a matter of hours from one of congratulatory euphoria, hugs and kisses to a circle-the-wagons, damage-control mode that made her the convenient scapegoat.

As the crescendo of claims that the documents were forged continued the day after the segment aired, Mapes writes that she was "incredulous."

"That couldn't be possible. When we'd shown the president's people the memos, the White House hadn't attempted to deny the truth of the documents," she wrote.

Mapes, who will appear at a CityClub luncheon in Seattle next week, characterizes the CBS communications team as totally unprepared for what she called "a brilliantly run national political campaign" to discredit the story, the network and Rather. After a while, she writes, it became apparent that senior-level network executives and corporate honchos, not news people, were calling all the shots.

Mapes chides the mainstream media for being spun into joining the attack on CBS, and paying no attention at all to the story about Bush's military service.

About the focus shifting to CBS, Mapes may be right. But given the historical significance of the whole episode, that focus is not entirely misplaced. While I've read only a snippet of it, I suspect that when historical scholars are looking back on this, Mapes' book is going to be a valuable and frequently used resource.

Source: This commentary appeared on 11 November 2005 and appears here by permission of the *Seattle Post-Intelligencer*.

Further Readings: "Kenneth Bunting." [Online]. Hearst Corporation Web site www.hearstcorp.com/biographies; "Ken Bunting." [Online, 2005]. Western Knight Center Web site www.wkconline.org; "P-I Outlines New Leadership Roles." [Online, 20 August 2005]. Seattle Post-Intelligencer site http://seattlepi.nwsource.com.

Bunyon, Maureen (?–)

Since February 1999, Maureen Bunyon has anchored the 6 PM and 11 PM news for ABC-7 at WJLA-TV in Washington, D.C. When she coanchored this program with Kathleen Matthews, the two were one of the nation's only two-woman anchor teams and the only such team in the District of Columbia market. She was born on the island of Aruba and grew up in southeastern Wisconsin. Bunyon received her undergraduate degree in English from the

University of Wisconsin in Milwaukee and a masters from Columbia University's School of Journalism. She also holds a masters in education from Harvard University. While in school, she freelanced for the *Milwaukee Journal*, and then moved to broadcasting, beginning in 1970 at Boston's public station WGBH-TV. She moved to New York City, working at WCBS-TV News, then in 1973, became lead anchor at CBS station WUSA-TV in Washington, D.C., cohosting with Gordon Peterson until 1995, also hosting the weekly news magazine shows "22:26 with Maureen Bunyon" and "Studio Nine." For the next three years she operated her own communications consulting firm, was chief correspondent for the PBS show "Religions and Ethics Newsweekly" and did substitute hosting on National Public Radio's "Talk of the Nation" and WAMU Radio's "The Derek McGinty Show," then joined the staff of WJLA-TV. She is a television news coverage fixture in the nation's capital.

Bunyon was a founder of the National Association of Black Journalists and the International Women's Media Foundation, which involves women who do media work in around 100 countries. She is on the national advisory board of the Casey Journalism Center on Children and Families and the advisory committee of Women in Film and Video and has been on the boards of the National Commission for Working Women and the National Council for Research on Women. She is also a member of the Broadcast Pioneers Club of Washington and is on the boards of Women of Washington, the National Women's Hall of Fame and the National Press Foundation. Over the years, she has won seven local Emmy awards, was named Journalist of the Year in 1992 by NABJ and won the Women in Communications Matrix Award in 2002. Another honor in that same year was the Immigrant Achievement Award given by the American Immigration Law Foundation. She has been inducted into the Hall of Fame of the D.C. chapter of the Society of Professional Journalists and the Silver Circle of the National Academy of Television Arts and Sciences and has also received the latter organization's Ted Yates Award for leadership in broadcasting. In 1998, she received an honorary doctorate from Trinity College.

Further Readings: "Maureen Bunyon." [Online, 29 September 2004]. WJLA/News Channel 8 Web site www.wjla.com; "Maureen Bunyan and Diane Rehm to Receive Matrix Award." [Onine]. Association for Women in Communication Web site www.womcom.org.

C

Caldwell, Earl (1938–)

Long a reporter and columnist, Earl Caldwell has a special place in twentieth-century journalism history because of his part in the precedent-setting Branzburg decision in 1972 dealing with the ability of news people to use anonymous sources for their stories. Today, he is Hampton University's Scripps Howard Professor of Journalism, producer/host of the Pacifica radio feature "The Caldwell Chronicle" and oral historian and director of the history project for the Robert C. Maynard Institute for Journalism Education. He was born in the town of Clearfield, Pennsylvania, put in six months of training as an Army Reservist and is a graduate of the University of Buffalo, where he majored in business with a specialty in insurance but was told that since he was black, he would have to look for work at a black-owned insurance firm. Back in Clearfield, a high school friend, Frank Cardon, who had become sports editor for Clearfield's daily paper, the *Progress*, suggested that he apply for a sports reporter opening there. Caldwell got the job and was mentored by editor George A. Scott, who Caldwell remembers as a master teacher in a green eyeshade, and one who would not tolerate racism. When Cardon moved on two years later, Caldwell became sports editor. In 1960, Scott encouraged him to move up to a bigger paper, the *Intelligencer-Journal* in Lancaster, Pennsylvania, where Caldwell joined the sports staff. Caldwell's chronicle of his career reveals that he was deeply touched by the pride that editor Scott, who was white, took in his former sports reporter's later career successes and that Scott always wrote about his protégé in his own column in the *Progress*. He also remembers Clearfield as a safe haven from the racism experienced by his parents, who had grown up in the South. His father, who lived to 104, had the reputation of being the strongest man in the county; he was a barber and helped run a lumber company in Clearfield. Caldwell grew up in a mostly Italian neighborhood in relative affluence, largely free of the sting of racism. In Lancaster, he took up golf and drove an MG-TD sports car, yet it was there that he joined his first civil rights demonstration. Eventually, he had the urge to move again to a still bigger paper and applied to the Harrisburg, Pennsylvania, *Patriot-News*. The sports editor informally offered him the job, but someone intervened, so Caldwell remained at the *Intelligencer-Journal* and arranged to be transferred to its news department. Soon thereafter, he met another young black reporter who was working only a few miles away in York, Pennsylvania. The young man was New York City-born Bob Maynard, fresh from the heady, invigorating atmosphere of Greenwich Village and the company of such luminaries as writer James Baldwin and columnist Murray Kempton. Maynard, who drove a Porsche, had secured a job at the *York Gazette*; both young men were the first black journalists to work at their respective mainstream papers. The two new friends went their separate ways, however, when Caldwell was hired in 1963 by the Rochester, New York, *Democrat and Chronicle* to help cover the growing civil rights struggle and Maynard got a 1965 Nieman Fellowship at Harvard. Once again Caldwell was his paper's first black reporter, only this time he immediately was called upon to write a race-connected story. He and fellow reporter Bill Vogler, who was white, each applied to rent a variety of local apartments. The white prospective renter was offered each apartment, but when Caldwell showed up, the apartment "had just been rented." The resulting story made Caldwell an instant hit among the African-American community of Rochester, who, in reference to an old song, nicknamed him "the boll weevil" in that he "was still looking for a home."

In July 1964, when rioting broke out in Harlem following the shooting of a black boy by a white policeman, the paper sent Caldwell, who had never before set foot in Harlem, to cover the story. Up to this point, Bob Maynard had been the only other black journalist of Caldwell's acquaintance, but while covering the riot, he saw and met several of the reporters who were the pioneering black journalists at the nation's big news weeklies and New York City's biggest dailies. Never before in U.S. history, Caldwell has recalled, were so many black reporters covering such a big story; and furthermore, some of the white reporters there were asking them for help. His dreams of working at a big-city daily suddenly looked a lot more possible to realize. Returning to Rochester, he found one of his journalistic idols, columnist Jimmy Breslin of the New York *Herald Tribune*, at a typewriter in the *Democrat and Chronicle* newsroom. Caldwell befriended Breslin, followed him around and watched him operate, and after a few days, Breslin requested that the young reporter take him to the toughest black bar in town. Before they could go, the bars were closed by violence-fearing city authorities, but before leaving, Breslin gave Caldwell the phone number of the *Herald Tribune*'s city editor. Eighteen months later, Caldwell was a reporter on that paper's staff. In 1966, he again found his services much in demand, inasmuch as he had far better access to the more militant side of the civil rights movement in Harlem than did his white counterparts. It was at this time that the word "black" rapidly became the preferred racial descriptor, replacing "Negro," and the expressions "Black power," "Black pride" and "Black is beautiful" began to be heard everywhere. It was the time of emphasized linking of U.S. blacks with all things African, and reporter Caldwell was right in the middle of it. His dream job lasted only a year, however, and the financially beleaguered *Herald Tribune* folded, after which Caldwell found a new job at the New York *Post*, becoming a protégé of fellow African-American journalist Ted Poston, who had been with that paper since 1935. Poston encouraged the younger man's ambition to work at the mighty *New York Times*, and in 1967, that dream became reality. He worked for the *Times* for two years in New York, also traveling to other parts of the nation wherever race-connected unrest was occurring. For example, he was dispatched to Chicago in 1968 to report on the protests surrounding the Democratic National Convention there. He is also said to have been the only reporter on the scene in 1968 when the Rev. Martin Luther King, Jr. was shot and killed. In 1969, the *Times* sent him to join the paper's staff in San Francisco. Another of the major stories he covered was that of Angela Davis, an African-American professor accused of complicity in the murder during a San Quentin Prison escape attempt. But events in 1970 would cement Caldwell's place in the history of U.S. journalism. The issue that made his name a household word among journalists was source confidentiality. Caldwell had been covering the militant Black Panther Party's activities in San Francisco and was summoned by a federal grand jury to appear and testify. This, he refused to do, arguing that to do so would cut off all future cooperation from his news sources, thereby depriving the newspaper-reading public of information about the Panthers. He was cited for contempt of court, but the Ninth Circuit Court of Appeals vacated the contempt citation against him. His case was thereafter combined with the similar cases of *Louisville Courier-Journal* reporter Paul Branzburg and Massachusetts television reporter Paul Pappas and examined by the U.S. Supreme Court in the case of *Branzburg v. Hayes* (408 U.S. 665, 92 S.Ct. 2646 (1972)). The upshot of this case was that the Supreme Court declined to create a federal shield law to protect the media's use of confidential sources. Nevertheless, most states have enacted some form of reporters' shield laws of their own, and the possibility of a standardized national shield law still generates lively controversy in 2006.

Caldwell became even better known to readers in 1979, when he was named the earliest black reporter to be given a column in a major mainstream metropolitan daily. The column appeared three times a week in the New York *Daily News*. He has compiled some of these columns into a book, *Black American Witness: Reports from the Front*, which appeared in 1994. Of special interest in this book are Caldwell's observations on many notables he interviewed or knew, such as Fidel Castro, Robert Mugabe, Cesar Chavez, David Dinkins, Jesse Jackson, Andrew Young, Dizzy Gillespie and Sammy Davis Jr.

After roughly 15 years at the *Daily News*, Caldwell's tenure there ended on a sour note in 1994. He apparently was fired by editorial page editor Arthur Browne over one of his columns that Browne considered too one-sided. The story involved charges that a white policeman had used his position of power to rape six black taxi drivers. Browne had spiked the column, saying that Caldwell had made no effort to get comments from the policeman. Caldwell claimed censorship pointing out that he felt justified in taking a position in a column, as opposed to a news story, where opinion would be altogether out of place. He was attempting to give voice to the voiceless, Caldwell said, and complained that in the year past, editor Browne had spiked perhaps six of his columns. Browne, on the other hand, said that Caldwell had voluntarily quit and promptly replaced Caldwell with two other African-American columnists, Stanley Crouch and Playthell Benjamin. Caldwell had also worked for several years as a CBS Radio Network commentator on "Spectrum." He accepted a position as writer-in-residence at Pennsylvania State University, and he now teaches at Hampton University in Virginia. He continued his radio work by producing and hosting "The Caldwell Chronicle" for Pacifica and is director of the history project for The Maynard Institute for Journalism Education.

Books by Earl Caldwell: With Lurma Rackley and Kenneth Walker, *Black American Witness: Reports From the Front* (Washington, D.C.: Lion House Pub., 1994).

Further Readings: "Earl Caldwell Biography." [Online, 2005]. Maynard Institute Web site www.maynardije.org; "Earl Caldwell: His Love for Journalism Began at His Hometown Paper." [Online, 2004]. Maynard Institute Web site www.maynardije.org; Garneau, George. "Dispute About Column Turns Racial." *Editor & Publisher*, 30 April 1994, pp. 9–10; Garneau, George. "N.Y. Daily News Reporters Charge Double Standard." *Editor & Publisher*, 14 May 1994, pp. 17, 29; Stein, M.L. Blacks in Communications: Journalism, Public Relations and Advertising. New York: Julian Messner, 1972, pp. 51–53.

Capehart, Jonathan (c.1967–)

Cowinner of the 1999 Pulitzer Prize for editorial writing, Jonathan Capehart is mainly known for his work at the New York *Daily News* but now works for communications consulting firm Hill and Knowlton. He also is known for his ties with New York City Mayor Michael Bloomberg and for his gay advocacy work. He holds a 1989 B.A. in political science from Carleton College and began his career as assistant to the president of the WNYC Foundation in New York writing speeches and doing other public relations work. In 1992 and 1993, he was a "Today Show" researcher at NBC, and with that background he joined America's oldest daily tabloid, the *Daily News*, in 1993 as an editorial writer remaining in that job until 2000, when he left the paper to work as a national affairs columnist and correspondent for Bloomberg News and to serve as policy advisor in the successful 2001 mayoral campaign of Michael Bloomberg, Democrat-turned-Republican and one of the world's

100 wealthiest individuals. Capehart also served on Bloomberg's transition committee. In 2002, he went back to Bloomberg News to write on global poverty and later in that year, re-joined the *Daily News* editorial department as deputy editorial page editor. In December 2004, he again left the paper, this time to become senior vice president and senior counselor of public affairs for Hill and Knowlton Inc. in New York, working under Hill and Knowlton USA CEO MaryLee Sachs. Capehart is also a political pundit for WABC-TV's "Eyewitness News Sunday" show. Other broadcast appearances have been on NPR's "Tavis Smiley Show," "Inside City Hall" on New York 1 News, MSNBC, CNN and Fox News channel. The openly gay Capehart has been a correspondent for the gay and lesbian PBS show "In the Life," as well.

The 1999 Pulitzer Prize that Capehart shared with Michael Aronson and the *Daily News* editorial staff was the result of the campaign Capehart orchestrated to revive the Apollo Theatre in Harlem. The 14 editorials that made up this campaign attacked the leadership of Rep. Charles B. Rangel, ranking member of the House Ways and Means Committee, who was head of the theater's foundation. Critics charged that the *Daily News*' campaign against Rangel was politically motivated. Capehart's role in the 2001 election of Michael Bloomberg, who was thought by many political observers to have little chance of defeating Mark Green for mayor but who had deep, deep pockets and the endorsement of outgoing mayor Rudy Giuliani, had more to do with Capehart's influence among the city's large gay population than with its African-American voters. Capehart had been listed in *OUT* magazine's tally of the 100 most influential gays in the Untied States in 1998 and 1999 and in *New York* magazine's 2001 Gay Power List of the 101 most influential gays in the city. He is an active member of the National Lesbian and Gay Journalists Association and is a man of many contacts. He has been a panelist for PrideFest and for the Empire State Pride Agenda group, and in 2001, he received the Angel Award of GMAD (Gay Men of African Descent), an award that honors people whose work benefits the black gay community. In an article Capehart wrote for the 1 February 2000 issue of the *Advocate*, he distinguished between behind-the-scenes activists for gay rights, such as himself, and what he called "barricade activists" who put themselves at physical risk protesting on the streets. Apart from his gay advocacy, Capehart is a member of the Council on Foreign Relations, the Japan America Young Leaders Project, The Century Association, and Global Leaders for Tomorrow of the World Economic Forum. In 2002, he participated in the Council for the Untied States and Italy conference and in 2003, in the BMW Foundation Herbert Quandt Transatlantic Forum. In 2000, he and the *Daily News* editorial board won the George Polk Award for another 14-part series, "New York's Harvest of Shame," about the plight of farm workers in the state.

Other Capehart stories published in the *Advocate* addressed the need for black Republicans, a visit with John F. Kennedy Jr. prior to Kennedy's tragic death, efforts of President Bill Clinton and presidential candidate Bill Bradley to be supportive of gays, and the work of gay online columnist Abigail Garner. In 2000, Capehart wrote a story for the *Los Angeles Business Journal* reflecting on the curious relationship between national politics and Hollywood. On one hand, he wrote, politicians put on a fine show for the folks back home about the moral failings of the movie industry, but on the other hand, they love rubbing elbows with the stars and getting actors' and directors' help in campaigning and fund raising. Some of his last editorials in the *Daily News* were a defense of Mayor Bloomberg, who had been charged with racism in city layoffs; Staten Island neighborhoods still "off limits" to blacks; New Jersey's Gov. Jim McGreevey, the nation's first openly gay governor; and the need for tighter regulation of street vendors in New York who do not pay business taxes. Capehart is unusual in that he worked for 11 years in the editorial department of a major newspaper but never worked as a reporter.

Further Readings: "Carleton Graduate Wins Pulitzer Prize for Editorial Writing." [Online, 13 April 1999]. Carleton College Web site www.carleton.edu/campus/newsbureau; "Jonathan Capehart." [Online]. David Patrick Columbia's New York Social Diary Web site www.newyorksocialdiary.com; "Johathan Capehart Joins Hill & Knowlton USA as Senior Counselor of Public Affairs." [Online, 14 December 2004]. Hill & Knowlton USA Web site www.hillandknowlton.com/us.

Chideya, Farai (c.1969–)

A woman who has worked in virtually every medium, Farai Chideya is now a correspondent and substitute host for National Public Radio's "News & Notes with Ed Gordon." She was born in Baltimore, Maryland, to parents who were both journalism graduate students, and she is a 1990 magna cum laude graduate of Harvard University. She interned at *Newsweek Magazine* and after graduating, she was, from 1990 to 1994, a researcher and reporter for this magazine working in Washington, New York and Chicago. At one point during this period, she was a pool reporter on Air Force One. From 1994 to 1996, she wrote for MTV News and in 1996 was a fellow at the Freedom Forum Media Studies Center, where she did research on why younger Americans are so often alienated from the news. Also during 1996, she covered the presidential race as a CNN political analyst. From 1997 to 1999, she was a correspondent for ABC News, reporting on racial issues, politics and youth issues. In 2000, Chideya moved from New York to Berkeley, California, and founded PopandPolitics.com, a site directed at young urban Americans. In founding this online journal, she had the help of the founder of BlackPlanet.com, Omar Wasow. Coverage on PopandPolitics.com has ranged from partisan politics to popular music, and Chideya was joined on the site by fellow African-American writers such as journalist and New York University journalism professor Pamela Newkirk and actress/playwright/performance art advocate Anna Deveare Smith.

In December 2003, the site languished for a time, but in 2004, it was relaunched in association with San Francisco State University's Center for Integration and Improvement of Journalism. Chideya was national affairs correspondent for *Vibe* magazine in 2000; during the same year was anchor of the primetime show "Pure Oxygen" on the women's-interest Oxygen Channel, in which Oprah Winfrey had a hand; and wrote a political column handled by the Los Angeles Times Syndicate (now Tribune Media Services International). In 2001, Chideya accepted a second fellowship, this time at Stanford University as a Knight Fellow. In October 2004, she moved to the Bay Area of California to become host of "Your Call," a talk/interview show on KALW 91.7 FM in San Francisco. In 2005, she joined NPR to work with the show "News & Notes with Ed Gordon." During her years as a media pro, she has written on music for *Vibe* and *Spin* and has also been published in *Time*, the *New York Times*, the *Los Angeles Times Magazine*, *Essence*, *Civil Rights Journal*, *O: The Oprah Magazine*, *Mademoiselle* and the *Nation*. She has appeared as a political analyst for CNN, BET, MSNBC and Fox as well, and she has been active on the university lecture circuit.

Chideya has published three books, the first of which appeared in 1995 aimed at debunking a variety of pervasive myths about African Americans. The second, in 1999, examined the shift from black-white to increasingly multiethnic racial perceptions on the part of younger Americans; and the third, in 2004, was a collection of essays about why so many Americans appear to be alienated from politics. Two big reasons for this disaffection, she writes, are lack of trust in the honesty and motivations of most politicians and the virtual inability of our system to accommodate third-party candidates. Her view of the Green Party is that as unsuccessful as it is, it might yet force the Democrats to be more liberal and less centrist in their policies. Her journalistic and book work, she has remarked, has literally enabled her to see the world. She has met and interviewed notables as different as Bill Clinton and Nelson Mandela. Politically, she describes herself as a populist. In January 2003, writing for PopandPolitics, Chideya made a rash prediction about the results of the 2004 presidential election. George W. Bush, she wrote, would be a one-term president. Centrist voters, she predicted, would eventually wake up and realize they had been bamboozled by "compassionate conservatism" and the tradeoff of, as she put it, "bodybags for oil" in Iraq. History would prove her wrong. Later that year, writing for Alternet.org, Chideya made another prediction that possibly was more accurate. Following the Jason Blair affair at the *New York Times*, which resulted in his firing and the forced resignations of editors Howell Raines and Gerald Boyd, she predicted there would be a flurry of breast beating, and then things at the *Times* would go back to business as usual, a style of journalism she regards as more sheep-like than hard-nosed. She called for more aggressive reporting on the growing debt situation of so many American families, more investigative work on corporate fraud and excess, and closer attention to the Bush administration's tax policies that tend to favor the wealthy.

She also argued that major news media should work up the courage to challenge the administration's reasons for having gone to war in Iraq. For *Essence* (1 May 2004), she wrote about that fascinating American original, the Rev. Al Sharpton. And in September of that year, on Alternet.org, she borrowed from her third book to examine why third-party candidates so seldom do well at courting the black vote. Her hope is for the emergence of a third party that will focus less on incarceration and more on providing opportunities for education and jobs, which might go far toward reducing crime rates. She mimics California governor Arnold Schwarzenegger, calling him "Ah-nult," and she jokes about Secretary of Defense Donald Rumsfeld continuing to serve in that capacity for an additional two terms under the nation's next chief executive, "President Jeb Bush."

NPR has allowed Chideya to interview or report on a wide range of interesting people and issues. Examples are the first black woman member of the British Parliament, Dianne Abbott; 2005 Pulitzer Prize winner Dele Olojede, a Nigerian working for *Newsday*; U2 singer Bono's campaign to alleviate the effects of AIDS and poverty in Africa; and the one-man show, "Not a Genuine Black Man," put on in San Francisco by Brian Copeland. She has also covered the issues of identity theft, mental illness as a taboo subject among black Americans, the need for wealth-building among African Americans and the millions of Africans who still die each year of malaria. Since Hurricane Katrina's widespread destruction along the Gulf Coast of America, many of Chideya's stories on NPR have been about rebuilding efforts in New Orleans and elsewhere in the region; the matter of what will happen to the devastated Ninth Ward, where much of the land is apt to be taken over by developers from the formerly black owners, and human-interest accounts of people uprooted by the storm.

In 1997, she was one of the 100 Americans selected by *Newsweek* as "people to watch." While at *Newsweek*, she won a national award for her education reporting, and she has been recognized as an AlterNet New Media Hero and has won a Gay and Lesbian Alliance Against Defamation award and a Marketing Opportunities in Business and Entertainment Internet and Technology award. PoliticsOnline.com has put her on its list of "25 Who Are Changing the World of Internet and Politics," and she won the 2004 Young Lion award from the Black Entertainment & Telecommunications Association. She has won a GLAAD Award for a *Spin* article on hip-hop music, has been included on the *New York Daily News'* "Dream Team" of political commentators and writers and has been selected for a WIN Young Women of Achievement award. In addition, she serves on the Knight Foundation's Journalism Advisory Committee.

Books by Farai Chideya: *Don't Believe the Hype: Fighting Cultural Misinformation about African-Americans* (New York: Plume, 1995); *The Color of Our Future* (New York: William Morrow, 1999); *Trust: Reaching the 11 Million Missing Voters (and Other Selected Essays)* (Brooklyn, N.Y.: Soft Skull Press, 2004).

Further Readings: Alger, Derek. "Interview with Farai Chideya." [Online, 10 May 2005]. Pif Magazine Web site www.pifmagazine.com; "Farai Chideya." [Online, 22 March 2006].

National Public Radio Web site www.npr.org; "Farai Chideya." [Online]. Pop and Politics Web site www.popandpolitics.com/bio; "Farai Chideya: Founder & Editor, PopandPolitics.com." [Online, 2006]. The Media Center at the American Press Institute Web site www.mediacenter.org; Sanders, Joshunda. "The Overachiever: Farai Chideya Moves to the Bay Area—And Into Radio." *San Francisco Chronicle*, 24 October 2004.

Ciara, Barbara (?–)

Barbara Ciara is managing editor and primary anchor for WTKR NewsChannel 3 in Hampton Roads, Virginia, and vice president–broadcast of the National Association of Black Journalists. She came up the hard way, having lived in public housing and having run away from home after ninth grade to live on her own in New York City, eventually taking night courses to earn her GED. She attended the University of Arizona and also worked for the campus newspaper at Tucson's Pima Community College. She dropped out during her junior year, 1976, to take a full-time job at Tucson station KZAZ-TV and did not complete her bachelor's degree until spring 2000, summa cum laude at Hampton University in Virginia. At KZAZ, she held a succession of jobs: reporter, photographer, audio director, technical director, assignment editor, producer, anchor and news director. When she was promoted to news director in 1978, she became the first African American to hold that job at a station in the U.S. Southwest. Moving to the Hampton Roads/Norfolk area of coastal Virginia, she went to work for WAVY-TV, then in 1988 for ABC affiliate station WVEC-TV. From autumn 1996 to summer 2000, she was managing editor of a joint venture between WVEC and public television station WHRO, producing and cohosting "This Week in Hampton Roads," a news magazine-format show. She became involved in media convergence work in February 1997, as managing editor of LNC, a venture combining WVEC, the *Virginian-Pilot* newspaper and cable television. In 1996, her bosses at WVEC wanted to replace her as coanchor of the 11 PM news, reportedly due to her weight gain. A petition was circulated to keep her as coanchor, but in January 1997, she left the job to become coanchor and managing editor of "Pilot 13 News," a new local news cable operation in Norfolk. The new show appeared throughout the day on LNC and was sent out to roughly 350,000 cable subscribers on Norfolk's Channel 4, Virginia Beach's Channel 8 and Newport News' Channel 29. Her coanchor was Mike Lewis. She held this job until July 2000 and, due to a no-compete clause in her contract, did not reappear on television news in the Norfolk area until July 2001, when she became a coanchor with Tom Randles for the 6 PM and 11 PM news on NBC affiliate WTKR-TV, channel 3. Before appearing on-camera at WTKR, she had worked since July 2000 as the station's managing editor, developing stories, assigning reporters and approving and editing news copy. Her new position has enabled her to travel to provide news coverage from Iraq during Operation Desert Storm and Operation Desert Shield, Cuba, Haiti, Mexico, Saudi Arabia and parts of Europe. In 2000, she won an Emmy for a series of stories titled "Guilty Till Proven Innocent," and the Columbia University Journalism School honored her for her reporting on race issues. One of her most controversial stories involved interviews with clergy, psychologists, entertainers and students—black and white—about current use of the N-word by African Americans. Ciara noted more casual use of this taboo word among younger blacks who are not old enough to have experienced the direct sting of segregation. She had been accorded many earlier honors, such as a variety of Associated Press and United Press International recognitions in the 1980s, a number of Excel awards given by the Hampton Roads Black Media Professionals, a 1995 Emmy nomination for her series "Letters from the Hood" about growing up on tough city streets, another Emmy nomination two years later for "Operation Haiti" and the 1997 Edward R. Murrow Award given by the Radio and Television News Directors Association. In 2004, she was inducted into the Scripps Howard School of Journalism and Communications hall of Fame at her alma mater.

Ciara has long been active with the NABJ serving two terms as national board representative for Region III and also as the organization's national vice president for broadcasting. In her role as vice president, she has spoken out to criticize columnist Armstrong Williams for having accepted $240,000 to push the Bush administration's No Child Left Behind policies, as well as a less widely publicized racial slur uttered during a weathercast in Las Vegas that resulted in the weatherman's dismissal. She has also pressed for more attention by U.S. broadcasting stations to hiring and retaining minority news employees. In 1996, she produced the NABJ's first awards program aired nationwide on Black Entertainment Television. She has also been on the boards of the American Red Cross, the American Heart Association, Habitat for Humanity, the American Cancer Society, the Virginia Marine Science Museum, the Tidewater AIDS Crisis Taskforce, the Urban League of Hampton Roads and the Children's Hospital of the Kings Daughters.

Further Readings: "HU Journalism School Announces 2003–2004 Hall of Fame Inductees." [Online, 6 May 2004]. Howard University Alumni Web site www.hualumni.com; "Loosening Up the Racial Dialogue." [Online]. Columbia University Graduate School of Journalism Web site www.jrn.columbia.edu/events/race/loosen.

Claiborne, Ron (?–)

Twenty-year broadcast veteran Ron Claiborne is news anchor of the "Good Morning America" weekend edition for ABC News. He was born in San Francisco and holds a 1974 B.A. in psychology from Yale University and a 1975 M.S. in journalism from Columbia University. His first job in 1976 was as a reporter for the *Richmond Independent* in California. From 1977 to 1980, he was a United Press International reporter and editor, and from 1980 to 1982, a metropolitan news reporter for the *New York Daily News*, for which he also covered city hall and state politics. He entered broadcasting as a general assignment correspondent at WNYW-TV in New York and worked there until 1986, when he joined the staff of ABC News. He was initially assigned to the network's bureaus in New York, Los Angeles, Chicago and Miami and went on to cover stories from the Middle East, Asia, Europe and the Caribbean. Claiborne reported on the Persian Gulf War of 1991 and the presidential campaign of Bill Clinton in 1992. In 1999, he reported on conflict in Belgrade and on the Elian Gonzalez controversy. He covered the problems caused by pedophile Roman Catholic priests in the Boston Archdiocese in 2002 and the November 2003 legalization of gay marriage in Massachusetts. In 2003, Claiborne became one of the American journalists embedded with the military in Iraq; he was assigned to the *USS Abraham Lincoln*, an aircraft carrier on duty in the Persian Gulf. In 2004, he covered the U.S. occupation of Iraq as an ABC News general assignment reporter for "World News Tonight," "World News Tonight Saturday/Sunday," "Nightline" and "Good Morning America." Claiborne has also contributed to the ABC Radio Network and to abcnews.com. He was based in Boston before becoming news anchor for the weekend edition of "Good Morning America" in early 2006. This news talk show first aired in 1975; its weekend edition premiered in 2004.

In 2003, a *Los Angeles Sentinel* article reported on the Church of Christian Fellowship's annual Men's Day event at which Claiborne was the speaker. His message was that men should challenge themselves as Christians to do more to combat community violence and to promote education, public health and attention to environmental needs. A standout story Claiborne did in that same year was an interview with William Pinkney, captain of the recreated slave ship the AmistadAmerica, constructed to be a traveling monument to freedom and a floating classroom for teaching about the history and evils of slavery. The ship's name was chosen after the original Amistad, a Spanish slaver famous because of the mutiny that took place in 1839 off Long Island. The slaves who mutinied were captured by the U.S. Navy and imprisoned on charges of murder, but thanks to the intervention of ex-president John Quincy Adams, the 35 men were released and returned to Africa in 1841. A more recent story, in January 2006, involved the implanting of a device into the brain of a small deaf boy. The story, a sidebar reported during the Winter Olympics at Turino, Italy, featured Claiborne's interview with Dr. Vittorio Colletti of the University of Verona. A month later, Claiborne himself made the news while reporting it on a topic that was quite personal. He had long wondered, he told his viewers, exactly where in Africa his own forebears had lived before being seized by slave traders. He had always assumed, he said, that this information would be forever unavailable to him but that thanks to new DNA-based genealogy testing innovations, African Americans could now trace their roots not only to geographic regions of Africa, but to specific tribal groups. Claiborne joined Oprah Winfrey, filmmaker Spike Lee, actor Isaiah Washington and other prominent African Americans and was able to trace his own heritage to Ghana. He reported that the database used to investigate his lineage contained 22,000 DNA samples from around 400 African sub-groups, that around 3,000 people had been tested by the company African Ancestry and that the cost of testing ranged between $130 and $650. In 2000, Claiborne was one of several ABC News staffers who won an Emmy for reporting on the Elian Gonzalez controversy. He was an Ochberg Fellow at the University of Washington-affiliated Dart Center for Journalism and Trauma in 2003.

Further Readings: "ABC-TV Newsman Ron Claiborne Prods Christian Men to Lead." *Los Angeles Sentinel*, 6 November 2003; "DNA Testing Allows African-Americans to Trace Ancestry." [Online, 21 October 2005]. Sorenson Genomics Web site www.sorensongeonomics.com; "Ron Claiborne." [Online, 2 March 2006]. ABC News Web site www.abcnews.go.com.

Clinkscales, Keith T. (1964–)

A shooting star in the firmament of African-American magazine publishing is Keith Clinkscales, the Harvard MBA who, with owner Quincy Jones, made a success of the music and urban lifestyle magazine *Vibe*, then launched his own ambitious but ill-fated company, Vanguarde Media, publisher of *Savoy* and other magazines. His more recent business launches are KTC Ventures, a consulting company, and First World Communications, an urban media and entertainment company. Clinkscales grew up in Bridgeport, Connecticut, is a magna cum laude graduate of Florida A&M University, and holds the MBA from Harvard Business School. While employed as an account officer at New York City's Chemical Bank, he identified a void in magazines aimed at urban African Americans, borrowed $3,000 from 15 friends and, at age 24, produced the prototype of *Urban Profile*. By the time he began the Harvard MBA program in 1988, the magazine was up and running as a quarterly, and when he completed his degree in 1990, *Urban Profile* had a respectable circulation of around 75,000. Meanwhile, music arranger and producer Quincy Jones had approached Time Warner about starting a magazine to compete against *Rolling Stone* by covering the predominantly black music scene, to include hip-hop, soul, and rhythm and blues. A test issue of *Vibe* appeared in September 1992, and the first regular issue, with rapper Snoop Doggy Dogg on its cover, came out in September 1993. Clinkscales had sent copies of *Urban Profile* to a conference held by the Harvard Business School's African-American Student Union, and an alumnus working for Time Warner later contacted him to ask him to edit *Vibe*. In 1996, Time Warner sold its interest in the magazine; Clinkscales and four partners formed their own company. In 1997, they bought the successful alternative rock music magazine *Spin* and formed Vibe/Spin Ventures.

In August 1998, the company added a third magazine, *Blaze*, a monthly targeting the 12- to 24-year-old segment of the market with content focusing on rap music: DJs, MCs, break dancing and graffiti. Soon the combined circulation of the three magazines had reached 1.5 million and Clinkscales was being hailed as the "boy wonder" of magazine publishing. The music they covered was by that time the fastest-growing segment of the U.S. popular music market. *Vibe* grew from 100,000 to 700,000 circulation in its first six years and was being published as an oversized monthly. Clinkscales directed the formation of a company web presence, Vibe Online, and, in partnership with Walt Disney, hosted Vibe Live, an annual music celebration held at Pleasure Island, Florida. In 1997, the company also sponsored "Jamizon" a music festival that toured 24 U.S. cities.

In May 1999, Clinkscales left his job as president of *Vibe* to found his own company, Vanguarde Media. A few months after acquiring funding from New York venture capital firm Provender Capital Group, LLC, he bought *Honey*, a hip-hop magazine aimed at young women readers from Harris Publications and the music magazine *Impact* from the Joseph Loris estate. He did an upscale redesign on *Honey*, giving it more emphasis on fashion and beauty, and, through his old college friend, Black Entertainment Television chairman Robert Johnson, who bought into Vanguarde, Clinkscales took control from BET of the black news magazine *Emerge*, the women's health magazine *Heart & Soul*, and the *BET Weekend* newspaper insert. In the spring of 2000, Clinkscales announced that *Emerge* and *BET Weekend* would be closed and that *Heart & Soul* would go from six to ten issues a year. Having accomplished these changes, Clinkscales made his most ambitious launch, *Savoy*, offering this magazine to the subscriber list of *Emerge*, which gave the new venture an immediate circulation of 120,000 when its initial issue appeared in January 2001. *Savoy* was billed as a magazine for sophisticated, well-to-do urban African Americans. Its title was taken from the legendary Savoy Ballroom, popular during the years of the Harlem Renaissance, and contained columns by Armstrong Williams and Deborah Mathis plus musical commentary by jazz great Branford Marsalis. *Savoy* was intended to be the African-American version of *Vanity Fair* and became the flagship title in Vanguarde's fleet of four magazines. It was edited by the man who had suggested its founding, Roy S. Johnson, who had worked as a writer for *Sports Illustrated* and as editor-at-large for *Fortune*. Circulation proved disappointing, topping out at around 325,000, leading Clinkscales to buy the magazine *Code* from Larry Flynt to make use of its subscription list. A new investor joined Vanguarde: Strauss Zelnick, who engineered a television special called "Savoy Life," also a disappointment.

A part of the company's problems stemmed from its online presence, Vanguarde Neomedia, which diverted too much money from the magazines into a variety of online ventures, some tied directly to the company's magazines and others, such as Urban IQ.com and SideHustle.com, independent of them. Another arm of the company was Vanguarde Nexus, a consulting firm that specialized in the entertainment industry. Eventually, investor Provender withdrew support, and in November 2003, Clinkscales had to announce that the company would file for Chapter 11 bankruptcy protection, putting 70 employees out of work. In hindsight, he had tried to do too much too fast.

Since the closing of Vanguarde Media, Clinkscales has founded two new companies. The first was KTC Ventures, a consulting firm specializing in media and marketing with an urban culture focus. The second, First World Communications, is an urban-oriented entertainment company that markets film and television programming. Clinkscales is CEO of both firms.

Clinkscales has retained connection to the magazine industry by teaching with Stanford Publishing Courses offered at Stanford University for mid-career magazine and book publishing professionals. He is an active supporter and treasurer of Harlem's Apollo Theater Foundation and in June 2005, was a judge in the Youth IT Challenge competition held in New York City and cosponsored by the National Urban League and Microsoft Corporation to interest 14-to 18 year-old minority youths in entrepreneurial careers in information technology. In January 2005, when Bridgeport, Connecticut, announced plans for a month-long celebration of black history, it was Clinkscales who accepted the key to the city from Bridgeport's mayor. He has served on PepsiCo's Advisory Board, has been inducted into the American Advertising Federation Hall of Fame and has been selected as a "40 Under 40" recipient from *The Network Journal*, a magazine devoted to black business people and professionals.

Further Readings: "A Vibrant Brand: Keith Clinkscales Takes Vibe Magazine to a New Level." [Online, April 1999]. Harvard Business School Bulletin Web site www.alumni.hbs.edu; Brown, Ethan. "Bad Vibes: Keith Clinkscales Leaves Behind Big Questions." [Online, 17 May 1999]. New York Metro site http://newyorkmetro.com; "Keith Clinkscales." [Online]. Greater Talent Network Web site www.greatertalent.com; Martin, Roland S. "Fade to Black: Vanguarde Media Files for Bankruptcy." [Online, 25 November 2003]. Black America Today Web site www.blackamericatoday.com; Prince, Richard. "Vanguarde Shuts 3 Mags: Going Out of Business." [Online, 25 November 2003]. Richard Prince's Journal-isms. Maynard Institute Web site www.maynardije.org; "Vanguarde Media Launches Savoy Magazine." [Online, 15 December 2000]. The Write News Web site www.writenews.com; Wynn, Ron. "Daring, Different 'Emerge' May Bring Quality Back." [Online, 22 December 2003]. The City Paper Web site www.nashvillecitypaper.com.

Cockfield, Errol A. Jr. (14 September 1973–)

Enterprising young Errol Cockfield is Albany Bureau chief for *Newsday*. He was born in the South American nation of Guyana, but due to political unrest there his family relocated to Trinidad in 1979. In 1984, they moved again, this time to Brooklyn, New York. Bright and bookish as a youngster, Cockfield skipped two grades and at age 16, was admitted to the University of Stony Brook. His parents, an electrical engineer and a social worker, wanted him to go into medicine, but his work at the school's African-American newspaper, *Black World*, headed him toward journalism instead. He majored in English, minored in journalism and was encouraged by one of his professors, Paul Schreiber, to apply for METPRO, the Tribune Company's Minority Editorial Training Program. That experience led him to a reporting job at the *Los Angeles Times* following his 1994 graduation. He worked there until 1997, when he was hired as a reporter by *Newsday*. He covered real estate and development news; two of his big stories concerned plans to build a partially tax-funded new stadium for the New York Jets football team and plans for rebuilding on the site of the World Trade Towers in Manhattan. He moved on to cover Nassau County politics and was named state capital bureau chief in late 2004. Cockfield's name began to become known in journalistic circles in large part due to his active involvement in the National Association of Black Journalists, which he first joined in 1994. He also has been active in that organization's local affiliate, the New York Association of Black Journalists. He was director of the NYABJ's annual workshop for journalism students, vice president–print, then NYABJ president. He helped organize Chapter Day at the 2004 UNITY conference in Washington, D.C. He has been on the board of directors for NABJ since being elected Region I Director, with responsibility for Connecticut, Maine, Massachusetts, New Hampshire, New Jersey, New York, Pennsylvania, Rhode Island and Vermont. He was also chair of the NABJ Council of Presidents from 2003 to 2005 and he has served on the NABJ membership committee.

While working in Los Angeles, Cockfield reported about attacks on African Americans by white supremacist "skinheads." In New York, he has covered debate over the death penalty and over draconian punishment for drug-related offenses. He reported on the lackluster monitoring by state officials in facilities that house New York's elderly. In 2001, he reported on pedestrian deaths in New York and efforts to install radar cameras in an attempt to slow traffic. In the same year, he also began writing about measures taken by state officials and the Coast Guard to protect New York Harbor; in 2005, he addressed jurisdictional confusion about patrolling the waters between New York and New Jersey. When the Jason Blair plagiarism story broke in 2003, Cockfield remarked that too many conservatives found it irresistible to use that incident as an opportunity to attack the institution of affirmative action, and he criticized what he termed the media's mob mentality in heaping abuse upon the *New York Times*. In spring 2004, he reported that one of the two observation decks planned for the project at Ground Zero would be, at 457 meters, the tallest such facility in the world. In December of that year, he reported on the state Senate's override of Gov. George Pataki's veto to give New York workers a $2 an hour increase in the minimum wage. The governor's criticism of Hamilton College for hosting radical academic Ward Churchill was the topic of a Cockfield story in February 2005; Churchill had called the victims of the September 11 attacks "little Eichmanns." The Jets stadium, which would cost taxpayers more than $1 billion and which was being supported by Pataki and New York City Mayor Michael Bloomberg, was the subject of a Cockfield story in May 2005. In later stories, he reported on vote delays as the proposed stadium continued to be debated, and in spring 2006, he reported on the state's politicians and their various suggested approaches to containing government spending.

In 2006, Cockfield was treasurer of the Legislative Correspondents Association of New York State. He has written freelance for such periodicals as *Upscale*, *Source* and *Vibe* and has made appearances on National Public Radio. He also writes poetry and does occasional readings at the Blue Moon Café and other poetry venues. One of his humorous poems, "Heads Ain't Ready for Poetry," won third-place in a Spirit of the Words competition sponsored by UNITY.

Further Readings: "Candidate's Biography—Errol Cockfield." [Online, 20 April 2005]. National Association of Black Journalists Web site www.nabj.org/members/elections/bios; "We Must Support NYABJ and NABJ." [Online, August 2002]. New York Association of Black Journalists Web site www.nyabj.org.

Cooper, Desiree (c.1959–)

National Public Radio commentator for "All Things Considered" and *Detroit Free Press* columnist Desiree Cooper was born in Itazuke, Japan, and grew up in the traveled life of an Air Force dependent, also residing in Florida, Texas, New Mexico, Colorado, Maryland and Michigan. She is a 1979 graduate of the University of Maryland and received her law degree at the University of Virginia Law School in 1984. She also has both accomplishments and further aspirations in fiction writing. Her page on the NPR Web site describes her as "a recovering attorney." In July 1997, she began a column titled "This Side of 30" for the Detroit *Metro Times*; her job in doing this column was to relate to younger readers. Thereafter, she began her *Free Press* column.

Cooper is a sprightly writer who turns an effective phrase and shows keen wit. In one of her "This Side of 30" columns in August 1998 she used an analogy with *Sesame Street*'s Kermit the Frog, who says it is not easy being green, relating that remark to Supreme Court Justice Clarence Thomas, who, she wrote, needed to be convinced by the larger black community that he is black. Another column from that same year related a shopping adventure she shared with a friend who had been a model, both dressed all in black. The two women, Cooper said, resembled the TJ Maxx Liberation Army. A holiday season column was less humorous but warm and inviting, as she described the way her family celebrates the season of Kwanzaa, which dates from 1966. Her focus was on the nurturing importance of family stories. A more complex column dwelt on her differing reactions to being pregnant, which, she explained, has both divine and sinister, fear-laden aspects.

Most of Cooper's columns dealt with race in some way. She wrote with sorrow about an eight-year-old Detroit girl shot to death when parties unknown fired into the house where she was sleeping and the troubling sight of a Ku Klux Klan robe displayed for sale in a local auction gallery. Others of her columns were about the need for arts education in poor city schools and Black Arts Movement poet Dudley Randall, who now publishes the work of black writers through his own firm, Broadside Press. She related unlikely success stories, such as that of a former teenage runaway with a drug problem who later succeeded in the film documentary business. When Naomi Tutu, daughter of the famous Anglican bishop in South Africa, visited Detroit and talked about 1994, the first year that black residents of her nation could vote, Cooper reminded her Detroit readers that in our own 2000 presidential election, 22 million single women who were eligible to vote, plus 16 million more who had never even registered, had passed up the privilege of voting. One of her most poignant columns described how her white great-grandfather and her mixed-race great-grandmother, living in rural Virginia, had not been allowed to marry or even to live in the same house, but managed to have and raise eight children. She pointed out the similarity of rhetoric between those who were against mixed-race marriages in her forbears' time and that of the politicians, clergy and others who use the same arguments today to oppose same-sex marriage. Another outstanding piece of her work was an explanation of the immense and remarkable popularity of television icon Oprah Winfrey.

Cooper has been nominated twice for a Pulitzer Prize. She has been recognized by Planned Parenthood, the Michigan Press Association and Radcliffe College. She has also won awards for her verse.

"Marriage Ban Only a Repeat of Injustice" by Desiree Cooper

Proposal 2 would have us revise the Michigan Constitution to ban gay marriages and civil unions. For guidance on how to vote, I need only to remember how another marriage ban robbed my ancestors of a basic human right.

A Love Story

My great-grandparents, Mary and Logan, met in rural Virginia in the late 1800s. He was a white planter descended from a family that built a fortune growing peanuts. She was a mixed-race midwife who also worked as a cook in Logan's kitchen.

By all accounts, they wee devoted to each other, but under Virginia's antimiscegenation laws, which dated to 1691, it was illegal for them to marry. According to attorney and author Phyl Newbeck in his book, "Virginia Hasn't Always Been for Lovers," the laws against interracial marriage were grounded in the desire to preserve slavery. Children who were half-white, half-black would "obscure the racial barriers necessary for the maintenance of the system," he writes.

But the more common justification was the enforcement of God's "natural law."

"Almighty God created the races white, black, yellow, malay and red and he placed them on separate continents," wrote a Virginia appeals court judge as late as 1965. "The fact that he separated the races shows that he did not intend for the races to mix."

Not only was intermarriage considered anti-Christian, it was deemed morally repugnant. "Intermarriage between whites and blacks is repulsive and averse to every sentiment of pure American spirit," said Georgia's Sen. Seaborn Roddenberry in 1912. "Let us uproot and exterminate now this debasing, ultra-demoralizing, un-American and inhuman leprosy."

As a result, my great-grandparents not only never married, they never even lived under the same roof. They managed to raise eight children, but the family never had the legal rights afforded families of married couples. The children could not be given their father's name. Even when the children later married, they hid their father's identity on their marriage certificates.

When Logan died in 1936, Mary and their children stood outside the church, forbidden to attend the funeral. Because he left no will, the sheriff rounded up Logan's possessions and divided them among 22 of even his most distant relatives, purposely excluding his "colored" family. When Mary died three years later, she wasn't buried beside the man she'd loved for 45 years, but in a separate graveyard for blacks.

Justice for All.

I know that history repeats itself, but I'm astounded that we are poised to ban civil unions and marriages between people of the same sex just 37 years after the U.S. Supreme Court recognized the stupidity of restricting marriage to those of the same race.

Supporters of Proposal 2 sound frighteningly like the judges, politicians, clergy and citizens who railed against interracial marriage as both ungodly and unpatriotic, claims that have proven to be bigoted and ignorant in the years since.

If there is one thing we learned from the civil rights movement, it is that we can't depend on popularity polls to validate basic human rights. Justice doesn't choose between the powerful and the weak, the mainstream and the marginalized. It belongs to everyone.

My vote against Proposal 2 may cause a lot of people to roll over in their graves, but among them won't be my great-grandparents. Despite scorn, they couldn't have had a more perfect union.

Source: Reprinted by permission of the *Detroit Free Press*. This column originally appeared on 14 October 2004.

Further Readings: "Desiree Cooper, NPR Biography." [Online]. National Public Radio Web site www.npr.org.

Corley, Cheryl (c.1956–)

Cheryl Corley covers the Midwest from the Chicago bureau of National Public Radio; her specialty topic is housing. She was born in Chicago and earned a B.A. cum laude at Bradley University in Peoria, Illinois. During her Peoria days, she was a reporter and news director for NPR station WCBU and was a director for WEEK-TV, an NBC affiliate station. Her next job was as news director for public radio at station WBEZ in Chicago. There she reported on city hall, with special attention to the administration of the city's first black mayor, Harold Washington, who was elected in 1983. She also reported for "Chicago Tonight" on station WTTW and appeared on news and issues programs on public television stations in the city. In 1995, Corley went to work for NPR as a general assignment reporter. She has covered a considerable variety of events and trends, including floods and other natural disasters; the death penalty; the pension fund woes of United Airlines and U.S. Airways in 2004; an interview with war crimes authority and Georgetown University professor Gary Solis regarding U.S. abuse of Iraqi prisoners, also done in 2004; the striking down by a circuit court judge of an Illinois statute that would have placed a cap on jury awards for pain and suffering; and the appeal and 2005 reversal of accounting/auditing firm Arthur Andersen, which had been found guilty in 2002 of obstruction of justice by shredding documents for client Enron Corporation. Other stories have been about the arts, such as an account of attempts in 2000 by blues musicians and others to preserve the musical heritage of Maxwell Street in Chicago, an area sought by the University of Illinois-Chicago for campus expansion and in 2002, a report on the Lorraine Hansbury play "A Raisin in the Sun," the title of which had been taken from a Langston Hughes poem; and an NPR interview with the music supervisor of the television program "The O.C." in 2004. A "Morning Edition" interview she did in 2001 profiled Ron Paige, secretary of education under the Bush administration, under fire at that time for not pushing hard enough for the president's agenda. She has also worked as a substitute host for the shows "Morning Edition" and "Weekend All Things Considered." As of early 2006, her assignment was reporting about the Midwest out of NPR's Chicago bureau, and she has developed a specialty on news and trends involving housing: urban renewal, home buying and public housing issues. In 2003, she reported on a real estate developer who had taken out advertisements to attract gays to a Chicago neighborhood undergoing renewal, on the premise that a substantial gay population helps to gentrify urban neighborhoods and stimulate their economies.

In an April 2002 interview of Corley done for Rtnda.org, she revealed some of her tricks of the trade as a radio interviewer, such as getting one's subject to chat informally while the interviewer sets sound levels, trying to capture as much natural sound as possible and not writing until first having listened to the sound recordings done for a story. The interviewer for that story remarked that Corley has an unflappable demeanor and a superior ability to put people at ease, even when they are being recorded. She has been accorded the Herman Kogan Award for her coverage of immigration issues, the Studs Terkel Award for reporting on Chicago's multiethnic neighborhoods and other awards given by the Associated Press, the Society of Professional Journalists and the National Association of Black Journalists.

Further Readings: "Cheryl Corley, Senior Reporter." [Online]. National Public Radio Web site www.npr.org; "Why Cities Are Courting the Gay and Lesbian Community." [Online, 3 June 2003]. The Urban Institute Web site www.urban.org; "Cheryl Corley: The Art of Persuasion." [Online, April 2002]. Radio-Television News Directors Association & Foundation Web site www.rtnda.org.

Crouch, Stanley (14 December 1945–)

New York Daily News columnist, renowned jazz critic, poet, novelist and essayist Stanley Crouch pulls no punches and dodges no confrontation. He was born in Los Angeles and attended, but never graduated from, two California schools: Los Angeles Junior College and Southwest Junior College. He is largely and successfully self-educated and has packed a lot of literary and journalistic accomplishment into his 62 years. In the early 1960s, he taught literacy in an East Los Angeles antipoverty program and was on the scene during the Watts Riots, which turned Crouch to black nationalism, which he soon repudiated after working from 1965 to 1967 as an actor and playwright in the Studio Watts Company. After spending 1968–1975 teaching at Claremont College, he relocated to New York City where he first was a drummer in his own jazz band, did bookings for an East Village club called the Tin Palace, then in 1979 began writing for the *Village Voice*, for which he worked until 1988. In 1972, he published his first book, provocatively titled *Ain't No Ambulances for No Nigguhs Tonight*, a collection of poetry. Over the years since that time, Crouch has written columns for the *Los Angeles Free Press*, *The Cricket* and the *SoHo Weekly News* as well as his more widely recognized column in the *Daily News*. He has been a contributing editor for *New Republic* and attracted considerable attention when he was fired in 2003 as a columnist for *JazzTimes* magazine. Apparently, Crouch's in-your-face attitude displeased the magazine's management; Crouch countered, responding that the magazine's editors bowed to music industry pressure from marketers who disliked his tough reviewing. Whatever the case, Crouch indisputably has been among the three or four most influential jazz critics in the nation, and he has widened the topical scope of his writing, often examining American culture through the lens of music.

An iconoclast by nature, Crouch has been outspokenly critical of a variety of generally well thought-of contemporaries. His 1990 book of essays *Notes of a Hanging Judge* pictured Nobel Prize winning writer Toni Morrison as a maudlin peddler of snake-oil. In other venues, he has attacked filmmaker Spike Lee, called Louis Farrakhan a nutcase, skewered *Roots* author Alex Haley as an abandoned plagiarist and opportunist, and consistently derided hip-hop rappers as tasteless thugs whose popularity increases according to the length of their arrest records. Those were verbal attacks. The burly Crouch has also made headlines for having occasionally escalated his attacks to the physical level. He is accused of having hit two of his *Village Voice* coworkers, punched Jazz Journalists Association president Howard Mandel, and slapped novelist and critic Dale Peck, whose review of one of Crouch's books was unfavorable. He is what might be described as an independent-minded, not especially compassionate conservative. He speaks out in his *Daily News* column and elsewhere against what he calls "the Afro-centric hustle," in which history is deliberately rewritten to give black Americans a more palatable past; this is the general topic of another of his books, *The All American Skin Game, or, the Decoy of Race*. Like most black conservatives, he stresses the importance of education, taking personal responsibility and the need for a more elevated cultural climate than the nation now enjoys. Since 1987, Crouch has been an artistic consultant for Lincoln Center and was founder of that center's jazz program.

Despite his reputation for occasional violence, Crouch the columnist shows considerable concern for human safety. He has urged New York mayor Michael Bloomberg to emulate former mayor Rudy Giuliani's tough stance on street crime and has urged the federal government to do something about the genocide in Sudan. Crouch appeared to think John Kerry would win a narrow victory in the 2004 presidential election, though he called Kerry a political stiff, so robot-like he sweats motor oil.

On the sunny side, Crouch has written glowingly about such music figures as Duke Ellington, the most patrician figure in black music; Louis Armstrong; Ray Charles; and longtime Café Carlyle entertainer Bobby Short. In his column on Short, who had spent 34 years entertaining at the Carlyle, Crouch complimented the musician not only for knowing all the songs, but for knowing why people like them. The columnist/critic is currently at work on a biography of alto saxophone great Charlie Parker. In his work for the *Daily News*, he continues to hammer away at what he considers the four great problems of society: corruption, folly, mediocrity and incompetence.

"The Descent of Michael" by Stanley Crouch

Celebrity is now something that comes about as much through attention as achievement. But the case of the Michael Jackson trial is more than a blip of photographs and prose loaded down with gush, hysteria and snoop. Michael Jackson is not Paris Hilton, though some might think he would like to be. He is such a master of step, spin and turn on the dance floor that Fred Astair called him a genius.

Yet Jackson the man is like many of the people and things that have emerged since the upheaval of the 1960s. We saw revolutionary social changes that made for a much better society, but nothing ever arrives alone, especially in America. Our enormous latitude for invention, lunacy and profit always allows the worst to come along almost immediately following a set of innovations.

In the case of the '60s, irrefutably important social changes were contrasted by the adolescent blob of rock culture that eventually swallowed up much of the taste and obscured much of the talent of the society. We saw the loud and the obvious take up more of our cultural space. Adolescent obsessions with sensation and the sensational pushed most subtle forms of expression into the margins as teenage angst became more and more dominant.

Michael Jackson is an expression of that part of our social history, but also a symbol of other things—plastic surgery, the kind of adolescent attraction to childhood fantasies that we see in his Neverland home and our threadbare rock and roll aristocracy, which we witnessed when he married Elvis Presley's daughter.

This trial brought up questions about all this, but it seems to me that illusions of the man have been on trial along with Jackson himself. These illusions are grounded in what people assumed their relationship to Jackson was during periods of being enthralled by his music and videos. The amount of emotion we heap on our pop celebrities is suspect. People are not good guys just because they have ability.

The descent of Michael Jackson is testing that whole arena. For all that Jackson has done to control our illusions over a career that became progressively eccentric, his powers have fallen before the forces of this trial.

The publicity, the infinitude of speculations and the images of him either dancing atop a car on his first day of court appearance or being admonished for coming to court dressed in what seemed to be pajamas have proved his undoing.

He will never again be able to get by as any more than a vastly talented eccentric. He has now joined the ranks of the great freaks of our age and has no one to blame other than himself and his own willingness to play with the carnivorous forces that created his illusion.

Source: *New York Daily News*, L.P., reprinted with permission. The above column appeared on 9 June 2005.

Books by Stanley Crouch: *Ain't No Ambulances for No Nigguhs Tonight* (New York: R.W. Baron, 1972); *Notes of a Hanging Judge: Essays and Reviews, 1979–1989* (New York: Oxford University Press, 1990); *The All-American Skin Game, or, The Decoy of Race: The Long and the Short of It, 1990–1994* (New York: Vintage Books, 1995); *Always in Pursuit: Fresh American Perspectives, 1995–1997* (New York: Vintage Books, 1998); *Don't the Moon Look Lonesome: A Novel in Blues and Swing* (New York: Vintage Books, 2000); with Deborah Willis and Teenie Harris, *One Shot Harris: The Photographs of Charles "Teenie" Harris* (New York: Harry N. Abrams, 2002); with Playthell Benjamin, *Reconsidering the Souls of Black Folk: Thoughts on the Groundbreaking Classic Work of W.E.B. Du Bois* (Philadelphia; London: Running, 2004); *The Artificial White Man: Essays on Authenticity* (New York: Basic Civitas, 2004).

Further Readings: Alexander, Amy. "The Bull in the Black-Intelligentsia China Shop." [Online]. Salon Brilliant Careers Web site www.salon.com; Coaes, Ta-Nehisi. "Crouching Stanley, Hidden Gangsta: Why the Hanging Judge Can't Keep His Hands to Himself." [Online, 24 July 2004]. The Village Voice Web site www.villagevoice.com; Gergen, David. "Politics of Blame." [Online, 22 February 1996]. NewsHour PBS Website www.pbs.org; King, Daniel. "Hanging the Judge." [Online]. The Village Voice Web site www.villagevoice.com; Masiello, Diane. "Crouch, Stanley" in Shari Dorantes Hatch and Michael R. Srickland, eds., *African-American Writers: A Dictionary*. Santa Barbara, Calif., Denver, Colo. And Oxford, England: ABC-CLIO, 2000; "Stanley Crouch: Jazz Critic & Essayist." [Online]. Greater Talent Network Web site www.greatertalent.com.

Crutchfield, James N. (1948–)

James Crutchfield became president and publisher of the *Beacon Journal* in Akron, Ohio, in 2001, capping a long career as a journalist. He announced in July 2006 that he was stepping down from this position. He was born in McKeesport, Pennsylvania, and grew up in the Hill District of Pittsburgh. He received a bachelor's in communication at Duquesne University and began his career in 1968, reporting for the *Pittsburgh Press*. In 1971, he worked for a brief time for the Pittsburgh Model Cities Program as its public information officer, then returned to newspaper journalism as a reporter for the *Pittsburgh Post-Gazette*. In 1976, he moved to Detroit to report for the *Detroit Free Press*, and in 1979, he took another breather from newspaper work to serve as press secretary to Michigan Senator Carl Levin. In 1981, he returned to the *Free Press* as its Lansing bureau head, holding that job for two years. He then moved up through four more assignments for that paper: assistant city editor, deputy city editor, city editor and deputy managing editor. In 1989, he left to become managing editor for the *Beacon Journal* in Akron. In 1993, he moved into the executive ranks as executive editor and senior vice president of the Long Beach, California, *Press-Telegram* and remained in that position until the paper was sold in 1997. At that time, he moved to Philadelphia and for one year was assistant to the publisher of Philadelphia Newspapers Inc., the parent company of the *Philadelphia Inquirer* and the Philadelphia *Daily News*. Thereafter, he was director of single-copy sales and distribution for the company until 2000, when he returned to Akron as general manager of the *Beacon*

Journal. In April 2001, he was promoted to president and publisher. Crutchfield chaired the Knight group's Akron Community Advisory Committee, and in June 2004, he was elected a trustee of the John S. and James L. Knight Foundation. He was able to solidify the *Beacon Journal*'s efforts to have a more diverse staff by promoting Debra Adams Simmons to editor and replacing her as managing editor with Mizell Stewart III, thereby making this mainstream newspaper quite unusual in that its publisher, editor and managing editor all were African American. An enormous complication arose, however, in March 2006, when word came that the Knight Ridder group was to be absorbed by the McClatchy Company and that 12 of the Knight Ridder's 32 dailies would be sold because they were not located in the nation's high-growth areas. The Akron paper is one that was divested by the new owners, so the paper's future and the jobs of its executives and staffers were under a cloud of doubt. In July 2006, Crutchfield announced that he would leave the paper, which in early August of that year was sold to Black Press Ltd. of Canada.

Crutchfield has served on a number of boards: Duquesne University, the Akron County Art Museum, the United Way of Summit County, the Summit Education Initiative and the Greater Akron Chamber of Commerce. He is on the diversity committee of the Weathervane Community Playhouse and is on the fundraising committee for the East Akron Community House. He is a member of the Accrediting Council of ACEJMC, which accredits the nation's journalism programs. Crutchfield belongs to the American Society of Newspaper Editors (ASNE), the Ohio Newspaper Association, the National Association of Black Journalists and the National Association of Minority Media Executives. He has been active with the ASNE's Journalism Values Institute, traveled to Cuba with an ASNE group in 2002 and was a member of the judging committee for spot news reporting for the 1997 Pulitzer Prize competition.

Further Readings: "Akron Publisher Elected to Knight Board of Trustees." [Online, 18 June 2004]. AScribe site http://newswire.ascribe.org; "James Crutchfield." [Online]. The Akron Roundtable Web site www.akronroundtable.org; Irwin, Gloria and Jim Mackinnon. "Turning the Page for the Beacon Journal." [Online, 14 May 2006]. Akron Beacon Journal Web site www.ohio.com.

Curry, George E. (23 February 1947–)

Formerly editor-in-chief of *Emerge: Black America's Newsmagazine* as well as president of the American Society of Magazine Editors, George Curry is now editor-in-chief of the National Newspaper Publishers Association News Service and BlackPressUSA.com and writes a weekly column that appears in roughly 200 historically black newspapers across the United States.

Curry, George E.

He was born in Tuscaloosa, Alabama. His mother did domestic work until getting a better job at an antipoverty agency, and his father was a mechanic who left the family when Curry was seven. In a June 2002 column, Curry compared the poverty he observed while in Cuba to his own beginnings remarking that his first home was a three-room shack in an all-black neighborhood of so-called shotgun houses known as "The Bottom." He quipped that he thought of his own house as a "B-B gun house"—not as nice as even a shotgun house. The family moved into public housing and, successful as he now is, Curry wears on one wrist a bracelet having a catch shaped like a screen door hook—to remind him of his roots and to make him grateful for his current prosperity. At Druid High School in Tuscaloosa, he was sports editor of the student newspaper and played football graduating in 1965. For the following year, he was a civil rights volunteer with the Student Nonviolent Coordinating Committee in New York City. He enrolled at Knoxville College and in 1970, completed his B.A. in history, and was hired as a *Sports Illustrated* reporter. He was the second black staffer hired by the then-new magazine. Two years later, he left *Sports Illustrated* to become a general-assignment reporter at the *St. Louis Post Dispatch*; from 1983 to 1989, he was a Washington correspondent for the *Chicago Tribune*. He next became the *Tribune*'s New York bureau chief, holding that job until 1993, when he was named top editor for *Emerge*, a news magazine aimed at black readers. He edited the magazine until it folded in June 2000 and entertains hopes of bring it back to life, either under the same title or a new one. During its brief life, *Emerge* won around 40 awards, and one of its 1993 covers gained nationwide publicity for its depiction of highly conservative Supreme Court Justice Clarence Thomas wearing an Aunt Jemima-style kerchief on his head. The magazine also gained national attention with its campaign to free Kemba Smith, a young black woman who received a remarkably long sentence for drug-related activities. In 2000, President Bill Clinton pardoned her, thanks in part to the three stories *Emerge* had run about her case. In May 2000, Curry was elected president of the ASNE becoming the first African American to serve in that capacity. At the time of his election, he was also working for Black Entertainment Television as a panelist on the program "Lead Story." In 2002, he began doing weekly radio commentaries syndicated by Capitol Radio News Service. These commentaries mainly covered elections, the war in Iraq and the various deficiencies of the George W. Bush administration. More recent commentaries have addressed the contributions—good and bad—of many contemporary luminaries: Al Sharpton, Jayson Blair, O.J. Simpson, Alan Keyes, Barack Obama, Colin Powell, Condoleezza Rice, Frances Berry, Shirley Chisholm, Rosa Parks, Louis Farrakhan, Johnnie Cochrane, Terri Schiavo and others. In 2003, Curry was named editor-in-chief of the National Newspaper Publishers Association News Service and BlackPress.com, at which time he also began writing a weekly column that goes to the historically black newspapers represented by the NNPA. His work with the NNPA has taken him to other pars of the globe; a page on his GeorgeCurry.com Web site displays photos of him taken with such news figures as Pope John Paul II, South Africa's Nelson Mandela, Archbishop Desmond Tutu, United Nations Secretary General Kofi Annan, U.S. Secretary of State Condoleezza Rice and sports figures Jim Brown and Magic Johnson. Curry was in Doha, Qatar, at the start of the U.S. invasion of Iraq and reported on the onset of hostilities.

Curry is also known for having founded a groundbreaking journalism workshop for aspiring black journalists in St. Louis in 1975. One of his February 2006 columns notes that the Urban Journalism Workshop he set up and directed so many years ago has been emulated in 15 other U.S. cities, and he listed some of the present-day journalists who went through these programs, including Russ Mitchell of CBS News; Nashville *Tennessean* editor Everett Mitchell; managing editor of the *Orlando Sentinel* Mark Russell and others. The column also noted that Curry had offered a summer program at the University of Missouri, and another in Washington, D.C., for Northwestern University. His accomplishments have earned him the honor of 2003 Journalist of the Year from the National Association of Black Journalists, and he is one of the individuals on that association's list of the most influential twentieth century journalists. Curry has authored one book in 1977 and edited two more, the first in 1999, the second in 2003. He also wrote a chapter for *Black Genius: African American Solutions to African American Problems* (New York: W.W. Norton, 1999), edited by Walter Mosley.

Of Curry's many accomplishments, the best might well be his weekly column. The lion's share of his columns during the past few years have dealt with various aspects of the national political scene as controlled by the George W. Bush administration, of which Curry clearly disapproves. He sees "compassionate conservatism" as translating in fact to having compassion for conservatives, and he disparages President Bush and his intimates for taking from the poor to give to the rich. In 2003, he took the Republican Party to task for trying to trick African Americans with lofty talk of "no child left behind" and then failing to back up the talk with funding and gave other examples of talking in one direction and acting in the opposite. As have so many other columnists, both black and white, Curry regards the U.S. invasion of Iraq as a huge mistake, especially the way the administration chose to ignore the opinions of our historic allies. He dislikes the notion of spending untold billions to rebuild Iraq when so much need exists to rebuild parts of our own country, and in 2005, he pointed out the displeasure of the black community as reflected in sharply declining enlistment for military duty on the part of young African Americans. While being proud of the achievements that brought Secretary of State Condoleezza Rice to such high office, he chides her for trying to bolster the increasingly unpopular Republican agenda by distorting history, giving specific examples. In a 2005 column headlined "George W. Is No LBJ," Curry attacks Bush's desire to use tax funds to subsidize private education, and he accuses the administration of cynically using Hurricane Katrina to the detriment of New Orleans' former black residents. A more recent column, in 2006, offers statistics that place New Orleans as having held fifth place among U.S. cities in terms of large black population, and he points out that in plans to rebuild the city, race is a highly important subtext. He has also written on what he terms "discrimination with a smile" in New Orleans, by which at some Bourbon Street bars, black patrons have been charged more for drinks than white patrons. What prompted this column was the beating to death of a black college student by three New Orleans bouncers. Curry has also opposed Samuel Alito as a Supreme Court nominee, blasted the Bush White House for its attacks on affirmative action programs and criticized the King family for rescinding their invitation to Bush critic Harry Belafonte as a speaker at the Coretta Scott King funeral after it was announced that President Bush would attend.

Another theme in Curry's columns is the importance of the historically black press. In June 2005, he decried the announcement that the *New York Times* would start a new Gainesville, Florida, paper specifically aimed at the black audience. It would be difficult, he pointed out, for struggling black-owned newspapers to compete with the deep pockets of the *Times*. In a column on the same general topic, he remarked that for deep and reliable coverage of the African-American community, the historically black press is indispensable. On other matters, he has written on the problem of AIDS in black America, citing figures that show blacks, who make up a little more that 12 percent of the U.S. population, now suffer 40 percent of AIDS cases. One of his most unusual column topics was the way funerals have replaced family reunions in fast-paced American life. Other Curry columns have been written about interesting public figures in contemporary America. Some of these columns are about individuals Curry does not admire, such as Jesse Jackson or Jayson Blair. Little as he thought of disgraced former *New York Times* reporter Blair, he thought even less of the relatively quiet way the similar case of white ex-*USA Today* reporter Jack Kelley was handled. Among people Curry has admired was lawyer Johnnie Cochran, who will be mainly remembered for the successful defense of O.J. Simpson even though Cochran had spent a lot of unpaid time defending impecunious clients he called his "No-Js." When CBS anchorman Dan Rather was attacked as a liberal, Curry defended him, citing studies that showed Rather as having been more nearly conservative over the years. And when magazine mogul John Johnson died, Curry wrote positively about the founding of *Ebony* and Johnson's other accomplishments, yet added that Johnson is often credited with having created the first media outlet that pictured black America in full, when, to Curry's mind, the black newspaper press deserves that honor.

"New Orleans: Chocolate, Vanilla or Neapolitan?" by George E. Curry

New Orleans Mayor Ray Nagin opened himself up for a torrent of criticism when he declared in a Martin Luther King Day speech that God wants New Orleans to again be a "chocolate city."

In his speech, he said, "It's time for us to come together. It's time for us to rebuild New Orleans—the one that should be a chocolate New Orleans." Nagin added, "This city will be a majority African American city. It's the way God wants it to be. You can't have New Orleans no other way. It wouldn't be New Orleans."

Under fire, Nagin backed away from his comments.

It's easy to criticize Nagin for his choice of words or for professing to speak for God—and many have done just that. But that's the easy way out. What's missing in the discussion about rebuilding New Orleans is a candid exchange about race. Now that the mayor has apologized for calling for the reconstruction of a chocolate city, let's discuss what's being avoided—the issue of race.

Of course, race is not the primary issue when pondering New Orleans' future. The paramount issue is one of safety and providing protection against future hurricanes in the below-sea-level city. But in deciding how to rebuild New Orleans, race becomes a salient factor, intended or not.

Prior to Hurricane Katrina, New Orleans had the fifth-highest concentration of African-Americans among major cities, according to the Census Bureau. With 84 percent, Gary, Ind. led the nation in that category, followed by Detroit, with 81.6 percent, Birmingham, Ala. at 73.5 percent, Jackson, Miss. with 70.6 percent and New Orleans, with Blacks representing 67.3 percent of the population. (The other leading chocolate cities were Baltimore, 64.3 percent, Atlanta, 61.4, Memphis, 61.4, Washington, D.C., 60 percent and Richmond, Va., 57.2.)

Mayor Nagin isn't the only person suggesting that New Orleans should maintain its chocolate majority. Secretary of Housing and Urban Development Alphonso Jackson, an African-American, predicted that New Orleans will become more vanilla-like. And even those who profess to want a Neapolitan city—similar to the equal stripes of chocolate, vanilla and strawberry in the brick-shaped block of ice cream—know that under current plans, vanilla will become the dominant flavor of the city.

Whatever the final product, race should be openly debated. New Orleans will, in effect, become a planned community and race should be part of that planning. New Orleans, like most major U.S. cities, has a largely segregated public school system that grew out of largely segregated residential patterns. If the city can be revived in a way that leaves no racial group isolated from important resources and services, Hurricane Katrina could be a blessing in disguise.

However, if the unstated plan is to rid the city of its Black majority, then everyone should return to the drawing board.

New Orleans' population approached 500,000 prior to Katrina. The special Bring New Orleans Back Commission places the current population at 144,000. The population is projected to rise to 181,000 by next September and 247,000 by September 2008. The commission says it is hoping to make New Orleans "the best city in the world."

But the commission has not helped its image by recommending a four-month moratorium on rebuilding the most damaged neighborhoods, most of them Black. The commission says a determination must be made to allow reconstruction or tear down these areas and allow others to redevelop them.

On January 22, the New York Times carried a candid headline: "In New Orleans, Smaller May Mean Whiter." That kind of candor and directness needs to be injected into the discussions about the new New Orleans.

"The city, nearly 70 percent African-American before Hurricane Katrina, has lost some of its largest black neighborhoods to the deluge, and many fear it will never be a predominantly black city again, as it has been since the 1970s," the New York Times article observed.

It continued, "Indeed, race has become a subtext for just about every contentious decision the city faces: where to put FEMA trailers; which neighborhoods to rebuild; how the troubled school system should be reorganized; when elections should be held. Many blacks see threats to their political domination in reconstruction plans that do not give them what they once had. But many whites see an opportunity to restore a broken city they fled decades ago."

It's an opportunity for Blacks and Whites to come together and determine what will be best for the city. But they can't do that by ignoring the elephant in the room—race.

Source: This column appeared on the GeorgeCurry.Com Web site on 23 January 2006 and is reprinted here by permission of Mr. Curry.

Books by George E. Curry: *Jake Gaither: America's Most Famous Black Coach* (New York, 1977); editor, *The Affirmative Action Debate* (New York, 1996); coeditor, with Cornell West, *The Best of Emerge Magazine* (Reading, Mass., 2003).

Further Readings: "About George Curry." [Online, June 2003]. George Curry Web site www.georgecurry.com; "George Curry." [Online]. The History Makers Web site www.thehistorymakers.com/biography; "George E. Curry elected President of American Society of Magazine Editors." [Online, 5 May 2000]. The Write News Web site www.writenews.com.

Curtis, Mary Cecelia (4 September 1953–)

Charlotte, N.C., *Observer* weekly columnist and executive features editor Mary Curtis was born in Baltimore and was a summa cum laude communications graduate of Fordham University in New York. From 1977 until 1981, she worked for the Associated Press in New York and Hartford, Connecticut, was marketing services coordinator for The Travelers Insurance Company and wrote freelance for various newspapers and magazines from 1977 to 1981. She was a copy editor at the *Arizona Daily Star* in Tucson from 1981 to 1983, when she joined the Baltimore *Sun* staff, first serving as travel editor and assistant features editor, then in 1984 and 1985 as arts and entertainment editor.

In 1985 Curtis moved to the *New York Times* as a copy editor and helped found and became assistant editor of the Living Arts section from 1988 to 1990, and its editor for the next two years. In 1992, she became editor of the Home section and was education life editor in 1993 and 1994. Since that time she has been with the *Charlotte Observer* in her present capacity. Her twice-weekly Carolina Living section column was picked up by Knight Ridder/Tribune Information Services as part of its "New Voices" package.

Curtis also has taught in the Maynard Institute's editing program for minority journalists and was a Nieman Fellow at Harvard University during 2005–2006.

Like many of the other columnists appearing in this book, Mary Curtis has a way of seeing societal issues clearly and holding them up to shake readers from their complacency. In a column headlined "Turning War into Feel-Good TV Moments," she used an Al Roker segment on the *Today Show* to address the too easy way many Americans have of giving lip-service appreciation for the troops fighting in Iraq and Afghanistan—feeling proud without personally giving up a thing. Feel-good moments, she remarks, are hollow. Public displays of affection, she adds, are our substitute for wartime personal sacrifice.

Curtis was also put off by those Southerners who would make a folk hero of convicted Atlanta bomber Eric Rudolph, who managed to elude authorities for five years. While understanding the appeal of an abortion-hating, eye-for-an-eye survivalist outwitting his pursuers and living off the rugged mountain land, she reminds readers of the people he killed with hidden bombs and expresses disgust over the threats that had been directed at the young police officer who captured Rudolph. In a later column written at the end of Rudolph's trial, she notes that his smirking lack of remorse was enough to make her at least temporarily favor capital punishment.

Occasionally her focus turns international, as in two columns inspired by the film "Hotel Rwanda," in which Hutu hotel manager Paul Rusesabagina risked his life by sheltering more than 1,200 Tutsis during the genocide that swept his country. The second column was written after Rusesabagina gave a talk at North Carolina's Davidson College in an attempt to raise awareness about similar ethnic cleansing that was taking place in Darfur in the Sudan.

At other times, her wide-ranging column deals with medical issues. In one of these instances, she advises readers to disregard what she terms the "yuck factor" and get regular colon screenings; in another, she recoils from the political pandering that went on in the Terri Schiavo life-support case, suggesting that politicians should be less quick to insert themselves into private medical decision making. In "Here's What to Love about Art You Hate," she addresses the 7,500 steel and fabric gates erected in New York's Central Park by artists Christo and Jeanne-Claude, pointing out that with publicly displayed art, there is seldom consensus. In 1995, Curtis won second place in the American Association of Sunday and Feature Editors' commentary contest. She had joined that organization in 1994 and has served on its board and also has been a member of the National Association of Black Journalists since 1984. She has been a member of the Society of Professional Journalists since 1972. In 2000, she took first place in the North Carolina Press Association's serious column category, coming in second in 2003. In 2004, this organization honored her with its Thomas Wolfe Award for the best newspaper story in the state; her story that won that award was "My Rebel Journey," which described Civil War heritage organizations. She won a first place Green Eyeshade Award in 2002 in the Society of Professional Journalists competition. In 2004, the NABJ awarded her first place in the commentary category and in the following year, inducted her into its Region IV Hall of Fame. She is on the executive board of the Charlotte-Mecklenburg Schools' Academic Internship Program and is active with Peace Journeys, a National Conference for Community and Justice program for teenagers. Curtis is also on the advisory board of the Charlotte Junior League.

"Turning War into Feel-Good Moments" by Mary C. Curtis

This is a tricky one.

As Al Roker slipped into his best pitchman voice, the "Today" show continued its salute to American "unsung heroes," military personnel and the men and women who love them.

If that sounds a little soap opera-ish, it's because that's what the scene at Fort Campbell in Kentucky resembled.

By the time Roker revealed that an entire family—husband and wife helicopter pilots with past and possibly future Iraq service, grandma and four kids—was headed to the "Weston Rio Mar Beach Resort Club in sunny Puerto Rico, "it was all very Queen for a Day."

They are unsung heroes, the best this country can offer. And they are part of a troubling trend: Soldiers as accessories.

Americans at home get to have it all. You don't have to give up a thing to feel proud.

Watch the beer commercial showcasing soldiers enveloped by appreciative applause as they walk through an airport. Then wipe the tears from the corner of your eye and go back to the Super Bowl.

Public displays of affection are the new substitute for personal sacrifice.

Adorning trees with ribbons and cars with bumper stickers of support are fine gestures. Unless there's a link to someone in service, though, it's too easy to honor and forget.

America is a country at war; at least that's what everyone keeps saying. How can we keep the home fires burning when we prefer tax cuts to more money for defense? And did you hear Prince Charles is getting married?

As I said at the start, I'm torn.

You can feel people tripping over each other to reward soldiers as, in part, a penance for the inability to separate the war from the warriors in the time of Vietnam.

That was a positive lesson learned. I say that as someone with relatives and friends who fought then and now. Some came back wounded and some didn't come back at all.

But that's also why it's jarring when every talk show features weeping spouses and children and surprise gift packages. (But no blood, of course.)

The reality of showing the faces and reading the names of the dead on "Nightline" was enough to stir controversy.

Soldiers surely deserve unlimited trips to fancy resorts, as well as generous veteran benefits and armored vehicles. I'd certainly rather watch a Marine—any Marine—then another update on the Michael Jackson trial.

Yet all the up-close-and-personal specials will never be good enough. A knitted brow of worry and concern is not the same as shared sacrifice, and we're nowhere near that.

In this American war on terrorism, there's a distance. This far-away conflict doesn't affect most Americans, save for a few feel-good, heart-tugging moments.

Though honored to serve, many joined the military for the opportunity to go to college or learn a skill. They made the best of limited choices. For others, the military is an option they wouldn't dare consider. They had other choices, other priorities.

When I see people play the game of whose flag is bigger, I have to cringe.

As war games go, it's a safe one.

Source: Reprinted with permission from *The Charlotte Observer*. Copyright owned by *The Charlotte Observer*.

Further Readings: "Observer's Curtis Gains Entry into Hall of Fame." [Online, 14 May 2005]. Charlotte Observer Web site www.charlotte.com.

D

Dash, Leon DeCosta Jr. (16 March 1944–)

Now a chaired professor at the University of Illinois, Leon Dash made his name as an "immersion journalist" at the *Washington Post*. Dash was born into a middle-class home in New Bedford, Massachusetts, but spent most of his formative years in New York's Harlem and Bronx sections. His father was a postal clerk, his mother, an administrator for the New York Health Department. Dash entered higher education at Lincoln University, where he edited the campus newspaper but after two years, transferred to Howard University. Once there, he found a job as a copy boy at the *Washington Post*, which in 1966 promoted him to reporter while he was still an undergraduate student. He received the B.A. in history in 1968, after which he joined the Peace Corps serving as a high school teacher in Kenya from 1969 to 1971. He rejoined the *Post* staff in 1971 as a reporter covering the suburban and local government beats. Dash's first book project was cowritten with media critic Ben Bagdikian; *The Shame of the Prisons* appeared in 1972. In 1973, he was sent to Angola to report on the antigovernment UNITA guerilla movement. He was there from June to September. He again went to Angola for the *Post* in October 1976 and is said to have hiked 2,100 miles with guerilla forces by May 1977. Back in the United States, he took time out from daily journalism in 1978 to work as a visiting professor of political science at the University of California at San Diego. Then he was back to Africa for the *Post*, this time as a correspondent and West African bureau chief working out of Abidjan in the Ivory Coast. In 1984, he returned to Washington and began gathering information for a series of stories on teenage pregnancy in urban America. His six-part series was a Pulitzer finalist in the explanatory journalism category in 1986 and was turned into a book titled *When Children Want Children*, which appeared in 1989. His next project for the *Post*'s special projects unit, which proved to be his masterwork, established him as a major "immersion journalist." To gather material for this series of stories, he spent six years—two part-time and four full-time, following the lives of one family that lived in a blighted section of Washington. The main character of his series was Rosa Lee Cunningham, a middle-aged black woman who was the poverty-mired granddaughter of North Carolina sharecroppers who had migrated north. Although eight of her ten siblings had escaped poverty, she had not done so and lived by welfare checks, prostitution, theft and drug dealing. Cunningham agreed to allow Dash to write about her, she told him, because her story of woeful degradation might help someone else avoid similar pitfalls. Cunningham herself had eight children by six different fathers. She taught the children how to shoplift, allowed them to watch as she worked as a prostitute, pushed one daughter into prostitution at age 11, and shared needles with her own children for injecting heroin. It should come as no surprise that six of her eight children also remained mired in a life of crime and drugs and that some of them, like their mother, contracted HIV. Rosa Cunningham died of AIDS at age 58 in July 1995, three months after Dash learned that his eight-part series done with photographer Lucian Perkins had won the 1995 Pulitzer Prize for explanatory journalism. His series, "Rosa Lee: Poverty and Survival in Washington," had appeared in the *Post* from September 18 to 25, 1994. Earlier, on the same day he received news about his Pulitzer, Dash had attended the funeral of one of Rosa's sons, a victim of drug-related violence. Not everyone was pleased by Dash's series. Critics appeared to think that he had exploited some of America's most pathetic, vulnerable people in telling Rosa's story and that doing so would underscore racial prejudice. The opposite view is that if society ignores the plight of Rosa and other people living in similar circumstances, improvement will be impaired or the need for improvement simply ignored. Her story was retold in Dash's 1996 book *Rosa Lee: a Mother and Her Family in Urban America*, which sold well and brought Dash considerable recognition. In 1995 and 1996, he was a Media Fellow with the Henry J. Kaiser Family Foundation. He retired from the *Post* in 1998 and became a professor of journalism and Afro-American studies at the University of Illinois at Urbana-Champaign. In 2000, he became the holder of a Swanlund Chair, his university's most prestigious faculty honor, and in 2003, he was appointed to the faculty of the university's Center for Advanced Study. For his part, Dash has housed his papers in the University of Illinois library archives.

Dash is fortunate to have worked for one of the very few American newspapers that can afford to support the kind of reporting that he has done so well. His insight into what he calls the "hyper-segregation" of the nation's under-underclass should, in a sane world, provide clues for improving public policy, which would be distinctly preferable to hearing well-off politicians in blue suits blathering about how people like Rosa need to "pull themselves up by their bootstraps." Dash's reporting has pointed out that such people do not even *have* bootstraps. Dash believes that education is the key to breaking the vicious cycle of poverty and crime, but that to accomplish this end, mentoring is needed. He also has remarked that the under-underclass is growing at a rate of about 8 percent a year and that this group of Americans are not even counted in our unemployment statistics, inasmuch as many of them have never had legal employment.

In addition to the Pulitzer, Dash has received many other recognitions. In 1974, he was given the George Polk Award by the Overseas Press Club and first place in international news reporting by the Washington-Baltimore Newspaper Guild. In 1984, he was honored for his international reporting by the Capitol Press Club and by Africare. The National Association of Black Journalists, of which he had been a founding member, awarded him first place in general news coverage in 1986; and that same year he received the Social Services Administration's Distinguished Service Award. In 1987, he took first place in the public service category from the Washington-Baltimore Newspaper Guild and first place from the organization Investigative Reporters and Editors. He won the President's Award for excellence in reporting urban affairs from the Washington Independent Writers in 1989 and a PEN/Martha Albrand citation for nonfiction in 1990 for *When Children Want Children*. In 1995, Dash and Lucian Perkins won a Robert F. Kennedy book award for their work on Rosa Cunningham. The National Academy of Television Arts and Sciences' Washington chapter accorded Dash and producer Luther Brown a 1996 Emmy for a televised version of Rosa's story, "Frontline: The Confessions of Rosa Lee." In 1997, the book on Rosa Lee won Best Book in the Harry Chapin Media Award competition, a recognition from the World Hunger Year organization and the PASS (Prevention for a Safer Society) Award from the National Council on Crime and Delinquency. New York University's journalism department in 1999 selected "Rosa Lee's Story" as one of the 100 best works of twentieth-century American journalism.

Books by Leon DeCosta Dash Jr.: With Ben H. Bagdikian, *The Shame of the Prisons* (New York: Pocket Books, 1972); *When Children Want Children: The Urban Crisis of Teenage Childbearing* (New York: William Morrow, 1989); *Rosa Lee: A Mother and Her Family in Urban America* (New York: Basic Books, 1996).

Further Readings: Besharov, Douglas J. "Inner City Blues." [Online, 13 October 1996]. Washington Post Web site www.washingtonpost.com; "Explanatory Journalism-Biography." [Online]. The Pulitzer Board Web site www.pulitzer.org/year/1995-journalism/bio; "Leon Dash." [Online, 2000]. The New New Journalism Web site www.newnewjournalism.com/bio; "Leon Dash Papers Open for Research." [Online, 24 October 2005]. Web Library site http://web.library.uiuc.edu.

Davidson, Joe (1950–)

A man of long experience in newspapers, magazines and radio, Joe Davidson is, in 2006, editor of the *Washington Post's District Extra*, the zoned weekly for

District of Columbia readers. He is also a political columnist for BET.com. Davidson was born in Detroit and began his career in newspapers working first for the *National Weekly*, a historically black paper. He then worked for the *Detroit News*, the *Philadelphia Bulletin* and the *Philadelphia Inquirer*. For 13 years, he was a Washington bureau correspondent and foreign correspondent for the *Wall Street Journal* as well; and from December 2001 to mid-2005, he was editor of *Focus Magazine*, a publication of the Joint Center for Political and Economic Studies, which aims its efforts at informing its audience of leaders, roughly half of whom are African American, on national issues. In 2004, the busy Davidson was also doing commentary for National Public Radio's "All Things Considered" and "Morning Edition," was writing for Washingtonpost.com and was covering the presidential campaign for BET.com. In addition, he interviewed Secretary of State Colin Powell in August of that same year for *Crisis Magazine*; perhaps the most interesting product of that interview was Powell's assertion that he had no interest in running for future political office. In April 2005, Davidson returned to newspapering as editor of *District Extra*, which goes to roughly 130,000 of the *Post*'s 700,000 subscribers.

Davidson was one of the founders of the National Association of Black Journalists and was once president of the Philadelphia Association of Black Journalists. He is also a member of the Trotter Group of African-American columnists and has twice been a Pulitzer Prize juror. Much of his effort in 2004 was directed at covering the campaign for the U.S. presidency. His stories in *Focus* and elsewhere had a common theme: the largely unsuccessful efforts of the Republican Party to woo black voters. An August 2004 story published on www.jointcenter.org noted that although the GOP sported more African-American delegates than ever before, black voters remained unconvinced of the party's good intentions. A month later, a *Focus* article noted that only 10 percent of black voters were Republicans, and Davidson pointed out that for African Americans as a whole, economic prosperity had declined during Bush's first term. He wrote about President Bush's polarizing influence noting that while Bush was being lauded by his party in Madison Square Garden, New York police were arresting protesters outside. He added that although most African Americans were in sympathy with the demonstrators, few of those marching were black. In another story, he remarked that the administration's rhetoric about compassionate conservatism did not match the reality of its actions. A Davidson story in the November/December issue pointed out a positive: that in the election, black voter participation had increased by 25 percent over participation in 2000. In one of his pre-election BET.com columns, he characterized the Bush administration's message about the war in Iraq as simplistic and dangerous and added that the U.S. invasion had turned Iraq into a magnet for terrorists. For both candidates for the presidency, Davidson wrote, the plight of the U.S. poor was a neglected issue. In guest appearances on NPR's "News & Notes with Ed Gordon," Davidson weighed in on such topics as the USA Patriot Act, the plight of Hurricane Katrina victims and black-on-black violence. Many of Davidson's stories, of course, have had nothing to do with election politics. In a Washingtonpost.com story in February 2002, he wrote about the abduction in Pakistan of *Wall Street Journal* reporter Daniel Pearl mentioning how he and Pearl had worked together at that paper's Washington bureau and praising Pearl's personal qualities. An August 2004 story for www.poynter.org addressed the overuse of anonymous sources and how that media tendency undermines media credibility, and in an "All Things Considered" appearance around that same, he discussed sexual assault accusations leveled at basketball player Kobe Bryant. In June 2006, the Philadelphia Association of Black Journalists celebrated its thirtieth anniversary; at the meeting, Joe Davidson received the organization's Trailblazer Award.

Further Readings: Prince, Richard. "Davidson to Edit Washington Post's D.C. 'Extra.'" [Online, 25 February 2005]. Richard Prince's Journal-isms. Maynard Institute Web site www.maynardije.org.

Davis, Allison J. (?–)

Current vice president of the Jackie Robinson Foundation, Allison Davis has enjoyed a long career in television and in new media for NBC and CBS. She is a native of New York City and holds two bachelor's degrees from Boston University: general college studies in 1972 and journalism in 1975. She has shown a strong interest in education for the modern, converging media environment, yet despite her direct involvement in the new technology of communication, she has continued to stress the importance of basic journalistic and storytelling skills. Also, she has taught as an adjunct faculty member in the John H. Johnson School of Communications at Howard University and more recently at City College in New York. From 1975 to 1978, she was a producer and investigative reporter for Boston's WBZ; she did similar work from 1978 to 1981 at KDKA-TV in Pittsburgh. In 1981, she joined NBC, working first on "NBC Nightly News" and, in 1983, was a producer for "Monitor." From 1984 to 1994, Davis was a writer/producer for NBC News' "Today" show and in 1984, worked with "First Camera." From 1993 to 1997, she originated and produced "The Scholastic NBC News Video"; and from 1994 to 1997, she was executive producer of MSNBC online, a high-ticket joint venture between the network and Microsoft Corporation. Thereafter, she produced two one-hour documentaries, "The Science of Sport," for The Learning Channel, after which she became executive producer of "The Reading Club," an educational venture of PBS in cooperation with Howard University's WHUT-TV. She became involved in this initiative through having worked on "Today" with Bryant Gumbel, who was a cohost of this show. The series was sponsored jointly by Dunbar Productions, a production company co-owned by Gumbel and CBS Eyemark Entertainment. The purpose of the series was to spur the reading of books by African-American women, bringing a new-media twist to the traditional book club. The series of 30-minute discussions aired nationally on at least 68 public television stations beginning in 1999. Davis was Dunbar Productions' senior vice president and was vice president–creative of KingWorld, the CBS syndication division. In 1999, Davis and NBC Nightly News producer Rod Prince taught an honors class in advanced media production for broadcast majors at Howard University. In 2004, Davis became vice president of The Jackie Robinson Foundation, which had been founded in 1973 by the widow of baseball great, Rachel Robinson, as a nonprofit organization that awarded college scholarships to academically gifted but needy African-American students. Many corporations have since joined the foundation's first corporate supporter, Cheseborough Ponds, in helping fund these scholarships.

Davis is now on the board of visitors of Howard University School of Communication. She was a founding member of the National Association of Black Journalists, for which she has served as both parliamentarian and vice president. She has also been on the boards of Episcopal Community Development and the National Visionary Leadership Project, Poets and Writers. Davis has received two Emmy nominations and two Women in Communication awards, in 1986 and 1998. She was honored in 1997 with Boston University's Distinguished Alumni Award for Service and in 2001 got the distinguished alumni award given by that university's College of General Studies. In addition, she contributed "Leading the Disadvantaged into the Information Age" to the book *Global News: Perspectives on the Information Age* (Ames, Iowa: Iowa State University Press, 2001), edited by Tony Silvia, and in 2005, she began teaching in the broadcasting program of City College in New York.

Further Readings: "Allison Davis." [Online, 2003]. The John H. Johnson School of Communications, Howard University Web site www.howard.edu/schoolcommunications/Development; Buchanan, Leigh. "The Peacock's New Feathers." [Online, September 1996]. CIO Communications, Inc. Web site www.cio.com; Lapham, Chris. "New Directions for New Media." [Online, August 1997]. CMC Magazine Web site www.december.com/cmc/mag.

Davis, Belva (13 October 1932–)

A journalist of rich experience, Belva Davis hosts a public-affairs program on Bay Area station KQED-TV and is a narrator and consultant for documentaries for KRON-TV, also in Northern California. She has been a journalist since 1957, and is a person who made it big in media work without benefit of college preparation and is national vice president of the American Federation of Television and Radio Artists. She was born Belvagene Melton in Monroe,

Louisiana, during the Great Depression and was part of a family of 11. Her father, who had taught himself how to read, operated heavy equipment for a lumber mill and became a mill supervisor. When one of Belva's uncles sued his employer, threats were made that resulted in several members of her family, including her father, leaving town on a freight train. For a time, she lived with her grandparents in Arkansas, then her father returned for her and the family moved to West Oakland, California. She reports never having had her own room, or even her own bed during her childhood. Her parents divorced and she spent parts of her girlhood living with relatives in other parts of the Bay Area. A shy girl with glasses, she read a great deal and was taken under the wing of a white physical education teacher at Berkeley High School. When a local bowling alley would not allow Davis to use its facilities except when she was there with the school bowling class, the teacher cancelled the entire bowling league in protest. A good student, Davis was admitted to San Francisco State University but could not afford the cost and instead went to work as a clerk following her 1951 graduation from high school. Within six months, she married a man who was in military service. She took a clerical test and found work as a GS-2 typist at a naval supply center. She moved with her husband when he was transferred to Andrews Air Force Base near Washington, D.C., where she found herself frightened by the city's tight racial segregation. Again she worked in a clerical job until the next move to Hawaii in 1953. In 1957, the couple returned to Oakland, where Davis worked with top-secret documents at the Naval Supply Center. She began experimenting with writing and was able to get an unpaid job writing a column for the black weekly newspaper the *Bay Street Independent*. The title of her column was the "East Bay Social News." She received on-the-job training from a white former Associated Press bureau chief who had experienced drinking problems and could find work only as editor of this paper. With this meager experience, she became the Northern California stringer for the then-new weekly news magazine *Jet*, a job that paid very little but allowed her to meet and interview a wide variety of newsmakers. She did her stringing while working full-time with the *Independent* besides doing extra clerical work. At the *Independent*, she met and interviewed activist Malcolm X and boxer Mohammed Ali. Having been rebuffed when she applied for openings at the area's mainstream newspapers, she decided to give radio work a try and in 1959, began reading social news on KSAN, a local black station. Most of what she read was cribbed from the area's five newspapers, she reported in one session of an extensive series of interviews she did with Shirley Biagi, now a journalism professor at California State-Sacramento. The interviews were done in 1992 as part of the Washington Press Club Foundation's oral history project "Women in Journalism." Davis got a show of her own, "The Belva Davis Show," on station KDIA in 1961; the two-hour Saturday show was recorded before a live audience and featured a mix of talk, interview and jazz music, both live and recorded. One of her interviews was with Bill Cosby at a time when he was doing stand-up comedy at the famous Hungry I. She also recalls that Martin Luther King, Jr. often came to the station. Her show's sponsor was Beauty Pleat draperies. By this time, she was divorced and she was remarried in 1963 to a photographer whose good qualities were pointed out to her by singer Nancy Wilson, also a guest on Davis' show. She left KDIA in 1966 when the station went to formatted radio, which made her work more prescheduled and impersonal than she was willing to tolerate. At that point in her career, she became a columnist and women's editor for another local black paper, the Oakland *Sun Reporter*, and she also began running the Miss Bronze California Beauty Pageant for Northern California. She lobbied successfully with area department stores to use some of the pageant contestants as models, and around the same time, began looking for a job in television. Her *entre* to the new medium came when she went to Channel 2 to argue for airtime for her pageant. Station management finally agreed but only if she would both host and produce the show. At the Oakland Public Library, she read up on the duties of a producer, began dieting and exercising and took the job. She was hired by San Francisco station KPIX-TV in 1966 to replace Nancy Reynolds as news anchor making her the first African-American news anchor in California, and on the West Coast, as well. She also hosted one of the first televised public affairs shows to focus on minorities, "All Together Now." Within two weeks of taking this job, she and her cameraman were covering a car chase after a robbery and somehow got between the robber and the police, who were firing at each other. In that same two weeks she saw her first corpse following a shooting in a drugstore. Davis quickly learned why it's called "hard news." During this period, she became friends with columnist Earl Caldwell and witnessed the beating he received at the hands of Berkeley police during a demonstration. On another assignment, observing conditions at the Yurok Indian reservation, she found herself seated in a helicopter next to Bobby Kennedy, a man she greatly admired. She also covered and befriended folk singer Joan Baez, an ardent supporter of civil rights. She went over to public television in 1977 anchoring the news shows "A Closer Look" and later "Evening Edition" for PBS station KQED but left this station in 1980. She took a new job in 1981 as anchor and urban affairs specialist at KRON-TV, channel 4, but continued working for KPIX on "All Together Now." She covered the activities of the Black Panther Party, traveled for KPIX to Cuba when President Jimmy Carter was considering normalizing relations, interviewed Bobby Seale prior to the Chicago 8 trial and interviewed Catherine Hearst, mother of the kidnapped heiress Patty Hearst. Other noteworthy interviews were with activist actress Jane Fonda, Jim Jones of the People's Temple and Jimmy Carter, who gave her a keepsake: a peanut dipped in gold. She also covered Dianne Feinstein's run for the U.S. vice presidency in the mid-1980s. In 1999, she began working as KRON's special projects reporter working on and narrating documentaries and in addition, doing "Bay Area Close-Up" stories on local people and organizations. Earlier, in 1993, she had become host of the KQED news analysis show "This Week in Northern California."

Like many individuals who have been in the media for a substantial period of years, Davis does not like the money-first approach of most news operations, which has diminished the media's watchdog role vis-à-vis government; and she abhors the violence that is brought to viewers in a steady stream on television. She has been actively involved in both professional and community organizations. She is national vice president of AFTRA, the American Federation of Television and Radio Artists, and chairs that organization's equal employment opportunity initiative. She is a trustee or board member of the Fine Arts Museum of San Francisco, Blue Shield of California, the Fort Mason Foundation, and the Glide Church Foundation. She is president of the board of the Museum of the African Diaspora project in San Francisco, which has been raising money for new space for the museum. Earlier, she had been active with the Women's Forum West, a national networking organization for African-American women, and she was on the board of the Howard Thurman Trust, which has provided small scholarships for study at historically black colleges and universities. She has won seven regional Emmy awards, the Lifetime Achievement Award given by the National Academy of Television Arts and Sciences, the Lifetime Achievement Award of the National Association of Black Journalists and the Lifetime Achievement Award from the International Women's Media Foundation. She is one of 500 journalists to be profiled in the Newseum in Washington, D.C., and she has received three honorary doctorates, from John F. Kennedy University, Golden Gate University and California State University at Sonoma. Davis has received other recognitions from Ohio State University, San Francisco State University, the Corporation for Public Broadcasting, the National Education Writers Association and the California Associated Press Television and Radio Association. The Belva Davis Diversity Scholarship is awarded annually by the group American Women in Radio & Television. Clearly, the 5'1" Davis is a woman who has fought the odds and won.

Further Readings: "Belva Davis." [Online]. Broadcast Legends Web site www.broadcastlegends.com; "Belva Davis, Biography." [Online]. The History Makers Web site www.thehistorymakers.com/biography; "Breaking Barriers: Television Journalist Belva Davis Continues to Bridge the Racial Divide." [Online, October 2004]. International Women's Media Foundation Web site www.iwmf.org; "In Honor of Belva Davis and Rollin Post." [Online, 20 May 1999]. U.S. House of Representatives Web site www.house.gov; "Interviews with Belva Davis, Recorded by Shirley Biagi." [Online, 1993]. The Washington Press Club Foundation site http://npc.press.org; "Political Reporting Veterans Belva Davis and Pete Golis Tell Stories from the Front Lines." [Online, 13 September 2004]. Sonoma State University Web site www.sonoma.edu.

Davis, Merlene (13 January 1951–)

Columnist Merlene Davis is a long-time employee of the *Lexington Herald-Leader* in Kentucky. She was born and grew up in Owensboro, Kentucky, and is a graduate of the University of Kentucky, having double-majored in journalism and English. Davis began her career at the now defunct *Memphis Press Scimitar* in Tennessee, in 1983, joined the *Herald-Leader* as a reporter. Her first column, headlined "I don't recall volunteering to be a mom," appeared on 25 October 1987, and since then, she has worked either full- or part-time as a columnist for this paper. Having contracted lung cancer, Davis took a brief leave from the paper just before the turn of 2005. The lower lobe of her right lung was removed and soon she was back writing her column.

In the column reprinted below, Davis reminds readers on the occasion of 4 July 2004, that on this day of national celebration, freedom means freedom for all. After comedian Bill Cosby's now famous criticism of inner-city African Americans, Davis replied that he had unfairly singled out blacks when white youth, too, were speaking Ebonics, reveling in the hip-hop scene and wearing jeans that sag to the absolute limit. She is no fan of George W. Bush and has characterized him as our unflinching leader against the terrorists and gay marriage. Watching Mr. Bush answer questions in the 2004 campaign, Davis wrote that she did not know if he was being serious or engaging in a parody. Politics are not her main stock in trade, however. More often, her columns deal with such things as her suggestion that in the 2004 Christmas season, some of her readers consider diverting a modest amount of their holiday spending for gifts to the children of Haiti, the hemisphere's poorest nation. She likes to celebrate good deeds, as in a column about a Lexington dentist who donates time to repairing the teeth of victims of domestic violence, or even the good work of Eagle, a celebrated human-remains detection dog that helped locate the boundaries of the city's oldest black cemetery. In 2002, she wrote about a Paris, Kentucky, couple who had been married 83 years, or, as she put it, longer than women have had the vote.

Davis was accorded the 1993 Women of Achievement Award by the Lexington YWCA, the 1997 Lyman T. Johnson Alumni Association award from the University of Kentucky and the YMCA's 2002 Black Achievers Community Achievers Award. She finished second in the 2003 National Headliners Award competition for column writing.

"Past Teaches Us That Freedom Is for Everyone" by Merlene Davis

The United States of America is celebrating its 228th birthday today, commemorating the signing of the Declaration of Independence by the Continental Congress on July 4, 1776.

That declaration quickly became world famous for the honor it gives to human rights and personal freedom, even though Thomas Jefferson, the author, owned more than 200 slaves at the time.

That bit of ambiguity, saying one thing but doing another, has defined this great nation ever since.

Turns out, the Declaration of Independence was meant for white men and, to a lesser degree, white women. White men are the only people who haven't had their rights added to the Constitution as an afterthought.

Jefferson and his fellow members of the Continental Congress did not include the slaves many of them owned.

So the freedom that was so dear to them didn't reach most black folk until the Emancipation Proclamation of 1863, 87 years after the nation was celebrating the Fourth of July.

It took a war and the deaths of more than half a million men and women before the leaders of this country made their first attempt to correct the tragic oversight of our Founding Fathers.

And still that didn't do it.

In fact, this country just celebrated the 40th anniversary of the passage of the Civil Rights Act of 1964, which gave blacks—188 years after the Declaration of Independence—rights enjoyed by white men and, by then, some white women.

That one act opened doors for blacks, other racial and cultural minorities and even white women, who saw glass ceilings transformed into sun roofs, albeit slowly.

Changes came, however, after violence and resistance.

You'd think we would have learned to include everyone when we hand out equality. Inclusion cuts down on having to go back and pencil in the disenfranchised every few years, to say nothing of the lives lost.

But we didn't learn. In 1990, Congress recognized another neglected group when it enacted the Americans with Disabilities Act, which prohibited discrimination against qualified people with disabilities.

Because of that, more avenues to personal freedoms and success have cleared for those who were excluded.

And now, just last week, the U.S. Supreme Court told the Bush administration that it can't incarcerate people, even suspected terrorists, indefinitely without giving them a chance to appeal their treatment in court.

The ruling pertained to the 600 "enemy combatants" from some 40 countries who have been held, uncharged and untried, at a naval base in Guantanamo Bay, Cuba, since most were captured in Afghanistan two years ago.

Supreme Court Justice Sandra Day O'Connor said, "history and common sense teach us that an unchecked system of detention carries the potential to become a means for oppression."

We speak of the freedoms hailed in the Declaration of Independence on one hand, but on the other hand try to give them only to special people.

Fortunately, the spirit of those Founding Fathers awakens from naps to remind us that if freedom and inalienable rights are good for some, let them be good for all.

Today, let us celebrate how we Americans are still trying to right the wrongs the first settlers came to this country to escape.

And let us take time to examine ourselves, those around us and anyone in our care, so that we can do it once and for all this time and in peace.

Source: This column, which appeared on 4 July 2004, is reprinted here by permission of Ms. Davis and *The Lexington Herald-Leader*.

Further Readings: "Merlene Davis: Good Old Southern Charm." *Knight Ridder News*, Fall 2003, pp. 21–22.

Dawkins, Wayne J. (19 September 1955–)

Longtime newspaper journalist and former associate editor and editorial writer for the *Daily Press* of Newport News, Virginia, Wayne Dawkins is now founder, president and CEO of August Press, a book publisher, a member of the journalism faculty at Hampton University and a contributing editor for BlackAmericaWeb.com. He was born in New York City, earned the B.A. in journalism from Long Island University in 1977 and the M.S. in 1980 from Columbia University's Graduate School of Journalism. Prior to receiving his masters, he was first an intern, then a reporter for the Trans-Urban News Service in Brooklyn, and from 1980 to 1984, he was a reporter for the *Daily Argus* in Mount Vernon, New York. From 1984 to 1988, Dawkins was a reporter for the *Courier-Post* in Camden/Cherry Hill, New Jersey and from 1988 to 1996 wrote editorials and was assistant metro editor for that paper. He added a general op-ed column in 1991 and in 1996, moved again to become an editor for the *Post-Tribune* in Gary, Indiana. He relocated to Virginia in 1998 and became associate editor for the *Daily Press* in Newport News. He retired from the *Daily News* in 2001 and became managing editor of BlackAmericaWeb.com. Later, in 2004, he began writing commentaries for this Web site, which was founded in June 2001 by Tom Joyner, host of radio's "Tom Joyner Morning Show." The site's purpose is to provide as comprehensive a source as possible for serving the needs of African Americans.

Dawkins' first book, *The NABJ Story*, appeared in 1993 and told the story of the organization's history. In 1992, he founded his own book publishing firm, the August Press, and since then he has published six books, including two of his own: *Rugged Waters: Black Journalists Swim the Mainstream* (2003), which, like his first, deals with the NABJ, and a revised edition of *The NABJ Story* (1997). Two of the other August Press books are collections of columns by Betty Baye and Elmer Smith, the remaining two, a novel by Raleigh, N.C., *News & Observer* editor Dan Holly and a memoir by Harlem-born writer Carla Thomson.

Dawkins cofounded the Black Alumni Network in 1980 and joined the NABJ in 1981, cofounding in 1988 and serving as president and treasurer of this organization's New Jersey chapter. He joined the Trotter Group of commentary writers in 1992 and the Publishers Marketing Association in 1994. He received awards from Columbia University in 1980 and 1990 and the Thomas Fortune Lifetime Achievement Award from the Golden State Association of Black Journalists in 1994. He teaches at Hampton University, where he offers courses in media writing, editing and media in a multicultural society.

"Despite Bush's Social Security Pitch to Blacks, Let the Buyer Beware" by Wayne Dawkins

Republican and Democrat voters in red and blue states can't even agree on the true color of the sky when they wake up each morning, yet on the question of Social Security reform, most of them see purple.

Numerous polls are reporting that Americans are not jumping enthusiastically at the Bush plan to privatize Social Security, then dump the 70-year-old system. Since senior citizens were not scared effectively by exaggerated claims that Social Security was about to go bankrupt, and young adults appear indifferent about the future of the program, the Bush administration late last week announced that it was going to step up their sales pitch and launch a rapid response campaign that posts op-ed essays and letters to the editor in response to critical press coverage.

Bush's Social Security plan is in trouble because of Bush himself. He tried a Chicken Little strategy, and most Americans understand that the sky is not falling, and Social Security will not collapse anytime soon. Plus, he didn't offer up enough specifics about shifting a reliable retirement program from the federal government to Wall Street.

Conservatives and liberals, Republicans and Democrats saw a big problem in accepting such a dramatic change with such flimsy detail.

Blacks, regardless of their political leanings, must eye his policy debate with the skepticism of hawks, then not hesitate to leap into the debate.

Jump in, please, because the Bush administration is trying to play us for fools. Bush has sold the private investment accounts proposal as a no-brainer to black self-interest.

Blacks on average live shorter lives than whites—goes the administration pitch—so that means most blacks pay more into the government-run Social Security system and get less from the program.

Right? Not quite. The Bush administration is misleading.

Right now, Social Security levels the playing field for many black retirees who don't have as much investment income as whites, a disadvantage that reveals the legacy of legal segregation and job discrimination. About 63 percent of whites have asset income for retirement; for blacks, asset income is 29 percent, reports the National Committee to Preserve Social Security and Medicare. Thirty seven percent of black beneficiaries rely on Social Security for all of their income because of a lack of other income at retirement.

The government system is also good to blacks who have suffered disabilities. On average, blacks get more out of the system than they put in.

Maya Rockeymoore, the Congressional Black Caucus Foundation's vice president of research and programs, wrote last year that 17 percent of blacks received Social Security disability benefits, despite representing 12 percent of the population. Furthermore, 68 percent of blacks are kept out of poverty because of disability benefits.

"African-Americans must take care to understand the importance of Social Security and the implications of privatizing the system," wrote Rockeymoore, words worth repeating in this wrongheaded push by the Bush administration to force privatized retirement accounts down Americans' throats.

Black conservatives like Alvin Williams and Star Parker published op-ed essays in the last week suggesting that blacks and advocates like the NAACP either go against their self-interest or are simply knee-jerk opponents in resisting the Bush plan.

Actually, the skeptics sense a shady scheme.

An article in the Wilmington, N.C. Journal this week explained: In targeting blacks—then telling them that Social Security cheats them out of money because of a significant disparity in life expectancy—what's not noted is that when you take the high black infant mortality rate out of the equation and compare the life expectancy of black and white young adults advancing to old age, a nine-year gap shrinks to a comparable two years.

According to a Reuters dispatch at the end of February, average life expectancy is now 77.6 years, but black men live 6.2 years less than whites, and black women live 4.4 years less, according to the Centers for Disease Control.

Right now, Social Security serves most blacks well. The Bush administration has acknowledged that private retirement accounts are not substitutes for what is fiscally troubling Social Security.

Most Americans right now are not feeling Bush's private accounts plans. So why are blacks being targeted to rally around a proposal that appears suspect?

Buyer, beware.

Source: "Despite Bush's Social Security Pitch to Blacks, Let the Buyer Beware" by Wayne Dawkins. This column appeared on 10 March 2005 on BlackAmerica.com and appears here by permission of the writer.

Books by Wayne J. Dawkins: *Black Journalists: The NABJ Story* (Sicklerville, N.J.: August Press, 1993; Merryville, Ind.: August Press, 1997); *Rugged Waters: Black Journalists Swim the Mainstream* (Newport News, Va.: August Press, 2003).

Further Readings: "Wayne Dawkins." [Online]. Black America Web Web site www.blackamericaweb.com.

Days, Michael (2 August 1953–)

Philadelphia-born Michael Days is editor and executive vice president of the *Philadelphia Daily News*. The first African American to hold this position at the *Daily News*, he took office in February 2005 at age 51 after having spent the previous 19 years with the paper. Days was raised in a neighborhood in North Philadelphia near Temple University. He graduated from Roman Catholic High School and went on for his bachelor's degree in philosophy (1975) at the College of the Holy Cross in Worcester, Massachusetts. He received his masters in journalism in 1976 at the University of Missouri and in addition, has completed Northwestern University Media Management Center's advanced executive program. His earlier work as a journalist was at the *Democrat and Chronicle* of Rochester, New York, from January 1978 to May 1980; the *Courier-Journal* in Louisville, Kentucky, from May 1980 to December 1984; and the Philadelphia bureau of the *Wall Street Journal* from January 1984 to January 1986. He joined the news staff of the *Daily News* in 1986 as a city hall reporter. He became the paper's business editor, then its assistant managing editor. In 1998, he was promoted to deputy managing editor. In April 2004, he was named managing editor, replacing Ellen Foley, who left to become editor of the *Wisconsin State Journal* in Madison. Only a year later, the paper's editor, Zachary Stalberg, announced that he was retiring after 20 years in that job and that his replacement would be Michael Days. Days took office on 11 February 2005. Press watchers hoped that his appointment would help heal the paper's rift with black readers that was particularly pronounced in 2002 when the paper was accused of racial insensitivity after publishing head shots of the city's most-wanted fugitives on its cover. All 41 were people of color. This created a serious problem in that roughly half the tabloid's 140,000 readers were minorities. In an era when the entire industry is under fiscal pressure, the paper badly needed to mend fences. Some predicted the paper's demise; others believed that its combination of colorful local news coverage and thorough attention to sports would see it through hard times, perhaps even better than its more dignified stable-mate, the *Philadelphia Inquirer*. Corporate bottom-line pressure being what it is, Days found himself having to announce a staff buyout program in September 2005. The goal was to cut 25 Guild staffers from the payroll by year's end. An unusual incident caused bruised feelings in 2006, when reporter Kurt Heine took a *Daily News* buyout and promptly landed a job at the *Inquirer*, which had been cutting an even larger number of its own staffers. On the happy side of developments, *Daily News* photographer Jim MacMillan was part of an Associated Press team that won the 2005 Pulitzer Prize for breaking news photography for their work in Baghdad, Iraq. In 2006, Days was a Pulitzer jury member in the 2006 beat reporting category.

In 2005, the *Daily News* joined the National Constitution Center in mounting an exhibit titled "Sports: Breaking Records, Breaking Barriers." Blowups of standout moments in Philadelphia sports were put on display at the Center from May to August of that year. The exhibit highlighted the increased presence of minorities and women in sports. In December 2005, the paper joined the Committee of Seventy, a city advocacy group in a multimedia project geared to the 2007 mayoral election. "The Next Mayor" project's aim is to carefully examine issues important in this election and to encourage citizen participation. Days himself is often involved in meetings in the city and beyond. He was a participant in an October 2005 National Liberty Museum seminar, "The News We Need: Finding Balance in an Age of Spin." He appeared on NJN Public Television in 2006, discussing "Headlines and Race." He was one of three main speakers at Temple University in a program titled "From MOVE to Katrina: Covering Communities of Color in Times of Crisis." The program's starting point was the 1985 police bombing of the MOVE house on Philadelphia's Osage Avenue. Days is a financial supporter of the National Association of Hispanic Journalists and was formerly on the board of the National Association of Black Journalists. He is an advisory board member of the Knight Center for Specialized Journalism at the University of Maryland.

Further Readings: Lewis, Monica. "Philadelphia Daily News Promotes Black Editor to Top Spot." [Online, 1 February 2005]. Black America Web site www.blackamericaweb.com; "Michael Days." [Online]. Meet PNI Web site www.pnionline.com.

Deggans, Eric (6 November 1965–)

Eric Deggans is the first person to work as full-time media critic for the *St. Petersburg Times* in Florida. Prior to assuming this position in August 2005, he was a *Times* columnist and editorial writer. He was born in Washington, D.C., and was raised in Gary, Indiana. He holds a 1990 B.A. in journalism and political science from Indiana University. A drummer, he played with the Motown group The Voyage Band in the 1980s. He still performs in St. Petersburg as a drummer, singer and bassist. Deggans began his journalism career in May 1990 as a reporter for the *Pittsburgh Press* and later, in January 1993, the *Pittsburgh Post-Gazette*. Before joining the *St. Petersburg Times* in November 1995 as its music critic, Deggans was, from May 1993 to October 1995, music critic for the *Asbury Park Press* in New Jersey. From December 1996 to 2004, he was the *Times*' television critic; he worked as columnist and editorial writer there from 2004 to August 2005.

Deggans was 2004 president of the Tampa Bay chapter of the National Association of Black Journalists. Earlier, he had been an NABJ vice president at chapters in New Jersey and Pennsylvania. He was on the boards of the Mid-Florida Society of Professional Journalists and the Television Critics Association and was instrumental in creating minority affairs reporting jobs at the *Pittsburgh Post-Gazette* in 1993 and the *Asbury Park Press* in 1994. In 2003, he began an ethics fellowship at the Poynter Institute in St. Petersburg, and in 2004, he was an instructor in the program. He has also been a lecturer or adjunct faculty member at St. Petersburg College, the University of Tampa, the University of South Florida, Eckerd College and Indiana University. In addition, he created a racial sensitivity training program for the State Troopers Academy in Pennsylvania. He has been a speaker at Columbia University in

New York and in Los Angeles at the 2005 National Critics Conference. His work won him recognition in 2005 from the Columbia University Graduate School of Journalism, which gave him its Let's Do It Better! Award for coverage of race and ethnicity. In 2005, he also won the NABJ's very first Chuck Stone Award for commentary for his column "Jason Blair and the Fear Factor." In 2003, he took first place in the criticism category from the Florida Society of Newspaper Editors, and he was named Best Newspaper Columnist by *Weekly Planet* magazine in 2000. In both 1999 and 2003, he was a finalist for criticism in the Atlanta Society of Professional Journalists' Green Eyeshade Award competition. Deggans has published freelance in the *Village Voice*, *Washington Post*, *Detroit News*, *Chicago Sun-Times* and *Seattle Times* and in such magazines as *VIBE*, *Hispanic*, *Smart Computing* and *Rolling Stone Online*. He has also written for MusicHound album guides. He has appeared on Black Entertainment Television's "The Tavis Smiley Show"; National Public Radio's "All Things Considered," "The Tony Cox Show" and "News & Notes with Ed Gordon"; the Public Broadcasting System's "Livelyhood" and "The Calling"; the Canadian Broadcasting System's "Crosscurrents"; and on MSNBC.

In April 2003, Deggans wrote about the dilemma of journalists who disagree with America's military presence in Iraq but do not want to appear unpatriotic or biased in their coverage. He was especially concerned about public demands that television news programs "wave the flag" in their war coverage. A month later, he wrote about Holocaust survivor Elie Wiesel's reservations about the CBS miniseries "Hitler: The Rise of Evil." In February 2004, he wrote about the increasing economic polarization among African Americans, commenting on so-called "black nihilism" in poor black communities where, he wrote, some residents scoff at education as a "white thing." In May of that year, Deggans wrote a tribute to the classic television sitcom "Frasier," which had aired for 11 years and which won 31 Emmy awards. His column lauded the show's merits and also pointed out the reasons for its eventual decline in popularity. In a June 2004 column, Deggans explored the matter of how television success can be measured: by popularity or by quality. His conclusion was that actual quality, as a way of "keeping score," is losing out rather badly in today's market. An August column examined the way so-called "reality television" evolved, and in September, he discussed the tendency of younger people to get their "news" from late-night television shows. An April 2005 column took National Public Radio to task for its overwhelming whiteness. In June, Deggans examined the potentially corrosive nature of celebrity as reflected in the troubles of entertainer Michael Jackson. An August column was on "diversity fatigue" in media hiring, a topic that had been raised by the Rev. Jesse Jackson at an appearance in Atlanta; and in October, Deggans wrote on the troubles of newspapers in today's on-demand media environment. In December, he wrote about plans by two Florida brothers, Glenn and Charles Cherry, to start a weekly newspaper, the *Florida Courier* that would attempt to appeal to the 3 million or so African Americans living in Florida. In January 2006, he wrote in more detail about on-demand television: customized RSS feeds, podcasting, the DVR and episodic television on demand. A February column was built around the recent redesign of the *Wall Street Journal* orchestrated by newspaper consultant Mario Garcia, and another column later that month was about the curious unpopularity of the 2006 Winter Olympics in Turin, Italy. A March column was an overview of various newspapers' attempts to attract younger readers by publishing tabloids or establishing special Web sites. Some of the new media he discussed were his own paper's tbt* (for *Tampa Bay Times*), the *Chicago Tribune*'s *RedEye*, the *Dallas Morning News*' *Quick* and the *Washington Post's Express*. An April 2006 column addressed CBS's questionable decision in replacing Bob Schieffer as nightly news anchor with celebrity Katie Couric, who clearly is more the perky entertainer than the seasoned journalist.

"Why the Rush to Protect 'Our Own'?" by Eric Deggans

Others may cite the Duke University rape scandal or the ongoing struggle to aid victims of Hurricane Katrina in New Orleans. But for Katheryn Russell-Brown, when talk turns to the way black people can unite publicly to protect their own, the discussion starts with one person.

O.J. Simpson.

Now serving as a law professor and expert on race relations at the University of Florida, Russell-Brown couldn't understand why black people widely celebrated the 1995 acquittal of a man who had barely acknowledged his status as a black American before he was charged with a double homicide.

"From everything I was able to tell at the time, Simpson did not particularly see himself as a member of the community or as someone who was particularly proud to be black," said Russell-Brown, who is black, citing polls at the time that showed black people's support for Simpson. "But the community was so fierce in its support for Simpson. A lot of it was historical. It wasn't just about O.J."

The professor eventually found a word for what was going on: black protectionism.

Her latest book, *Protecting Our Own: Race, Crime and African Americans* (Rowman & Littlefield, $19.95, 216 pp), attempts to dissect why many black people often reflexively defend and protest public criticism of other black people...even when the subject of their protectionism may not deserve it.

Beyond the shadow of O.J., the topic brings to mind issues ranging from the rape allegations lodged by a black stripper against members of Duke University's mostly white lacrosse team, to congresswoman Cynthia McKinney's largely unsuccessful effort to turn a scuffle with a security guard into an indictment of modern-day race relations.

Based on an examination of previously published polls and her own focus group of 30 Gainesville-area residents, Russell-Brown explains why the reflex benefits men more than women, how other ethnic groups employ it, and how it even stretched to include Bill Clinton—a white president beloved by black people who saw the Monica Lewinsky-fueled impeachment as an unfair prosecution.

Reached at her Gainesville office, the author offered more thoughts on a reaction she has called "a kind of blues expression, a lyric, a voice that sings when called to action."

Why does this protectionism happen?

This isn't something new and this isn't something crazy and it isn't illogical; that fear, since the time African-Americans have been here, and the need for the community to support one another so we weren't taken to another plantation as punishment. This really is a protective mechanism for saving community members. But also at the same time, it's an acknowledgement that the justice system is flawed and black people have been treated shabbily. Now it's about figuring out when it's in our best interests to provide this protective cloak. The cloak makes sense. I think we need to be a little more circumspect, a little more critical about who gets to wear it. The question I always ask is: "What has O.J. done for us lately?"

I think he's still searching for the real killer.

Deggans, Eric

Kobe Bryant was saying he didn't see himself as part of the black community and he thought that most black people didn't care that much about him. He was surprised at the response of the community towards him following allegations he raped a woman in 2004. It's available for black men, generally. But that was a question for me: Who should get it and under what circumstances? How was it that Clarence Thomas could get it, but not Cynthia McKinney? I'm not making a judgment about any particular case, but that's a fair question.

It seems, sometimes, black protectionism is almost required to get movement on race issues. It's as if white and black America is stuck in this relationship where, if black people don't raise a protest, their fairness concerns won't be fully addressed.

I hadn't thought of it in those terms but protectionism is a cry... a yell. It is saying, "Are we being treated fairly?" It probably does make a lot of white folks ask "Are they crazy? They're always talking about race, screaming out in the streets." But otherwise, nobody is paying any attention. Because, to white people, it looks like things are working the way they are supposed to. Black protectionism is important. My argument is that it should be used more critically. But it's a necessary response to continuing racial injustice.

You criticize those who assume all black people think the same way. But isn't presenting black protectionism as a valid response to racism encouraging such perceptions?

To me, it's not about rallying behind anyone and throwing all your support in the biggest embrace possible. The kind of thing we saw with O.J. should be reserved for very special cases. Everybody shouldn't get the full embrace of black protectionism. You need to earn that. We also need to acknowledge wrongdoing. That's why it's interesting to watch the Duke rape case unfold. The smear campaign against this accuser has been the impetus for black protectionism, particularly in Durham.

But isn't there a danger of making race-based excuses for guilty people? Particularly when celebrities facing legal trouble such as Michael Jackson or O.J. Simpson seem to encourage it?

We should expand it beyond black celebrities and see it as a call for racial justice. It's about creating justice in our communities for victims and offenders. Saying you're opposed to draconian sentencing laws doesn't mean you're soft on crime. We just want justice and fairness.

Why don't black women get this benefit?

One of my students said to me, "Black men get it because they need it more than the sisters do." If you're comparing black women to black men and you have to pick which one needs help... I think most African-Americans will point to black men. And that's not just about today, but in terms of looking at black men throughout history... whether it's Emmett Till, or any number of black men who are falsely accused of crimes, strung up and dumped in the river.

Isn't it possible that people are just being sexist?

Sure. And it doesn't have to be either/or. We shouldn't have to pick one. Because many of the cases facing black women were not serious felonies, I think the perception is the onslaught is against black men. As I did focus groups and talked to people, I've seen the dismissive treatment of black women. If folks can defend singer and accused pedophile R. Kelly, then why can't they stand up for Cynthia MdKinney?

What's your recommendation for a better response?

First of all, the community should assert that it's not condoning the crime that occurred. As far as I'm concerned that's where most cases should begin and end. You can't just chip away at racial capital for anybody. It can't be that Clarence Thomas and Jesse Jackson get the same support.

But if protectionism is about ensuring justice is done, why should it matter whether they have been associated with black culture or causes before?

That's what a lot of people have said... protectionism is not about the person, it's about the community. But making sure that Clarence Thomas isn't railroaded isn't the same thing as making Anita Hill out to be this delusional black woman out to bring down a black man. So yes, Clarence Thomas deserves to be treated fairly. But do we have to come out and see 68 percent of black people supporting his confirmation? You hardly heard any African-Americans talking about sexual assault and sexual violence.

Aren't you seeking to control something that is uncontrollable?

I believe many African-Americans think any time one African-American is in trouble, "That could be me." There's a real sense that there's a need to protect our own.

Source: The above column first appeared on 7 May 2006 and appears here by permission of the *St. Petersburg Times*.

Further Readings: "Bio: Eric Deggans." [Online]. The Huffington Post Web site www.huffingtonpost.com/contributors/bio.

Delaney, Paul (13 January 1933–)

Longtime journalist Paul Delaney is director of Howard University's Center for the Study of Race and Media and was for 23 years a correspondent and editor with the *New York Times*. He was born in Montgomery, Alabama, and earned the B.A. in journalism from Ohio State University. He entered journalism during the Civil Rights Era as a reporter for the *Atlanta Daily World*, and from 1961 to 1963, he was a probation officer in Atlanta. He returned to journalism to report for the *Dayton Daily News* in Ohio and from that job moved on to the *Washington Star* in the nation's capital. In 1969, he became a correspondent for the *New York Times*, where during the next two decades he held a number of jobs. He was an urban affairs reporter, covering politics and civil rights, and a national desk editor. He worked as the *Times*' Madrid bureau chief and also in the paper's Chicago bureau. He later became a national desk editor and senior editor for newsroom administration. Delaney wrote about the rise of Elijah Muhammad and the Nation of Islam, better known as the Black Muslims, and about the policy changes made by Wallace D. Muhammad after his father's death in 1975. These changes, in the main, relaxed the strict code of conduct for practicing Black Muslims and moved toward reconciliation with whites. He also wrote about Wallace Muhammad's disagreements with Louis Farrakhan. Muhammad assumed the title Imam and changed the name of his religious organization to the American Muslim Mission; Farrakhan broke away and revived the Nation of Islam under his own leadership. The two rivals at least partially reconciled in 2000.

While with the *Times*, Delaney reported in 1976 on the efforts of African Americans to help Jimmy Carter win the presidency. Years later, working in Madrid, Spain, Delaney filed stories about protests against the government of Prime Minister Felipe Gonzalez. Commenting in 1987 about the large collection of documents in Spain's Archive of the Indies, Delaney wrote a memorable story headlined "Was Columbus a Whiner?" in which he detailed some of the explorer's many complaints about compensation, health problems and the like. He wrote about the history of Spain's Jewish population and as early as 1988 was reporting on the activities of the Palestine Liberation Organization (PLO). He described for *Times* readers another kind of battle: the efforts in Tunisia, Morocco and Algeria to combat an enormous 1988 infestation of locusts. He reported on Tunisia's moves to align its government with that of Libya's Muammar Qaddafi and with the PLO. In addition, he wrote about efforts by the nations of North Africa to attract more Western tourists as a source of needed revenue.

In 1992, Delaney retired from the *Times* and served from then until 1996 as chair of the University of Alabama department of journalism. From 1996 to 1998, he edited the editorial page of *Our World News*, and during 1999 and 2000, he contributed editorials to the *Baltimore Sun*. Since 1999, he has directed the Center for the Study of Race and Media at Howard University in Washington, D.C. He was a founding member of the National Association of Black Journalists and has held membership in the Society of Professional Journalists and the Overseas Press Club. Another of his memberships is in the not-so-well-known Society of Silurians, a New York club founded in 1924 and open only to individuals who have been newspaper journalists for 30 years or longer. In 2001, Delaney took part in a University of Michigan program on press coverage of racial matters. He has been a board member of both National Public Radio and the University of Maryland's Philip Merrill College of Journalism, is on the committee that selects media fellows for the Henry J. Kiser Foundation and is director of the Syracuse University Initiative on Racial Mythology.

Further Readings: "Paul Delaney." [Online]. The History Makers Web site www.thehistorymakers.com/biogrpahy; "Race: The Conversation You're Not Hearing in Your Newsroom." [Online, 21 March 1997]. American Society of Newspaper Editors Web site www.asne.org.

Diuguid, Lewis Walter (17 July 1955–)

A twice weekly opinion page columnist for the *Kansas City Star*, Lewis Diuguid is also the paper's vice president for community resources and a member of its editorial board. He has trained the paper's staffers in diversity workshops since 1993 and cochaired its diversity program since 1995. He is facilitator for meetings of the Diversity Coalition in Kansas City, which attracts white, black, Asian, Native American and people of various faiths and ages. Diuguid was born in St. Louis and is a 1977 graduate of the University of Missouri's well known School of Journalism. He joined the *Star* immediately after graduation and has worked in a long progression of jobs there: reporter/photographer, copy editor, automotive editor, Southland assistant bureau chief and bureau chief, assistant city editor, associate editor and columnist. He helped found the Kansas City Association of Black Journalists and has served as its treasurer, awards chairman and newsletter editor. He is also a member of the National Association of Black Journalists, the Trotter Group of Black Voices in Commentary and the National Society of Newspaper Columnists. From 1995 to 1999, he spent a great deal of time at Washington High School in Kansas City, which resulted in the publication of around 100 columns and one book about problems in public education, such at bureaucratic bullying of teachers, the unfortunate aspects of the George W. Bush administration's No Child Left

Behind initiative, and the need for more parental involvement in their children's education.

In his column, Diuguid has expressed a strong dislike for the Bush White House and has criticized the administration's skillful use of appeals to patriotism and fear, which he has termed "patriotic Viagra," employed to whip up support for invading Iraq. He has likened the president's use of lofty rhetoric, faulty generalizations and ridicule of opposing views to the empty calories in the junk food. He cheered Michael Moore's 2004 film "Fahrenheit 9/11" for dramatically pointing up the bluster and bravado that led to a military invasion of another nation for dubious reasons. His view is that the forces of terrorism are not so much changing the United States as unveiling the aspects of our culture that we would prefer to ignore or hide, to the great detriment of our international image. Another frequent theme of his column is what he calls America's "prisonindustrial complex," a term he borrowed from President Dwight Eisenhower's comments about our "military-industrial complex." The growth of for-profit prisons concerns him, as does what he sees as the greater likelihood of minority people to be arrested, jailed and given disproportionately long sentences. The expanding gap in wealth between whites and blacks is another worry, as is the recent internal squabbling in civil rights organizations, mainly the NAACP and the Southern Christian Leadership Conference. Although his column usually addresses problems, Diuguid also uses it to celebrate the positive as in a 1999 column about an Eli Lilly-sponsored scholarship program to help schizophrenics and other people having mental illnesses. Among his awards has been the 2000 Missouri Honor Medal for Distinguished Service in Journalism.

"Fear Taints Patriotism" by Lewis W. Diuguid

Like a rock star, U.S. Attorney General John Ashcroft has started a multicity tour, singing praises for the Patriot Act.

His Web site, www.lifeandliberty.gov, quotes the Declaration of Independence, and in a recent speech Ashcroft cited the need to prevent another tragedy like Sept. 11, 2001, as the reason for the law. He said the Patriot Act provides the "tools necessary to preserve the lives and liberty of the American people."

Ashcroft is among many Bush administration officials who repeatedly use the terrorist attacks, terror alerts, the unending wars against terrorism and fear to keep patriotism up in America. But the bad law Ashcroft is peddling takes away civil liberties, and that's not good. Proponents like him cleverly put the "patriot" label on the law.

That reframing helps generate what I call "patriotic Viagra." Government spin doctors dump the tonic into America's information streams to win the public's support for the Bush administration and get people to feel safer.

The truth is U.S. troops keep dying in battles. Amnesty International also reports the U.S.-led war on terror has made the world more dangerous and repressive. Amnesty' report said human rights have been usurped and international law has been undermined.

Yet in this country, patriotic Viagra inspires allegiance to President Bush, acceptance of lost civil liberties and support for U.S.-led wars in Afghanistan and Iraq. Opponents are labeled un-American and unpatriotic. But blind compliance isn't patriotic. To find the true meaning of patriot I used an English/Latin dictionary.

Elpida Anthan, who teaches classical Greek and classical Latin at the University of Missouri-Kansas City, said the Latin and Greek roots of English words reveal their real meaning. That cleanses them of political additives, which cause people to impulsively act without thinking. In Latin, "patriot" is civis bonus. In English that means good citizen.

"A good citizen refers to someone active in the republic," Anthan said.

Good citizens are people who vote regularly, pay taxes, give blood, donate to charities, volunteer, work with youths, remain active in civic and church groups, support the community and defend what this country stands for. That includes civil liberties but not phantom weapons of mass destruction.

Anthan showed the Greek derivative of "patriot." It is philopatris, meaning "loving one's country." True patriots also show that love when they insist that the Patriot Act goes too far, taking away civil liberties, which laws are supposed to protect. But the Bush administration has effectively narcotized the public into just playing along.

It's reminiscent of Hermann Goering's infamous quote in April 1946. He told it to Gustave Gilbert, a German-speaking intelligence officer and psychologist, who was granted free access by the Allies to prisoners in the Nuremberg jail at the Nuremberg trials. Gilbert kept a journal, which he published as the *Nuremberg Diary*.

"Why of course the people don't want war," said Goering, who was second in command to Adolph Hitler in Nazi Germany. "But, after all, it's leaders of the country who determine the policy and it is always a simple matter to drag the people along, whether it's a democracy or a fascist dictatorship or a parliament or a Communist dictatorship."

Here is the chilling part: "But, voice or no voice, the people can always be brought to the bidding of the leaders. That is easy. All you have to do is tell them they are being attacked, and denounce the pacifists for lack of patriotism and exposing the country to greater danger."

That isn't good government. But that is what the nation is being forced to stomach.

Source: This column appears here by permission of *The Kansas City Star*. It originally appeared on 31 August 2003.

Books by Lewis Walter Diuguid: *A Teacher's Cry: Expose the Truth about Education Today* (Boca Raton, Fla.: Universal Publishers, 2004).

Further Readings: "Biography: Lewis W. Diuguid." [Online]. Project Equality Web site www.projectequality.org.

Donovan, Kyle (1971–)

Early in 1999, 27-year-old Kyle Donovan founded Envy Publishing Group and launched *NV* magazine, a combination business and lifestyle periodical for young urban professionals. The initials NV had a double meaning: envy, as reflected in the magazine's parent company name, and "New Visions in Business," the periodical's subtitle, indicating that the magazine is intended to serve the needs of a rising population of financially successful new urban capitalists. Donovan was raised from ages 9 through 15 in Brooklyn, New York, by his grandmother, Mary Lou Raby, who is probably the individual he most admires. He finished high school in Brooklyn and in the publisher's note on his Web site, www.nvmagazine.com, he remarks that he went to the best university in the world: the university of MLR, meaning the things he learned from his overworked but uncomplaining grandmother. Donovan, as a businessman, is largely self-taught. He started his own photography business at age 19 and built an impressive list of clients. His Web site mentions that among these clients were the *New York Times*, *Barrons*, The Dow Jones Corporation and EMI-Capitol Records. His success in photography and with stock market trades helped him raise the funds needed to start his magazine. When he did so, he became perhaps the youngest publisher of a U.S. national magazine. His success has earned Donovan more than a little attention. His work is mentioned in the 1999 book *It's about the Money! The Fourth Movement of the Freedom Symphony: How to Build Wealth, Get Access to Capital, and Achieve Your Financial Dreams* (New York: Times Business), by the Rev. Jesse Jackson and Jesse Jackson Jr., written with the help of Mary Gotschall. His story also has been told in *Crain's Business Magazine*, *Advertising Age* and *Entrepreneur Magazine*.

In 2002, Donovan was a member of the U.S. delegation that participated in the German-American Young Leaders Conference in Berlin. He has been a speaker at the business schools of Columbia University, the University of Pennsylvania and Howard University and has spoken at conferences sponsored by the National Urban League Young Professionals, the Association of African Americans in Advertising, the National Association of Minorities in Communication and the North Alabama African American Chamber of Commerce.

Donovan describes the readers of his bimonthly magazine as "NVisionaries"—people who want to define the minority urban professional as someone known for what he or she creates rather than what he or she consumes. A stylish-looking young man with a distinctive, well-trimmed moustache and beard—made especially so by the narrow vertical strip of beard that extends downward from the middle of his lower lip to the top of his modified goatee—he publishes an annual issue devoted to women in business and another geared to the needs of urban singles. Themes of other issues are sports and entertainment, information technology, and politics. Three issues thus far have been themed to appeal to Latino readers. The May/June 2006 issue of *NV* features lawyer/novelist/producer Tonya Lewis Lee, who is also filmmaker Spike Lee's wife. The issue's other main feature piece titled "She Hate Me," examines the multiple obstacles confronting today's successful black women, not the least of which is the animosity directed at them by lower-ranking women employees in their companies. The issue also includes a tribute to the late Coretta Scott King. Like most other lifestyle magazines, *NV* provides travel articles and fashion coverage. Most of the remainder of its editorial content is devoted to various aspects of business and to legal information pertinent to the magazine's readers.

Future business plans include publishing a line of children's books to be called the Do 'Bees series. The Do 'Bees are six bees who do something so they can be something. The theme of the series will be to encourage children to try to be whatever they want to be.

Further Readings: "About NV." [Online]. New Vision Web site www.nvmagazine.com; "Kyle Donovan." [Online]. New Vision in Business Web site www.nvmagazine.com.

Douglas, William (?–)

Longtime newsman Bill Douglas is White House correspondent for Knight Ridder and prior to taking this job, he reported for *Newsday* out of New York City and Washington, D.C. He was born in Long Beach, California, and grew up mainly in Philadelphia. He studied journalism at the University of South Carolina, graduating in 1980 and going to work at that time as a general assignment reporter for North Carolina's *Charlotte Observer*. He also covered the education beat for the *Observer* before moving in 1983 to write features for the *Atlanta Journal-Constitution*. He returned to reporting in 1984, when he again moved, this time joining the Baltimore *Evening Sun*. At the *Sun*, he did both general assignment and higher education reporting. He joined the staff of *Newsday* in New York City in 1987, where he first covered New York's congressional delegation. He reported on Speaker of the House Newt Gingrich's dramatic rise and fall between 1994 and 1998 and the presidential campaign of Sen. Bob Dole in 1996 and was put on the White House beat during Bill Clinton's second term in office. In 2000, Douglas reported on the Al Gore bid for the presidency and thereafter was a foreign affairs reporter. He covered the Iraq war while on the Pentagon beat. His move to Knight Ridder's Washington Bureau came in 2003. In that year, he was assigned the State Department beat; at that time, *Newsday* was one of only 12 U.S. newspapers to assign a correspondent to this highly important beat. He has won awards from the National Association of Black Journalists' Atlanta chapter, the South Carolina chapter of the Society of Professional Journalists and the Associated Press Sports Editors.

Some of his most dramatic coverage in 1999 was on the bombing of Kosovo, Yugoslavia, by NATO warplanes and on President Clinton's efforts to use the bombing to persuade Serb forces to leave the city. Another of his stories in 1999 reported on the dissatisfaction of Jewish voters in New York with Hillary Rodham Clinton's lack of response to accusations made by Suha Arafat, wife of Palestinian leader Yasser Arafat, that Israelis had harmed Palestinian women and children by using toxic tear gas. In 2001, Douglas reported on the Bush administration's ill-fated use of the Advertising Council in an attempt to "sell America" to the Muslim world. In 2003, Douglas reported on the angry response by British Prime Minister Tony Blair to U.S. Secretary of Defense Donald Rumsfeld's comments during a press briefing that questioned Britain's resolve in the fight against terrorism. He wrote about the Pentagon's attempts to promote Iraqi banker Ahmad Chalabi for a leadership role in that nation's new government, a move opposed by the U.S. State Department and the CIA, and about covert Pentagon plans that attempted to destabilize the political might of Iran's clergy. In June 2003, he reported on an extensive Pew Global Attitudes Project poll conducted in 20 nations that showed the extent of damage to America's image caused by the Iraq war. In 2006, some of Douglas' stories have addressed the red-carpet reception in Washington of Africa's first female head of state, Liberian president, Ellen Johnson-Sirleaf; President Bush's remarks that U.S. troops would remain in Iraq past his own presidency; the administration's successful efforts to defuse the legal troubles of Cheney aide Lewis "Scooter" Libby and presidential advisor Karl Rove, who had been charged with "outing" CIA agent Valerie Plame; and Bush's continued support of Donald Rusmfeld and the president's defense of Big Oil's soaring profits. Other 2006 stories concerned the president's decision to send National Guard troops to patrol the U.S. border with Mexico and President Bush's recommendation that the Senate support a constitutional amendment that would ban gay marriage.

"U.S. Turns to Madison Avenue for PR War" by William Douglas

The Bush administration, fearing that it might lose the public relations war in Muslim and Arab nations to Osama bin Laden, is turning to Madison Avenue for help.

The State Department is talking to the Advertising Council, a New York-based nonprofit group that develops advertising strategies for national causes, about crafting a "public diplomacy" campaign on the military action in Afghanistan and the war on terrorism.

Overseeing those talks is Charlotte Beers, the new undersecretary of state for public diplomacy and a former J. Walter Thompson advertising executive who started in the industry marketing Uncle Ben's Rice. Beers was named to the post by President George W. Bush early in his administration and was sworn in Oct. 2.

Her job is to sell America, a difficult task in some Arab and Muslim countries where citizens are protesting the U.S. military response to the Sept. 11 attacks on the World Trade Center and the Pentagon.

"I think the fact is, there is a battle for hearts and minds," said Philip Reeker, a State Department spokesman. "There's a lot of disinformation... The difficulties we face in getting our message out are quite clear."

Several advertising executives and media analysts say the administration's increased efforts will do little to sway Muslims and Arabs overseas, many of whom say their distrust of the United States goes beyond the situation in Afghanistan.

The U.S. handling of the Palestine-Israeli conflict, for example, fuels Arab and Muslim anger and prompts many to tune out the rationale for going after bin Laden in Afghanistan, said newspaper owner Osama Siblani.

"The Untied States lost the public relations war in the Muslim world a long time ago," said Siblani, publisher of the Arab American News, a weekly newspaper in Dearborn. "They could have the prophet Muhammad doing public relations and it wouldn't help."

That apprehension increased after Sept. 11 because of what Siblani and some advertising executives called the administration's muddled public relations strategy.

Two weeks ago, the White House went on an information defensive, with National Security Advisor Condoleezza Rice urging television networks not to air any more statements by bin Laden live and unedited. The networks, which showed a taped message of a defiant bin Laden from the Arabic-language Al-Jazeera network on Oct. 7, refused, but pledged to view the tapes first.

Secretary of State Colin Powell unsuccessfully lobbied Qatari Emir Sheikh Hamad bin Khalifa al-Thani to "tone down" what he considered inflammatory, anti-American rhetoric on the government-financed Al-Jazeera offensive. Powell, Defense Secretary Donald Rumsfeld and Rice found themselves defending America's position in exclusive interviews on the network that's becoming the CNN of the Arab and Muslim world.

Beers told Advertising Age last week that she would consider buying air time on Al-Jazeera to get America's message across to a foreign audience.

The State Department and the council, which has done pro bono public service campaigns for the government, are discussing the possibility of putting together a campaign for foreign consumption. Several advertising executives and media analysts expressed skepticism about the administration's strategy.

Jeff Odiorne, chairman of Odiorne Wilde Narraway and Partners, a San Francisco advertising firm, questioned the benefit of top administration officials doing Al-Jazeera interviews.

"Can you imagine being an 18-year-old Arab kid, going to religious school and being taught to hate Americans and we put on a pasty, 60-year-old white guy to tell you that what we are doing is just?" Odiorne asked. "Talk about reaching your target audience. Doing the stuff that we're doing is only adding salt to the wounds."

Source: Copyright, 2001, *Newsday*. Reprinted by permission. The story originally appeared on 23 October 2001.

Further Readings: "Bill Douglas." [Online, Fall 2004]. School of Journalism & Mass Communications, University of South Carolina Web site www.jour.sc.edu; "William Douglas." [Online]. Knight Ridder Washington Bureau Web site www.realcities.com/mld/krwashington/news/columnists.

Dow, Harold (?–)

Since 1990, Harold Dow has worked as a CBS correspondent for the show "48 Hours." He was born in Hackensack, New Jersey, and studied at the University of Nebraska in Omaha. His earliest television experience was at KETV in Omaha, where he was a reporter, coanchor and talk show host. He was a news anchor for WPAT Radio in Paterson, New Jersey, and did freelance reporting for KCOP-TV in Los Angeles. He was a reporter and anchor for Theta Cable TV in Santa Monica, California, prior to joining CBS in 1972. As a CBS reporter and from 1977 to 1982 as the network's Los Angeles bureau correspondent, he covered a variety of big stories, such as the Patricia Hearst kidnapping by the Symbionese Liberation Army and the return of U.S. prisoners of war from Vietnam. In 1982, he moved to New York City to work as coanchor and interviewer for "CBS Nightwatch." He held that position until 1983, then was a reporter for the "CBS Evening News with Dan Rather," "CBS News Sunday Morning," and the CBS News series "Verdict." Dow began his present job as a "48 Hours" correspondent in 1990 and for two years prior to this time contributed to the show, which first appeared in 1988. Moreover, he had worked on a 1986 documentary about crack cocaine that led to the creation of "48 Hours" as a weekly news magazine show, and his interview with O.J. Simpson after the murders of Simpson's wife Nicole and friend Ron Goldman was the first segment aired on the new program in 1988.

Dow also worked on recent developments in a 1946 hanging death that had been ruled suicide. He and his "48 Hours" crew went to Gainesville, Florida, to cover the case of cabinet-maker Harold "Buddy" Vest, who had been found hanged wearing women's underwear in the restroom of his cabinet shop. In 2003, Vest's son, Herb Vest, caused his father's body to be exhumed and examined by a forensic pathologist, who found evidence of a struggle on the night of the hanging. The coroner changed the ruling to homicide, probably the result of an argument over a woman. Dow has also done numerous celebrity interviews for the show, including one in 2001 with entertainer Eartha Kitt, then age 74; one in 2003 with hot-selling rap singer Lil' Romeo (Percy Romeo Miller III); and another in 2004 with country singer Reba McEntire. He has also reported for "48 Hours" on the troubles of entertainer Michael Jackson, whose remarkable musical career started at age five. The interview covered Jackson's phenomenal rise, his having become the first music video megastar, his smart acquisition of rights to the Beatles' music and his odd, lavish lifestyle at his Neverland Ranch home.

Further Readings: Dow, Harold. "The Tower Is Down." [Online, September 2001]. CBS News Web site www.cbsnews.com; "Harold Dow." [Online]. CBS News Web site www.cbsnews.com.

Dreyfuss, Joel P. (17 September 1945–)

Joel Dreyfuss, currently editor-in-chief of *Red Herring* magazine and Web site, has in his long career worked in virtually every medium. He was born in Port-au-Prince, Haiti, and holds a 1971 B.S. from City College of the City University of New York. Prior to graduating, he worked part-time as a *New York Post* reporter (1969–1971). He reported for the *Washington Post* from 1971 to 1973, after which he was an Urban Journalism Fellow at the University of Chicago in 1973, then an Associated Press reporter until 1976. From 1977 to 1979, he worked in broadcasting as a writer/producer for San Francisco station KPIX-TV, a CBS affiliate. In 1980, he switched media to become executive editor of *Black Enterprise* magazine, leaving this job in 1982 to become New York bureau chief for the newly launched national newspaper *USA Today*. A year later, he returned to magazine work, as associate editor of *Fortune* magazine. He held this position until 1990; from 1986 to 1988, he was also *Fortune*'s Tokyo bureau chief. From 1990 to 1991, he was managing editor of *Business Tokyo*, and from 1991 to 1994, editor-in-chief of *PC Magazine*, also in New York City. Dreyfuss was, from 1994 to 1996, editor-in-chief and later editorial director and associate publisher of *InformationWeek*, a periodical devoted to technological innovation in business settings. Next, he was editor of *Our World News*, an online weekly that offered black perspectives on the news, and in 1997, he returned to *Fortune* as a senior editor. In this position, he revamped *Fortune*'s spin-off magazine *FSB*, which covered small business, worked on the launch of a new Web site for small business, and wrote "The Dreyfuss Report," a column on information technology.

In 2000, the attraction of new media work lured him away to become editor-in-chief of *Urban Box Office*, a news and information Web site that targeted the young, multiracial urban audience. *UBO* was one of many online ventures that went under during the dot com crash. In this specific case, founder George Jackson had died, dissention developed among the staff, and management was unable to achieve sufficient capitalization. From the demise of *UBO* until 2004, Dreyfuss was a senior editor and writer for *Bloomberg Markets* magazine in New York, again focusing on information technology and venture financing. Then in 2004, he became editor-in-chief of *Red Herring*, directing the company's Web site and the relaunch of its paper magazine of the same title. The magazine *Red Herring* had been founded in 1993 and became popular with dot com entrepreneurs. Its reappearance in paper form occurred in November 2004.

During his remarkable and varied career, Dreyfuss has cowritten one book and has made numerous television appearances, to include the Charlie Rose show, Bloomberg TV, and MSNBC. He has been a member of the Council on Foreign Relations as well as the Japan Society, a Pulitzer Prize juror, a board member of the American Society of Magazine Editors and a founding member of the National Association of Black Journalists.

"Black People Must Be Stupid" by Joel Dreyfuss

Black people must be stupid. That's the conclusion implied by David Horowitz's "Baa Baa Black Sheep" column following the November elections. Horowitz is baffled that blacks continue to vote for Democrats in majorities "like the populations of communist countries." He complains that Rep. Charles Rangel, D-NY, won 94 percent of the vote in his Harlem district and suggests there would be uproar if a white candidate defeated a black candidate because more than 90 percent of whites voted for the white candidate.

Horowitz follows in a long tradition of lamenting the willingness of black people to vote their interests. I can understand why he's upset: Unusually high black turnouts in key races had a lot to do with upsetting the Republican apple cart in November. Until the day after the election, the impact of black voters was barely discussed on the talk shows, a state of affairs reflected on election night, when being white seemed to be the primary qualification for on-air pundits.

Lamentations about black voters are often thinly disguised efforts to set them aside. In 1984, after Ronald Reagan won reelection with majorities among all constituencies except African-Americans, a number of political experts suggested that blacks were isolated because of their unwillingness to join the coronation. Yet within weeks, this same "isolated" group launched protests that would force a change in the Reagan administration's "constructive engagement" policy toward South Africa—protests that eventually helped end apartheid and free Nelson Mandela.

One of the favorite devices of conservatives is the mythical "double standard." Blacks get away with behavior that would not be acceptable among whites because of white guilt. "Black Sheep" is full of such insinuations. Massive black support for black candidates is one example. Yet in races involving black candidates who are not incumbents, 80 percent of the white vote usually goes to the white candidate—no matter how qualified the black candidate. Even Andrew Young, that paragon of integration and moderation, could barely gather 15 percent of the white vote when he first ran for Congress in 1972.

The red herring of the double standard is actually a cover for another favorite conservative hot button: moral equivalency. The fact that most black people only got the right to vote in the last 30 years; that they represent just 12 percent of the population; or that they are the only ethnic group whose rights were specifically limited by this nation from its inception seem not to matter to critics like Horowitz. So 90 percent of blacks voting as a bloc is rendered equal to 90 percent of whites voting to maintain their dominance.

While Horowitz laments the refusal of blacks to vote for most Republican candidates (strange that he doesn't mention the Govs. Bush), he ignores the GOP's long history of race baiting and appealing to white interests. In fact, Republican gains in the South are largely the result of thinly veiled appeals to white voters who feared black political gains. From Richard Nixon's 1968 "Southern strategy" through Willie Horton to anti-affirmative action appeals in this last election, the message to white voters has been clear: Let's keep *them* under control. In other words, white voters are asked to vote their interests, although white voters' interests are usually equated with *everyone's* interests. Once again, black voters just don't seem to understand.

Horowitz cites welfare reform as an example of Republican policies that have helped blacks, but even many who favored ending the old dependencies warn that an unusually long economic boom may have masked the long-term effects of throwing tens of thousands off the rolls with little or no safety net. One of the issues he and other conservatives ignore is that African-Americans have been among the chief critics of the damaging effects of welfare. But blacks favored a more gradual, well-planned process to avoid the chaos that could hit many cities in an economic downturn—cities still viewed as alien territory among suburban white voters.

Why is it that white conservatives use black conservatives to support their arguments? If their ideas can stand on their own merits, why must they drag in blacks making the same arguments? It suggests that for all the posturing about merit, white conservatives feel they need someone with a different skin color to make their positions more credible. Horowitz laments the harsh criticism of black conservatives like Larry Elder, Clarence Thomas, Ward Connerly and others by mainstream blacks. But isn't the wholesale rejection of their arguments by African-Americans a sign of maturity? Blacks have looked beyond the color of their skin to the content of their character, and rejected their positions.

As one who has closely followed the arguments of conservatives of all colors for years, I think one of the problems with many of these black conservatives is that they simply restate old arguments made by white conservatives. When black conservatives try to make more nuanced arguments—such as economist Glenn Loury's complaint that white conservatives offer no constructive alternatives to the programs they don't like—they are expelled from the circles that initially welcomed them.

Conservatives like Horowitz cannot admit that black people have enemies. They are willing to give every opponent of affirmative action, set-asides and minority election districts the benefit of the doubt: that they are really taking positions because they have the best interests of black people at heart. Maybe that's why he doesn't bring up the cynical Republican strategy in the first part of this decade to push blacks into majority-minority districts—so Republicans could win all-white suburban districts.

And like most conservatives—and a lot of liberals—Horowitz is willing to dismiss the worldview of the black majority as simply wrong. African-Americans live in a world more finely nuanced than conservative ideology can comfortably embrace. Polls show that black people believe they have friends and enemies in all colors. Black people feel they still need affirmative action because of their real experiences with white people. That is why middle-class black people are more ardent supporters of affirmative action than poor blacks. They find that even the most well-meaning whites cannot always overcome hundreds of years of legislated and implied superiority. Just as African-Americans see real progress, they also see continuing obstacles, slights, unintended insults and exclusions. And that is why they won't embrace the Larry Elders and Clarence Thomases as heroes, no matter how often they get called black sheep.

Source: This commentary piece appeared on Salon.com on 1 December 1998 and is reproduced here by permission of Mr. Dreyfuss.

Books by Joel P. Dreyfuss: With Charles Lawrence, *The Bakke Case: The Politics of Inequality* (New York: Harcourt Brace Jovanovich, 1979).

Further Readings: Fost, Dan. "Red Herring Resurfaces with Plans to Go Weekly." [Online, 27 October 2004]. San Francisco Chronicle Web site www.sfgate.com; "Joel Dreyfuss." [Online, 2005]. The Media Center of The American Press Institute Web site www.mediacenter.org; "Joel Dreyfuss Joins Red Herring as Editor-in-Chief." [Online, 23 August 2004]. Quote.com site http://finance.lycos.com; Joyce, Cynthia. "Race Matters in Cyberspace, Too." [Online, 5 June 1997]. Salon Magazine site http://archive.salon.com.

Dunlap, Karen Brown (1951–)

In 2002, Karen Dunlap, president and managing director of the Poynter Institute became the first African American named to the board of directors of the Times Publishing Company, owner of Florida's *St. Petersburg Times*, *Congressional Quarterly* and regional business magazine *Florida Trend*. She was born in Tennessee, and when she was a seventh-grader in Haynes School in Nashville, one of her teachers suggested that she would make a good journalist. While in high school, she interned at the *Nashville Banner*. She earned a 1971 bachelor's in mass communications from Michigan State University, after which she became editor of a small paper, the *Warner Robins Enterprise* in Georgia. In a brief story published in 1997 on the Web site of the American Society of Newspaper Editors, Dunlap revealed that not only did she do most of the writing for that paper, but she was photographer, substitute typesetter and ghost writer of the publisher's column as well. To make the staff appear larger than its actual size, she used the byline Karen Brown, her first and married names, on some stories, and on others, the name Lavette Fitzgerald, her middle and maiden names. Her next job, in 1973, was with the much larger Georgia paper the *Macon News*. She returned to school in 1974 and completed the M.S. in speech communications at Tennessee State University in 1976. Continuing her formal education, Dunlap earned the Ph.D. in mass communications in 1982 at the University of Tennessee in Knoxville. She worked during the summers of 1983–1985 as associate editor of the minority youth program at the *Nashville Banner* and in the summer of 1986 and the autumn of 1992, was a staff writer for the *St. Petersburg Times*. After receiving her M.S. in 1976, Dunlap joined the journalism faculty of Tennessee State University in Nashville. In 1985, she took a new teaching position in the journalism program at the University of South Florida in Tampa. In 1989, she joined the Poynter Institute, which offers seminars for journalists. The institute owns the *St. Petersburg Times*, Florida's largest newspaper, and hence is very well funded. She initially worked as an instructor, then became dean of the faculty. As dean, she added to the institute's offerings in newspaper management and newsroom leadership. In August 2003, she replaced the retiring James Naughton as president and managing director of the institute. In 2006, her salary was reported as being just under $250,000 a year. Dunlap was coauthor, with Jane T. Harrigan, of *The Editorial Eye* in 2004 and earlier had cowritten with Foster Davis the 2000 book *The Effective Editor: How to Lead Your Staff to Better Writing and Teamwork*. She also has done editing for and contributed to the institute's *Best Newspaper Writing* series and was a contributor to Roy Peter Clark and Cole C. Campbell's *The Values and Craft of American Journalism* (Gainesville, Fla.: University of Florida Press, 2002, 2005).

Managing and teaching at Poynter, Dunlap has offered advice on such topics as the need for newspapers to provide some content that will surprise readers, how to address the challenges of the changing media environment and how editors can get along more smoothly with their reporters. Her position is that editors should do more coaching and less fixing. She offers those who attend the institute a 10-point list of how to edit one's own copy. She has twice served as a Pulitzer Prize juror, is on the foundation board of the Newspaper Association of America and is on the boards of Eckerd Youth Alternatives Inc., a nonprofit organization dedicated to helping troubled youth, and the Florida Education Fund. In April 2004, she was an ethics panelist at the joint annual convention of the NAA and the American Society of Newspaper Editors in Washington, D.C. In October of that year, she was keynote speaker at the European Journalism Centre in Maastricht, the Netherlands. Dunlap was the 2005 commencement speaker for the College of Communication and Information at the University of Tennessee and performed the same function in 2006 at Eckerd College. In 2005, she was recipient of the University of Tennessee's Hileman Award.

"Year of Storms: Lessons Learned & Stories Yet to Be Told"
by Karen Brown Dunlap

As the plane began its descent toward New Orleans and the terrain came into view, the passenger next to me became chatty. He offered to explain what we'd see of his home region, pointing out the blue roof tarps that carpeted an area beneath us. He talked about the slow recovery of the economy, the problems with schools, the huge amount of work to be done, and doubts about the levee system.

He's thinking about moving away, he said, thinking of starting over in another state.

"Will things get better here?" I asked.

He paused, and then answered, "Only if the news media keep covering it. Only if they don't stop covering it."

It didn't occur to me to ask his name, but I wish I had. I'd like to share with him what happened on the ground over the next couple of days.

That evening about 40 members of the region's news media gathered in New Orleans for a two day conference on covering the hurricanes and their effects, sponsored by Poynter and the Dart Center for Journalism and Trauma. Another group of journalists gathered near Biloxi for a similar conference.

News directors and editors, reporters, photojournalists and others told and retold stories of the storms: Katrina, Rita, and for at least one Miami journalist, stories of Wilma.

They talked about the shocks. David Vincent, news director of WLOX-TV Biloxi, told of his station's work while Hurricane Katrina blew off portions of the station's roof. "We huddled in the hall and kept reporting," he said. "We had a table set up for the anchors. It was really pretty dangerous."

Earlier, Anzio Williams, news director at WDSU-TV, New Orleans, told of sending out teams of journalists to the Superdome, an emergency response headquarters in the Hyatt Regency hotel and other sites that were supposed to be safe. As the hurricane hit and the levees broke, all the locations failed. He and others went from telephones to cell phones—and then to text messaging—in efforts to find staffers and report the news.

Stories abounded of living in offices or in the homes of colleagues for weeks at a time. The pre-hurricane drill for staffers included evacuating families. Like other residents, many members of news staffs found that damage prevented them from returning home after the storm had subsided.

"The station's generator provided power so many of us stayed there," said Dan Gresham, morning anchor/producer at KFDM-TV Beaumont.

Vicki Zimmerman, news director of WAFB-TV in Baton Rouge, said her house became a camp-out site for some, including journalists sent from out of town by her corporate office. "There were about 11 there at one point," she said. "We worked long hours and they were a big help."

Much of the conversation during the conferences revealed pride in the coverage. Zimmerman said one of her station's goals was "to minimize harm." That caused the station to shy away from some stories on weapons sales in Baton Rouge to avoid inflaming a city rife with rumors of rapes and gunfire.

Paul Cross, assistant managing editor of the Mobile Register, said his station sent a reporter to New Orleans after readers in Mobile kept telling the newspaper stories of violence in New Orleans. He said the result was that the Register was among the first to report that many of the claims of violence were untrue.

As conversations continued, a deeper effect of the storm emerged. Roger Simpson, executive director of the Dart Center for Journalism and Trauma, led participants in the Biloxi/Gulfport group in talking about how they have changed. They spoke of sleeplessness, irritability and anxiety about next year's hurricane season. Some spoke of guilt at suffering only minor damage as they witnessed so much loss around them.

The roads from New Orleans to Gulfport reveal the long-term destruction from the storm that greets residents. Along I-10, some shopping areas and housing complexes are quiet. Houses sit askew and windows are missing. Highway billboards sag at odd angles, some large metal poles bend in half.

Across from the beaches of Gulfport, trees dangle ghostly white and colored objects: paper, clothes, shredded sheets and towels, pieces of businesses and lives. Only the inner frames of hotels remain. All that's left of restaurants are signs, some saying they will return. The steeples of historic, stately churches rise but missing windows and doors reveal that the insides are empty.

A car pulls over and two tourists jump out. One takes a picture while the other smiles before a backdrop of what used to be. Nearby, an older woman wanders through a yard, searching through what's left. Small signs crowd the ground near intersections advertising for painters, haulers and roofers. For some poorer areas, the devastation doesn't look new. It's a reminder that some folks have lived in the middle of a storm much of their lives.

Traffic hassles add to the misery. A westbound bridge is out along I-10 near Slidell, so the eastbound lanes divide to serve both directions. That causes major back-ups for those leaving New Orleans in the afternoon. Many intersections operate as four-way stops in the absence of swept away traffic signals or electricity.

Journalists live with their own stresses while reporting on those of others. At last week's meetings, they spoke quietly of friends who avoid church because they don't want to see others, of loved ones who had white collar jobs but now spend their days as laborers in the clean-up and repair.

Roger Simpson of the Dart Center explained that post-traumatic stress was once believed to be caused by unexpected events, but doctors are beginning to agree that it also results from the cumulative effects of listening to others' distress. Journalists in the gulf would qualify for both causes.

Simpson reminded them that the symptoms they described, including headaches and forgetfulness, were typical of stress. He led them through a process aimed at helping them understand it and deal with it.

"We need to look at stress in individuals, in the newsroom and in the community," he said.

Most organizations have stories of staffers who left their jobs after the storm. Some took early retirements, jobs elsewhere or simply decided to leave.

In the long post-hurricane phase, journalists continue to inform and lead their communities. As the groups met Friday, the Orleans Times Picayune front page announced plans for a $3.1 billion outlay to rebuild levees. The page featured a picture of Mayor Ray Nagin and President George Bush shaking hands. There was also news about phone service and a feature on the reunion of two Canadian tourists and the New Orleans family that helped them escape flooding.

On the day before the conference the Biloxi Sun Herald carried an editorial saying attention is turning away from destruction in Mississippi. It said the devastation of the storm, particularly in Mississippi, cannot be forgotten.

The weekend gave journalists a chance to repair and compare. To hear from others who have covered communities after devastation and to rethink their craft skills and their approaches to the news. After guests fly away, these journalists continue on. If things are to change in the battered coast, the news media will have to bind its wounds and keep covering the storm.

Source: The above story appeared on www.poynter.org on 23 December 2005 and appears here by permission of Poynter Online.

Books by Karen Brown Dunlap: *The Effective Editor: How to Lead Your Staff to Better Writing and Teamwork* (Chicago: Bonus, 2000); with Jane T. Harrigan, *The Editorial Eye* (Boston: Bedford/St. Martins, 2004).

Further Readings: Nohlgren, Stephen. "African-American Woman Joins Times Board." [Online, 12 December 2002]. St. Petersburg Times Web site www.sptimes.com; Nohlgren. Stephen. "Poynter Dean Will Be Next President: Karen Brown Dunlap Will Lead the Journalism School When President James Naughton Retires." [Online, 17 January 2003]. St. Petersburg Times Web site www.sptimes.com.

E

Edmond, Alfred Adam Jr. (8 March 1960–)

Alfred Edmond is editor-in-chief and senior vice president of *Black Enterprise* magazine and executive editor of the publishing company Earl G. Graves Ltd. in New York City. He was born in Long Branch, New Jersey, and is a 1983 graduate of Rutgers University, where he majored in studio art and minored in economics. His career in journalism began as managing editor of *Big Red News*, now retitled the *New York Beacon*, a historically black weekly paper in Brooklyn, New York. He worked there from 1983 to 1985, when he became associate editor of the *Daily Challenge*, and again switched jobs in 1986 to become senior editor of *MBM/Modern Black Men Magazine*, also in New York. In 1987, he moved to *Black Enterprise*, where he has worked since that time. Here, he began as assistant editor and soon was made business editor. By 1990, he was associate editor for administration and became managing editor in 1992. In 1995, he was promoted to executive editor and in 2000, editor-in-chief of *Black Enterprise*. His responsibilities currently include serving as a member of the magazine's editorial board, exercising control of the editorial staff and editorial content, and doing long-range planning for the magazine. He also supervises the magazine's new media affiliates: the juvenile business periodical *Teenpreneur*, blackenterprise.com, Black Enterprise Report, a television program, and Black Enterprise Radio Report. *Black Enterprise* itself now has a readership of around 4 million and addresses personal finance, entrepreneurship, trend analysis, workplace technology, consumer spending and lifestyle, career planning and international business. It also profiles successful black business people and offers other editorial matter designed to inspire. The magazine's overarching aim is entrepreneurial: providing information that will help its readers become able to work for themselves instead of for others.

In a 2005 BlackAmericaWeb.com series on the state of Black America, Edmond stressed two needs of U.S. blacks: earlier home ownership—he suggested buying rather than renting within three years after finishing college or starting one's first job—and learning to save, regularly, roughly 15 percent of what one earns.

Edmond has been a member of the New York Association of Black Journalists since 1985, the National Association of Black Journalists since 1987, and the American Society of Magazine Editors since 1988. From 1994 to 1995, he was a member of the Society of American Business Editors & Writers. He has actively supported his alma mater as a Rutgers Alumni Federation board member and founding member of the university's African-American Alumni Alliance, both in 1990, and as an editorial board member of the *Rutgers Alumni Magazine* since 1991. He also taught journalism part-time for Rutgers during 1994 and 1995. He has been accorded a number of recognitions, among which are Lincoln University's Unity Award for Excellence in Media (1989–1992) and the Recognition for Excellence, 1996, given by Rutgers' Paul Robeson Cultural Center. He often appears on CNNfn's "Market Call" and on America's Black Forum and is known for his expertise in business and economics. During his tenure as editor-in-chief, *Black Enterprise* has won three editorial excellence in business and finance awards from the magazine industry trade magazine *Folio* and a Griot Award from the New York Association of Black Journalists.

Further Readings: "Alfred Edmond." [Online 1 November 2004]. Black Enterprise Web site www.blackenterprise.com; Farrow, Nicole and Osakwe Beale. "Black Enterprise Magazine, Creating Economic Leaders for the World." [Online]. Harlem Live Web site www.harlemlive.org; McNeal, Natalie P. "Black Women's Economic Clout Increases." [Online, 14 February 2005]. Miami Herald Web site www.mcaon.com/mld/miamiherald.

Edwards, Tamala (?–)

Tamala Edwards is news anchor at Philadelphia's station WPVI-TV and prior to taking this job in January 2005, was anchor of ABC's "World News Now" and "World News This Morning." She was born in Georgia but grew up in Texas. Edwards received the B.A. with honors in international relations at Stanford University, where she worked on the student newspaper, and began her career as an intern-researcher with Time International in New York in 1993. In 1995, she moved to Washington to work as a reporter at *Time Magazine*'s bureau there and went with candidate Pat Buchanan to Alaska, reported on the candidacy of Sen. Phil Graham, and spent another part of her two-year tenure at the bureau following the unsuccessful 1996 presidential campaign of Bob Dole. Her reporting covered the hard-to-explain absence from the campaign of the candidate's wife, Elizabeth Dole, and the painful self-destruction of Sen. Dole as a candidate, with his sad and off-putting way of constantly referring to himself in third person. In 1997, the photogenic Edwards became a correspondent for ABC News, where she joined chief White House correspondent Terry Moran and covered the presidential campaigns of Vice President Al Gore and New Jersey's senator, Bill Bradley. Many American viewers met her as one of the panelists in the Apollo Theater debate between Bradley and Gore, where she focused attention on the black community's enthusiastic support for school vouchers, putting Gore on the spot by pointing out that while he opposed vouchers, his own son attended an expensive private school, Sidwell Friends. She also moderated the October 2000 debate held at Wake Forest University in Winston-Salem, North Carolina. Younger viewers got to know her from MTV's campaign "Choose or Lose," which was intended to boost the number of youthful voters, and she was also a frequent guest on the talk shows "Inside Politics," "Hardball with Chris Matthews" and "Washington Journal" and was a panelist on CNN's "Take Five," where she looked askance at President George W. Bush's push for faith-based initiatives, fearing a new wave of discrimination against non-Christians and gays. Apart from her campaign coverage, she specialized in religion, education and culture stories, usually for "World News Tonight" with anchor Peter Jennings and "Good Morning America." She also became an embedded reporter during the early part of the war in Iraq. She was one of a modest number of female embeds and was stationed with the 332nd Air Expeditionary Wing at an Air Force base at Tallil, near Nasiriyah, a base from which fighter pilots made bombing raids. Some critics accused her on being biased against the U.S. invasion of Iraq and the Bush administration's hawkish policies. Later, Edwards appeared as part of a panel at American University, along with Martin Turner, BBC's Washington bureau chief; Michael Getler, ombudsman for the *Washington Post*; and Capt. T. McCreary, public affairs advisor to the Joint Chiefs of Staff. The panel's topic was "Embedded Journalists: Is Truth the First Casualty of War?" Edwards' main contribution to the discussion was that the concept of embedded journalists produces very good human-interest material because of the reporter's close relationship with the troops, yet the individual reporter feels that she or he is reporting in a vacuum, not knowing what is taking place elsewhere in the war and lacking context for their news stories.

In December 2003, Edwards moved to New York and became anchor for "World News Now," the ABC overnight news program that was launched in 1992 and that combines serious news coverage with soft-news accounts of the odd, offbeat and amusing. She was one of several young anchors rotated through this late-night program with its undesirable work hours, and she also did some work for the network's "World News This Morning." In January 2005, she moved to Philadelphia to become morning coanchor with Matt O'Donnell for WPVI-TV, a property of the Disney Corporation, which also owns ABC. Over her career, Edwards has covered a great variety of stories: China's Madame Chang's visit to Washington, removal of home rule from the financially troubled District of Columbia, sexual harassment on college campuses, the lucrative college preparation industry, the increasing number of U.S. women philanthropists, the dangers to children of over-aggressive games of dodge ball, the anger of black voters at being either ignored or taken for granted in presidential election campaigns and the enormous growth of financially successful but unmarried women in the United States.

Further Readings: "ABC News Names Tamala Edwards 'World News Now' Anchor." [Online, 2 December 2003]. All Your TV Web site www.allyourtv.com; Emery, Mike. "War Leaves Family Members Watching, Wondering." [Online, 16 April 2001]. University of Houston Web site www.uh.edu; Huff, Richard. "The Nets' Gender Gulf: A Few Women Are Covering Conflict." [Online, 24 March 2003]. New York Daily News Web site www.nydailynews.com; Ponte, Lowell. "Odds and Ends." [Online, 23 April 2000]. Front Page Magazine Web site www.frontpagemag.com; "Tamala Edwards." [Online]. ABC News site http://abcnews.go.com.

Elder, Laurence (Larry) A. (1952–)

Syndicated columnist and radio/television personality Larry Elder was born and raised in South Los Angeles. He graduated from Brown University in 1974 with a degree in political science and earned a 1977 law degree at the University of Michigan. He joined a law firm in Cleveland, Ohio, then founded his own business Laurence A. Elder and Associates, which specialized in recruiting lawyers. In addition, he began his media career in Cleveland, hosting a talk show for PBS and later Fox. Clearly a conservative, although he prefers to call himself an independent, Elder writes a column distributed nationally by Creators Syndicate, has freelanced widely in newspapers, and publishes "The Elder Statement," a monthly newsletter.

The debonair Elder has been profiled on "60 Minutes" and has appeared on practically every television talk show, including "Larry King Live," "Oprah," "MacNeil-Lehrer," "Hard Copy," "The Today Show," and "Geraldo." He has been a presence on KABC Talk Radio in Los Angeles since 1994 and hosts the nationally syndicated "Larry Elder Show" daily on KABC 790. He has authored two books on public issues.

Elder has been one of President George W. Bush's staunchest defenders. In a column headlined "Two Americas"—Bush-Haters and the Rest of Us," Elder applauded vice-presidential candidate John Edwards' comment to the effect that there is really no red states, no blue states, just one United States of America. We do have two Americas, concludes Elder, in the sense of those who see President Bush as the exemplar of all that is decent, and those who despise him almost as much as Osama bin Laden.

Answering Sen. Ted Kennedy's charge about the invasion of Iraq—that the administration had told the public lie after lie—Elder replied that there are more self-reported conservatives today because the liberals keep getting things wrong. In the face of apparent lack of progress in Iraq and growing public unrest, Elder cites lessons from the past about the unpopularity of the earlier wars and conflicts, showing that World War II was the only war that enjoyed widespread public support. To critics of the Bush plan to partially privatize Social Security, thereby cutting benefits, Elder has responded by reframing the issue, suggesting that the Democrats do not seem to think that ordinary people have enough sense to manage their own money. In another column he crossed swords with Walter Cronkite as to what Elder sees as journalism's liberal bias. To attacks on President Bush for using religion to gain political advantage, Elder wrote a column that was ostensibly about Ronald Reagan's many mentions of his faith. This column never once mentioned President Bush, but was clearly written in his defense. When Sen. Hillary Rodham Clinton charged President Bush with trying to "undo the New Deal," Elder dubbed her "Shrillary" and described her "capacity to build falsehood upon exaggeration, upon anger." And when a variety of Hollywood liberals harshly criticized candidate Bush, Elder needled them for out-of-their-league naivety.

No fan of the Rev. Al Sharpton, Elder took a swipe at that flamboyant gentleman for responding to a slowing market for his main product, combating racism, by campaigning for KFC to treat chickens more humanely. Elder did, however, defend comedian Bill Cosby against University of Pennsylvania professor Michael Eric Dyson, author of the 2005 book *Is Bill Cosby Right? Or Has the Black Middle Class Lost Its Mind?* (New York: Basic Civitas), which castigates Cosby for unfairly attacking the poor and downtrodden. Elder also criticized the "Today Show" for its uneasy blend of journalism and entertainment, saying that Al Roker was the wrong choice for conducting an interview on such a serious topic as the Dyson-Cosby matter.

Elder has authored two books about contemporary American culture.

"Christmas Encounter with a 'Radical Socialist'" by Larry Elder

Moonie, my neighbor's cat, sits predictably outside my front door every morning at 7 A.M. Moonie expects breakfast, and if unhappy with that day's selection—fish, chicken, beef—Moonie sniffs indignantly and walks over to the front door and meows for his immediate release. Who knows where he goes? Perhaps he ravels back home or to yet another accommodating neighbor with more appealing offerings. Safe, happy, full and entitled, Moonie sometimes sunbathes in my driveway, requiring me to literally get out off the car and move him when the roar of the engine and the car's horn fail to rouse him.

One day last week, Moonie ate most of his ritual morning delicacies. I then went clothes shopping, taking my uncle and dad. He Lebanese store manager, Walid, waited on us and told a harrowing tale of how he came to America at age 7.

Neighboring Syrians assassinated the leaders of Lebanon, establishing a leadership more amenable to Syrian demands, which included taking Lebanese oil, leaving Lebanon with little compensation.

Syrian authorities routinely patrol Lebanon's streets, acting toward the Lebanese with Hussein-like arrogance and brutality. Many Christians live in Lebanon—including, at one time, the salesman—surrounded by Muslims, living an uncomfortable and frequently perilous day-to-day existence. For this reason, his family applied for a visa to America and waited over seven years before being accepted.

Moments after hearing the salesman's story, I ran into another shopper. Recognizing me from television and radio, the shopper said, "We probably won't like each other. I'm a committed radical socialist." Now understand the scene. This clothing store touts its high quality at reasonable prices.

Tell me, does my "radical socialist" understand that the American system of capitalism competition and free enterprise enable her to shop at this sore where she, like my father, my uncle and me, sought reasonably priced quality?

Did some bureaucrat at the Department of Labor or Commerce use command-and-control edicts to compel this hard-working Lebanese immigrant to improve himself? If the shopper drove to the store, she benefited from free-market competition between automakers. She used fuel resulting from the competition between oil discoverers, producers, refiners and retailers. And, frankly, given her ample girth, she did not appear to miss too many meals in America, despite her "radical socialist" view.

Some contrast. The appreciation for America shown by the Lebanese salesman vs. the lack of same demonstrated by the "radical socialist." The socialist showed little appreciation or understanding of the greatness of this country and its abundance, which results from economic freedom, separation of church and state, respect for individual rights, and relatively low taxes and regulation, all of which create an incentive for people like the Lebanese salesman to take risks that mutually benefit both himself and the "radical socialist."

This country allowed my father, a child of the Depression who never knew his biological father, to overcome Southern racism through pride, hard work and focus. My entrepreneurial-minded dad applied for a taxi license in a Southern court but was denied by the judge, who referred to my father as "a nigger."

Dad became a Marine in World War II, stationed as a cook on Guam, while America prepared for the invasion of the island of Japan, an invasion aborted by the dropping off the bombs on Hiroshima and Nagasaki. Yet when my dad returned to the South to get a job as a cook, the racist restaurant refused to hire him, claiming that he "lacked references."

My father applied the same attitude he later taught my brothers and me and said, "What can I do about it?" He then relocated to Los Angeles, a city he visited pre-war as a train Pullman porter, in a search for better employment opportunities. There, too, no restaurant hired him, claiming he "lacked references."

He went to an unemployment office, taking the first job that presented itself—that of a janitor. He worked that job for nearly 12 years, taking a second full-time janitor position elsewhere. He also went to night school three nights a week to get his G.E.D. He managed all this with a stay-at-home wife while raising three boys, finally saving enough to open his won café. Unlike our "radical socialist," he never complained about America's inequality, lack of opportunity or roadblocks placed in the paths of less-advantaged people.

Work hard, get an education, learn a trade, and don't make bad moral mistakes, he always told us. Don't blame others, and "the sky is wide open" if one only sees the opportunities.

Some, however, like the "radical socialist," shopper—and my neighbor's cat, Moonie—seem oblivious to the comfort, freedom and abundance that flow from America's historically unparalleled opportunities. At least Moonie, however, in an occasional display of affection, will from time to time rub against my leg in appreciation.

Source: Published by permission of Larry Elder and Creators Syndicate, Inc. This column originally appeared on 26 December 2003.

Books by Larry Elder: *The Ten Things You Can't Say in America* (New York: St. Martin's Press, 2000); *Showdown: Confronting Bias, Lies, and the Special Interests That Divide America* (New York: St. Martin's Press, 2002).

Further Readings: About Larry Elder [Online]. Creators Syndicate Web site. Creators.com/opinion.

Elie, Lolis Eric (10 April 1963–)

New Orleans *Times-Picayune* columnist Lolis Eric Elie is also a well-known food writer, especially in regard to that great American favorite, barbecue. A native of New Orleans, Elie has an undergraduate degree from the University of Pennsylvania's Wharton School of Finance and two masters degrees: one from the Columbia School of Journalism in New York, the other in creative writing from the University of Virginia. He has taught in both these academic areas at the University of Virginia and at Southern University in New Orleans. He worked for three years as a business reporter at the *Atlanta Journal & Constitution* and in 1989 and 1990, was assistant managing editor for the African/African-American arts journal *Callaloo*. Working for Operation Crossroads Africa, he conducted tours for U.S. college students during two summers; the groups worked on small agricultural, public health and construction projects. Prior to joining the *Times-Picayune* in 1995, he was road manager for New Orleans-born jazz great Wynton Marsalis, and it was at this time that he and photographer Frank Stewart planned their edited book *Smokestack Lightning: Adventures in the Heart of Barbecue Country*, which appeared in 1996 and contained a collection of 43 articles, columns, and poems. Elie's second, solo-authored barbecue book, *Cornbread Nation 2: the United States of Barbecue*, came out in 2004. Elie seems to view both barbecue and cornbread as a sort of a gustatory metaphor for life in the South. Both are foods that exhibit considerable regional diversity in the way they are prepared, and both are loved by blacks and whites alike. In short, he sees these foods as quintessentially American. A similar theme is evident in his 2003 column "Architecture Is a Gumbo of Cultures," in which he explained how Creole architecture in his home city is not simply French, but a blend of European and African influences, especially in joinery technique and in the intricate ironwork for which the city is noted.

Elie's column often concerns itself with cultural and artistic topics. He has cheered on such efforts as uptown jazz club Tipitina's efforts to raise money to help buy musical instruments for public school students who could not otherwise afford them and expressed disgust at a New Orleans statute that makes unsold art on consignment in galleries a taxable item for the artists—before the artworks are sold. He fondly remembered black musician Willie Metcalf Jr., who gave free lessons to young would-be jazz performers; Elie himself played guitar in Metcalf's Academy of Black Arts jazz group during part of his youth. In a city that has an enormous historic area filled with a curious mix of beautifully restored houses interspersed with houses that look virtually abandoned, Elie has written a glowing copy about pre-Hurricane Kristina restoration and revitalization projects, in either such neighborhoods as Algiers or Gert Town, or on once dilapidated but again thriving streets such as Dryades Street, now renamed after civil rights leader Oretha Haley. He has a dim view of professional sports in his city, and of Louisiana politicians in general, especially those who use tough-on-crime posturing to get elected and those who seem determined to make New Orleans look like "everywhere else, U.S.A."

"Messages Aplenty, But No Meeting" by Lolis Eric Elie

On May 27 of last year, my City Council person called me.

I had written about my trip to Udine, a city in northeastern Italy. I had wandered the streets of that old place, ignoring the art and architecture, devoting my full attention to the search for a parking space.

I quoted a traveling companion who said of Italy, "Tintorettos and Michelangelos, you can find everywhere," she said, "but a parking space..." I mused that the Italians would be wise to hire some of our City Council members as consultants.

Here in New Orleans, where our priorities are clear, our civic leaders would never let an old castle stand in the way if a developer thought a parking lot would look nice in its place.

Respect for Credentials

Jacquelyn Brechtel Clarkson was not amused. She said so in a voice-mail message. She wanted me to know that she had been elected by a large margin.

She praised her opponents in that race as a means of ensuring that I would fully comprehend the magnitude of her victory over such top-notch competition.

The people of the district respected her business credentials, she explained. The voters felt a person with her credentials was needed on the City Council.

Somewhere in Clarkson's voice message, I vaguely recall her saying something about her dedication to the preservation of the city's diminishing stock of historic buildings.

First-name Basis

Clarkson and I still haven't had a chance to talk about her philosophy.

I haven't been able to ask her about her efforts to ban tap dancers from the streets of the French Quarter. Nor have I been able to ask her about the alleged police harassment of homeless people in the Vieux Carre.

We had an appointment on Sept. 24, 2002, but she had to reschedule. We had another one Oct. 7, but something came up. Ditto for Feb. 28.

In the meantime, I have called Clarkson's appointment secretary so often that we are on a first-name basis.

Clarkson did call me once recently. She left a voice-mail message saying she liked one of my columns. Her message didn't include a suggested date for an actual conversation, however. Unfortunately, I didn't save that message or its predecessor.

Some of my friends have begun to doubt that I actually have a City Council representative. Each time Clarkson and I make an appointment, I tell them that I will take a picture of our meeting and prove that she exists. They just laugh.

They compare me to Linus, the Peanuts comic strip character who used to spend Halloween waiting for the Great Pumpkin.

"But my council member is real," I tell them. "Watch, I'll get an appointment with her before the end of the month."

"The end of the month?" they ask. "What a coincidence. That's when the Easter Bunny will be here."

Source: © 2005 *The Times-Picayune* Publishing Co. All rights reserved. Used with permission of *The Times-Picayune.* This column originally appeared on 11 April 2003.

Books by Lolis Erie Elie: Ed. With Frank Stewart, *Smokestack Lightning: Adventures in the Heart of Barbecue Country* (New York: North Point Press, 1996); *Cornbread Nation 2: The United States of Barbecue* (Chapel Hill, N.C.: University of North Carolina Press, 2004).

Further Readings: "America's Barbeculture: Who Owns It? Panel Discussion." [Online, 13 June 2004]. The Egullet Society for Culinary Arts & Letters Web site www.forums.egullet.com; Pendleton, Nicki. "Talkin' Pig with Food Writer Lolis Eric Elie." [Online]. BookPage Web site www.bookpage.com.

Ellington, E. David (?–)

Corporate and tax lawyer David Ellington is now trustee and commissioner of the San Francisco Employees Retirement System and before assuming that position was founder and CEO of NetNoir Inc, a venture capital-backed Internet service company specializing in African-American culture and lifestyles. He holds a B.A. in history from Adelphi University, an M.A. in comparative politics and government from Howard University and the J.D.

from Georgetown University Law Center, where he focused on international, corporate and tax law. In addition, he completed a year-long study of Japanese at Cornell University. He then opened his own law practice in Los Angeles specializing in international, new technology and multimedia entertainment law. He is a member of the State Bar of California and has been chairman of the international law component of the Beverly Hills Bar Association.

Ellington had a chance meeting with a man he describes as a "friend of a friend" who was working on a masters in computer science. The younger man, Malcolm CasSelle, gave Ellington a crash course in multimedia and CD-ROM technology, and the two men decided to start a business venture aimed at better involving African Americans in the digital revolution. By August 1994, they had put together a business plan and they obtained funding from America Online's Greenhouse Division. They named their company NetNoir Inc.; its central purpose was bringing African-American culture to a mainstream audience. Their multimedia service company provided media solutions and market research to other businesses that wanted to reach the black audience. With a staff of 25, they competed with Black Entertainment Television and BlackFamilies.com.

Next he turned his attention to a not-for-profit educational venture in response to a 1997 proposal from Dan Geiger, consultant to the Bay Area's Local Economic Assistance Program (LEAP). With financial help from LEAP, the two men cofounded OpNet, a high-tech training program for disadvantaged 17- to 24-year-olds in San Francisco. During the five-week course, students learn Photoshop, basic HTML programming skills, java-scripting and social skills, then are placed in a four-month paid internship with a multimedia company in the city. A little more than half of these internships have led to full-time jobs with good salaries and often with stock options. Ellington's hope is to help these students learn about wealth-building and how to invest.

In 1997, Ellington also became commissioner and president of the Telecommunications Commission for the City and County of San Francisco. Thereafter, he joined the board of the city's employee retirement system, SFERS, and in 2002–2003, chaired its governance committee and was on its alternative investments committee. He was board chairman in 2003 and 2004, then became trustee and commissioner for this fund, which has more than $13 billion in assets. He is active in local and state affairs and serves on the board of the San Francisco Jazz Organization, which produces the yearly San Francisco Jazz Festival, and is on the boards of the Commonwealth Club of California and CompuMentor, which gives technical help to companies or other entities involved in serving the disadvantaged. In 2001 and 2002, he was on the San Francisco Workforce Investment Board and in 2000 was a member of the Federal Trade Commission's Committee on Online Access and Security. He also served on the advisory board for Rutgers University's Center for Media Studies from 1999 to 2002. In 1996, he was recipient of *Black Enterprise* magazine's Entrepreneurs Award for having been Innovator of the Year.

Further Readings: "Can E-Biz Become as Diverse as America?" [Online, 16 September 1999]. Business Week e.biz Web site www.businessweek.com/ebiz; "E. David Ellington." [Online]. Graduating Engineer & Computer Careers Web site www.graduatingengineer.com; "E. David Ellington." [Online, 2005]. Kauffman Foundation's Entre World Web site www.entreworld.org/Content/AuthorsBio; Ellington, E. David. "Giving Resources to Create Wealth." [Online, June 2000]. Entire World.org Web site www.inc.com; Krigel, Beth Lipton. "NetNoir Expands Offerings." [Online, 24 November 1997]. CNET Networks, Inc. site http://news.com.com; "Redefining Leadership: Letting Go." [Online]. Chief Executive Web site www.chiefexecutive.net/specialreport/lettinggo.

Estes-Sumpter, Sidmel Karen (27 November 1954–)

With WAGA-TV/Fox Five News since 1987 and currently executive producer of its highly rated morning show "Good Day, Atlanta," Sidmel Estes-Sumpter was also the first woman elected president of the National Association of Black Journalists (NABJ). She was born in Marysville, California, and was a 1976 honor graduate of Northwestern University's Medill School of Journalism, where she also received her masters in 1977. During her years at Medill, she worked part-time as a reporter for the *Chicago Daily Defender* in 1974 and in 1975 as a desk assistant for the *Chicago Daily News*. She was a founder of both a new campus literary magazine, *New Sense*, and *Blackboard*, a newsletter for Medill's African-American journalism students. Her first job after graduation was reporting, anchoring and producing for Guam Cable TV. A year later she became an assignment editor for WAGA-TV/Fox Five in Atlanta. She was elevated to associate producer and still later to producer of "Eyewitness News" and in 1993, was named executive producer of "Good Day, Atlanta." Two years before, in 1991, at age 36, she became the first woman to lead NABJ after having been a regional director for this organization and since 1982, a member of the Atlanta Association of Black Journalists, which she had also served as president. Following her term as president of NABJ, she became president of Unity, a more inclusive organization of minority journalists that includes African-American, Hispanic, Asian and Native American media people. The first Unity convention was held in 1994 in Atlanta, with an attendance of 6,000. She has also been an adjunct faculty member, teaching journalism at Emory University, a Robert R. McCormick Tribune Foundation Fellow in 2000 and owner of her own media management company, BreakThrough Inc., in Atlanta.

Estes-Sumpter has been a board member of the Atlanta Press Club and has been active with her city's chapter of NAACP, Leadership Atlanta, Atlanta Exchange and the Society of Professional Journalists. In addition, she has been active in support of her alma mater, helping found the first student chapter of NABJ there, serving on the Medill board of advisors and Northwestern's Black Alumni Association and diversity council. In 1997, she became a charter member of the Medill School's Hall of Achievement. She has been accorded an impressive list of other honors. In 1988, Atlanta Mayor Andrew Young declared 18 November "Sidmel Estes-Sumpter Day," and in that same year, the National Association of Media Women named her Media Woman of the Year. Atlanta's Association of Black Journalists gave her its Pioneer Black Journalist Award in 1990, and in 1992, *Crisis Magazine* gave her its award for Lifetime Achievement and *Ebony* magazine listed her among the 100 most influential African Americans.

Further Readings: "A Salute to NABJ's Presidents: Sidmel Estes-Sumpter." [Online]. National Association of Black Journalists site http://members.nabj.org; "Alumni Service Award: Sidmel Estes-Sumpter." [Online]. Northwestern University site http://alumni.northwestern.edu; Davis, April. "News Coverage Still Misses Minorities, Speakers Say." [Online, 12 June 2000]. Freedom Forum Web site www.freedomforum.org.

F

Fancher, Faith (23 August 1950–19 October 2003)

Faith Fancher, who died at age 53 in 2003 after a six-year battle with breast cancer, was a long-time television reporter in Oakland, California, and earlier had been the first African-American television reporter in Knoxille, Tennessee. She was born in Franklin, Tennessee, and was a graduate of the St. Francis de Salle Boarding School for Girls in Powatan, Virginia, and a 1972 summa cum laude graduate of the University of Tennessee at Knoxville, where she had majored in English and education. In 1973, she was hired by Knoxville station WBR becoming the city's first black reporter; one of her competitors for the job was Oprah Winfrey. In Knoxville, Fancher also worked for station WSM-TV. Later she moved to Washington, D.C., and became the first African-American woman to work in CNN's D.C. bureau. She also reported for the National Black Network and for National Public Radio and married NPR colleague William Drummond, who is now a professor of journalism at the University of California, Berkeley. In 1983, the couple moved to the San Francisco Bay area, where Fancher was employed as a coanchor on the 10 o'clock news for station KTVU-TV. According to one of her colleagues there, she was often given the tough, gritty stories, such as executions at San Quentin, and was considered the station's best live reporter. On the personal side, she is remembered as a warm, positive person with a mega-watt smile and a hearty laugh.

In May 1997, Fancher was diagnosed with breast cancer. She decided to go public with her health troubles in the hope of convincing other women to be more attentive regarding early detection, and partially, she said, because in her long broadcast career, she had stuck her mike in front of so many other people at times when they might have preferred privacy. With her friend and coanchor Elaine Corral Kendall, she documented her seven operations: lumpectomy, mastectomy and reconstructive surgery, as well as radiation and chemotherapy treatments. Surgeries and treatments left her too weak to continue on the air—she retired in September 1997—but during her years of remissions and recurrences, she not only continued to make her experiences public on KTVU, but helped attract donations to help others through the Friends of Faith, an organization of area media people who raised around $750,000. The funds went to area clinics and agencies dedicated to helping low-income women who had breast cancer. Friends of Faith also established the East Bay Breast Cancer Emergency Fund, which made direct small grants to pay for rent and groceries, cab fare, child care, medical insurance premiums and medical costs for disadvantaged women suffering from this disease. Fancher was concerned that although African-American women are somewhat less likely to contract breast cancer, they are more apt to die from it, largely due to insufficient access to medical care. She continued to make public appearances, bald of head but still bright of smile, to lobby for more funds and to increase public awareness of breast cancer. She was emcee of a benefit for Circle of Care, a support group for children and families of breast cancer victims and in 2002, was the keynote speaker at a symposium held by the California Breast Cancer Research Program, the nation's largest state-funded research program dedicated to fighting this disease. She also took part in the annual fund-raising efforts of the Oakland A's baseball team to help fund research and treatment efforts.

Fancher won numerous honors, including local Emmys, the 1991 Scripps-Howard Foundation's National Award for Journalistic Excellence in Radio News, the Bay Area Black Media Coalition's 1993 Beverly Johnson Award, the California division of the American Cancer Society's 1998 Excalibur Award, and also in 1998, the Sojourner Truth Award given by the San Francisco Business and Professional Women. Also, the California Breast Cancer Research Program created an annual research award in her honor: the Faith Fancher Award. Fancher died in her home in October 2003.

Thank you. I have always wanted to make an entrance into Survivor since I heard Destiny's Child. I have been thinking very hard since I was asked to talk to you about what I could say to such a distinguished group of researchers, doctors, nurses, experts from all across the country on the subject of breast cancer. What could I add to the body of knowledge that hasn't already been said? And then it hit me. I am an expert in one thing. I have faced breast cancer up close and personal, and I am still living to tell the tale.

So sit back and relax and get ready for one hell of a story, because it continues to be one hell of a journey. Oh, yeah, better tighten your seatbelts because it is going to be a bumpy and interesting ride.

I call cancer the B-goddess, and I can tell you the B does not stand for beautiful. I first met the B in March of 1997. She didn't have the decency to wait for a formal introduction... just a routine mammogram, and bam, you've got breast cancer.

Now, there are two ways you can react to the worst news of your life. You can despair and wail at the fates... pull the covers over our head, or you can stand up and find your courage and fight back.

I decided that the B was no match for my faith and the journey began.

It continues to be a surprising journey that has taught me more than I ever imagined...a formula for survival that is working for me.

It begins with three words that are very hard for many of us to say: I need help. I have always been good at giving help but accepting it, now that is a different story. But when I said those words, first to myself and then out loud to others, magical things began to happen.

Source: The above untitled remarks were made on 2 March 2002 by Faith Fancher as part of a mainly extemporaneous speech before a cancer support group. They appear here by permission of her surviving husband, Bill Drummond.

Further Readings: Ashley, Guy. "Faith Fancher Eulogized in Oakland." [Online, 23 October 2003]. Contra Cosa Times Web site www.contracostatimes.com; "Faith Fancher Loses Battle with Cancer." [Online, 19 October 2003]. KTVU.Com Web site www.ktvu.com/news; Montague, Ave with Kelly and Pan McDonald. "About Faith." [Online]. SF Bay View.com Web site www.sfbayview.com; Walsh, Diana. "KTVU's Faith Fancher—Breast Cancer." [Online, 20 October 2003]. San Francisco Chronicle Web site www.sfgate.com.

Faulkner, Harris (1965–)

In February 2006, Harris Faulkner became news anchor of Fox News. In March 2005, she had become a correspondent for the then-new Fox magazine-format show "A Current Affair." Prior to that time, she was best known for her work at WDAF-TV in Kansas City, where she had been a reporter and anchor. She was born at Fort McPherson in the Atlanta area. Her father was an Army pilot, and she and her mother lived for three years in Stuttgart, Germany, awaiting her father's return from duty in Vietnam. She and her family returned to the United States in 1969, and Faulkner attended the University of California at Santa Barbara, where she studied both mass communications and business administration. She began her work life as an accountant in Los Angeles and later became a freelance business writer for the *L.A. Weekly*. After a reporter for KCLP-TV told her that her voice was well suited to broadcasting, she secured an internship at this station and at first worked behind the cameras. Her good looks got her some on-camera experience at KCLP, which in turn helped her get a full-time job as a general assignment reporter at station WNCT-TV in Greenville, North Carolina. At this point her family was living in Texas and in order to live nearer them, she relocated to Kansas City in 1992 for a reporting job at WDAF-TV. She moved into anchoring the news at this station, but her time on this job was marred by an experience with a stalker. The man was someone she had dated while living in North Carolina, a coworker at WNCT. She had ended the relationship, but the man followed her to Kansas City, moved across the street from where she was living, began phoning her 50 or 60 times a night and repeatedly sent her flowers. He refused her requests to be let alone, vandalized her car and threatened other men she dated. Finally, she discovered that he had been breaking into her apartment while she was out. He was arrested and jailed, but after being released, he resumed his stalking. In 2000, he finally stopped calling, yet she worries that even though she is now married, he might someday reappear. This terrible experience led Faulkner to become a motivational speaker in an attempt to help other women who are the victims of stalkers. Her positive message to the effect that bad experiences often can make us stronger people also found its way into a book published in 1999: *Breaking News: God Has a Plan. An Anchorwoman's Journey Through Faith.* In 2001, she sold rights to the book to AOL Time Warner Telepictures division. She held the primary evening news anchor job at WDAF until 2000, when she moved up to take the same job in a bigger market, Minneapolis/St. Paul, where she worked at KSTP-TV and KSTC-TV through 2004. In May 2003, she began coanchoring with Asian-American newscaster Kent Ninomiya. In 2002, she also began hosting the "Harris Faulkner Show" in Twin Cities, Minnesota, on all-talk station FM 107. In February 2005, she moved to New York City where she, Tina Malave and Michel James Bryant became correspondents for "A Current Affair," a nationally syndicated new program on Fox. She was an occasional host of "Court TV" and a newsreader for the Fox News Channel. Then in February 2006, she became news anchor of Fox News and a relief host of "A Current Affair."

Faulkner has been interviewed about her stalker experience on "The Montel Williams Show," and was on the A&E show "Investigative Reports with Bill Curtis" and has guest-hosted the "Nancy Grace Show." She has won six Emmy awards. Stories she has covered have included natural disasters: tornadoes, floods, snow storms and hurricanes; the Oklahoma City bombing of 1995; the air crash that killed Minnesota Sen. Paul Wellstone in 2002; and the 2005 disappearance in Aruba of 18-year-old Natalee Holloway. Liberal viewers of her work on highly conservative Fox News accuse her of being a "patsy" for the Bush administration and an apologist for Halliburton and its controversial no-bid contracts associated with the war effort in Iraq, but she volunteers time for worthy projects such as having coemceed the Twin Cities' Oscar-related fundraiser to benefit the Minnesota AIDS project and Planned Parenthood. She has also served as emcee of Minnesota's Human Rights Day.

Books by Harris Faulkner: *Breaking News: God Has a Plan. An Anchorwoman's Journey Through Faith* (Overland Park, Kansas: Leathers Pub, 1999).

Further Readings: Barnhart, Aaron. "Faulkner Puts Rumor on Ice." [Online, 22 February 2001]. The Kansas City Star Web site ww.icriticus.com; "Introducing Harris Faulkner." [Online, 23 March 2006]. Fox News.com Web site www.foxnews.com; Prince, Richard. "Asian-Black Anchor Team in Minneapolis." [Online, 9 May 2003]. Richard Prince's Journal-isms. Maynard Institute Web site www.maynardije.org; Prince, Richard. "Harris Faulker Joins 'A Current Affair.'" [Online, 2 March 2005]. Richard Price's Journal-isms. Maynard Institute Web site www.maynardije.org.

Fennell, Arthur (1954–)

The dapper Arthur Fennell is principal anchor and managing editor of the Comcast Network's CN8 News in Philadelphia. He was born into a family of 12 children; spent his boyhood in Bennettsville, South Carolina; and remained in his home state for his bachelor's degree, which he earned in 1982 in communications and dramatic arts at South Carolina State College (now University) in Orangeburg. His early work life included posts with WBTW-TV in Florence, S.C.; the South Carolina Educational Television Network; Charleston, S.C., station WCBD-TV; Savannah, Georgia's WSAV-TV, and WAVY-TV in Portsmouth, Virginia. After working in Portsmouth, he relocated to Philadelphia and station WCAU-TV, where he was a news anchor. At NBC 10 in Philadelphia, he held a variety of jobs: reporter, anchor and producer. In 1997, he left NBC 10 to found his own media consulting firm and some time later, went with Comcast's CN8, anchoring a regional news show at 7 and 10 PM.

Fennell has received a reported 75 awards, one of which was the Philadelphia Association of Black Journalists' Vanguard Award. He was founding president of the Hampton Roads Black Media Professionals group, belongs to the Philadelphia local chapter of the National Association of Black Journalists and has served as a regional director of NABJ. From 1995 to 1997, he was this organization's national president—its first president who was an on-air broadcaster. He led the organization through successful fundraising; relocated the national office from Reston, Virginia, to the University of Maryland at College Park; appointed a committee charged with creating a five-year plan for the organization; presided over the founding of the NABJ Institute; mounted two conventions—in Nashville and Chicago—that paid for themselves; and increased national publicity for NABJ, such as when he arranged for the organization's awards ceremony to be taped for airing on Black Entertainment Television. He also arranged for President Bill Clinton to appear at the Chicago convention, the first presidential visit to an NABJ meeting. He held off Secret Service demands to scale back the size and duration of an awards luncheon meeting and successfully negotiated a similar problem when security people for the Nation of Islam wanted to body-search NABJ members before they could enter a session in which Louis Farrakhan was to speak. Fennell has also made appearances with then vice president Al Gore, presidential candidate Bob Dole and nationally known defense lawyer Johnnie Cochran.

Fennell has done consulting on communication skills and image enhancement and has worked briefly as an adjunct instructor of communications for Delaware State University. He founded the Arthur Fennell Foundation in 2001 to help raise funds for education about and prevention of chronic diseases to the benefit of such organizations as the American Cancer Society, the American Heart Association and the Sickle Cell Anemia Society. The foundation's primary annual fundraiser has been the Arthur Fennell Celebrity Billiards Championship, which in 2003, became the Arthur Fennell and Kenny Gamble Celebrity Billiards Championship; part of the proceeds now go to the charities supported by music writer/producer and founder of Philadelphia International Records company Gamble, whose Universal Companies community development corporation benefits the rebuilding of urban America. Celebrity participants have included such music figures as Pat Croce, Kathy Sledge and the group Boyz II Men, as well as quarterback Donovan McNabb and other standouts from Philadelphia's various professional sports teams. The billiards fundraiser is aired as a one-hour special on CN8. In a January 1996 article published in *Ebony* magazine, Fennell addressed the question of how African Americans might prepare for the next 50 years. He commented on such topics as changes in technology, work decentralization, job shrinkage in the United States and consequent downsizing, and the improved yet lingering problem of racism. In 1995, he appeared in the movie "Twelve Monkeys," playing a role he knows well: anchorman.

Further Readings: "About Arthur Fennell." [Online]. CN8 The Comcast Network Web site www.cn8.tv/channel; "Arthur Fennell." [Online, 4 August 2004]. Unity Online Web site www.unityjournalists.org; Hendren, Lee. "TV Anchor Recalls Lessons Learned at SCSU." [Online]. South Carolina State University Web site www.scsu.edu; Lowe, Herbert. "A Salute to NABJ's Presidents: Arthur Fennell." [Online]. National Association of Black Journalists site http://members.nabj.org.

Ferguson, Renee (22 August 1949–)

Since March 1987, Renee Ferguson has been an award-winning investigative and general-assignment reporter for NBC5 News at WMAQ-TV in Chicago. She might very well be the first African American to be assigned as a full-time broadcast investigative reporter. She was born in Oklahoma City and in 1971 and earned the B.A. in journalism at Indiana University. Later, she had journalism fellowships at the University of Chicago and the University of Southern California. She worked initially in the newspaper business as a reporter for the *Indianapolis News* during 1971 and 1972. She moved to broadcasting working as a reporter from 1972 until 1976 at Indianapolis station WLWI-TV. This job led to a position in a bigger market, Chicago, where she reported until 1982 for station WBBM-TV. Thereafter, she was a CBS reporter working out of New York and Atlanta before taking her present job in 1987 with WMAQ-TV. During her more than 30 years in news, she has been the recipient of many honors, mainly for her investigative stories. For one such story,

Ferguson did undercover work on charges of sexual harassment at Ford Motor Company plants; her story resulted in a class action lawsuit and eventually, a multimillion-dollar settlement. Another of her stories began when she received a call from an angry African-American woman who had been strip-searched for drugs by U.S. Customs officials at Chicago's O'Hare Airport. Officials had been profiling—mainly black airline passengers. Ferguson discovered that roughly 2,000 such strip searches had occurred and that blacks were being disproportionately targeted. Drugs were found in about one-fourth of these searches, but in three-fourths of the cases, individuals had been embarrassed or humiliated needlessly. Congressional hearings resulted, new training was given to Customs workers and $9 million was spent on body-scanning devices to reduce the need for airport strip-searching. Another of her investigations looked into corruption in Chicago's Head Start Program, and still another examined working conditions in the city's water-treatment plants. She has also done stories on problems with guns and drugs at a Chicago high school, the use of children in clinical drug tests and allegations of guns and drugs taken from a police property room in Gary, Indiana. Her investigative work helped in the 1995 arrest of serial killer Hubert Geralds, who had killed seven women, and a documentary she did profiled a group of school children from Chicago public housing projects who visited West Africa. Ferguson also went to South Africa to cover that nation's first race-free elections.

Ferguson has won a total of seven Emmys in Chicago, the Goldsmith Award from Harvard's Kennedy School of Government, the American Women in Radio and Television's Gracie Award, a Best Investigative Reporting Award from the Associated Press and the national Alfred I. duPont-Columbia Award, plus awards from the National Association of Black Journalists and from this organization's Chicago chapter. She has been recognized by the American Civil Liberties Union, the Lawyers Committee for Civil Rights Under the Law, the National Organization for Women and the Black Women's Lawyers Association in Chicago. Ferguson is on the board of directors of Criminal Justice Journalists, the national organization of journalists who work in a variety of media, covering crime, the courts and prisons.

Fields, Michael (?–)

Since May 1999, Michael Fields has been Southern bureau chief for National Public Radio. He is, as of early 2007, the only person to hold that job. Fields hails from Washington, D.C., and earned a 1969 B.A. from Swarthmore College in Pennsylvania. After graduating, he worked for three years as a freelance writer/photographer leaving this difficult pursuit for another tough job: teaching emotionally challenged children at a private school in Washington, D.C.

Fitzpatrick, Albert E.

His radio career began in 1979 at WGBH-FM in Boston. He was director of public affairs for this NPR member station before moving to another NPR station in the city, WBUR-FM, where he was a reporter and later a producer and assistant news director. He again moved to a new station in 1982: WEEI-AM, an all-news station where he became executive editor and producer of the midday news show. Four years later, he took a job with NPR as assistant producer of "All Things Considered." He became associate producer of this show a year later and in 1989, became Midwest editor for the NPR national desk, with responsibility for covering eight states. He took over the Southern region in 1992 and in 1993 was promoted to deputy senior editor of the national desk. From 1997 to late 1998 his title was acting senior editor of the network's national desk. Then in May 1999, he assumed his present position at the time the Southern bureau was set up in Atlanta. He was charged with increasing coverage of the nation's large Southeast region and to do so, works with the network's own reporters, individual NPR stations in the region and freelancers.

Some of the major stories Fields has reported for NPR include the April 1993 storming of the Branch Davidian compound in Waco, Texas, in which religious cult leader David Koresh and 80 followers perished by fire; the 1994 elections in South Africa; the 1995 bombing of the Oklahoma City Federal Building by Timothy McVeigh and Terry Nichols that killed 168 people; and domestic terrorism at the 1996 Atlanta Olympics perpetrated by Eric Rudolph. Fields' work has been recognized by a Robert F. Kennedy award, a John S. Knight fellowship at Stanford and two Silver Baton awards from the Alfred I. duPont Columbia University awards program. Fields' part in the banning from further NPR exposure of Steven Emerson, authority on Islamic extremism and producer of the PBS documentary "Jihad in America," brought him considerable criticism in 2001. Emerson had appeared in 1998 in an NPR "Talk of the Nation" interview after having been blacklisted by the network; Fields was quoted as saying that the Emerson appearance had been a mistake and would not be repeated. Emerson had been branded an anti-Islam bigot by various American Muslim organizations. NPR in general has often been accused of favoring the Palestinian side of the Arab-Israeli conflict.

Further Readings: "Michael Fields, Southern Bureau Chief." [Online]. National Public Radio Web site www.npr.org.

Fitzpatrick, Albert E. (30 December 1928–)

Retired Akron *Beacon Journal* and Knight Ridder executive Al Fitzpatrick will be remembered for his efforts to foster African-American leadership talent in newspaper work and for his service as president of the National Association of Black Journalists. He was born in Elyria, Ohio, in the Cleveland suburbs, wrote sports copy while in high school, served six years in first the Army and then the Air Force and received the B.A. in journalism and sociology in 1956 at Kent State University. Following graduation, he became a reporter for the Akron *Beacon Journal*, where he was the sole African American in the newsroom. Then, through 1984, he moved through a succession of other positions. He was assistant news editor, moving up to news editor in 1970; in this position he directed coverage of the Kent State protest in which National Guard troops shot and killed four student demonstrators. For its coverage of this story, the *Beacon Journal* won a Pulitzer Prize for reporting. He worked briefly as city editor, then in 1973 as managing editor—the first African American to hold this position with a mainstream metropolitan newspaper. In 1977, he became the paper's executive editor. In 1985, he was named Knight-Ridder's director of minority affairs and in 1987, he relocated to Miami to become this organization's assistant vice president for minority affairs.

The genial Fitzpatrick was president of the still-young NABJ from 1985 to 1987. His connections with mainstream journalism helped secure new funding. His primary initiative was to raise enough money to secure space for the organization's headquarters. Thanks in large part to contributions from the Knight Foundation and the Gannett Foundation, the NABJ moved into offices in Reston, Virginia, in the same building as the American Newspaper Publishers Association and the American Society of Newspaper Editors. During Fitzpatrick's presidency, the number of scholarships the organization sponsored doubled and membership reached 1,000.

In 1991, Fitzpatrick became the founding chairman of the National Association of Minority Media Managers, an organization that was the brainchild of his associate Carl Morris, whom he had hired as NABJ's executive director. The purpose of the new organization was to foster management talent among African Americans working in a variety of media. One of its programs is the Albert E. Fitzpatrick Leadership Development Institute, which provides short courses for aspiring media executives. Fitzpatrick is the institute's dean.

During 1979 and 1980, he taught on the journalism faculty of Northwestern University's Medill School, and after his retirement from Knight Ridder, he taught again, this time at Kent State, where in 2006, he was an adjunct professor. He was president of the Akron Press Club from 1981 to 1983 and has served on the boards of the Boy Scouts of America, the American Cancer Society and the Center on Economics Education. He has been honored with both the Ida B. Wells Award and the Frederick Douglass Lifetime Achievement Award given by the NABJ, the Outstanding Alumnus Award and the Community Service Award from Kent State University, and, in 2004, the American Journalism Historians Association Local Journalists Award for career accomplishment. In October 2005, he was accorded the Robert G. McGruder Award for fostering media diversity; the award is given by the Kent State School of Journalism and Mass Communication and was created by Knight Ridder. In April 2006, he was named a member of the NABJ Hall of Fame. Fitzpatrick now lives in semi-retirement in Akron.

Further Readings: Dotson, John L. Jr. "A Salute to NABJ's Presidents: Al Fitzpatrick." [Online]. National Association of Black Journalists Web site www.nabj.org; "Former Akron Beacon Journal Editor Al Fitzpatrick Named Recipient of 2005 McGruder Award for Media Diversity at Kent State University." [Online, 19 October 2005]. Kent State University site http://imagine.kent.edu/media.

Fletcher, Michael A. (?–)

Michael Fletcher is White House reporter for the *Washington Post* and has worked for this paper since 1995. He was born and grew up in New York City, went to public schools there and is a graduate of Boston University. Prior to joining the *Post*. He reported for 13 years for the *Baltimore Sun*, for which he covered state government and city hall in Baltimore. His initial assignment for the *Post* was covering education and racial issues. He and *Post* colleague Kevin Merida have coauthored a book for Doubleday about Supreme Court Justice Clarence Thomas.

In April 2000, Fletcher and Philip P. Pan wrote on the split in the Latino community caused by the Elian Gonzalez controversy as to whether the boy should remain in the United States or be returned to his native Cuba. A story Fletcher wrote a month after the September 2001 World Trade Center disaster examined the shrinkage in tolerance on university campuses for critics of U.S. foreign policy. It was a time of increased conformity when disagreement with Bush administration policy was seen by many Americans as unpatriotic. A June 2002 Fletcher story was about an Ohio proposal that would require teaching "intelligent design" alongside evolution in the state's schools, and later that summer, he and Kevin Merida published "The Lonely Stand of Clarence Thomas" in the 4 August issue of the *Washington Post Magazine*. An insightful story written by Fletcher in May 2003 was on a damned if you do, damned if you don't topic: the practice on some U.S. college and university campuses of holding separate graduation ceremonies for African-American students, as well as for Latino and Asian-American graduates. Critics call it a new form of segregation, namely, self-segregation; proponents say that these ceremonies are merely a way to foster pride and give special recognition to minority students. In October 2004, the *Post* ran two stories on Clarence Thomas, written by Fletcher and Kevin Merida. Early in 2005, Fletcher wrote about the Bush administration's ill-fated plans to partially privatize Social Security. In a July 2005 story, Fletcher reported on then-Supreme Court nominee John Roberts and whether he had or had not been a member of the Federalist Society for Law and Public Policy, a group of right-leaning law students who have helped put the conservative in "compassionate conservative" for more than two decades. In September of that year, Fletcher and Richard Morin wrote about the political damage to President Bush's approval ratings following the federal government's limp reaction to the immense damage caused by Hurricane Katrina. Continuing to collaborate with fellow *Post* staffers, Fletcher wrote with Charles Babington on Supreme Court nominee Samuel Alito, who had just indicated that if seated on the Court, he would be unlikely to vote to overturn the 1973 Roe v. Wade abortion ruling, and in May 2006, he and Jonathan Weisman reported on President Bush's plan to use the National Guard to tighten the U.S. border with Mexico and slow illegal immigration.

"The New Segregation" by Michael Fletcher

As the master of ceremonies called their names, the black seniors proudly strode to the front of the room to receive colorful pieces of kente cloth marking their impending graduation from the University of Pennsylvania.

The students solemnly called out the names of their elders as poet and social worker Kamau McRae poured water on a plant in an African libation ritual. Afterward, the students laughed and cried as they leafed through their black student yearbooks and offered heartfelt tributes to their favorite professors, to staff members and to one another.

The presentation of the class of 2003 was the central event at this year's Black Senior Celebration. The ceremony here, attended by almost half of the university's 140 black graduating seniors, followed separate celebrations that honored Asian American and Latino seniors in the weeks leading up to Penn's general graduation ceremony today. University officials say these racially and ethnically themed ceremonies are a way for minority students to celebrate their cultural connections as well as their ability to overcome the special challenges they face at predominantly white universities.

"Our students need the support they get from one another," said Patricia Williams, dean of the W.E.B. Du Bois College House, a Penn dormitory geared toward the exploration of African American culture. "Often, they don't receive the same recognition and psychological support as other students at the university."

But opponents of these separate ceremonies see them as a manifestation of self-segregation, which they say is too common at colleges and universities that proudly cite their racial diversity. It is a debate that has swirled at the nation's colleges since black, Latino and Asian American students became a substantial presence on campus a generation ago. But it is taking on new significance as the higher education community braces for the Supreme Court's decision in coming weeks on two cases that challenge the legality of race-conscious college admissions.

This year, various schools are hosting racially separate graduation events, in addition to their regular ceremonies. Vanderbilt University had a separate recognition ceremony for black graduates. Washington University in St. Louis hosted a black senior alliance ceremony. The University of Michigan and Michigan State University held black celebratory ceremonies. Stanford University will host a black graduation ceremony next month, and the University of California at Berkeley hosted its Black Graduation on Saturday. Many other schools also have special ceremonies honoring Latino and Asian American students.

"The fact that these ceremonies are so prevalent nicely shows that the common defense of racial preferences—that it puts whites and blacks on the same campus to learn about and become comfortable with each other—is senseless," said John H. McWhorter, a UC-Berkeley professor who is an outspoken critic of race-conscious college admissions. "On the contrary, campuses are precisely where many black students learn a new separatist conception of being 'black' that they didn't have before."

College officials say the ceremonies offer a way for minority students to support and recognize one another in an environment that they often find isolating. Black and Latino students, particularly, are far more likely not to finish college than whites or Asian Americans. While educators blame that on flaws in the academic preparation of some black and Latino students, they also say students are more likely to founder if they feel adrift at predominantly white schools.

"When black students come together, the assumption is often that they are being separatist," said Karlene Burrell-McRae, director off the Makuu Black Cultural Resource Center, which organized the black graduation celebration at Penn. "But the reality is that they are full members of the university community who take on responsibility for contributing to their community while also contributing to the larger community."

Ajay T. Nair, director of the Pan-Asian American Community House and director of Asian American studies at Penn, called the separate celebrations a way to honor students who might otherwise be overlooked. Earlier this month, the house hosted a 150-guest celebration for the Asian graduates.

"We are celebrating the graduation of students who have a specific interest," he said. "It probably is not realistic to expect these students to be recognized in the larger context of the university."

But some opponents of affirmative action argue that although many of the nation's colleges now have substantial minority populations, those students often operate in parallel worlds that are frequently defined by race or ethnicity. They attend the same classes, these opponents say, but they often are members of separate fraternities, sororities and cultural centers, they study in separate groups, they eat at segregated dining tables and they unwind at separate parties.

Ward Connerly, a member of the University of California Board of Regents and a leading opponent of affirmative action, called separate graduation ceremonies part of a well-intentioned but counterproductive approach to diversity.

"These celebrations are part of a larger context of cultural centers, black orientations, black studies, black housing," he said. "They are part of an infrastructure of programs aimed at making students feel welcome. The problem is that this whole entourage of efforts has formed to isolate students in cultural ghettos."

Surveys have found that students are no more likely to closely engage one another across racial lines when they finish college than when they arrive. The National Survey of Black Student Engagement [A correction published on 10 June showed that this survey was actually The National Survey of Student Engagement.] released last fall found that 50 percent of college freshmen reported "often" having serious conversations with a student of another race or ethnicity. The same survey found that 49 percent of seniors reported the same level of interracial dialogue.

With a freshman class last year that was 43 percent minority, the University of Pennsylvania has a long history of supporting racial diversity and allowing students to gather in culturally and racially separate support centers. There is the Hillel House, a cultural center for Jewish students, the Newman Center, which promotes Catholic traditions, and the W.E.B. Du Bois College House, which holds black cultural forums and houses about a quarter of the university's black students, according to the Journal of Blacks in Higher Education.

Penn officials say that type of diversity is indispensable to the learning environment at any world-class institution.

"Our mission, at its core, is to educate. And we believe that homogeneity stifles learning," said a statement on affirmative action issued by Judith Rodin, president of the University of Pennsylvania, and James S. Riepe, chairman of the university's board of trustees.

Makuu, the black student center at Penn, teaches study skills and publishes a directory of black faculty members and a black resource guide to the university.

"The students describe Makuu as a safe space," said director Burrell-McRae. "It is a place where they don't have to explain who they are."

And for the past two years, it has hosted black graduation celebrations. The cost of the celebration is negligible: about $2,000, mainly for kente cloths and a sumptuous buffet. Penn is paying for the celebration, as many schools do. For the students, it is one of the high points of their senior year.

"Being at Penn has not been easy for me," said Nicole Andrewin, 21, an accounting major who helped plan the celebration. "Penn can be a place where you can more easily get lost if you're not in the majority. This celebration is a way for us to say to each other, 'Congratulations, we made it.'"

Source: © 2003, *The Washington Post*. Reprinted with permission. The above story appeared on 19 May 2003.

Books by Michael A. Fletcher: With Merida, Kevin. *Supreme Discomfort: The Divided Soul of Clarence Thomas* (New York: Doubleday, 2007).

Further Readings: A. Cillizza, Chris. "Post Politics Hour: Wonky vs. Warm from the Bully Pulpit." [Online, 27 March 2006]. Washington Post blog site http://blog.washingtonpost.com.

Fraser, Charles Gerald Jr. (30 July 1925–)

C. Gerald Fraser, now in his eighties, writes for the *San Diego Earth Times*, spent 28 years working at the *New York Daily News* and the *New York Times*, began his career at the historically black New York *Amsterdam News* and is old enough to have vivid memories of racial discrimination's full horror. The story of the difficulties he faced while trying to get into journalism is enough to make anyone's skin crawl. He was born in Boston to a Jamaican father and a mother from Guyana; by age 12 he had decided to be a newspaperman. He worked as a *Boston Globe* copy boy during his high school years and thereafter went to college at the University of Wisconsin, where he majored in economics, wrote for the student paper, the *Daily Cardinal*, and worked during his summers as a New York Central Railroad dining car waiter. Armed with a college degree, he applied for a reporting job with the *Boston Globe*. Rebuffed there, he tried the tabloid *Boston Herald*—in a most unusual manner. He and a friend who delivered the *Boston Record* to the *Herald* newsroom handed a copy of the paper to a man working late at his typewriter. Told that Fraser had a college degree and wanted work as a reporter, the man agreed to hire him, directing him to visit the paper's personnel office the next morning. Fraser arrived there only to find that the man who had "hired" him was a theater critic who had been drinking and had no authority to hire anyone. Again Fraser came away without a job. He lived with his parents, washed cars to meet expenses and had a temporary job with the postal service. Informed that the Urban League in New York City was making efforts to match black college graduates with white-collar jobs, he went there by train and got a job referral that produced no results. He next attempted to get a job at the *Amsterdam News*, one of New York City's oldest black papers, but again was unsuccessful. In answer to another message from the Urban League, he returned to New York and was handed a referral for what he thought was a reporting job at the *Boston Herald*. When he arrived for the interview, he found to his humiliation that the person he was sent to interview was hiring janitors. At that point, he had been a college graduate for a full year. He took temporary summer work washing pots and pans on a cruise ship of the Eastern Steamship Lines, which ran between New York and Nova Scotia. He was promoted to assistant to the chef and later joked that at least he could lay claim to being upwardly mobile. He applied repeatedly to the New York City papers, with the exception of the *Daily News, Mirror* and *Journal American*, which he considered too blatantly racist. Even though he was disgusted with the Urban League by this time, he tried this organization once again when he heard that Tex and Jinx McCrary, whose radio show was the forerunner of daytime talk shows were hoping to hire a young black reporter. He applied but lost the job to the daughter of a Philadelphia politician, even though she had no journalistic training or experience. When he was informed that the *Amsterdam News* had a new editor, he went back for another try. The editor, G. James Fleming, had also graduated from the University of Wisconsin and hired Fraser after giving him a story to write on a freelance basis. Thirty-five months after his college graduation, Fraser finally had a reporting job. He worked for is paper from 1952 to 1956, covering crime and education. Thereafter, he was able to increase his compensation by editing military manuals and editing a union newspaper for the Building Service Employees Union, Local 144, and he also wrote about United Nations initiatives for various periodicals in the Caribbean. When the grip of segregation and discrimination began to ease, he was able to get a reporting job with the New York *Daily News*, working there from 1963 to 1967. The following 24 years he spent with the *New York Times*, much of this time writing about city news, books, television and places in the city that were of interest to tourists.

Fraser also put his long experience to work in academe by teaching for both Columbia University's graduate journalism program and its John Jay College of Criminal Justice. After retiring from the *Times*, he began writing for the United Nations-affiliated *San Diego Earth Times*, a monthly first published in 1993 that covers a wide range of environmental issues. He has also written for the Robert C. Maynard Institute for Journalism Education; in May 2003, he wrote for the institute on implications of the Jayson Blair plagiarism scandal, which had occurred at his old newspaper, the *Times*. Fraser was one of the founders of Black Perspective, a New York City organization for black journalists that appeared in the 1960s. He was later given a lifetime achievement award by the New York Association of Black Journalists.

"Jayson Blair: Implications for Journalists of Color" by C. Gerald Fraser

Has Jayson Blair, the New York Times' prodigious plagiarizer and fabricator destroyed the news gathering industry's aims to provide equal opportunity employment?

Enemies of newsroom diversity now see Blair as exhibit A in their argument that diversity programs promote double standards. They are wrong. But that doesn't mean the implementation of such programs can't be critiqued. And diversity pressure is only a thread in a story with many ragged edges," says a Columbia Journalism Review online commentary, "Trouble at the Times."

Those "ragged edges" include many negative implications for African Americans. Will the newspaper industry maintain diversity programs? Are all African American journalists these days considered diversity, or as some whites say, "affirmative action hires"? How can newsroom diversity be achieved? Can one essentially nondescript 27-year-old black guy cocooned in a lifetime of lies shut down job opportunities for black men and women in the nation's journalistic corporations?

Diversity initiatives, never popular in white America, are viewed as "mechanisms to avoid discrimination lawsuits," says Diversity Inc., an online magazine. And now, says the publication, because of Blair, a "diversity poster child for dishonesty, journalistic fakery and tokenism," The Times has damaged the credibility of diversity initiatives and insulted all the qualified journalists of color who have loved a chance to work there."

Journalists of Color Stigmatized

On ABC-TV's "Nightline," May 15, anchor Chris Bury asked National

Association of Black Journalists president Condace Pressley, "Do you worry that, fairly or unfairly, this whole episode may stigmatize African American journalists?"

Pressley ignored the bizarre "fairly or unfairly" phrase and said yes she did. "There are some 300-plus members of my organization who are under 30 and upholding the tenets of journalism very well every day. And I know that they are just terrified that their editors are going to look at them in a different way because of this incident."

The perceived collateral damage issue may affect all minorities—African Americans, Asians, Native Americans, and Hispanics. Blair fallout could stimulate anti-diversity stances by hesitant employers such as publishers of small newspapers away from urban areas. These papers offer young journalists the best opportunities for solid professional growth.

Star System Failure or Diversity Failure?

It is important not to identify Blair as a "diversity failure." His individual biting-the-teat-that-nursed-him, is from a diversity perspective unimportant. He is a college dropout with no moral compass—a characteristic that, fortunately for him, does not rule out success in today's United States of America.

It is more important in this affair to differentiate between routine newsroom activity and newsroom diversity activity. Inside the newsroom of the New York Times Blair's race didn't matter—regardless of his level of experience. Big newspapers, especially, like to hire journalists who are already stars. But top editors also seek young people with star potential.

These neophytes are then anointed, which translates to encouragement-plus. Within the newsroom the anointed may be envied or detested by colleagues and scorned by some editors, but he or she is shielded. Anointment means top editors want this man or woman to succeed so the road must be cleared of obstacles. It means middling and bottom editors block up-and-coming's path to stardom at their peril. Not surprising is the fact that one below-the-top Times editor said reports of Blair's record of inaccuracies "got socked in the back of my head."

There have been black journalists at The Times with star potential. Some were encouraged, but none was anointed. Until Blair, the anointed were white. Because of this aspect of newsroom culture, Blair's race need not have been a significant element affecting his career.

White Fabricators vs. Black Fabricators

Now, outside the newsroom, Blair's blackness is the only thing that matters. Scott Simon, anchor of National Public Radio's "Weekend Edition," spoke May 17 of journalistic fabricators. He mentioned Stephen Glass whose prevarications at the New Republic magazine led to his dismissal there. Glass, subsequently fired, is now promoting his roman a clef about his misdeeds on, among other places, CBS's "60 Minutes." Simon ended his comments about journalistic fakers by saying Glass "wasn't an affirmative action hire." He didn't explain how he knew.

Actually, everybody knows. That's the tag that's hung on practically all blacks hired these days by journalistic enterprises. And by equating Blair with affirmative action, and diversity, it becomes possible for the "anti" crowd to chop down two undesirables—blacks and diversity—with one swing of an axe.

It's not the same when a white journalist fabricates. The Boston Globe columnist, Mike Barnicle; fired, apparently reluctantly, by the Globe. Now he's on television and writing for the New York Daily News. Michael Daly, fired by the same Daily News, now back there writing a column. No weeping and wailing by white journalists about their future in the news business; Ruth Shalit, fired for fakery by the New Republic. No questions about whether, fairly or unfairly, the various episodes would stigmatize white journalists. No "terrified" young journalists. These white journalists are simply "bad apples."

Which Double Standard Applies?

Columnist Richard Coehn, of the Washington Post's Kurtz and Cohen platoon out to scuttle Blair and bias-free employment, said" "A close reading of the Times' account of what went wrong suggests that the paper itself does not fully comprehend what happened...The Times denies favoritism based on race. Blair is black, and The Times, like other media organizations, is intent on achieving diversity. Sometimes this noble and essential goal comes down to a parody of affirmative action."

Kurtz pats himself on the back for "working on this story when nobody had heard of Blair."

Fraser, Charles Gerald Jr.

On ABC's "Nightline," May 15, anchor Chris Bury asked Kurtz whether The Times wanted to "push him [Blair] ahead faster because of his race." Kurtz said that with Blair's substandard work known, the paper's failure "to come to grips with this is what raises the perception, at least, of a double standard." For Kurtz the double standard means one for whites, another for blacks. Although he must know, the primary newsroom double standard is: one rule for stars, another for everybody else.

The Past Is Past

Many, if not most, Americans abhor history. They say, for example, they own no slaves; their parents owned none, and they bear no responsibility for or are obliged to do anything about United States slavery.

Carl Cohen thinks along that line. Cohen is a University of Michigan professor who stoked the fires of the anti-affirmative action suit now under consideration at the U.S. Supreme Court.

In his book, "Naked Preference: The Case Against Affirmative Action," Cohen wrote, "deliberately visiting the sins of the fathers upon their innocent children and grandchildren, to the special advantage of persons not connected with the original sinning, is conduct neither lawful nor morally right... The nature and degree of the injury done to many Americans because they were black, or brown or yellow varies greatly from case to case. Some such injuries may justify compensatory advantage now to those injured. But the calculation of who is due what from whom is a sticky business; compensatory instruments are likely to compound injustice unless the individual circumstances of all involved—those who were originally hurt, those who benefit now, and those who will bear the cost, are carefully considered."

Affirmative Action as Part of U.S. History

For Cornell West, another academic, the past lingers. He writes in "Race Matters" that there were "de facto affirmative action measures in the American past's contracts, jobs, and loans to select immigrants granted by political machines, subsidies to certain farmers, FHA mortgage loans to specific home buyers, or GI Bill benefits to particular courageous Americans."

West adds: "Given the history of this country, it is a virtual certainty that without affirmative action, racial and sexual discrimination would return with a vengeance...without affirmative action, black access to America's prosperity would be even more difficult to obtain and racism in the workplace would persist anyway."

Torn between the need to protect white dominance on one hand and recognizing that African Americans can be troublesome when it comes to racial discrimination, about three decades ago white America devised equal opportunity procedures for African Americans and called them affirmative action.

Affirmative action in practice eventually made many white men belligerent. The thought of a finite number of "white men's slots," of jobs or admissions to universities and professional schools going to black men and women roiled white America. White males felt buffeted by blacks demanding the right to vote and an end to poverty and racial discrimination; beset by women insisting on an end to gender discrimination; angered by homosexuals who protested rejection because of sexual orientation; and criticized for overlooking obstacles faced by the disabled. The men denounced affirmative action, diversity, and everything like it.

Nevertheless, diversity-employment based on merit, not whiteness, has worked at The New York Times. African Americans, Asians, Hispanics, and Native Americans can be found on The Times' corporate board, on the editorial board, on the op-ed page, as foreign correspondents, in the Washington Bureau, working for the national desk and the metropolitan desk, as sports writers and columnists, in the book review, as critics, and writing business news. Not many newspaper can make that claim.

Source: The story above appeared on 21 May 2003 on the Web site of the Robert C. Maynard Institute for Journalism Education. It appears here by permission of Mr. Fraser.

Further Readings: "C. Gerald Fraser." [Online]. Reporting Civil Rights: Reporters and Writers Web site www. reportingcivilrights.org/authors/bio; Fraser, C. Gerald. "Getting My Foot in the Door." [Online]. The first in a series of memoirs written for the Maynard Institute Web site www.maynardije.org.

Fulwood, Sam III (28 August 1956–)

In the year 2000, Sam Fulwood left his job as a Washington reporter for the *Los Angeles Times* to become a thrice-weekly metro columnist for the *Plain Dealer* in Cleveland, Ohio. He was born in Monroe, North Carolina, and holds a 1978 B.A. in journalism from the University of North Carolina, Chapel Hill. His career began at the *Charlotte Observer* in the same year. Years later, he wrote that he was told at the time he was hired that he got the *Observer* job more for his pigmentation than for the paper's appreciation of his talent—a sobering thing to hear when one is beginning a career. While in Charlotte, he covered the crime, sports and business beats, then was hired by the *Baltimore Sun*, where he was assistant city editor, business reporter, Johannesburg correspondent and editorial writer. He moved again and from 1987 to 1989 worked for the *Atlanta Journal & Constitution*, serving as state political editor and assistant business editor. Thereafter, he became a Washington correspondent for the *Los Angeles Times* covering the presidential elections of 1992 and 1996, and starting a race-relations beat. During his 10 years with the *Times*, he was also part of a team that won a Pulitzer for reporting on the Los Angeles riots of 1992, and he covered the Clarence Thomas Supreme Court hearings. In 1997 he published a book, *Waking from the Dream: My Life in the Black Middle Class*, which presents a not at all optimistic view of relations between blacks and whites in America at the end of the twentieth century. Having grown up in prosperous circumstances, Fulwood found himself surprised that inclusion in mainstream society was still so far from complete for successful African Americans. He describes the black middle class as an isolated, comfortable cocoon that provides a lifestyle apart from both whites and less prosperous blacks. In 2000, he moved to Cleveland and began writing his column, a chance to interpret as well as report. His column frequently deals with racial concerns, crime and politics; promotional copy from his paper says that he looks for "the steel beneath the rust" in this Rust-Belt city. Fulwood was a Nieman Fellow at Harvard University in 1993 and 1994 and an Institute of Politics Fellow at Harvard's John F. Kennedy School of Government. He taught media literacy in 1994 at Cleveland's Case Western Reserve University as a Presidential Fellow and has published a second book, a collection of his columns.

Fulwood quite possibly has written more about comedian Bill Cosby's tough-love message to black America than any other U.S. columnist. Soon after Cosby made his now-famous 2004 Washington speech, Fulwood praised him for saying things that needed to be said. A few days later, another of his columns reported unusual agreement—by black and white readers alike—in calls, letters and e-mails that endorsed his, and Cosby's stand on the matter. Two weeks thereafter, another column reported on meeting with a Cleveland representative of the

Nation of Islam, Richard Muham, who took the opposite stance on Cosby's message, and months later, in January 2005, still another column told Fulwood's readers about a call from Cosby asking the columnist to help him arrange a visit to Cleveland. Fulwood did so, but in late February, the meeting was cancelled after allegations made by a former Temple University basketball official who accused the comedian of sexual misconduct.

Many of Fulwood's columns address local topics: praise for St. Martin de Porres High School, named for the first black saint from the Americas and successful in meeting the needs of poor inner-city children; a hole-in-the-wall restaurant frequented by Cleveland's Somali taxi drivers who do not feel welcome elsewhere; and the controversial coming of another huge Wal-Mart store and the concomitant threat to small, independent retailers nearby. Other columns are about state controversies: a new entrance fee for Ohio state parks, which Fulwood accepted with resignation; a bill that would allow more people to carry concealed handguns, which he opposed, the legislature's vote to ban same-sex marriages, which the liberal Fulwood described as a form of bigotry. An especially hard-hitting column took the governor of the state to task for waffling over the mysterious disappearance of $55 million from the Bureau of Workers' Compensation funds under the watch of one of the governor's cronies. At the national level, Fulwood has not often leveled his guns at President George W. Bush, but he wrote about the nation's military recruitment problems and the strange case of an underage Cleveland boy who received recurring phone calls from Navy recruiters after their having been asked to stop. Below appears a frank column expressing Fulwood's dissatisfaction with America's most avuncular of presidents, Ronald Reagan. In a telephone conversation with the author, the topic turned to column subject matter that had extra power to stir readers up; Fulwood expressed the view that newspaper editors often try to avoid controversy and fail to "give the readers credit for enjoying being offended." Finally, like many columnists, Fulwood occasionally gets very personal, building columns around "Darling Daughter" and her progress through the teen years. He has won the Livingston Award for international reporting and the Salute to Excellence Award given by the National Association of Black Journalists.

"President Reagan: A Bad Leading Man" by Sam Fulwood III

I never liked Ronald Reagan.

I didn't like him as a B-movie star in eyewash like "Bedtime for Bonzo," a 1951 movie in which the future president of the United States was upstaged by a chimpanzee.

I didn't respect him for turning away from President Franklin D. Roosevelt, whose New Deal policies helped lift Reagan's own family out of the depths of the Great Depression.

He was a hypocrite who started out as a Democrat and proud union man but turned Republican after he became rich and famous in Hollywood by pretending to be a common man.

But it was as president that I disliked Reagan most. Actually, the way he announced his decision to run ruined any chance of redemption.

On Aug. 3, 1980, the former California governor went to Philadelphia, Miss. Of all the places in this great nation, Reagan chose the infamous town where the bodies of three murdered heroes of the civil rights movement—Michael Schwerner, Andrew Goodman and James Chaney—had been found in 1964. He never mentioned them or civil rights in his announcement speech.

Instead, on that hot, summer day in Mississippi, he stole a line from Strom Thurmond's 1948 segregationist campaign.

"I believe in states' rights," Reagan said.

I haven't been able to stomach him ever since.

Of course, a great many people loved Reagan for his optimism and never-say-die confidence in this nation. I tip my hat to him for that.

But judging from the accolades following news of Reagan's death, at 93, last weekend, many people only note the best about the 40th president.

I remember the downside, too.

Much of the bad that has happened in America's public life started with the Reagan Revolution. Racial polarization widened during his two terms in the White House.

Reaganism let loose a sense of entitlement and lawlessness among corporate executives, spawning that famous line by actor Michael Douglas in his 1987 movie, "Wall Street." Said Gordon Gekko, "Greed is good."

Before Reagan, the national GOP contained moderates and conservatives in equal measure. After his rise to power, the relatively liberal Rockefeller wing of the party was clipped, leaving only the red-meat conservatives and intolerant Christian fundamentalists.

And that wasn't the worst of it. Reagan and his powerful allies poisoned the nation against government. Out of misguided populism, he threatened to starve the federal government out of existence.

Such a notion was impossible. But it didn't prevent Reagan from overseeing record deficits, rampant unemployment, desperate homelessness and rising poverty. Meanwhile, he spent liberally on military hardware, which helped end the Cold War.

Little is said about how he waged war on this nation's poor people. Reagan loved to tell stories, and he invented whoppers about "welfare queens" and "people on welfare driving Cadillacs to cash food stamps."

Reagan understood the power of an exaggerated metaphor. He used his movie-honed skills to inspire affluent Americans and to scapegoat poor ones.

It was mostly smoke and mirrors, honed from a life and career lived in La-La-Land. I am saddened by his passing, but I can't indulge in the fiction that he represented the best of our national character. He didn't.

First and everlasting, Reagan was a bad actor.

Source: This column is reprinted here with permission of Mr. Fulwood and the *Plain Dealer*. It originally appeared in the *Plain Dealer* on 8 June 2004.

Books by Sam Fulwood III: *Waking from the Dream: My Life in the Black Middle Class* (New York: Anchor Books, 1996); *Full of It: Strong Words and Fresh Thinking for Cleveland* (Cleveland, Ohio: Gray and Co., 2004).

Further Readings: "About Sam Fulwood III." [Online]. Cleveland Plain Dealer Web site www.cleveland.com; Rose, Sonya. "Sam Fulwood III: Biography and Sociology." [Online]. Life Traces Web site ww.nhc.rtp.nc.us; "The Full Cleveland: Sam Fulwood III Leaves the Los Angeles Times Washington Bureau to Write a Column for Cleveland's Plain Dealer." [Online, September 2000]. American Journalism Review Web site www.ajr.org.

G

Gilliam, Dorothy Pearl Butler (24 November 1936–)

In July 2003, Dorothy Gilliam was honored for her 35-year career at the *Washington Post*, which she joined in 1961 as that paper's first black woman reporter and for which she wrote around 1,500 columns. She was born Dorothy Butler in Memphis, Tennessee, and moved with her mother and her father, who was a preacher, to Louisville, Kentucky, in 1941, arriving there on 7 December, the day Pearl Harbor was attacked by the Japanese. Her earliest contact with newspaper journalism was delivering the weekly *Louisville Defender*, a historically black paper—one of the two newspapers her father read each day. She, too, was an avid reader, and her family sent her to study at Lincoln Institute located between Louisville and Shelbyville, Kentucky. Thereafter, she got a scholarship to newly integrated Ursuline College in Louisville and studied there for two years. Her typing skills got her a part-time job as a secretary at the *Defender*, and when the paper's society editor became ill, Gilliam, age 17, took her place. This heady experience for one so young hooked her on journalism and showed her how the job was a key that opened doors previously closed to her. Two years later, she was offered another scholarship, this time at predominantly black Lincoln University in Jefferson City, Missouri. She graduated cum laude in 1957 and was hired as a reporter for the *Tri-State Defender*, another member paper of the small *Defender* chain; here her editors encouraged her to give crime stories the dramatic treatment. Against the orders of her editor, who was concerned for her safety, she went to Little Rock in September 1957 to cover the integration of the city's high school. In Chicago she met editors from *Jet* magazine, the nation's leading black news weekly and after only two months at the *Tri-State Defender*, she moved to Chicago to become an associate editor for *Jet*. There she benefited from the periodical's national scope while writing interview stories and features in addition to performing rewrite duties. After two years in Chicago, she began to chafe at the magazine's emphasis on celebrity and felt a need to write about more substantive topics. She applied to the graduate journalism program at New York's Columbia University but lacked the number of liberal arts courses that program required for admission. A friend who was leaving *Ebony* magazine to do public relations for Tuskegee Institute hired her as his assistant and there she took the courses she needed and secured admission to Columbia, from which she received the M.A. in 1961. She applied to the *Washington Post* but was told she needed more experience. Instead, she went to Kenya with Operation Crossroads Africa, a predecessor of the Peace Corps, lived in a tent and helped build a road to a children's hospital near Nairobi.

While in Africa, Gilliam attempted to freelance for the *Post*, and when she returned to the United States later in 1961, she was hired as the paper's first black woman reporter. Only four African-American men had worked in the *Post* newsroom before she was hired: Simeon Booker, Luther Jackson Jr., Wallace Terry and Roscoe Lewis. The earliest, Booker, had been hired in 1952. Segregation was still rampant in the early 1960s, and her working environment was sometimes difficult because of it. In a 1993 interview with Donita Moorhus, however, Gilliam recalled the kindness of *Post* publisher Phillip Graham, who would visit her at her desk to ask how she was doing. She was in an advantageous position to cover the civil rights movement, interviewed Medgar Evers before his murder, and, by happenstance, was having lunch with her old Columbia school chum Nina Auchincloss Steers, Jacqueline Kennedy's half-sister, when news came of President Kennedy's assassination. Gilliam left the paper from 1965 until 1972 to spend time with her growing family, freelanced for *Redbook*, *McCall's* and other magazines, taught for a term at American University and began a four-year part-time job doing a WTTG-TV talk show, "Panorama," for which she won an Emmy. The *Post* invited her back in 1972 as editor of the Style section, a redesigned version of the paper's old women's section. At this time she was the paper's only black editor. She held this position until 1979, also writing a book about the remarkable actor and singer Paul Robeson, and she was a cofounder of the Maynard Institute for Journalism Education in California in 1976. She was chair of its board for eight years. In 1979, she moved to the *Post*'s Metro section, which was then edited by Bob Woodward, and began writing a twice-weekly column. The column usually addressed a mixture of politics, education and race. In 1997, she became director of the paper's Young Journalists Development Project, which promoted journalism education in Washington high schools. From 1993 to 1995 she was president of the National Association of Black Journalists; her primary agenda in that role was encouraging inclusiveness for other ethnic minorities, which led to the inaugural 1994 Unity convention that brought members of the NABJ into closer contact with Hispanic, Asian-American and Native-American journalists. She had worked during 1991 and

1992 as the NABJ's print task force chair; in that role, she was instrumental in protests when the New York *Daily News* fired all its black male reporters and some female reporters. She also worked on a survey of black journalists after the acquittal of the police who had beaten Rodney King in Los Angeles.

In 2000, Gilliam was named Virginia Commonwealth University's Distinguished Professor and taught a brief, intensive course in feature writing for the university's journalism program; and in 2003–2004, she was the J.S. and Maurice C. Shapiro Fellow at George Washington University, teaching and developing a minority outreach program for the School of Media and Public Affairs. In considerable contrast to 1961, when Gilliam was the *Post*'s lone black newswoman, at the time of her 2003 retirement, 90 African Americans and 40 other people of color were employed in this newsroom. Her honors have included the New York Newspaper Woman's Club Ann O'Hare McCormick Award, the Alumni of the Year honor from the Columbia University journalism program and the Unity Award given by Lincoln University in Jefferson City, Missouri. She has also received the Journalist of the Year award and other recognitions from the Capital Press Club.

Books by Dorothy Pearl Butler Gilliam: *Paul Robeson, All-American* (Washington, D.C.: New Republic Book Co., 1976).

Further Readings: "Biography: Dorothy Gilliam." [Online]. Media Makers Web site www.thehistory makers.com; Case, Tony. "Abu-Jamal Dominates NABJ Convention." *Editor & Publisher*, 26 August 1995, p. 12; "Dorothy Gilliam Interview." (With Donita Moorhus) [Online]. Washington Press Club Foundation Web site http://npc.press.org; Hernandez, Debra Gersh. "Unequal Terms." *Editor & Publisher*, 16 September 1995, p. 28; Prince, Richard. "Dorothy Gilliam Honored After 25 Years at Post." [Online, 2 July 2003]. "Richard Prince's Journal-isms, Maynard Institute Web site www.maynardije.org; Trescott, Jacqueline E. "Committed to the Cause: A Salute to NABJ's Presidents: Dorothy Butler Gilliam." [Online]. NABJ Web site http://members.nabj.org.

Goler, Wendell (July 1949–)

Wendell Goler is a White House correspondent for FOX News Channel in Washington, D.C. He is originally from Detroit and attended the University of Michigan from 1967 to 1971 majoring in political science and psychology but leaving school prior to graduating. Goler's initial interest in journalism was photography; he was a photographer for the Jackson, Michigan, *Citizen Patriot*. He added reporting skills and covered local news. He left Jackson and, he said, lived pleasantly but nonproductively in Colorado and Missouri, then returned to Jackson to work as a disc jockey and later news director for radio station WKHM. His next broadcasting experience, in 1976, was with WRC radio in Washington. In 1979, he switched to WRC-TV and worked there for about a year until he ripped his Achilles tendon playing basketball. From 1981 to 1996, he was with the Associated Press Radio Network, for which he covered the

White House beat starting in summer 1986. He joined FOX when it went on air in 1996. Perhaps his biggest stories have been the impeachment of President Bill Clinton and White House reaction to the terrorist attacks of 11 September 2001. He also reported on a 1997 memorandum from Louis Freeh, then director of the FBI that accused the Justice Department of inaction after charges were made that Vice President Al Gore's campaign fundraising had not been in order. In September 2001, rival news organization CNN quoted FOX's Goler regarding President George W. Bush's first official state visitor, Mexican President Vincente Fox. Goler's point was that being invited as the first official visitor to a new U.S. administration should be viewed as an honor. In November 2004, Goler noted in a FOX special report that whereas President Bush's immediate concern was North Korea's nuclear program, Secretary of State Colin Powell had told the press that Iran might be a more immediate threat in that intelligence reports had indicated Iran was trying to arm a nuclear warhead using North Korean and Pakistani technology. A big story for Goler in December 2004 was the enormous death toll from a tsunami that struck Thailand and other nearby countries. He also reported President Bush's displeasure at the U.S. promise of $15 million in aid having been criticized abroad as stingy. In February 2005, Goler scooped the competition with advance word of the president's ideas on Social Security reform to be presented in his upcoming State of the Union address. Like other FOX correspondents and anchors, Goler has been criticized for giving the national news a rightward spin.

Further Readings: Jones, Graham. "End of a Special Relationship?" [Online, 6 September 2001]. CNN Archives site http://cnn.com; Stanley, Alessandra. "Fast, Frisky and Caffeinated, Fox News Looked Right at Home All Week." [Online, 3 September 2004]. Free Press News Web site www.freepress.net/news; "Wendell Goler." [Online, 23 June 2004]. Fox News.com Web site www.foxnews.com.

Gonsalves, Sean (25 January 1971–)

Sean Gonsalves (pronounced GON-zals) is a self-syndicated columnist and reporter/columnist with the *Cape Cod Times*. His column was previously distributed by Universal Press Syndicate. He was born in Hyannis, Massachusetts, on Cape Cod, and at age three, moved with his family to Oakland, California. His last name is of Portuguese/Cape Verdean origin. Gonsalves is largely self-educated, having dropped out of a private high school during his senior year. Although he has no high school diploma or college degree, he earned the GED and read voraciously while taking some classes at Cape Cod Community College, where one of his professors was Dan McCullough, a Sunday columnist for the *Cape Cod Times*. From 1990 to 1992, Gonsalves worked as a porter at the Cape Cod Hospital, and from 1993 to 1994 he was employed here in outpatient billing. He began freelancing commentary pieces to the *Cape Cod Times* in 1992, and three years later, when he was 24, he signed a column-writing contract with Universal Press Syndicate. He wrote this column for three years and had 22 clients, including the *Oakland Tribune, Kansas City Star* and *Seattle Post-Intelligencer*; but the column was dropped by the syndicate as insufficiently profitable. At that point, he began to self-syndicate. His work has also appeared in the *Washington Post, Boston Globe, USA Today* and the *International Herald Tribune*. Following a very brief taste of union representative work in late 1994 and early 1995 for the organization that represented the employees at the hospital in Cape Cod, he became a local reporter and columnist at the *Times* in May 1995. Gonsalves often has appeared on talk radio—on NPR, BBC and Air America. He has also spoken at churches, schools and universities. In May 2000, he was conducting a roadside interview with an unusually religious man named Arthur Blessit, who was carrying a 12-foot cross. Police were summoned by someone who thought that Gonsalves was robbing the man, and Gonsavles was detained and searched before he could convince the officers to look at his press credentials.

A columnist of decidedly liberal orientation, he frequently delivers jabs at the presidency of George W. Bush. In a 2002 column, he recalled President Bush's promise to bring honor and integrity back to the Oval Office, after which Bush appointed Henry Kissinger to chair a federal commission on national security. Gonsalves likened this choice to appointing Don King to investigate irregularities in boxing. Soon thereafter, he noted that the nation had become "Fortress America" and that we were losing the global image war. In a column that took the form of a letter to former president Jimmy Carter, who had just published a book on the use of negotiation rather than military force, Gonsalves noted that a just war should have a just cause and that any war should be a last resort. His Christmas column for 2004 addressed the way Americans mix worship and consumerism during the season, and how consumerism now clearly has the upper hand. A summer 2005 column attacked neoconservatives for tarring would-be peacemakers as unpatriotic "appeasers." Soon thereafter, he accused the Bush administration of whipping up fears of a possible bird flu pandemic as a means of keeping the public frightened and easily controlled. He also mentioned the matter of spending billions of dollars to stockpile the medicine Tamiflu manufactured by a company that was, he wrote, formerly chaired by Bush's Secretary of Defense, Donald Rumsfeld. From time to time, Gonsalves makes use of a fictitious literary character, Dr. Oxy Moron, to point up logical inconsistencies in government policy. An example was the White House simultaneously claiming not to condone torture yet arguing that the CIA should not be bound by a ban on torture's use. Another issue of interest to Gonsalves has been the Bush administration's efforts to eliminate the federal estate tax, which conservatives call the "death tax," mainly to the advantage of the extremely wealthy.

"Say Hello to the New PC" by Sean Gonsalves

The term "political correctness" was invented by sensitive "liberal" academics who wanted to raise awareness about the power of language to dehumanize, but has now become a cynical wisecrack in the mouths of "conservatives" who have made it politically correct to be politically incorrect—"I know this isn't politically correct but...(hee, hee)."

Mostly made up of "angry white males" who cry victim over the "victim mentality" of historically oppressed groups in America, the old PC backlashers do make a good point. "Progressives" and other assorted leftists need to lighten up.

On the other hand, being politically incorrect is not the same thing as having the courage to "speak truth to power." There's nothing courageous or truthful in publicly proclaiming that Indians, for example, shouldn't be "so sensitive" about the racist imagery of sports team mascots. It's downright callous.

Say hello to the new PC, which turns Jesus' famous words on their head by condemning the splinter in other people's eyes while ignoring the lumber in their own. The new PC is about doling out Scarlet Letters through public moralistic scrutiny of individual private behavior with little or no concern for matters of public interest or institutional morality.

So the new PC, for example, considers President Clinton's sex sins and his lying about something that all unfaithful men lie about to be worthy of impeachment hearings.

But devotees of the new PC are apparently willing to accept, at face value, the word of war planners that the Iraq WMD hype was the result of "mistaken" intelligence, and the "war on terror" torture scandal is essentially a "liberal media" conspiracy to "aid and abet the terrorists" by sensationalizing the behavior of "a few bad apples," despite overwhelming evidence to the contrary.

The inadequate funding of the "No Child Left Behind Act" (doublespeak at its best)? So what, says the new PC. Cut my taxes! Teachers, who are arguably the most socially valuable asset this country has, make too much money anyway, right?

Enticing desperate, poor teenagers to join the "all volunteer" military with promises of employment and education benefits while exposing them to the horrors of war? No big deal for the new PCs, just don't burn my flag.

And now, here comes the "baseball steroid controversy" with Congress holding high-profile hearings this week. The central question: how widespread is/was steroids in pro baseball?—a question that ranks right up there with the other great inquiries of modern times like Who Framed Roger Rabbit? And Got Milk?

Where are all the "free-market" scholars and cheerleaders complaining about big government sticking its nose into the private business of baseball?

On a baseball talk show on XM Radio the other day, one co-host suggested there were more important things Congress ought to be concerned about, like the rising price of gasoline.

His colleague agreed but took issue with the analogy. There's a big difference between "kids dying of steroids" and the price at the pump. Point taken. But is the analogy that far off-base? To the extent that the war in Iraq is about extending American hegemony in the Middle East (the lifeblood of the U.S. dominated energy industry), one could argue that kids are dying over the price of gas.

The war in Iraq isn't just about oil, as leftist critics rightly point out. But, as many hawks refuse to acknowledge, if Iraq's major industry was the exportation of pomegranates, there never would have been any talk about a nonexistent "grave and gathering threat."

Nor would we have intelligent people pretending that Bush's "pre-emptive" invasion of Iraq is fundamentally an expression of compassion for the Iraqi people whose "liberation" is so important to us that we're willing to sacrifice thousands of young lives to, once again, pay "the price of freedom."

So to be down with the new PC, I suggest Congress hold hearings about the rampant use of the performance-enhancing drug caffeine in journalism. Subpoena me. I'll testify about how reporters, "juiced" on caffeine, are "cheating" and how we need to put an asterisk in Pulitzer-prize record books because coffee has tainted some accomplishments.

Where's the outrage?

Source: This column appeared on 17 March 2005 and is reproduced here by permission of Mr. Gonsalves.

Further Readings: Brennan, Anne. "Cape Police Questioned on Treatment of Black Reporter." [Online]. SouthCoast Today Web site www.s-t.com; White, Dick. "Unlawful Search Procedure Reveals Symptoms of Social Epidemic." [Online]. SouthCoast Today Web site www.s-t.com.

Goode, Malvin "Mal" Russell (1908–12 September 1995)

Mal Goode was the first African-American television network news correspondent and the first black member of the National Association of Radio and TV News Directors, best remembered for his news bulletins during the Cuban Missile Crisis of 1962. He was born in White Plains, Virginia, attended public schools in Homestead, Pennsylvania, and was a 1931 graduate of the University of Pittsburgh. Goode put himself through school working in Pittsburgh steel mills during both high school and college and remained in that job after graduating college until in 1936, he got a job in the juvenile court system in Pittsburgh. Later, he worked for the Centre Avenue YMCA and still later in 1942, for the city's housing authority. In 1948, he went to work for the *Pittsburgh Courier*'s circulation department. His first strictly journalistic work came in 1949, in radio at Pittsburgh's station KQV. Television was being introduced in the larger markets at that time, and owners of radio stations were running scared. Many people thought radio would disappear, and cheap air time was available on the older medium. KQV approached the historically black *Courier* for possible programming and Goode was assigned to do radio commentaries. In a 1984 interview for the Teaneck, New Jersey, Oral History Project, Goode reported that within six months, he had gained a considerable following and that after financial disagreements with the station's management, which by that time wanted the *Courier* to pay for Goode's air time, he switched stations to WHOD, where Goode's sister, Mary Dudley, was a disk jockey. Her gospel music show was called "The Mary D Program." Goode initially offered not commentary, but a five-minute news program from 3:00 to 3:05 PM daily. He was sponsored by the *Courier* and soon his news show was increased to 15 minutes duration. Baseball was being integrated at that time, and next, Goode and the *Courier* added a 10-minute sports program during which he would interview the early African-American ballplayers, such as Jackie Robinson, Roy Campenella, Don Newcomb and Satchel Paige. His programs gained popularity and worked well for the *Courier*, which used Goode's programs to build an unusually strong classified ad section. In 1956, station WHOD was sold to a new owner, who fired Goode and his sister. She relocated to WSIB in Baltimore and he to WMCK in Mckeesport, Pennsylvania, near Pittsburgh. He worked there for two years, then freelanced with various stations and began attempting to get a job in television. He appeared as a guest on stations KDKA, WTAE and WWIC, but none of the white-owned television stations in the area would take the first step toward integrating the airwaves by hiring a black reporter. Finally, in 1962, a white sportscaster friend of Goode's, Bob Prince, allowed him to fill in on one of Prince's WTAE shows. Goode's performance reportedly was well received by the show's largely white viewers, many of whom called the station with positive comments. Only one negative, racist call was received, but that was enough to keep Goode from reappearing on that station. Four more years passed until Goode got his big break. His friend Jackie Robinson, by that time a highly popular baseball player, alerted him that ABC was building a news program under the leadership of President Dwight Eisenhower's former press secretary, Jim Haggerty. With Robinson's encouragement, Goode applied for a job and three months later was brought by Haggerty to New York to do a test show in competition with other candidates. He memorized most of his script and did not have to rely on the teleprompter, which impressed the network decisionmakers. In September 1962, at 54 years of age, he got the job and in 1963, moved his family from Pittsburgh to Teaneck, New Jersey.

Goode had succeeded in becoming the first black network newsman on television, but management did not put him on the fast track. Instead, they gave him the United Nations beat, one of the quietest beats possible, where few big stories were expected to materialize. Then the unexpected happened. In October 1962, during the presidency of John F. Kennedy, Russian missiles were discovered in Cuba, and Kennedy and Soviet head of state Nikita Khrushchev began playing a potentially deadly game of "chicken" while the U.N. Security Council met in emergency session. At that moment, Goode was the only broadcast reporter on the scene at United Nations headquarters, and as the American television audience waited nervously, fearing war with Russia and the possible launching of missiles by both sides, viewers had their first look at an African-American newscaster. Reporting on both television and radio, Goode appeared a total of 17 times, introduced by the words, "We interrupt this program" ... His brief news bulletins kept the nation abreast of breaking news about the crisis, which at last was resolved when Russia backed down and agreed to remove all its missiles from Cuba, thereby averting what might well have become World War III. The country's first look at a black newscaster simply could not have happened in a more dramatic way. Although his first television appearance was to be his most heralded, he went on to report on the difficulties encountered by poor black Americans and interviewed on ABC such luminaries as civil rights figures Martin Luther King, Jr. and Malcolm X; boxer and war protester Mohammad Ali; and singer Nat King Cole. In 1963, he also was one of several broadcasters who traveled to Africa to offer journalism instruction to students in Ethiopia, Nigeria and Tanzania. Goode continued working into his seventies and died in 1995 of a stroke at age 87. Although his story of breaking the color barrier in television network news is one of triumph, he remarked late in life that never a day went by at work that he was not in some way reminded of his race.

Gordon, Ed (c.1960–)

With more than 20 years of broadcast journalism behind him, Ed Gordon filled the void on Black Entertainment Television that was created when Tavis

Smiley's contract was not renewed. Also, Gordon's new public affairs show, "News & Notes with Ed Gordon," premiered on National Public Radio in January 2005. Gordon was born in Detroit, is a graduate of Cass Tech and holds a bachelor's in communication and political science from Western Michigan University. While at Western Michigan, he had an internship at WTVS, Channel 56, in Detroit. From 1985 to 1988, he hosted the public affairs show "Detroit Black Journal" and with Detroit Pistons basketball star Isaiah Thomas, cohosted "No Crime Day," a show that attempted to steer young people away from crime. Hired by BET, Gordon hosted the interview program "Personal Diary" from 1989 to 1991. His guests included fellow television journalist Ed Bradley of "60 Minutes," tennis star Arthur Ashe, and poet Myra Angelou. He hosted specials, such as "President Clinton Face to Face: A White House Special"; another special broadcast, "Murder Madness," on crime in America; and "BET Town Hall" broadcasts on a variety of issues. Also on BET, he hosted two popular public affairs talk shows: "Lead Story," which began airing in September 1991, and "BET Tonight." "Lead Story" had its troubles, which resulted in the resignation of journalists and roundtable regulars Cheryl Martin and, later, DeWayne Wickham. Two other regulars, George E. Curry and Armstrong Williams, clashed with one another, and Williams eventually had much worse troubles of his own due to his too-close relationship with the Bush administration. Following the 2001 sale of BET to media giant Viacom, the new ownership canceled most of its public affairs programs, including "Lead Story" and "BET Tonight with Ed Gordon" in favor of the more cheaply produced pabulum of entertainment programming. Cancelled at the same time was "Teen Summit," which had been the concept of Robert Johnson's ex-wife, Sheila Johnson. Gordon's handling of the explosive O.J. Simpson murder case, especially his interview with the former football star, had attracted the attention of MSNBC-TV, which hired Gordon. He anchored and hosted at MSNBC and did interviews for "Dateline NBC" for three years, part of that time on the talk show "Internight." For "Dateline NBC," he conducted an interview with Autumn Jackson, who had sued entertainer Bill Cosby unsuccessfully for patrimony. Gordon entered talk radio with a weekly ABC show, "On Point with Ed Gordon," and in January 2005, he began hosting a National Public Radio show, "News & Notes with Ed Gordon," an assignment that partially resulted from a presidential election special he had hosted in October 2004 for NPR. The one-hour show, which airs Monday through Friday on 86 member stations covers a wide range of topics from politics to popular culture. On this show, Gordon is joined from Culver City, California, by regular contributor Farai Chideya. Around that same time, he became a contributing correspondent for "60 Minutes" on CBS.

Gordon returned to BET in 2000 as a contributor to "The Today Show" and "Dateline." In January 2005, he began anchoring "BET News with Ed Gordon," for which he is also managing editor. He continues to host the interview program, "Conversation with Ed Gordon." Over his years in broadcasting,

Gordon has become known for his interviewing. Politicians he has interviewed include presidents George H.W. Bush and Bill Clinton, presidential hopefuls Sen. John Kerry and Al Sharpton, the ever-outspoken Newt Gingrich, the equally outspoken Lewis Farrakhan of the Nation of Islam, Gov. Arnold Schwarzenegger of California, Sen. Trent Lott and South Africa's President Nelson Mandela. Other interviews have been with media superstar Oprah Winfrey, Ed Bradley of "60 Minutes," singers Janet Jackson and Whitney Houston, actor Jamie Foxx and songwriter-singer R. Kelly, who had been charged with sexual misconduct with a minor. As a reporter or commentator, Gordon has covered such major stories as the untimely death of Princess Diana of Great Britain, the release from prison of Nelson Mandela, the Rodney King beating and its aftermath and the terrorist attacks on the World Trade Center and the Pentagon. He has taken on such topics as the spread of AIDS in Africa, the immigration question at home, negative images of black women in the popular media and the question of imminent domain. The Emmy-winning broadcaster has also received the Award of Excellence given by the National Association of Black Journalists and the Communication Excellence to Black Audiences award. *People* magazine once named him one of the "50 most beautiful people," and in 2005, the Association of Black Harvard Women recognized him as their Outstanding Man of the Year.

Further Readings: Covington, Artelia C. "BET Cancels Ed Gordon's Show, 'Lead Story' and 'Teen Summit." [Online, 16 December 2005]. Black Press US Web site www.blackpressusa.com; "Ed Gordon Biography." [Online]. California State University Multi-Cultural Center Web site www.csus.edu/mcult; "News & Notes with Ed Gordon." [Online, NPR Web site www.npr.org; "NPR to Launch News & Notes; Ed Gordon Selected as Host." [Online, 21 December 2004]. NPR Web site www.npr.org.

Graves, Earl Gilbert (9 January 1935–)

Founder of *Black Enterprise* magazine, Chairman and CEO of Earl G. Graves, Ltd. and a tireless supporter of black entrepreneurship, Earl Graves is one of America's outstanding African-American businessmen. He was born in Brooklyn, New York, to parents who emigrated there from Barbados. He grew up in the Bedford-Stuyvesant section of Brooklyn and, like so many people raised in humble circumstances, began making money at an early age. He attended mostly black Morgan State University in Baltimore, working as a lifeguard to help pay his way. He majored in economics, went through the ROTC program and graduated in 1957, after which he was commissioned as a lieutenant in the Army. He did Airborne training and rose to the rank of captain in the Green Berets. He returned to Brooklyn after his tour of duty, was a U.S. Treasury Department narcotics agent in 1962, began selling real estate and became active in Democratic Party politics. Due to prejudice, his first attempts to volunteer locally were rebuffed, but he wrote to the Democratic National Committee and was put to work on the 1964 presidential campaign working for the Johnson-Humphrey ticket and for Robert Kennedy's campaign for the U.S. Senate. Graves' big break came when an event he planned came off far better than similar events elsewhere, and Robert Kennedy hired him as an administrative assistant. Graves was present when Kennedy was shot and killed on 5 June 1968; following that tragic event, Graves received two offers: a Ford Foundation fellowship and a job with IBM. Inasmuch as he was more interested in entrepreneurship than in a salaried position, he chose the fellowship and spent it studying economic development in Barbados with an eye toward becoming a consultant for black-oriented business. After beginning in this line of work, he pondered starting a newsletter for his clients and potential clients, but Howard Samuels, a friend from his time working with Kennedy and by then head of the Small Business Administration, persuaded him to instead start a magazine. The result was *Black Enterprise*, which, with the help of a $150,000 loan from Chase Manhattan Bank, first appeared in August 1970. Despite the usual difficulties that most black media have experienced in attracting major advertisers, the magazine became profitable in less than a year—a rarity in magazine publishing. It filled a niche: providing the African-American business news that had long been ignored by the mainstream media. Beginning in 1973, the new magazine dramatized the increasing economic clout of black America with an annual list of the one hundred largest black-owned business firms. The magazine has remained profitable, enjoys a circulation of around 500,000, received *FOLIO*'s 1996 award for editorial excellence in the business/finance category and has made Graves a very wealthy man. From 1978 to 1980, he took time out to work as an aide to the U.S. Secretary of the Army. Since 1968, *Black Enterprise* has been the lynchpin property of Earl G. Graves, Ltd., a privately held company with its headquarters on Fifth Avenue in New York City. The firm operates a magazine-related Web site; publishes books, one of which is *Black Enterprise* (1986); produces radio stories; and operates an event-planning subsidiary called Black Enterprise Unlimited. All three of Graves's sons are active in the business, with the eldest, Earl Jr., or "Butch," serving as president and chief operating officer since January 2006. In 1990, the elder Graves became the largest minority bottling franchisee of Pepsi-Cola, with operations in the Washington, D.C., area. He sold the franchise back to Pepsi Co in 1998 and is now chair of that corporation's committee for ethnic marketing. He is on many other companies' boards, including Aetna, Federated Department Stores, DaimlerChrysler, Rohm & Haas and the parent company of American Airlines, AMR Corporation.

Graves volunteers time to many nonprofit enterprises, such as the Schomburg Center for Research in Black Culture, the National Underground Railroad Freedom Center, the presidential commission for a National Museum of African American History and Culture, and the Steadman-Hawkins Sports Medicine Foundation. He is on the board of trustees of Howard University, is a member of the Committee for Economic Development and the New York Economic Club and is vice president of the national executive board of Boy Scouts of America. His awards are many, including the Dow Jones Award for Entrepreneurial Excellence in 1992, Ernst & Young's New York City Entrepreneur of the Year award in 1995, the NAACP's CEO of the Year in 1997 and its Springarn Medal in 1999, election to the American Academy of Arts and Sciences in 2000. To date, he has received more than 50 honorary degrees, and following his $1 million gift to his alma mater's business school in 1995, he was honored by having the school named for him: the Earl G. Graves School of Business and Management; the program has a full-time faculty of roughly 50, more than 900 majors and a Ph.D. program. Graves has also set up the Earl G. Graves scholarship program through the NAACP, which gives $5,000 grants for the study of business administration to students in seven geographic regions. Graves has written one book. In 2006, Graves drew criticism for requiring a student to cut his dreadlocks if he wanted to intern at *Black Enterprise*. Raleigh, North Carolina, *News & Observer* columnist Barry Saunders was one such critic. Saunders pointed out that Graves himself still sports unusual "porkchop sideburns" but conceded that for better or for worse, Graves was within his legal rights in that he owns the magazine.

Books by Earl Gilbert Graves: *How to Succeed in Business without Being White: Straight Talk on Making It* (New York: HarperBusiness, 1997).

Further Readings: Bell, Gregory S. "Graves, Earl." In *African American Lives*. Ed. by Henry Louis Gates Jr. and Evelyn Brooks Higginbotham. New York: Oxford University Press, 2004, 349–50; "Earl Graves, An Image of Black Business Success." [Online]. The African American Registry Web site www.aaregisry.com/africa_american_history; "Earl Graves, Publisher." [Online, February 2002]. CNN Web site www.cnn.com/SPECIALS/2002/black.history/stories; Graves, Earl. "How We Got Started." [Online, September 2003]. Fortune Small Business Magazine Web site www.fortune.com/fortune/smallbusiness/articles.

Green, Lauren (?–)

The comely Lauren Green covers the arts and works as news update anchor for the FOX News Channel's A.M. show "Fox & Friends," and is also a talented pianist. She studied piano at the University of Minnesota, from which she graduated summa cum laude with a BFA. She also has a master's degree from the Medill School of Journalism at Northwestern University. She was active in beauty pageants and was the 1984 Miss Minnesota and third runner-up for Miss America the following year. She considered a career as a concert pianist but opted instead for broadcasting. From 1988 to 1993, Green was a general assignment reporter for St. Paul, Minnesota, station KSTP-TV, an ABC affiliate, then moved to Chicago to work as a correspondent and weekend anchor for WBBM-TV, a CBS station. In 1996, she joined FOX News, where she covers the arts and gives news updates on the hour and half-hour for the successful morning program "Fox & Friends," a right-leaning talk show that first aired as "FOX News Live," then as "Fox Xpress," and, following a reader contest, as "Fox & Friends." With her formal training in music, she has provided informed coverage of various musical events and the work of professional musicians, such as the Metropolitan Opera, the Van Cliburn International Competition for Outstanding Amateurs, violinist Joshua Bell, Spanish tenor Placido Domingo and French composer/conductor Pierre Boulez.

Green herself has performed during her years in broadcasting. In April 2002, she performed a piano recital at the Van Cliburn competition held at Big Canoe, Georgia, playing pieces by Brahms, Chopin, Tschaikovsky, Beethoven, Rachmaninoff, Ginastera and George Walker. In November of that same year, she teamed with another Lauren Green, this one a male conductor, to perform a work by Mendelssohn in Bartlesville, Oklahoma. A CD of classical favorites played by Green, titled "Classic Beauty," was released in 2004. The CD cover shows her reclining languidly on the keyboard of a concert grand. That cover somehow seemed to point up a career challenge for Green, an intelligent, dignified and talented individual: not to be perceived as merely a pretty face among the sizeable bevy of beautiful young women who do anchor duty for FOX. To further succeed in broadcast journalism she must guard against being seen as just another "FOX Barbie" in a short skirt. She was badly used in the autumn of 2005 when fellow FOX News correspondent James Rosen, during an interview with U.S. Secretary of State Condoleezza Rice, who is single, suggested that the secretary should meet fellow pianist Green, also single. Fox viewers seized upon Rosen's remarks as suggesting the possibility of a romantic connection between the two, causing quite a stir. For her part, Green assured the press that she is not gay. Also in 2005, Green served as mistress of ceremonies at New York City's Waldorf-Astoria Hotel for the awarding of the Simon Wiesenthal Center's Humanitarian Laureate Award to her boss, media mogul Rupert Murdoch.

Further Readings: Johnson, Peter. "Fox Wakes Up Morning TV." [Online, 17 August 2003]. USA Today Web site www.usatoday.com; "Lauren Green." [Online, 13 June 2004]. Fox News Channel Web site www.foxnews.com; Whipple, Bennett. "Fox News Anchor Lauren Green Performs Her Van Cliburn Program." [Online, May 2002]. Big Canoe Web site www.bigcanoehoa.org.

Grosvenor, Vertamae (c.1938–)

Multiaccomplished Vertamae Grosvenor (who sometimes uses Smart-Grosvenor) is a cultural correspondent for National Public Radio and has hosted NPR's " series "The Americas' Family Kitchen with Vertamae Grosvenor," "Seasonings" specials about African-American cooking, and the documentary series "Horizons." She is also a poet, an actress and a culinary writer who has specialized in describing ties between food and the culture of the people who prepare and eat that food. She was born in coastal Hampton County, South Carolina, in what is called Geechee or Gullah country. She and a twin brother were born premature. The brother was too weak to survive, but she clung to life, fed goat's milk from a medicine dropper; she was warmed in a shoebox placed on the oven door of the family's wood-burning stove. Her family nicknamed her "Kuta," the Gullah term for the turtle, and she grew up speaking that lyrical, rapid-fire blend of English, French Creole and African languages still spoken by some residents of the Sea Islands of South Carolina and Georgia. She moved to Philadelphia when she was 10 and, partially as a retreat from being picked on by children who thought she "sounded funny," she became a voracious reader. She traveled to Paris when she was 18 and, thanks to seeing more of the world, gained a sharper appreciation of her own Gullah culture. She has been with NPR for many years. In the 1980s, she produced several documentaries for the "Horizons" series, among which were "Slave Voices: Things Past Telling" "and "Daufuskie: Never Enough Too Soon," about beautiful Daufuskie Island. The latter program won Grosvenor the Robert F. Kennedy Award plus another recognition from Ohio State University. She went on to host the "Horizons" series from 1988 until it was cancelled in 1995.

Grosvenor also represented the area of her birth in the *National Geographic Explorer* series documentary "Gullah," for which she was a writer and consultant, and on WUSA-TV's "Capitol Edition," with her Emmy-winning story "Growing Up Gullah." Her freelance writing has included stories for *Ebony* magazine, *Essence Magazine*, *Elan Magazine*, *Life*, *Redbook*, *Viva*, the *New York Times*, the *Washington Post* and the *Village Voice*. Her television appearances have included "The Today Show," "The Phil Donahue Show," "Nightline" on ABC, "Our Voices" on BET and "The Galloping Gourmet." She was a language consultant for and an actress in the 1991 "American Playhouse" production "Daughters of the Dust," by Julie Dash. Another of her performances was in the 1998 movie "Beloved," starring Oprah Winfrey and Danny Glover. She narrated the film "The Language You Cry In," about the Sierra Leone roots of many of today's Gullah people, and "Goin' to Chicago," a 1994 University of Mississippi-sponsored film about the Great Migration. She spoke on the Harlem Renaissance poet and columnist Langston Hughes on the PBS series "Slavery in America." Another of her contributions to this series was about a lesser known figure: Mary "Crazy Bet" Bowser, who had been born a slave in Richmond, Virginia, and who was a Civil War spy for the North while working in Richmond as a house servant for Jefferson Davis, President of the Confederacy. Grosvenor has been a writer-in-residence at the Penn Center, located on St. Helena Island, South Carolina, near Beaufort, and she has worked with the South Carolina Arts Commission's Literary Task Force. Grosvenor was narrator of and one of the writers for the NPR documentary series "Will the Circle Be Unbroken?" which combined music with a look at the civil rights movement in the South. She was one of the voices in

"Tell About the South," produced and directed by Ross Spears. One of her most recent projects was hosting NPR's one-hour tribute to the late singer Nina Simone, which aired in January 2006 as "Nina Simone: Forever Young, Gifted & Black." She has authored four books and is at work on others. Her first book appeared in 1970, a combined autobiography and cookbook titled *Vibration Cooking; or, The Travel Notes of a Geechee Girl*. In 2003, she was a presenter at the Kentucky Women Writers Conference at the University of Kentucky. In 1998, she was a speaker at the Hannaian Educational Conference in the Bahamas, and she was a founding member of the organization Southern Foodways Alliance, which sponsored an oral history project.

Grosvenor won both the Ohio State Award and the duPont-Columbia Award in 1990 for her work on NPR's series "AIDS and Black America: Breaking the Silence." In 1991, she received the Communications Excellence to Black America award for "Marcus Garvey: 20th Century Pan-Africanist," and in 1992, she won a National Association of Black Journalists award for "South Africa and the African-American Experience," which had aired on "All Things Considered." In 1996, her show "Seasonings" was the 1996 winner of the best culinary radio program in the nation award from The James Beard Foundation.

Books by Vertamae Grosvenor: *Vibration Cooking; or, The Travel Notes of a Geechee Girl* (Garden City, N.J.: Doubleday, 1970); *Thursdays and Every Other Sunday Off; a Domestic Rap* (Garden City, N.J.: Doubleday, 1972); *Vertamae Cooks in the Americas' Family Kitchen* (San Francisco, Calif.: KQED Books, 1996); *Vertamae Cooks Again: More Recipes from the Americas' Family Kitchen* (San Francisco, Calif.: Bay Books, 1999).

Further Readings: "Vertamae Grosvenor, Cultural Correspondent." [Online]. National Public Radio Web site www.npr.org; "Vertamae Grosvenor on a Civil War Spy." Slavery and the Making of America. [Online, 19 April 2002]. PBS Web site www.pbs.org; "Vertamae Grosvenor on the Legacy of Langston Hughes." Slavery and the Making of America. [Online, 8 February 2002]. PBS Web site www.pbs.org; "Vertamae Smart-Grosvenor." [Online, April 1994]. South Carolina African American History Online Web site www.scafam-hist.org.

Gumbel, Bryant (29 September 1948–)

Now the host of Home Box Office's "Real Sports with Bryant Gumbel," this longtime news/features/sports personality is also known for his years as host of NBC's "Today Show" and later, the "Early Show" on CBS. He was born in New Orleans; his father had served in World War II and following the war, put himself through Xavier University and Georgetown Law School. In 1953, the family moved to Chicago, where the elder Gumbel became a probate judge. The future broadcaster grew up in Chicago's Hyde Park section and attended Roman Catholic schools there. He was a 1970 liberal arts graduate of prestigious Bates College in Lewiston, Maine, after which he took a job with Westvaco, a paper products manufacturer, but quit after six months. He tried his hand at freelance writing and in 1971, sold his first story to *Black Sports* magazine. He was hired by this magazine in 1972 and became its editor-in-chief eight months later. Gumbel also became a broadcaster in 1972, taking a weekend sports job in Burbank, California, for NBC affiliate KNBC-TV. He auditioned for and won the station's weekend sports anchor job, then from 1976 to 1981 was the station's sports director. During some of this period, he commuted on weekends from New York to Burbank. He cohosted Rose Bowl Parade coverage in 1975, and an Olympics special he did won him his first Emmy in 1976. He cohosted the Super Bowl in 1977; and in 1978 and 1979, he was winner of the Los Angeles Press Club's Golden Mike Award. Gumbel had been slated to host the 1980 Summer Olympics in Moscow, but the assignment fell through when the United States decided to boycott the games. He had developed a widespread reputation by this time, and in June 1980, he signed a deal with NBC that guaranteed him three sports features a week for the "Today Show." In January 1982, he became that show's cohost with Jane Pauley and Chris Wallace, replacing the departing Tom Brokaw. The show, which had been in second place among the three major networks' morning shows, soon moved into first place, and Gumbel held this job until 1997, also covering the Seoul Olympics in 1988. More awards came his way: the Overseas Press Club's Edward R. Murrow Award for foreign affairs coverage in 1984, a sports Emmy for his Olympics work in 1988, and both a news Emmy for an interview with Sen. Ted Kennedy and the NAACP Presidents Award in 1997. In April 1995, Gumbel began hosting his long-running HBO sports show "Real Sports with Bryant Gumbel." Since that time, the show has won at least 10 Emmy awards.

In May 1997, he left NBC for CBS and a $5 million a year plus stock options contract with CBS plus a new magazine-format news show, "Public Eye With Bryant Gumbel." Although the new show won two Emmy awards, two Peabody Awards and an Overseas Press Club Award during its short life, ratings were not up to expectations and the show was cancelled in 1998. His CBS contract also gave him three specials a year and his own production company. From 1999 to 2002, he anchored "The Early Show" for CBS. This show replaced the declining "CBS This Morning," but despite the $30 million the network spent on a showy new 5,000 square-foot Manhattan studio, ratings continued to fall, leaving Gumbel's show a distant third to competitors "Today" on NBC and "Good Morning America" on ABC. Gumbel was unable to repeat the spectacular ratings success he had enjoyed with the "Today Show" and left both the show and the network in 2002, saying that it was time to do something else. He continued his work with "Real Sports" and in 2003, began a PBS public affairs series, "Flashpoints USA," cohosted with newswoman Gwen Ifill.

A liberal, Gumbel has frequently incurred the wrath of the conservative right. One conservative Web site, run by the Brent Bozell-led Media Research Center, referred to some of the broadcaster's left-leaning remarks as "Gumbel's stumbles," another online conservative dismissively called him "Gumball" and a third referred to the morning show host as the head chef of petit dejeuner liberalism.

Probably the far right will never forgive Gumbel for daring to criticize President Ronald Reagan's policies that, he contended, mainly benefited the very wealthy, demonized the poor and polarized the nation. He has continued to level the same basic criticisms at the George W. Bush administration, which some conservatives regard as bias masquerading as news or commentary and the Web site FreeRepublic.com terms "nincompoopery." Criticism of Gumbel's opinions ran especially high in 1992 following the Los Angeles riots, after the commentator said that the violent unrest was attributable to policies initiated by the Reagan administration. At times, Gumbel has brought anger and resentment upon himself by criticizing his colleagues. In 1989, he wrote a memo to his producer, Marty Ryan, in which he accused "Today" weatherman Willard Scott of displaying bad taste. After fallout from the memo subsided, however, the two appeared to make up their differences. Gumbel also complained that "Today" movie critic Gene Shalit's reviews were frequently late and of unsatisfactory quality. In 1999, in a *New York Times Magazine* interview, Gumbel remarked that a person who would remain nameless was not really as sweet and perky as she appeared to television viewers, an obvious reference to his former "Today" cohost Katie Couric. He also criticized her for frequently replacing her assistants and makeup people. Three interview stories he conducted in 1998 cast doubt on the veracity of Kathleen Willey regarding her claims that she had had sexual encounters with President Bill Clinton. These stories also generated considerable fire from the right, as did a remark he made to a *Washington Post* reporter in 1994 to the effect that to be a black person in the Untied States was like being a witness at one's own lynching. In 2000, Gumbel had conducted an "Early Show" interview with the Family Research Council's Robert Knight, who had defended a recent Supreme Court decision that allowed the Boy Scouts of America to refuse to employ gay scoutmasters. The interview had concluded and, thinking the microphone was off, Gumbel appeared to mutter "He's a f------idiot," setting off a firestorm of conservative anger; CBS spokesmen denied that he had made this comment. Earlier, when celebrity commentator Geraldo Rivera was cut from a "Today Show" segment in which he was to have discussed the O.J. Simpson case, Rivera not only fired back that being canceled was retribution for a story he had run about Gumbel's alleged marital infidelity, but he challenged Gumbel to a boxing match, calling him a wimp and a hypocrite. This episode recalled another Gumbel controversy dating back to 1989, when the commentator criticized the Rev. Ralph Abernathy for publishing information about the extramarital affairs of Martin Luther King, Jr. These comments appeared in Abernathy's book *And the Walls Came Tumbling Down* (New York: Harper & Row, 1989). Gumbel was again accused of hypocrisy in 2002 for interviewing National Council of Women's Organizations chairwoman Martha Burk, who was campaigning to secure membership for women in the no-women-allowed Augusta National Golf Club when he himself was a member of several similarly exclusive golf clubs, some of which did not allow women members.

Also in 2002, his conservative critics charged special celebrity treatment after the quick release of Gumbel's son, who had been arrested in New York for assault and attempted robbery.

Surely even Gumbel's detractors must admit that his broadcasting career has been long and varied. He has reported from all over the world and covered some of the biggest news stories of his time, including the fall of Saigon, the cold war relationship between the United States and Russia, and the Persian Gulf War. He did a 1985 telecast with Pope John Paul II from the Coliseum at Rome and also did a televised interview in the Pope's private Vatican apartment, a first. On a different level, he got an Emmy in 1999 for a segment he did on the selling of counterfeit golf clubs, and in 2003, he interviewed black Vanderbilt University athlete Marcus Dixon of Lindale, Georgia, who had received a mandatory 10-year prison sentence for having had sex with a 15-year-old white girl. Dixon was the first person to be sentenced under a stiff new Georgia law, and in 2004, his 10-year sentence was invalidated. The girl had claimed rape; Dixon said the sexual encounter had been consensual. Gumbel hosted the television series "Games People Play" and appeared in the role of a sportscaster in the movie "Heaven Can Wait" in 1978 and the series "Main Street" and "NBC's 60th Anniversary Tribute" in 1986 and the series "The More You Know" in 1989. Other television work includes the 21st NAACP Image Awards show in 1989, "The Hard Way" in 1991, "Seinfeld" in 1993, "Arthur Ashe: Citizen of the World" in 1994, "Muhammad Ali: The Whole Story" in 1996, "The Nanny" in 1997, "Cosby" in 1999, a number of "Survivor" shows from 2000 to 2002, numerous appearances on the "Late Show with David Letterman," and two flying saucer specials: "The Roswell Crash: Startling New Evidence" in 2002 and "The New Roswell: Kecksburg Exposed" in 2003. In 2004, he appeared in "The N-Word."

Gumbel has produced an Oprah Winfrey-like book show for PBS affiliate WHUT at Howard University in Washington. Called "The Reading Club," it is syndicated to public stations nationwide by Dunbar Productions, owned by Gumbel. The show, which first aired in 2004, and which is anchored by newswoman Carol Martin, gives practical experience to Howard student interns, targets black women and attempts to generate increased awareness of and interest in the work of African-American authors. Examples of "Reading Club" choices are Lawrence Otis Graham's book *Our Kind of People: Inside America's Black Upper Class* (New York: HarperPerennial, 1999) and Benilde Little's *The Itch: A Novel* (New York: Simon & Schuster, 1998).

Further Readings: Armstrong, Mark. "Gumbel Makes an 'Early' Exit." [Online, 4 April 2002]. E Online Web site www.eonline.com; "Bryant Gumbel." [Online]. The Early Show. CBS News Web site www.cbsnews.com/earlyshow/bios; Elder, Sean. "Free Bryant Gumbel!" [Online, 7 April 2000]. Salon.com site http://archive.salon.com; Goldberg, Jonah. "Biased Gumbel: A Breakfast Serving of Liberalism—Television Personality Bryant Gumbel." *National Review*, 31st July 2000; Waggoner, Glan. "Gumbel at the Turn." [Online] TL Golf Web site www.tlgolf.com/features.

Gumbel, Greg (3 May 1946–)

A sportscaster of long experience, the affable Greg Gumbel is currently host of "NFL Live," which covers the National Football League, and host of NCAA men's basketball tournament coverage. He was the first African American to do play-by-play for a Super Bowl, in 2001. He was born in New Orleans and moved with his family to Chicago when he was a child. He is the older brother of fellow sportscaster and former morning show host Bryant Gumbel. In 1967, he received the bachelor's degree in English from Loras College in Dubuque, Iowa, where he played baseball. His first job was as an advertising director for a clothing company in Chicago; next he was a paper buyer for Time Inc.; then he became a sales representative for American Hospital Supply Company. Gumbel worked part-time as a weekend sportscaster for station KNBC in Los Angeles, and in 1973, he determined to have a full-time career in broadcasting, going to Chicago's WMAQ-TV and working there as sports anchor until 1981. From 1981 to 1986, he was a coanchor for the ESPN show "SportsCenter," after which he worked for three years for Madison Square Garden Network, covering college basketball and backing up announcer Marv Albert. In 1988, he worked for CBS doing NFL play-by-play announcing and hosted a morning radio show on WFAN in New York City. Then NBC got the contract to handle the NFL, and in 1994, Gumbel began a four-year stint with the network as host of "NFL on NBC," as an anchor of pre-game shows and doing play-by-play for "Baseball Night in America." He hosted coverage of the New York Nicks basketball team and, in baseball, the New York Yankees. He was host of "NFL Live" as well. Thereafter, in 1998, he rejoined CBS. From that time until early summer 2004 he was the network's leading NFL play-by-play man and has been host of the NCASA basketball championship games. In June 2004, the network made a switch whereby then "NFL Today" host Jim Nantz and play-by-play head Gumbel exchanged roles. Gumbel has been coanchor of morning broadcasts of the 1992 Olympics in Albertville, France; host for coverage of the 1994 Winter Olympics in Lillehammer, Norway; and announcer for the 1996 Summer Olympics in Atlanta, Georgia. He has also done play-by-play for the 1993 American League championship games and the College World Series and has hosted coverage of the Daytona 500 automobile race and the World Figure Skating championships. He has hosted Super Bowls in Minneapolis, Tempe, San Diego, Tampa and Houston. In 2004, he began working as a host of "The NFL Today" with Boomer Esiason, Shannon Sharpe and Dan Marino. He has also shared the microphone with such sports luminaries as Joe Montana, Terry Bradshaw, John Madden, Bill Walton and Mike Ditka.

Gumbel's sports work has earned him three Emmy awards, and as an entertaining and motivational speaker he commands fees of $10,000–$20,000.

His intimate knowledge of sports has made him a popular speaker with the likes of Bell South, Toshiba, Shearson-Lehman, BMW, civic groups and school audiences. He is in his second term as a member of the National Board of Trustees of the March of Dimes. He has also made appearances on such shows as "Evening Shade," "3rd Rock from the Sun," "The Chris Rock Show," "Cosby," and "Cheap Seats."

Further Readings: "Greg Gumbel." *The African American Almanac*, 9th ed. (Detroit: Gale Group, 2003), p. 869; "Greg Gumbel." [Online]. Capitol City Speakers Bureau Web site www.capcityspeakers.com. Griffith, Bill. "Gumbel Enjoying Super Run." [Online, 11 January 2004]. Boston Globe Web site www.boston.com/sports; Martzke, Rudy. "Greg Gumbel Returns to 'NFL Today.'" *USA Today*, 21 June 2004; Sandomir, Richard. [Online, 22 June 2004]. New York Times Web site www.nytimes.com.

H

Hair, Princell (1965–)

A talented and pleasant young man who has been caught between journalistic principles and television's insatiable demand for maximized ratings, Princell Hair was for slightly more than one year the executive vice president and general manager of CNN/US, a very powerful position in television broadcasting. After being replaced in that position, he remained with CNN as a programming and talent-development executive. Hair, whose unusual first name came from an aunt who gazed down at him when he was a newborn and remarked that he looked like a little prince, grew up in Ft. Lauderdale, Florida, earned the B.S. in broadcast journalism from Florida International University and took MBA coursework at the University of Baltimore until his studies were interrupted by a move to the West Coast. His first connection with the news media was delivering newspapers at age 16. His first job out of college was in Miami, where he worked during 1990 and 1991 as a writer and producer at WPLG-TV. Next, he switched stations to the city's WSVN-TV, known for its crime coverage. During 1991 and 1992, he worked here under Joel Cheatwood, who later became a CBS executive and who has recommended Hair for at least three different jobs. Hair's dizzying career path took him next to Detroit and a producer job at WDIV-TV, where he worked in 1992 and 1993; after that to the night executive producer job at WBBM-TV in Chicago (1993–1994); and thereafter to the assistant news director spot at Orlando's Channel 6, WCPX-TV (1995–1997). As he continued to hop-scotch upward through the ranks, he returned to Chicago as news director for WMAQ-TV (1997–1998), became news director for WBAL-TV in Baltimore (2000–2001), corporate news director of Viacom in 2001, and KCBS-TV news director in Los Angeles, succeeding Roger Bell. He was replaced in June 2002 by Nancy Gonzales after a management shakeup. In September 2002, Hair became vice president for news at Viacom. In his new Viacom position, he was in charge of news coverage for the company's 39 television stations, which serve 15 out of the 20 largest U.S. market areas. Throughout his many moves, Hair developed the reputation of a quiet, thoughtful, rather conservative manager, and his ratings success from 1995 to 1997 in Orlando at WCPX, which became WKMG, made him an attractive hire. The pinnacle of his rise occurred in September 2003, when he left his Viacom vice presidency to succeed Teya Ryan as the executive in charge of all U.S. news operations for CNN, which placed him over roughly 3,600 of the company's employees. He was the first African American to hold this position and was brought in to attempt to catch up to or surpass the ratings of the rival Fox News Channel. Jim Walton, president of CNN News Group, hired Hair, he said, for the 36-year-old's ability to work with high-end talent and for his leadership abilities. As he took over the job, Hair said that he planned no dramatic changes, just a renewed emphasis on news fundamentals and connecting more meaningfully with the viewing audience. Some industry onlookers predicted a quick demise for Hair, whose primary experience had been in local news work. Others pointed to a regrettable move he had made at Chicago's WMAQ-TV when he hired Jerry Springer, host of a talk show that must surely rank at or near the bottom of television history in taste level, to be a commentator, causing two of the station's anchors to resign. By January 2004, Hair had begun making changes at CNN, consolidating the network's reporting and programming divisions and creating new units. Ratings failed to improve enough to please top management, however, and in November 2004, Hair was replaced by Jonathan Klein, who had been executive vice president of CBS News during the mid-to late-1990s. It appears that Hair was not willing to do anything sufficiently outlandish to overtake the rabid programming of Fox. Running a major television news operation in the Age of Entertainment is not a simple matter.

Hair is on the board of the Radio and Television News Directors Association and the board of visitors of Florida International University. From time to time, he lectures on broadcast journalism at Florida's Poynter Institute. In 1994, he won a Emmy for a special on inner-city violence he produced while working in Chicago, and he was also recognized by the Associated Press as best newscaster in Michigan.

Further Readings: Boedeker, Hal. "Princell Hair May Not Be on Camera, But the 36-Year-Old Executive Is in the Spotlight." [Online, 8 January 2004]. Florida International University Communicator site http://jmc.fiu.edu; de Moraes, Lisa. "At CNN/U.S., Another Quick Change of Suits." [Online, 23 November 2004]. Washington Post Web site www.washingtonpost.com; Johnson, Peter. "Young CNN Chief Has Lots to Prove." [Online, 29 September 2003]. USA Today Web site www.usatoday.com; Martin, Ed. "CNN's Princell Hair Assesses His Network (and Gives Fox News a New Nickname." [Online, 7 January 2004]. Jack Myers Entertainment Report Web site www.jackmyers.com; Prince, Richard. "Hair Out as CNN's U.S. News Chief." [Online, 22 November 2004]. Richard Prince's Journal-isms. Maynard Institute Web site www.maynardije.org; "Princell Hair." [Online]. CNN Web site www.cnn.com.

Hall, Arsenio (12 February 1956–)

Show host, actor and comedian Arsenio Hall is probably best known for hosting the first black late-night talk show, "The Arsenio Hall Show," from 1989 to 1994. He was born in Cleveland, Ohio, and as a boy growing up in the hard inner-city conditions of a public-housing project, daydreamed of being a show host like his favorite entertainer, Johnny Carson. Like Carson, he became an amateur magician while in grade school and later worked weddings, bar mitzvahs and parties. An adept student, he was admitted to Ohio University in 1973. His original intent was a career in law, but instead, he became a communications major. He transferred to Kent State University, was a member of the forensics team, worked part-time at local comedy clubs and graduated in 1977 with a bachelor's degree in speech communication. He worked the comedy club circuit in Chicago, was master of ceremonies at the Sheba Lounge and was "discovered" on Christmas night 1979 by jazz singer Nancy Wilson, who helped him relocate to Hollywood. He arrived there in 1980 and worked as an opening act for Wilson and such other performers as Dionne Warwick, Patti LaBelle, Aretha Franklin, Tina Turner, Wayne Newton, Tom Jones and Stevie Wonder. In 1983, he appeared on the "Merv Griffin Show" and was host of a soon-to-be-cancelled show titled "The Half Hour Comedy Hour." From these beginnings, he was able to book appearances on the "Thicke of the Night" series in 1983 and 1984, "The New Love American Style" and "Motown Revue" in 1985, and the series "Solid Gold" in 1986 and 1987. His first movie appearance was a small role in "Amazon Women on the Moon," which premiered in 1987. Hall became a friend of former "Saturday Night Live" star and enormously successful movie comedian Eddie Murphy and appeared with Murphy in the 1988 Paramount Pictures hit movie "Coming to America," playing multiple characters, one of which was reportedly based on his own father, a Baptist minister. In the following year, he and Murphy worked together a second time in the less successful movie "Harlem Nights." Also in 1987, Hall signed a deal with Paramount that included both movie and television work. Another Hollywood friend, comedienne Joan Rivers, made Hall a frequent guest on her Fox network program "The Late Show." In May 1987, when the network fired Rivers, Hall, with a megawatt smile and hip banter, took her place as the show's host. Then, in January 1989, "The Arsenio Hall Show" began its five-year run, with Hall as host and executive producer. Perhaps more than any other such show, Hall's heralded the sea change from the older guests who populated the Carson show to the younger, more hip, more multicultural performers and other celebrities who appeared on Arsenio's Paramount-syndicated show. Rappers and hip-hop performers such as Snoop Doggy Dogg popularized gangsta rap attracting a much younger and more racially diverse audience. Other singing stars who appeared were Prince (or, the performer formerly known as Prince), Barry Manilow and Madonna. In June 1992, presidential candidate Bill Clinton played two saxophone numbers—fairly well—and in doing so, ingratiated himself with younger voters. Occasionally, Hall would offer more serious content: Jesse Jackson, Louis Farrakhan of the Nation of Islam, and appeals for viewers to practice safe sex and to be aware of the danger of AIDS. Arsenio's friend and basketball great Magic Johnson appeared on the show just after having announced that he was HIV positive. Hall's show made headlines after the second appearance of comedian Andrew Dice Clay and the accompanying protests by the groups ACT UP and Queer Nation, who regarded some of Clay's and Hall's humor as harmful and homophobic. Other show guests included Eddie Murphy, Bill Cosby and MC Hammer. Hall wrote his own theme song, "Hall or Nothing," and as a show host, he differed from Carson in that he used no desk and had no "sidekick" or "straight man," in the manner of Carson's Ed McMahon. Another difference between the two shows was that next to the band, stage left, Hall's show had an audience-participation section, known as the "dog pound"; these individuals would cheer him on with fist pumping done in a circular movement and cries of "Woof, woof, woof" in place of applause. When Johnny Carson retired in 1992, Jay Leno was hired as his replacement, which caused Hall feelings of resentment. Also at that time, David Letterman moved his youth-appeal late-night show from NBC to CBS to compete directly with Leno, which reduced the viewer ratings for Hall's show. Largely due to the Letterman factor, "The Arsenio Hall Show," which had been second only to Carson in late night viewing, was brought to a close in May 1994.

In 1990, Hall had opened Arsenio Hall Productions in what had been the Gloria Swanson Building. His popularity was high, and in that year, he was selected as *TV Guide*'s "Television Personality of the Year" and "Entertainer of the Year" in a poll conducted by *US* magazine. Also in 1990, he was given his own star on Hollywood's much-visited Walk of Fame. In the following year, his production company created and syndicated the series "The Party Machine with Nia Peeples." He was executive producer of the movie "Bopha!" in 1993; Morgan Freeman was director of this story about a family living under apartheid. Not as successful was Hall's return to television in 1997 with the show "Arsenio," a sitcom in which he played an Atlanta sportscaster; and in a change from comedic work to an action role, he appeared as a Los Angeles policeman in "Martial Law," which starred the Hong Kong martial arts actor Sammo Hung. The show aired during 1998 and 1999. He has also done other hosting and narration work, including hosting the MTV Video Music Awards in 1990 and 1991 and "Soul Train's 25th Anniversary" show in 1990. He cohosted the "World's Greatest Commercials" special in 2002 and in 1998, narrated "Intimate Portrait: Josephine Baker." In 2005, he did the voice of the character Dr. Carver in the Disney Channel's "The Proud Family Movie." During 2003 and 2004, Hall was host of the popular "Star Search" series on CBS. The year 2004 found Hall caught up in a paternity suit.

At this writing, his star seems to have dimmed, and he reports spending most of his time being a single dad.

Further Readings: "Arsenio Hall." [Online]. Internet Movie Database Inc. site http://us.imdb.com; "Arsenio Tries for Dramatic Comeback." [Online, 19 September 1997]. E Online Web site www.eonline.com/News; Hawkins, Walter L. In *African American Biographies: Profiles of 558 Current Men and Women* (Jefferson, N.C.: McFarland & Co., 1992); Joyce, Aileen. *Arsenio: the Prince of Late Night, an Unauthorized Biography.* New York: HarperPaperbacks, 1993; King, Norman. *Arsenio Hall.* New York: Morrow, 1992; Neville, Ken. "Hall, Arsenio." [Online, 2000]. A&E Television Networks Web site www.biography.com.

Hall, Charlotte H. (1946–)

Experienced newspaperwoman Charlotte Hall is, in 2006, editor and vice president of Florida's *Orlando Sentinel*. Her early experience was gained in Hackensack, New Jersey, at the *Record*, the *Boston Herald-American* and the *Washington Star*. In 1981, she began working as copy chief for *Newsday*, which serves the New York City and Long Island markets. Other positions she held at this newspaper were metropolitan editor of the city edition, editor for Nassau County, Washington news editor, and assistant managing editor of the Long Island edition. She worked for two years as marketing director of *Newsday*, with responsibility not only for marketing but also for the paper's research department and its newspaper-in-education program. In 1996, under editor Anthony Marro, she became the newspaper's managing editor, a job she would hold for seven years. In this position she had responsibility for all news desks, the photo department and editorial art. Her final job with this paper came in October 2003, when she was named *Newsday*'s vice president for planning. She reportedly lost the job of *Newsday* editor to Howard Schneider in July 2003, and her move to the *Orlando Sentinel* came in March 2004. Both *Newsday* and the *Sentinel* are Tribune Company properties. In a somewhat unusual move, Orlando Sentinel Communications president, Kathleen M. Waltz, also made the paper's editorial page editor, Jane E. Healey, a vice president and directed that the editorial department would henceforth report to the president rather than to the editor. The stated reason for the change was to underscore the division between the paper's news and editorial functions. As editor, Hall directs all newsgathering and news reporting functions for the paper and for its subsidiaries, OrlandoSentinel.com, the bilingual Spanish-language paper *El Sentinel*, elSentinel.com and the paper's radio and television partnerships through which broadcasts are done in both English and Spanish.

Hall became a board of directors member of the American Society of Newspaper Editors in 2001 after having chaired the organization's diversity committee. She later chaired the ASNE high school journalism committee. She was elected treasurer in October 2004, which means she will be ASNE president in 2008. In 2005, Hall also served on the Pulitzer Prize jury for the investigative reporting category. Her recognitions include the Tribune Values Award in 2001 for her efforts to promote staff diversity and the 2004 Robert G. McGruder Award for Diversity Leadership, which is given jointly by the Associated Press Managing Editors and The Freedom Fund.

Further Readings: "Editors Elect Charlotte Hall to Leadership Ladder." [Online, 4 October 2004]. American Society of Newspaper Editors Web site www.asne.org; "Orlando Sentinel Editor Named—Charlotte H. Hall." [Online]. Hispanic Business.com Web site www.hispanicbusiness.com; Prince, Richard. "Charlotte Hall, Diversity Advocate, to Edit in Orlando." [Online, 31 March 2004]. Richard Prince's Journal-isms, Maynard Institute Web site www.maynardije.org.

Hamblin, Ken (1941–)

A former *Denver Post* columnist who was syndicated by the New York Times Syndicate in the 1990s and a longtime presence on conservative talk radio, Ken Hamblin has been a scourge of the Clinton White House and of liberals everywhere. He gave himself the nickname "The Black Avenger" for his advocacy of patriotism, capital punishment, gun rights and self-reliance and for his longtime campaign against affirmative action, welfare and other forms of dependence upon government, as well as "gangsta rap" music. His parents were immigrants from Barbados, and he grew up on welfare in the Bedford-Stuyvesant section of Brooklyn, New York. He has recalled once having to ride the A-train all night with his family after they were evicted from their apartment. He joined the military to escape a life of poverty and served with the One Hundred First Airborne's Screaming Eagles, an experience that helped him educate himself and that greatly influenced his take-no-prisoners brand of conservatism. Conservatives have applauded him as a good example for disadvantaged youth; liberals have mocked him as an "Uncle Tom." His overall message to black America is essentially that voiced more recently by entertainer Bill Cosby. Hamblin long has chided his fellow African Americans that they must take charge of their own destinies and light candles of hard work instead of blaming whites and cursing the darkness of self-perpetuating poverty. What he so passionately suggests sounds easier than it really is, yet he himself is an example of how it can be done. During the late 1960s, he secured his first media job as a photographer for the *Detroit Free Press*; there he specialized in urban street photography that recorded the Detroit race riots, the 1968 Democratic Convention and protests such as the march on Washington. Some of his pictures were published in other venues, such as the *New York Times*, *Time* and *Life*. His next move was into film. He produced and filmed "Arson for Profit" and on the effects of drug abuse, "Take a Sad Song and Make It Better." His cinematography got him hired as a producer and host on WTVS-TV, Channel 56, Detroit's public television station, and in 1982, he moved to Denver, Colorado, to begin his first radio talk show at station KOA. His show excited interest and he achieved national syndication in 38 states, working out of Denver. Hamblin also moved into newspaper journalism in 1990 writing a weekly column for the *Denver Post*, and soon thereafter added a new twice-weekly column distributed by the New York Times Syndicate. In both his radio and newspaper work, Hamblin has crossed swords with a wide variety of both liberals and fellow conservatives and also has made some unexpected bedfellows. An example of the latter was his highly sympathetic reception of Richard Barrett, general counsel for The Nationalist Movement, a group that espoused a right-wing brand of patriotism that appeared to many onlookers as essentially antiminority. The two men were in full agreement as to what they considered the political opportunism of President Bill Clinton and black spokesmen Jesse Jackson and Al Sharpton. They also agreed that paying reparations to African Americans to redress the lingering ills of slavery was a bad idea and that being able to live in the United States constituted reparations aplenty. On the anger-producing issue of abortion, Hamblin has taken a safer stand: that men should leave the issue to women. His support of the Second Amendment has placed him at loggerheads with such people as Kristin Rand of the Violence Policy Center, which Hamblin considers an alarmist group. He has excoriated the *New York Times* for its editors' stand against a bill to allow airline pilots to be armed while in the air. When conservative demigod Rush Limbaugh's substance abuse problems surfaced in the news, Hamblin raked him over the coals of conservatism, while other media right-wingers such as Sean Hannity rose to Limbaugh's defense. When events took the wind out right-winger Newt Gingrich's political sails, Hamblin was similarly unflinching in his criticism. A conservative politician who fit Hamblin's preferred mold, however, was columnist/presidential candidate Patrick Buchanan. Some observers have called Hamblin "the black Patrick Buchanan," but Hamblin has responded that he would prefer to say that Buchanan is "the white Ken Hamblin." In 1992, remarks Hamblin made to the effect that Native American medicine was nothing but hocus-pocus and superstition drew angry responses from such American Indian Movement spokesmen as Russell Means and Glenn Morris, who were quick to point out some of the contributions to mainstream medicine made by emulating traditional American Indian cures. Other Hamblin targets have been Ebonics and other street argot, feel-good education policies and dependence on illegal drugs in lieu of hard work. And, like most conservatives, Hamblin has been supportive of President George W. Bush and his administration's military intervention in Iraq. In all these things, Hamblin's written and broadcast commentary has benefited from his wide range of interests: chess, motorcycle riding, camping, horseback riding, fly fishing and scuba diving. He also has his twin-engine pilot's license. His admirers have enjoyed his feisty, provocative language: "poverty pimps," "white trash," "black trash," "brood mares" (teenage mothers on welfare), "egg-sucking dog liberals" and the like. His detractors, such as fellow commentator Tavis Smiley, have characterized his commentaries as shallow and uneven and as "rants." Hamblin's recent radio affiliations have included American View Radio Networks, from which he resigned in a dispute over money, and KBIM Radio of Roswell, New Mexico. He has won a variety of broadcast awards, including recognition from Sigma Delta Chi. Hamblin has published two books: *Pick a Better Country* (1996), in which he pictures a black American underclass passive in its acceptance of ghetto living, and *Plain Talk and Common Sense from the Black Avenger* (1999), which touches on Bill Clinton, O.J. Simpson, capital punishment, affirmative action and more.

Books by Ken Hamblin: *Pick a Better Country: An Unassuming Colored Guy Speaks His Mind about America* (New York: Simon & Schuster, 1996); *Plain Talk and Common Sense from the Black Avenger* (New York: Simon & Schuster, 1999).

Further Readings: Leverette, Slater G. "The Black Avenger." [Online]. Sgt Grit Web site www.grunt.com; "Ken Hamblin." [Online, 11 February 2000]. Quest Educational Foundation Speaker Series Web site www.questeducationalfoundation.org/speakers; "NYTS Syndicating Radio Host's Column." *Editor & Publisher*, 12 March 1994, p. 43.

Hanif, C.B. (1952–)

C.B. Hanif, ombudsman and editorial columnist for the *Palm Beach Post*, came to his present job by, as he puts it, a nontraditional path. A native of Baltimore, he attended high school at the Baltimore Polytechnic Institute, graduating in 1970. He left Carnegie-Mellon University after five semesters and edited books and journals for several publishing houses, including The Waverly Press (1980–1982), and from 1982 to 1983, the Johns Hopkins University Press, University Park Press of Baltimore, and Scripta Technica of Silver Spring, Maryland, which publishes English-language translations of Japanese and Russian technical journals. His first newspaper job was with the *Atlanta Voice*, an African-American audience weekly, for which Hanif was news editor. He relocated to West Palm Beach in July 1986 to write opinion copy for the *Post*. The following year, he was made ombudsman, or Listening Post editor, and in 1990, he became a member of the paper's editorial board. The columns he writes as ombudsman to address readers' concerns about fairness or accuracy appear under the standing headline "Listening Post"; his more general columns, such as the one appearing below, do not. An October 2004 column chided the Florida and national news media for being too quick to assume guilt on the part of tenured University of South Florida professor Sami Al-Arian, accused of aiding terrorists. He also has concerns about the nation's lack of Arab voices in the media and their attempts to bomb an Arab country into democracy.

Hanif was born Charles Bond—no relation, he says, to either James or Julian. As an adherent of Islam, he had his name legally changed in the 1990s, "giving Mr. Bond's name back to him" but retaining the C.B. initials. In doing so, he sought a stronger tie to roots severed generations ago when his ancestors were brought to America.

"War Appealed to Americans' Fear" by C.B. Hanif

So this is what we get when they let Clarence Thomas pick the president. For sure, the Supreme Court's stand-in for the late Justice Thurgood Marshall isn't solely to blame, even if it was his deciding vote that put George W. Bush in the White House. But that doesn't change the fact that this latest administration underwritten by all the millionaires necessary has shown little more imagination than what Rabbi Michael Lerner of *Tikkun* magazine has called "the triumph of fear."

Even before all the crowing over Iraq began, Rabbi Lerner was asking: "How could it have come to this? The fundamentally decent people of the United States destroying the homes and lives of innocent Iraqis... How did we get to a place where the carnage of another people is seen as an 'acceptable cost' and a pragmatic path?"

Well, "everybody's got a thing," as Stevie Wonder once sang, "but some don't know how to handle it." At the helm of the mightiest military ever, President Bush seems unable to make it a true instrument of peace, and instead has successfully exploited polarizing language to appeal to Americans' fears. But even worse is the culpability of the news media in parroting everything from "war on terrorism" to "weapons of mass destruction."

"Bush won his support for this war through deception," observes MSNBC commentator Eric Alterman, "and the media helped." He cited a *Los Angeles Times* report that despite the CIA's evidence to the contrary, nearly 80 percent of Americans believed the administration's claim that Saddam Hussein had "close ties" to Al-Qaeda, while 60 percent said they believed Hussein had some responsibility for the Sept. 11, 2001, attacks.

"If 60 percent of Americans believe something we know to be false, and are in support of the war for that reason," Alterman said, "isn't that a significant aspect of the story? How did they get that view? Who has been misleading them? What are the media doing about setting them straight?"

He predicted that future wars will work much the same. Meanwhile, *The New York Times* has reported that "most notable" in last week's meeting between the foreign ministers of France and Britain "was their agreement on the need to end the cycle of violence in the Middle East as the only way to bring stability to the world."

The *Times* also reported that "some in the administration expect Mr. Bush to press (Israel's Ariel) Sharon to make the hard steps toward peace that the Israeli leader has said Israel would have to make someday. But Europeans remain skeptical that Mr. Bush would do anything to alienate American supporters of Israel. The end of the Iraq war, both sides say, will pose a test to see who is right."

But it's likely that the media will help Mr. Bush continue to tiptoe around what many Americans and greater numbers of people around the world consider the U.S. policy of turning a blind eye in the Palestine-Israeli confrontation to policies that we condemn elsewhere.

With the free press going down before a full-court press instead of questioning and clarifying the administration's assumptions, it's small wonder that amid all the crowing over Iraq there has been little notice of what *New York Times* columnist Bob Herbert called the divergence of interest "between the grunts who are fighting this war, spilling their blood in the desert, and the power brokers who fought like crazy to make the war happen and are profiting from it every step of the way."

That's partly because most Americans never have heard of the Defense Policy Group that Mr. Herbert said made the invasion of Iraq "one of the clearest examples ever of the influence of the military-industrial complex that President Dwight Eisenhower warned against so eloquently in 1961." It's also due to the fact that Americans, as Rabbi Lerner said, "are in a state of fear, and that fear has been manipulated by militarists and political opportunists to lead ordinarily decent people to the conclusion that we can only be safe by wiping out others."

Source: The above column appears with the permission of Mr. Hanif and the Palm Beach Post.

Harris, Jay T. (3 December 1948–)

Having been with the Knight Ridder organization since 1985, Jay T. Harris resigned in 2001 as chairman and publisher of the chain's *San Jose Mercury News*, the most influential newspaper in Silicon Valley, California. He currently holds the Wallis Annenberg Chair in Journalism and Communication at the University of Southern California's Annenberg School of Communication and is director of the Center for the Study of Journalism and Democracy at that university. He left his newspaper position in protest of the insatiable bottom-line demands of his corporate headquarters. Harris was born in Washington, D.C., to a disabled veteran father and a social worker mother. He received his B.A. in journalism from Lincoln University in 1970, having been attracted to newspaper work, he has said, because of his enjoyment of writing and his desire to contribute to the public betterment. His entry to newspaper journalism, directly following graduation, was as a general-assignment reporter at the Wilmington, Delaware, *News-Journal* papers. He moved from reporting into editing then left in 1975 to teach at Northwestern University's Medill School of Journalism; before returning to newspapering in 1982, he also had worked as an assistant dean at Medill. In 1982, he became a columnist and national correspondent for Gannett News Service, and in 1985, he was hired by Knight Ridder as executive editor of the *Daily News* in Philadelphia. In 1988, he became assistant to the president of Knight Ridder Newspapers, Tony Ridder, and thereafter he became vice president of operations for the chain, with responsibility for nine newspapers. He became chairman and publisher of the *San Jose Mercury News* in 1994. In this position, Harris set out to appeal to his paper's multicultural, multilingual readership. In 1996, the paper launched the first of two affiliated weeklies: the Spanish-language *Nuevo Mundo*, and in 1999, the Vietnamese-language *Viet Mercury*. Also, during his seven years as publisher, the percentage of minority staffers at the *Mercury News* grew to 30 percent, and female staffers to 50 percent. Other of his priorities were improving the paper's coverage of Silicon Valley business and technology. Profits remained strong despite a drop in advertising revenue, and until 2001, Harris was enjoying success in a powerful newspaper position at a quality paper that had increased in national reputation. On 19 March 2001, he announced in an e-mail to his staff that he had resigned to protest the company's bottom-line mentality at the expense of good journalism. He apparently made this decision following a meeting with Tony Ridder and Steve Rossi. About three hours after Harris' announcement, union workers held a walkout in support of his position. Like so many of today's "corporatized" newspapers and magazines, the *Mercury News* was under pressure to reduce content costs in order to meet ever-higher profit-margin targets, which in turn would bolster share prices of company stock. The danger inherent in this approach is that reducing editorial quality of product might make the product less attractive to readers, thereby eventually killing the goose that lays the golden egg. Harris resigned when he concluded that financial values had dangerously supplanted journalistic values, thus aligning himself with such earlier newspaper leaders as David Lawrence in Miami and Gene Roberts in Philadelphia, who also took the long view as to maintaining journalistic quality. Speaking before the ASNE less than a month after his resignation, Harris remarked that the high salaries paid to top newspaper management were functioning as "golden handcuffs" as the industry lurched toward a possible financially induced institutional suicide. He also drew a parallel between newspaper cost-cutting and the similar situation in medicine, with HMOs' constant efforts to cut costs. These remarks were repeated in an article Harris contributed to the *Nation* that appeared in the 28 May 2001 issue.

After a brief rest, Harris resurfaced in October 2002 as the holder of the Wallis Annenberg Chair in Journalism and Communications at the Annenberg School of the University of Southern California. At the same time, he became the founding director of the Center for the Study of Journalism and Democracy there. Harris also teaches as one of three presidential professors at Santa Clara University. With Eva M. Terrazas, he has cofounded Deep River Associates, a firm that works with nonprofits in support of the public good.

Harris is on the Pulitzer Prize Board of Directors, the National Advisory Board of the Poynter Institute in Florida and the boards of the Salzburg Seminar, the Community Foundation of Silicon Valley, the Silicon Valley Manufacturing Group, the Silicon Valley chapter of the American Leadership Forum and the Pacific Council on International Policy. He is a member of the Council on Foreign Relations and the American Society of Newspaper Editors. For the latter organization, he created in 1978 an annual census of minority employment in daily newspapers. He has been active in recruiting minority journalism students from historically black colleges and universities and has served on the board of visitors of the Medill School at Northwestern University. He has also been chair of the board of the Bay Area Council and chair of the executive committee of the San Jose Symphony. At his university, he is a member of a task force charged with investigating overly generous compensation for University of California administrators. He has received honorary degrees from Santa Clara University and from Lincoln University. He is a sought-after public speaker, and one of his remarks at a recent Poynter Leadership Academy commencement has been quoted many times. He credited the thoughts to Chinese philosopher Lao Tzu, who once observed that the mark of the best leader is that he or she does not strive for personal aggrandizement, so that after good results have been achieved, subordinates will think that they, not their leader, were responsible for the accomplishments.

Harris, Jay T.

"News and Profits" by Jay T. Harris

It was the conviction that newspapers are a public trust that brought me to Knight Ridder in 1985. I understood then and understand even better today that a good newspaper and a good business go hand in hand. Indeed, without a good business it would be impossible for a newspaper to do good journalism over the long haul. But at some point one comes to ask, What is meant by a good business? What is good enough in terms of profitability and sustained year-to-year profit improvement? And how do you balance maintaining a strong business with your responsibilities as the steward of a public trust?

Most businesses can reduce expenses more or less proportionally with demand and revenue without doing irreparable damage to their core capabilities, their market position or their mission. But news and readers' interests do not contract with declining advertising. Nor does our responsibility to the public to get smaller as revenue declines or newsprint becomes more expensive. In the same way that hospitals are important to the health of individuals and communities, good newspapers are important to the health of our communities, our nation and our democracy. My argument today is that a freedom, a resource, so essential to our national democracy that it is protected in our Constitution, should not be managed primarily according to the demands of the market or the dictates of a handful of large shareholders.

I thought the tension and its sources were captured clearly and succinctly in a recent segment on *The NewsHour* With Jim Lehrer during which correspondent Terrence Smith asked Lauren Rich Fine, a Merrill Lynch media analyst, "What profit margin does Wall Street expect from a newspaper, a publicly held newspaper company? If they average in the twenties, is that enough? What does it have to be?" To which Fine responded: "Well, it's never enough, of course. This is Wall Street we're talking about."

That is an honest and unabashed statement of what some of us see as the tyranny of the current situation. It matters not whether the source of that tyranny is the demand of analysts and major shareholders, the reaction of corporate executives to those demands or merely the demands of owners of privately held newspapers for an unreasonably high return.

The trend threatening newspapers' historic public service mission is clear—if we're willing to see it.

And it can be challenged and reversed—if we're willing to speak out. Of course, many are unable, or unwilling, to see or speak the truth of the situation. One reason is that the high salaries many of our leaders receive, in newsrooms and business offices as well as corporate headquarters, have turned into golden handcuffs. And those handcuffs have morphed into blindfolds and gags as well.

But this muffle of good fortune has not produced absolute silence. Today, we hear a growing chorus of brave souls, inside and outside the industry, protesting vigorously—and an audible grumbling of discontent from within the ranks of journalists and readers alike.

So where do we go from here? I am hopeful and optimistic about the future of American newspapers—both as a business and as key contributors to the vitality of our democracy. I neither believe nor will I accept that the current trend can't be changed, that the proper balance can't be restored, that the unwise is somehow unavoidable or that a course that is inconsistent with our principles and values must be followed. I believe that if we are willing to speak the truth, willing to talk together and work together to determine what the proper balance is and how it can be restored, we can achieve that end. Here are a few thoughts on how this might be done:

- The discussion needs to include all the stakeholders, not just publishers, editors, large shareholders and institutional investors. Journalists and employees from the business side need to be at the table as well. So do readers, scholars and a diverse group of community representatives.
- One goal of the effort should be to develop a working definition of what being a good and faithful steward of the public trust requires of newspaper managers and newspaper owners.
- The moral, social and business dimensions of the issue should be fully explored and given equal priority.
- The discussion should build the case for a steady and reliable investment, insofar as prudent business allows, in news, circulation, research and promotion.
- The case needs to be made that editors must seek equal access to the publisher's chair. Journalists cannot leave the helm to those who do not have a deep commitment to a newspaper's responsibilities to its readers and its community.

- And finally, a way must be found to give the public a sense of "ownership" in its community newspaper. It should hold the paper—its managers and owners—to reasonably high standards and accept nothing less.

Source: This article is reprinted with permission from the 28 May 2001 issue of the *Nation*. For subscription information, call 1-800-333-8536. Portions of each week's *Nation* magazine can be accessed at http://www.thenation.com.

Further Readings: Denardo, Christina and Icess Fernandez. "Jay Harris Goes on the Record." [Online, 6 April 2001]. American Society of Newspaper Editors Web site www.asne.org; Halstead, Dirck. "The Bloody 20%." [Online]. The Digital Journalist site http://digitaljurnalist.org; "Jay T. Harris." [Online, 2005]. Annenberg School of Communication, University of Southern California site http://asweb.suc.edu; "Jay T. Harris." [Online, 2001]. Medill School of Journalism, Northwestern University Web site www.medill.northeestern.edu; "Jay T. Harris." [Online]. United Church of Christ Web site www.ucc.org/ocinc/parker/harris; Lewis, Johnny. "Jay Harris Emphasizes Newspapers' Need to Balance Public Trust with Bottom Line." [Online, 6 April 2001]. American Society of Newspaper Editors Web site www.asne.org; McManus, John. "The Question Behind Jay Harris' Resignation: Does Wall Street Have to Trump Main Street?" [Online]. Grade The News Web site www.fradethenews.org; Vargas, Jose Antonio. "A Year Later, Jay Harris Has No Regrets." [Online, 12 April 2002]. American Society of Newspaper Editors Web site www.asne.org.

Harris, Leon M. Jr. (1961–)

With CNN from 1983 to 2001, Leon Harris is now anchor of the 5 PM, 6 PM and 11 PM news and cohost of "Capital Sunday" at ABC7/WJLA-TV in the nation's capital. He was born and raised in Akron, Ohio, and while at Buchtel High School, from which he graduated in 1979, he got a National Merit Scholarship to Ohio University. He interned at CNN, and after graduating from college cum laude with a communication degree in 1983, he joined this network in Atlanta as a cameraman. Next, he worked in the network's satellite department becoming its assistant director. In working out agreements for national and international satellite services, he often traveled with the White House press. In 1992, he sat in as substitute on-camera talent to enable a new show to be set up for broadcast. A pair of network vice presidents noticed his on-camera presence and made him a reporter and coanchor for "Prime News" and "The World Today." Later he became coanchor of "Early Edition," "CNN Live Today" and "American Stories." Some of the big stories Harris covered for CNN were the 1992 Rodney King beating and the subsequent Los Angeles riots, the 1993 siege of the Russian Parliament, the 1995 Oklahoma City bombing, the 1997 murder of fashion great Gianni Versace, the 1999 plane crash of John Kennedy Jr., the World Trade Center attacks of 2001 and tornado damage in 2003 at Jackson, Tennessee. He also covered the 2000 presidential election and reported live from the Republican National Convention that year. In 2001, changes were underway at CNN that appeared to be substituting glamour and conservatism for old-style objective journalism, which seemed an unfortunate trend to any journalist who had been with the network during its years of gradual professional improvement. He also wanted to do more war coverage than management wished, and Harris was hired away by Washington station WJLA which having merged in 1999 with NewsChannel 8, was striving to be the city's predominant television news operation. He began at WJLA in October 2003 joining Maureen Bunyan and Kathleen Matthews.

The multiple Emmy winner has also received two CableAce awards as Best Newscaster, a National Headliner Award and the Louis R. Lautier Memorial Award. His favorite charities are those that benefit children, and he is on the boards of the YMCA, 100 Black Men and the Ohio University's Foundation Board. He is also on the advisory board of his alma mater's College of Communications for which he has established the Leon M. Harris Jr. Scholarship for minority students.

Further Readings: Baker, Chris. "WJLA Reels in CNN Anchor." [Online, 29 October 2003]. The Washington Times.com Web site www.washtimes.com; "Leon Harris." [Online, 17 February 2006]. ABC7 News Web site www.wjla.com/news; "Leon Harris." [Online]. The Akron Roundtable Web site www.akronroundtable.org/speakers; Rowe, Sean. "Anchor Leon Harris Leaving CNN." [Online, 4 September 2003]. WXIA-TV Atlanta Web site www.11alive.com/news.

Harshaw, Karla Garrett (23 January 1955–)

Karla Harshaw is editor of the *Springfield News-Sun* in Springfield, Ohio, and is also senior editor of Cox Community Newspapers. She was born in Cleveland, Ohio, and began writing for newspapers at age 13 in Dayton, Ohio; one of her middle school teachers was editor of the historically black *Dayton Express* and gave her a taste of newspaper reporting. Still earlier in her life, she had wanted to study nursing, largely based, she has said, on the snappy cape and crisp uniform worn by one of her aunts who was a nurse. Then a girl in her neighborhood was bitten by a dog, and the nursing career went out the window when she discovered she and the sight of blood did not mesh well. Harshaw also wrote for a local magazine while very young and after her sophomore year of high school participated in a summer training program at the *Dayton Daily News*. After this program ended, she became a stringer for the paper, an intern and finally a regular reporter. Harshaw attended and graduated in 1984 from Wright State University, where she majored in secondary education and minored in English. After graduation she remained with the *Daily News*, working as reporter, assistant city editor, features editor and assistant business manager until August 1990, when she left to edit another Cox newspaper, the *Springfield News-Sun*. In May 2000, she was given an additional assignment for the Cox papers: she was made senior editor for the chain's 12 community newspapers, meaning those having circulations of 55,000 or less. In this capacity, her primary concerns are to attract and retain good employees and to encourage cooperation among these papers and within the various departments of each paper.

Harshaw's participation in journalistic organizations has included membership in the National Association of Black Journalists, the National Association of Minority Media Executives, and the Ohio Newspaper Women's Association. She was also a founding member of the Dayton Association of Black Journalists. She was on the board of the American Society of Newspaper Editors beginning in 1995, was vice chair of this organization's 1998–1999 convention program committee and in April 2004, at age 49, she replaced Peter K. Bhatia, executive editor of the *Oregonian*, when she was elected president of ASNE—the first African-American woman to hold this position. In 1995, 1996 and 2002, she participated in selecting nominees for the Pulitzer Prize in various categories. She is on the board of trustees of Wilberforce University; the board of the Clark County, Ohio, Opportunities Industrialization Center; and the board of the Maynard Institute in California. She has been a frequent participant at roundtables, institutes and other venues where journalism is discussed. She was a keynote speaker in 1994 at the Inland Press Association Convention. In 1999, she took part in a Scripps Howard Foundation-sponsored roundtable on media credibility, was one of several editors joining host Marvin Kalb in 2001 to discuss newspaper leadership and credibility before the National Press Club and in 2005, speaking as immediate past president of ASNE, addressed teachers attending that organization's High School Journalism Institute and was a speaker for Communication Week at Central State University in Wilberforce, Ohio. She has been quoted in various stories and on several Web sites on journalism-related topics. Examples from 2004 are a CapitolHillBlue.com story by Lance Gay that quoted her as expressing concern about the way the George W. Bush administration was attempting to foster secrecy in transportation policy in the name of national security, and in an Associated Press story by David Brauder, she was quoted on the subject of how U.S. efforts in Iraq had become a war of images, with pictures providing war-related reality for the public and hence affecting public opinion and even war policy. In particular, she spoke about news photos of Army private Lynndie England and how those graphic photos of prisoner abuse caused a major change in public perception of the war in Iraq. Among her earliest recognitions were two Ohio Newspaper Women's Association awards for religion writing, in 1981 and 1982. Harshaw won the "Best of Cox" award for column writing in 1995 and took third place in 1997 for editorial writing in the Ohio Associated Press competition and second place in 1999. In April 1997, she was inducted into the NABJ Region IV Hall of Fame. Her many activities were interrupted for a time in July 2005, when she had surgery for removal of a brain tumor. Following surgery, she took a seven-month leave of absence, returning to work at the end of January 2006.

Further Readings: "Editors Elect Karla Garrett Harshaw to Lead ASNE." [Online, 23 April 2004]. American Society of Newspaper Editors Web site www.asne.org; Harshaw, Karla Garrett.

Hartman, Hermene Demaris

"My First Job." [Online, 2 January 2006]. Chips Quinn Scholars Web site www.chipsquinn.org/jobs/first; Prince, Richard. "Operation to Remove Editor's Tumor Successful." [Online, 12 July 2005]. Richard Prince's Journal-isms. Maynard Institute Web site www.maynardije.org.

Hartman, Hermene Demaris (24 September 1948–)

Magazine publisher Hermene Hartman established her reputation with *N'Digo*, a successful Chicago "magapaper" that also is probably the best-known black weekly in the nation, and more recently for reviving the slick, sophisticated magazine *Savoy*. She was born into affluence in Chicago, the only child of Pepsi distributor Herbert Hartman. Her educational background includes a 1970 B.A. in fine arts and 1974 master's degrees in sociology and education from Roosevelt University, plus a 1994 MBA from the University of Illinois. Her work life began in the civil rights movement working with the Southern Christian Leadership Conference's Operation Breadbasket under Jesse Jackson and after his break with the SCLC, Jackson's new organization called Operation Push; her job was coordinating this organization's Black Expo event. Next, she was a public service programming producer for station WBBM-TV in Chicago; in this position, she was best known for producing a community affairs program called "Common Ground." From 1978 to 1984, she taught behavioral science courses at Truman College and at City Colleges of Chicago, the nation's largest community college system. At the latter school, she became director of development and communications, then vice chancellor for external affairs. Concurrent with her academic work, she founded The Hartman Group, a Chicago public relations firm that she continues to operate.

Feeling the need to provide a forum for black success stories in Chicago, she launched *N'Digo*, which she termed "a Magapaper for the Urbane," in 1989. It began as a monthly lifestyle periodical, printed black-and-white on newsprint but containing editorial copy more nearly like that of a magazine, to include material about black celebrities, travel, politics, entertainment, the arts and city gossip. Having had a startup circulation of 50,000, the periodical was converted to a weekly and now reports readership of roughly 500,000. Its present focus is on successful African Americans and on business news and lifestyle topics of interest to the city's prosperous black middle class. She herself has written her publisher's page commentary on issues affecting life in the city, and a new feature in *N'Digo* is "West Side Story," which focuses on life in the city's not-so-prosperous West Side. *N'Digo*'s success has enabled Hartman to spin off three related periodicals: the annual *N'Digo Profiles*, said to reach a readership of 1.2 million; *N'Digo Profiles Educational Guide*, aimed at classroom use; and *Jr. Wings*, an on-board magazine published twice yearly to serve young travelers. She is also founder and president of the N'Digo Foundation, which she created in 1995 to do fundraising for education. The foundation sponsors an annual black-tie gala called N'Digo Live and hosts other music events that raise money for educational purposes, such as college scholarships for Chicago students.

Hartman's latest and riskiest magazine venture is her resurrecting of *Savoy*, an upscale magazine that first appeared in 2001, the brainchild of publisher Keith Clinkscales, CEO of Vanguarde Publishing in New York, and closed in Chapter 11 bankruptcy three years thereafter. In a bankruptcy auction on 3 May 2004, *Savoy*'s remains were purchased for $375,000 and assumption of up to $516,000 in its liabilities by another New York company, Jungle Media. In turn, the property was bought by Hermene Hartman through Hartman Publishing Company's new subsidiary, Jazzy Communications, for $600,000. Eight months later, in February 2005, the magazine was relaunched, looking much as it had before, remaining a slick, full-color general-interest magazine geared to the black urban elite. The magazine's new editor was Monroe Anderson, and its 116-page first issue's cover pictured Illinois Sen. Barack Obama and his wife, Michelle. Inside were 14 articles, among which were two summary pieces, one on 50 great civil rights moments since that involving Rosa Parks, the other a spread on 21 African-American standouts from different walks of life. In addition to the editor's social/political commentary column, "Monroe's Doctrine," were columns by economist Julianne Malveaux, motivational specialist Terri Williams and the "Today" show's Wayne Johnson, who deals with lifestyle topics. A horoscope column and a social column titled "The Rhumboogie" also appeared. Aside from these five columns, *Savoy*'s content includes the arts, travel, current events and issues, a profile of a newsworthy African American and a department called "It's About Time," covering issues of special interest to black Americans. The new magazine, which honored all remaining subscriptions, will appear 10 times yearly. Circulation at relaunch was 325,000 and Hartman's plan was to seek outside capital that would enable the company to attract more subscriptions so as to depend less heavily on newsstand sales. Among the initial advertisers were Wal-Mart, Mercedes, General Motors, Toyota, Citibank, McDonalds and Hennessy. Success or failure will depend largely on the magazine's ability to attract a strong advertising base and Hartman's ability to secure the necessary capital from venture firms or other sources. Taking over a national magazine and moving it to Chicago was a bold move, even though her only direct general-interest competitors are *Ebony*, *Black Enterprise*, *Essence*, and *Suede*.

Hartman has been active in many organizations apart from her business interests. She has served on the national advisory committee of the John F. Kennedy Center for the Performing Arts, was vice president of the Chicago Association of Black Journalists, a board member of Boy Scouts of America, an advisory board member for the School of Arts and Design at the University of Illinois, a 2003–2004 member of the Hearings Board in Illinois in 2004, and president of ABLE, the Alliance of Business Leaders and Entrepreneurs. She is on the board of the Illinois Community College Trustees Association and is on the advisory board for Chicago's Children's Advocacy Center. She has received dozens of awards and recognitions, and as a public relations media consultant, she has worked with such clients as Phillip Morris, the Chicago public schools, Shell Oil, the Goodman Theater and the Chicago Symphony Orchestra. In 1983, she collaborated on editing a book of photographs taken of the Rev. Martin Luther King, Jr.

Books by Hermene Demaris Hartman: With John Tweedle, eds., *A Lasting Impression: A Collection of Photographs of Martin Luther King, Jr.* (Columbia, S.C.: University of South Carolina Press, 1983).

Further Readings: Cottman, Michael H. "Savoy Magazine Gears Up for Its Long-Awaited Relaunch." [Online, 28 January 2005]. Black America Web site www.blackamericaweb.com; "Hermene Hartman." [Online, August 2005]. Kellogg School of Management Web site www.kellogg,northwestern.edu; "Hermene Hartman." [Online]. The History Makers Web site www.thehistorymakers.com/biography; Maymon, Jason. "Thriving Magpaper Changes the Image of African Americans One Issue at a Time." [Online, 2003]. Echo Magazine site http://echo.colum.edu; "Payne, Allison. "Chicago's Very Own: Hermeme Hartman." WGN9, Chicago site http://wgntv.trb.com/news/local/eveningnews.

Haygood, Wil (1954–)

Known to many as a book author, Wil Haygood is also a staff writer for the Style section of the *Washington Post*. He was born in Columbus, Ohio, and was raised by his mother and various relatives after his father abandoned the family. He grew up in the Bolivar Arms housing project on Mount Vernon Avenue in Columbus, a street, and neighborhood, known for music and nightlife, which his mother found irresistible. In consequence, he was mainly brought up by his grandparents with the assistance of his grandfather's no-nonsense brothers. He has described his youth as a happy one, playing sports and fishing, watched over by supportive family members. After finishing at Franklin Heights High School, where he was on the basketball team, he attended Miami University in Oxford, Ohio, majoring in urban studies. His first job after graduating in 1976 was with Macy's in New York City, but when he lost that position, he took a job reporting at the Columbus bureau of the historically black weekly newspaper the *Call & Post*. Here, he discovered his talent for writing that eventually led him to much more high-profile jobs at the *Boston Globe* and the *Washington Post*. First, however, he was a copy editor at the *Charleston Gazette* in West Virginia for two years and worked at the *Pittsburgh Post-Gazette* for the following year. Then in 1984, he joined the *Boston Globe*, where he worked for 17 years as a feature writer, national correspondent and foreign correspondent. In a January 2000 interview with Tran Ha of Poynter.org, Haygood said that his favorite interview was with former Alabama governor and segregationist George Wallace. At the time of the interview, Wallace was bedridden and in need of constant care, most of which was provided by his African-American nurse, his African-American physical therapist and even an African-American deputy assigned to guard him. The dramatic irony of a man who had so opposed racial integration being tended and comforted by blacks as he neared life's end made for an excellent story. Another story that Haygood regards as one of his best took him in 1989 to interview soul singer James Brown in prison confined there after having been convicted on assault and weapons charges, and from there to search out Brown's scattered backup singers, whose livelihoods had been severely affected by the star's legal troubles. In April 1992, he covered the Los Angeles race riots that erupted after the clearing of several white policemen who had been charged with brutality to minorities. The rioting resulted in 50 deaths, 12,000 arrests and around $1 billion in property damage. More recently, at the end of the 1990s, Haygood and a *Globe* colleague traveled to Africa to write a series about the awful effects of AIDS on this continent. Another major story at around the same time was headlined "A Black Writer's Journey into Poor White America." For this story, Haygood spent a month traveling around a thousand miles in three states, observing and interviewing. A standout interview for this story was with a white American Nazi Party member in a jail near St. Louis. Although he had great affection for the *Globe*, Haygood could not turn down a 2001 invitation to join the Style section of the *Washington Post*. In December 2002, Haygood's story "Crossed Paths in Africa" detailed the polarized state of health care in Kenya, where little care is available for the poor. "The Promised Land" appeared in October 2004; it was the two-part story of black Virginia farmer Ricky Haynie's legal battle with the U.S. Department of Agriculture. Haynie, who had leased and farmed thousands of acres of land, charged racial discrimination in the government's handling of agricultural loans. Haygood wrote a touching story about the effects of Hurricane Katrina on the poor black sections of New Orleans in September 2005, and in October of the same year appeared stories that drew their inspiration from the death of civil rights icon Rosa Parks and Alice Yaeger Kaplan's book *The Interpreter* (New York: Free Press, 2005), which charged differential punishment along racial lines for World War II soldiers who had been charged with crimes. A December 2005 story reported Haygood's interview with Liberia's president-elect Ellen Johnson Sirleaf, who recently had been elected as the first woman president in all of Africa. Also in that month appeared a human-interest account of former Washington, D.C., police chief Isaac Fulwood, who had been faced with arresting his own brother. Possibly the story had special appeal for Haygood in that both of his own brothers have been in frequent trouble with the law.

Aside from his newspaper work, Haygood has written books and magazine stories. A fine example of his magazine work, reprinted below, is a December 2000 article in the *American Prospect* titled "Why Negro Humor Is So Black." In it, he discusses the rise of African-American comedy from vaudeville to the so-called "chitlin circuit" in the South and finally to the mainstream entertainment media, and how black comedians' central challenge was to mirror social wrongs without alienating the white audience. Noting that the world of black comedy has been mainly male, Haygood gives special credit to the late comic Moms Mabley, born Loretta Mary Aiken. The first of Haygood's four books appeared in 1986; *Two on the River* was set on the Mississippi and was done with photographer Stan Grossfeld. The second book received a great deal more attention. It was on the life of flamboyant New York Congressman Adam Clayton Powell, Jr., and was titled *King of the Cats*. In it, Haygood presents Powell as a man ahead of his time and as someone the Eisenhower administration did not quite know how to handle. At that time in history, Powell was the primary political spokesman for the rights of black Americans, and Haygood relates the informal deal struck between the congressman and the White House that helped chip away at some of the nation's most blatant aspects of racial discrimination. To gather material for his third book, Haygood took a leave from his duties at the *Boston Globe* and returned to his Ohio roots. In 1997 appeared *The Haygoods of Columbus*, his memoir about growing up in this city, and his particular section of the city, during a time of change as urban renewal was changing the black community there. His most recent book, *In Black and White*, was his 2003 biography of entertainer Sammy Davis, Jr., a man literally caught between black roots and white aspirations and who, with religion absent in his early life, suddenly turned to Judaism. Becoming a Jew, wrote Haygood, gave Davis a new and unusual role to play during a show business career that, in the main, appealed more strongly to whites than to blacks. The film rights to Haygood's book were optioned in 2004 by Universal Pictures and Imagine Entertainment with plans for Denzel Washington to direct the movie.

Haygood has been a three-time winner of the National Association of Black Journalists Award and has also won the Sunday Magazine Editors Award twice and the New England Associated Press Award once. While at the *Globe*, he was a Pulitzer Prize finalist for his story "From Memphis to Cape Town—A Writer's Journey Around the World." *The Haygoods of Columbus* won the Great Lakes Book Award in 1997 and the Ohioana Book Award for nonfiction in 1998. He has been awarded the James Thurber Literary Fellowship, the Alicia Patterson Foundation Fellowship and the Yaddo Fellowship given by the Trask Society. He has been a workshop leader for the Zora Neale Hurston/Richard Wright Foundation's annual Writers' Week summer short-course for black writers.

"Why Negro Humor Is So Black" by Wil Haygood

Let us now, at long last, praise all those Negro humorists from years gone by. Some still with us, but so many gone. Moms Mabley and Pigmeat Markham and Redd Foxx and Flip Wilson and Bert Williams and Amos 'n' Andy, gone. Stepin Fetchit, gone. Dick Gregory and Richard Pryor and Chris Rock and Steve Harvey and Eddie Murphy and Bill Cosby are very much still with us, though Gregory and Pryor are ailing and far removed from the comic stage. Altogether, through the years, they've held on.

The Negro comics' trajectory has gone from minstrel shows to outdoor tents, from honky-tonks to Greenwich Village salons, from amphitheaters to the big screen. Laughter washing over them like brittle sunshine. Sometimes the laughter is of a confused sort, owing to misinterpretation, the joke merged with history and the ears of whites placed at awkward angles.

"I was a nigger for 23 years," the great Richard Pryor once explained. "I gave it up—no room for advancement."

So much social pain, endured. But that didn't stop the curtain from opening. Hell, it opened wider. And there they stood, mike in hand, a on of history on their backs, free to strangle it or reinterpret it. History written by the jokesters. Just trying to get a laugh. Just holding on to freedom's ticket.

The Negro humorists began their huge rise after the death of vaudeville, on the chitlin circuit. To a comic, the chitlin circuit meant the South, out-of-the-way theaters, low paychecks, funky hotel rooms, hot plates, and checks that might bounce. The smart comic demanded pay in advance.

They were spawned by he society in which they worked and sweated. They were Negroes, and they were America, too. But the Negro comic always had to be careful. How to find jokes and—in a land where pain was everywhere, or most everywhere—share them with civility? If Nat King Cole could be dragged off a stage by white thugs in Alabama, worse could befall a Negro comic with a chip on the shoulder. The sly challenge was to hold a mirror up to America. Because there sat, either in the audience or on the other side of the TV screen, white America. Welcome to Negro life, at a safe remove.

There is nothing like Negro humor. It is loud, profane, juicy, wondrous, scabrous, willful, tricky, and sometimes delivered in coded language. It is steeped, as well, in American history, in blackface and Jim Crow laws and segregation. And also in the stuttering integration we all still participate in. And it is funny as hell.

Comedy is hard. And when it is awash in racial battling, it is even harder. Imagine looking in the mirror and watching the mirror crack and trying to put it back together for a laugh.

"Take a nigger to bed with you tonight," Dick Gregory had once said to the whites attending a civil rights rally in the state of Mississippi. He held aloft a copy of his autobiography, titled *nigger*. It drew laughter, gales of it. So it was, all at once, publicity and a sexual joke and a nod to the pangs of history.

At the height of civil rights unrest in Mississippi 38 years ago, President John Kennedy went on national TV. He looked somber and spoke somberly, holding a piece of paper in his hands, reading from it. He talked of Negro rights and the long arc of history that was now circling the country regarding the Negro. James Meredith, an eccentric black man, had entered the all-white University of Mississippi. His enrollment set off riots and killings. Kennedy looked out into the TV audience (needless to say, he assumed it was all white) and asked who among them were willing to "change places with the Negro." Negroes might have gotten a sure laugh out of that one, rushing to their tenement windows, looking for whites who might be yelling, "Me! I will change places with the Negro!"

Now fast-forward to years later, and listen to comic Chris Rock doing stand-up. Looking out over his audience, into all those white faces, and saying, "Ain't no white man here willing to trade places with me." Long pause. "And I'm rich!" From Jack Kennedy to Chris Rock. Who'll trade places with the Negro? The black funny bone is razor sharp.

Negro humor continues to perplex segments of America (translation: white America). You can see it, almost feel it, in the white audience reaction to *The Original Kings of Comedy*, a film directed by Spike Lee. The movie stars four stand-up comics: Bernie Mac, D.L. Hughley, Steve Harvey, and Cedric the Entertainer. It was shot in a cavernous auditorium in Charlotte, North Carolina, one of those southern cities that used to be a stop on the chitlin circuit.

Lee lets his comics talk about anything they want to: sex, marriage, whites, blacks, hip-hop. The movie serves as a kind of explainer, actually—blacks explaining, sometimes in inside-joke fashion, our dilemma of existing tranquilly in society and hoping whites get it. It is a kind of history lesson of the American Negro laugh track. The whites in the audience stand out. They are the integrators; for once, it is not the other way around. There is a nervous sweetness when the camera pans the audience, settling, momentarily, upon whites seated next to blacks.

One need only take apart the subjects that Lee's comics cover to find serious interludes, riffs on history and historical perspective, dollops of pain. Cedric the Entertainer talks about golf. Barred from all those country clubs and golf courses, blacks haven't played much golf, let alone talked about it. Before Tiger Woods, there had been only two Negro golfers of note. Lee Elder and Charlie Sifford. Rolling across golf courses on national TV in the 1970s, they were as rare as aliens. Cedric notes that Woods is propelling blacks in large numbers onto the golf courses. He talks of a recent outing, of running into "the brothers" on the golf course, of one of those brothers asking him to "let me ride your golf cart to the store, man." It's a funny line, a great line, of blacks breaking the rules, stylishly and comically upsetting them. Yes, Cedric seems to be saying, blacks will golf, but we will do it in our own imagination, our own way: With some soul. Or how else cope with the blighted history of the sport?

The mixing of comedy and raced can indeed be tricky terrain. If there is, as many sociologists contend, a little truth in every stereotype, how far does the black comic go in bull's-eyeing the stereotype? How massive can a backfire become? Consider *The Secret Diary of Desmond Pfeiffer*, a television series that premiered on UPN in 1998, described as a "Lincoln-era comedy." The show was about an imaginary black Englishman who served as a smart-alecky servant to President Abraham Lincoln. The black actor who played Desmond Pfeiffer, right along with the show itself, was howled off the air. The NAACP was at the forefront of the protests.

There are some blacks, tending toward upper-crust society, who feel that the rumblings in the Negro closet of humor, when taken to the edge, would best be forced back inside that closet. For years Bill Crosby—whose comedy is decidedly more congenial and less feisty than many of the younger comics'—has expressed displeasure at the scintillating brand of humor propelled by he likes of Eddie Murphy and Bernie Mac. Cosby is your father's best comic; Bernie Mac, maybe secretly, is yours.

If Mac might remind some of the stereotype—his outlandishness, his vulgarity—the stereotype cuts two ways. It swings history at us, hoping we're sophisticated enough to understand that Mac understands. Some blacks hoard artifacts from the Jim Crow era, the Colored Only signs, the posters of the mammy musicals. Other blacks sometimes don't understand such a hobby. It could be sophistication taken to a new and bold level. Shattered images don't have to be forgotten.

Lee delves into race and history, and the degrees of separation among blacks on the issue of race. Along with *The Original Kings of Comedy*, Lee recently made another movie on race and comedy. *Bamboozled* is about blackface, that tortured period of entertainment that saw whites blacking their faces to present their stereotyped images of black folk. One of the intriguing sidelights to *Bamboozled* was *The New York Times*'s refusal to run one of Lee's ads for the movie. Reportedly, it portrayed a man in blackface eating watermelon. For many blacks, there is nothing like the watermelon joke to rush the adrenaline. Cartoonists in the 1930s often depicted some grand activity—a parade, a march—and in the background had Negroes sitting on fence posts, chomping on watermelon. I remember vividly my grandmother in Columbus, Ohio, refusing to let her grandchildren eat watermelon on the front porch. Less neighbors see us. Less the world think we had no couth.

The Original Kings of Comedy performed well at the box office, but *Bamboozled* bombed. Whites did not wish to see the film, but neither did blacks. In a different time, blackface got laughs. And Lee updates the story in *Bamboozled*: The movie is about a blackface act done by blacks that becomes strangely popular. But blackface presents a uniquely painful portrait of America. Even Lee's sophisticated reworking—blacks in blackface—draws too much blood. It anguishes too many hearts. It might take years more before we understand the damaging psyche of cinematic blackface.

Better financial fortune befell Robert Redford's film *The Legend of Bagger Vance*, a movie about a white golfer, played by Matt Damon, who has lost his swing and has it revived by Bagger Vance, a mystical Negro played by Will Smith. It is set circa the 1930s, when there were no blacks in professional golf tournaments in the South. So it is fable and myth. It is also a silly movie that runs in the opposite direction of hard racial truths. The Negro character, seemingly ripped from an earlier time in American film history, appears to exist only for the betterment and soul enrichment of white folks. As *The Washington Post*'s film critic mused about *Vance* and the character portrayed by Smith: "Isn't it time to put Stepin Fetchit to rest?"

Negro comedy is hard. But it can also be redemptive when it is shared. Let loose, it flies like birds, as Lee's quarter of comics shows. So often Negro life, lived in the trenches, provides just enough comic relief to keep us going, smiling.

In 1936 a young Negro minister by the name of Adam Clayton Powell—so fair-skinned he could have passed as white—was hustling toward a first-class train compartment in Atlanta. A porter who had looked over his shoulder out of curiosity wondered if the man he has just seen stepping into the train was a Negro. Maybe. Maybe not. But damn if he wasn't going to check it out, go fetch a superior. Upon entering the first-class compartment, the superior looked around and yelled out: "Hey, we believe there might be a nigger in here!" Before eyes could rest suspiciously upon him, Powell hopped up. "Where! You better find him and get him the hell out of here! What kind of train are you running?" Then the young minister sat down, like a king, like a rich white man. And the train pulled off. Powell must have been laughing uproariously on the inside. Couldn't laugh on the outside, though. Negro life was too risky to do that.

Negro laughter, then, is hard earned, has been for so very long; and the kings and queens of comedy knew it.

How do women deal with the male-dominated world of Negro comedy? Black women, for years, shied from the women's movement, contending they were wrapped up in the movement of the black race as a whole. Their men needed them. Many of the male comics' observations are directed at them, at their expense—rollicking lines about divorce proceedings and sex in the bedroom. The humor does lie somewhere between sexist and raw. It's not meant to be feminist or antifeminist; it is meant to be funny. And sometimes it is just plain contagious. Many of the heartiest laughs in *Kings* during the bawdy sex jokes come from women. As if they are saying: Together, we shall laugh at ourselves. Or, as James Baldwin once said about a particular thorny truism: "It be's that way sometimes."

Moms Mabley knew how to deal with male egos. "There ain't nothing an old man can do for me," she once said, "but bring me a message from a young one."

Moms walked out on stage one night, looked around. "Hi, children. How ya'll doin' tonight?" she asked the audience. She stood staring. It was as if she was sucking in all the years, all the woes of Negro life, all the travails that had come and were yet to come. All the jokes born from pain, all the pain that led to laughter. She seemed to answer her own question: "Yeah, I know! I know how ya'll feel. Moms is tired too."

Long live Moms.

Source: The above article originally appeared in the 18 December 2000 issue of *The American Prospect* (vol. 11 no. 26). It appears here by permission of *The American Prospect.*

Books by Wil Haygood: With Stan Grossfeld, *Two on the River* (Boston: Atlantic Monthly Press, 1986); *King of the Cats: the Life and Times of Adam Clayton Powell, Jr.* (Boston: Houghton Mifflin, 1993); *The Haygoods of Columbus: A Love Story* (Boston: Houghton Mifflin, 1997); *In Black and White: The Life of Sammy Davis, Jr.* (New York: Billboard, 2003).

Further Readings: Ha, Tran. "Journalism Is a Calling," Parts 1 and 2. [Online, 14 January 2000 and 18 January 2000]. Poynter Online Web site www.poynter.org; Prince, Richard. "Wil Haygood Hooks Up With Denzel Washington." [Online, 7 July 2005]. Richard Prince's Journal-isms. Maynard Institute Web site www.maynardije.org; "Wil Haygood: Leading African American Biographer to Speak at Washington University." [Online]. Washington University in St. Louis site http://news-info.wustl.edu.

Henderson, Angelo B. (14 October 1962–)

From Pulitzer Prize-winning *Wall Street Journal* feature writer to ordained minister is an unusual career progression, but it is the one chosen by one-time automotive reporter Angelo Henderson. Alongside his pastoral duties, he is also a media consultant, motivational speaker and popular radio talk-show host in Detroit. Henderson was born in Louisville, Kentucky, and although his family moved to Oakland, California, during his teenage years, he is a 1985 journalism graduate of the University of Kentucky. During high school he was a section editor of the school yearbook and went to a summer journalism workshop at Northwestern University. During college, he not only worked on the *Kentucky Kernel* campus newspaper, but set a near record with the number of internships he completed, which include Walt Disney World, CBS affiliate WHAS-TV, the *Wall Street Journal*, the *Lexington Herald-Leader* and the *Detroit Free Press*. Following graduation, his first employment was with the *St. Petersburg Times*, for which he was a staff writer in 1985 and 1986. In this job he covered tourism for the paper's business section and reported on largely black South St. Petersburg for the Neighborhoods section. In 1986, he became a business writer for the *Courier-Journal* in Lexington, Kentucky, and remained there until leaving in 1989 to work as a business reporter and columnist for the *Detroit News*, covering small-and minority business in Michigan. His next newspaper job was at the *Wall Street Journal*, for which he worked during 1995 through 1997 as a reporter and then in 1997 and 1998 as a deputy bureau chief in Detroit. His initial beat was the U.S.-based operations of Honda, Toyota and other non-U.S. automobile manufacturers. Next, he covered Chrysler Corporation. He reported on the company's negotiations with the United Auto Workers union and on the failed takeover attempt of Kirk Kerkorian. As bureau chief, he supervised and contributed to coverage of the newly globalized automobile industry. From 1998 through 2000, he was a special Page One writer for the *Journal*, working with editor Ken Wells. It was during this time that Henderson wrote "Crime Scene," the story that won him the 1999 Pulitzer for feature writing. This story required considerable time to research and write; it involved the fatal shooting by a white pharmacist of a young black robbery suspect. It took Henderson months to gain the confidence of the pharmacist, Dennis Grehl, who eventually opened up and talked with Henderson at great length about his fears and feelings. Henderson also interviewed the mother of the man who was shot, Tony Williams. The result was a story of unusual depth and feeling. In 1999, Henderson was hired as associate editor by Real Times Newspapers, which had bought the old *Chicago Defender* chain: the *Defender, Michigan Chronicle, New Pittsburgh Courier, Memphis Tri-State Defender* and *Michigan Front Page*. Henderson's charge was to focus on content and to try to build the new group into an African-American Gannett or Knight-Ridder. In 2001, at age 39, he took his last newspaper job to date, as special projects reporter for the *Detroit News*, for which he wrote on crime and race, usually in urban settings. He also began hosting, every other week, a weekday morning talk show, "Inside Detroit," on WCHB-AM. His cohost is Mildred Gaddis. In addition, the busy Henderson started his own media-consulting firm, Angelo Ink L.L.C., to handle his training and development sessions for journalists, civic organizations, and corporate executives and to book his engagements as a motivational speaker. He has conducted training workshops for such clients as the *Charlotte Observer, Atlanta Journal-Constitution, Providence Journal* and Cleveland *Plain Dealer* and has spoken to college groups at the University of Kentucky, Dartmouth, Brown, Columbia, Vanderbilt, Florida A&M, Alabama State and the University of Iowa. He has taught training sessions for the American

Society of Newspaper Editors, the Freedom Forum, the Poynter Institute and the Asian American Journalists Association. Examples of his writing appear in two anthologies: Ken Wells' *Floating Off the Page: The Best Stories from The Wall Street Journal's "Middle Column"* (New York: Simon & Schuster, 2002) and David Garlock's *Pulitzer Prize Feature Stories: America's Best Writing 1979–2003* (Ames, Iowa: Iowa State Press, 2003), plus Edward Jay Friedlander and John Lee's writing text *Feature Writing for Newspapers and Magazines*, 5th edition (Boston: Allyn and Bacon, 2004). Aside from his Pulitzer, he has received other honors, such as the Detroit Press Club Award, the NABJ award for coverage of the black condition, and the Unity Award for excellence in minority reporting for public affairs and social issues. Not bad for a fellow who was once told by a *St. Petersburg Times* editor that he was not suited for journalism.

Henderson's personal needs had begun to change toward the spiritual, and in 1999, on the very day he received news of his Pulitzer Prize, he became an ordained deacon in the Baptist Church. He enrolled in the Ecumenical Theological Seminary of Detroit and in December 2003, he was ordained and licensed as a minister. In January 2004, became associate pastor of Hope United Methodist Church in Southfield, Michigan, a rapidly growing African-American congregation. At that time, he gave up his newspaper job at the *Detroit News*. In his church work, Henderson directs the church's efforts to utilize the Internet, broadcasting and e-mail, and he travels to speak to other congregations and church organizations.

"Jarrett's Years as a Journalist, as an Educator"
by Angelo B. Henderson

He challenged us, chastised us and changed us as Black people.

Vernon Jarrett wasn't afraid to fight for us. In fact, he was created to do just that—not with his hands, but with his head.

Strategic. Uncompromising. Fearless.

He knew who he was and he'd tell you who you were if you ever forgot.

Cantankerous about education, freedom and fairness for his people because he cared; impatient because he was passionate.

It wasn't often that anyone was confused about what Vernon Jarrett said.

Flustered or frustrated by his comments, maybe, but never fuzzy about the message.

As a columnist, editorial board member, television show host, reporter, author and founder of NAACP's ACT-SO (Academic, Cultural, Technological and Scientific Olympics), Vernon Jarrett was never scared to say exactly what he meant. That's why no one could ever speak for him.

We can't even do that today, and he's no longer with us.

The fact is he started his journalism life with us as a reporter here at the Chicago Defender, a Black-owned newspaper, and he ended it here as a columnist. He believed in the Black press.

In this section, you will hear from Vernon Jarrett—in his own words. He's going to talk about education, the war, the church, and you know Vernon—whatever else he wants to.

Farewell to another civil rights pioneer, who has joined the heavenly list of civil rights greats. There was DuBois, Langston, Truth, Wells—and now there's Jarrett.

Source: This selection originally appeared on the Angelo Ink Web site and appears here by permission of the Rev. Henderson.

Further Readings: "Angelo Henderson." [Online]. The History Makers Web site www.thehistorymakers.com/biography; Hunt, Charis and Latrisha Jackson. "Journalist Journey to Valor." Soul Source (July 2004). Also Online on Angelo Ink Web site www.angeloink.com/articles; Newkirk, Pamela T. "Guess Who's Leaving the Newsrooms? Too Many Journalists of Color Don't Stick Around. Why?" [Online, September/October 2000]. Columbia Journalism Review site http://archives.cjr.org; Russell. Mark. "One Creative Mind, One Off-Center Idea, One Pulitzer Prize: Observations on Reporting from The Wall Street Journal's Angelo Henderson." [Online]. Angelo Ink Web site www.angeloink.com/articles; Scharfemberger, John. "Pulitzer Prize Winner Angelo Henderson Credits Kentucky Roots in His Success." [Online]. Angelo Ink Web site www.angeloink.com/articles; SinhaRoy, Sanhita. "Number of Minority Journalists Declining." [Online, 17 April 2001]. The Progressive Media Project Web site www.progressive.org.

Herbert, Bob (7 March 1945–)

Bob Herbert's twice weekly op-ed column in the *New York Times* is also syndicated nationally by the New York Times News Service. He is, in 2006, the *Times*' only African-American columnist. Herbert was born in Brooklyn, New York, and served in the military during the Vietnam war, stationed in Korea with an engineer battalion. In 1988 he earned a B.S. in journalism from Empire State College, part of the State University of New York system. His career had begun years earlier, in 1970, as a reporter for the *Star-Ledger* in Newark, New Jersey. He also moonlighted at that time by working in his father's upholstery shop. He was promoted to night city editor in 1973 and remained with the paper until 1976, when he was hired by the *Daily News* in New York City. There, he was a reporter until 1981, when he was promoted to City Hall bureau chief, then to city editor in 1983. In 1985, he was given a column, which he wrote until 1993, and membership on the paper's editorial board. It was at this time that he began work on his college degree. The athletic-looking Herbert broke into television journalism in 1990 as a panelist on the new weekly news show "Sunday Edition" on WCBS-TV. He also became host of a New York public television show, "Hotline." In 1991, he became a national correspondent for NBC, working for the "NBC Nightly News" and "The Today Show." Finally, in 1993, he returned to newspapering as a *New York Times* columnist and at present is one of only seven columnists syndicated by the New York Times News Service. Like fellow NYTNS columnist Maureen Dowd, Herbert is a liberal and is one of U.S. journalism's most outspoken critics of President George W. Bush, his administration and the war in Iraq. Herbert's columns deal with political and social issues ranging from the eternal battle between Republicans and Democrats, the criminal justice system, race relations in America and contemporary pop culture. In her review of Herbert's one book, *Promises Betrayed* (2005), essayist Barbara Ehrenreich called him the *Times*' conscience and a writer of unflinching candor. She likened his columns to the writing of Charles Dickens in that they enable readers to understand life as lived by people different from themselves. Edward Deevy of "The Deevy Report" blog credits Herbert with being the only mainstream journalist willing to write about what Deevy considers the present-day class war in America that is progressively making the rich richer and the less affluent even more so.

In recent years, Herbert has written against the growing official secrecy favored by the Bush administration and epitomized by Vice President Dick Cheney. He has spoken out against law enforcement efforts that seem to unfairly single out minorities, as in the clumsy 2002 sting operation in Tulia, Texas, that reportedly had the result of arresting ten percent of that town's black population. George W. Bush was governor at that time, and, in Herbert's view, President Bush's former attorney general John Ashcroft later closed the case to prevent further embarrassment. From the start, Herbert opposed the U.S.-led invasion of Iraq. He has called the invasion one of America's darkest moments, which has raided the federal treasury, alienated many of our former international allies and besmirched the national honor. In 2003, he referred to President Bush as The Reverse Robin Hood, an enabler of the nation's fattest fat cats, mean-spirited and hostile to poor and working citizens. In 2004, he protested the unchecked globalization of business, which, he wrote, might be good for the profits of multinational corporations, but has had a severe impact on working Americans. Another of his targets has been the medical insurance industry, which he considers a prime cause of higher medical costs. Another 2004 column dealt with possible voter intimidation in Florida, whereby officials, operating under presidential brother Gov. Jeb Bush, "investigated" elderly black Orlando voters, most of whom were expected to favor the Democratic ticket. When George Bush won re-election in November 2004, Herbert expressed dismay at the results of a University of Maryland survey showing that roughly 70 percent of Bush supporters believed Saddam Hussein had been working closely with Al Qaeda, about a third thought that weapons of mass destruction had been found in Iraq, and a third believed that most of our foreign allies were in agreement that we should invade Iraq. Such widespread ignorance of that which had appeared in the news, Herbert remarked, is absolutely frightening. In 2005, the columnist took on the Army's hard-sell tactics to recruit troops from the nation's high schools, protested the government's willingness to resort to torture and other degrading treatment of prisoners and called the network of secret prisons run by the CIA shameful and Dante-esque pointing out that out of fear we appear to be morphing into the very kind of country we have always despised. Herbert suggests that the military draft should be reinstated, in that if the nation's citizens really think the war on terror is important, they should be more willing to take part in it or sacrifice for it. The federal government's response to Hurricane Katrina's devastation of the Gulf Coast has also drawn stiff criticism from Herbert and appeared to strengthen his belief that the Bush administration is engaged in what amounts to class warfare against the poor in America. Herbert also has blasted "gangsta culture," which he considers self-destructive in that it glorifies crime, drugs, gangs and anti-intellectualism.

Herbert has done part-time teaching of journalism at Columbia University and at Brooklyn College. He served as chair of the Pulitzer Prize jury for the spot news reporting category in 1993 and has won an award for his own work from the American Society of Newspaper Editors. He also has been a winner of the Meyer Berger Award.

"The Army's Hard Sell" by Bob Herbert

The all-volunteer Army is not working. The problem with such an Army is that there are limited numbers of people who will freely choose to participate in an enterprise in which they may well be shot, blown up, burned to death or suffer some other excruciating fate.

The all-volunteer Army is fine in peacetime, and in military routs like the first gulf war. But when the troops are locked in a prolonged war that yields high casualties, and they look over their shoulders to see if reinforcements are coming from the general population, they find—as they're finding now—that no one is there.

Although it has been lowering standards, raising bonuses and all but begging on its knees, the Army hasn't reached its recruitment quota in months. There are always plenty of hawks in America. But the hawks want their wars fought with other people's children.

The problem now is that most Americans have had plenty of time to digest the images of people being blown up in Baghdad and mutilated in Fallujah, and they know that thousands of our troops are coming home in coffins, or without their arms, or without their legs, or paralyzed, or horribly burned.

War in the abstract can often seem like a good idea. Politicians get the patriotic blood flowing with their bombast and lies. But the flesh-and-blood reality of war is very different.

The war in Iraq was sold to the American public the way a cheap car salesman sells a lemon. Dick Cheney assured the nation that Americans in Iraq would be "greeted as liberators." Kenneth Adelman of the Pentagon's Defense Policy Board said the war would be a "cakewalk," and Donald Rumsfeld said on National Public Radio: "I can't say if the use of force would last five days or five weeks or five months, but it certainly isn't going to last any longer than that."

The hot-for-war crowd never mentioned young men and women being shipped back to their families deceased or maimed. Nor was there any suggestion that a broad swath of the population should share in the sacrifice.

Now, with the war going badly and the Army chasing potential recruits with a ferocity that is alarming, a backlash is developing that could cripple the nation's ability to wage war without a draft. Even as the ranks of new recruits are dwindling, many parents and public school officials are battling the increasingly heavy-handed tactics being used by military recruiters who are desperately trying to sign up high school kids.

"I started getting calls and people coming to the school board meeting testifying that they were getting inundated with phone calls from military recruiters," said Sandra Lowe, a board member and former president of the Sonoma Valley Unified School District in California.

She said parents complained that in some schools, "the military recruiters were on campus all the time," sometimes handing out "things that the parents did not want in their homes, including very violent video games."

Ms. Lowe said she was especially disturbed by a joint effort of the Defense Department and a private contractor, disclosed last week, to build a database of 30 million 16-to 25-year-olds, complete with Social Security numbers, racial and ethnic identification codes, grade point averages and phone numbers. The database is to be scoured for youngsters that the Pentagon believes can be persuaded to join the military.

"To have this national data collection is just over the top," Ms. Lowe said.

Like many other parents resisting aggressive recruitment measures, Ms. Lowe has turned to a Web site—leavemychildalone.org—that counsels parents on their rights and the rights of their children. She described the site as "wonderful."

What's not so wonderful is that this war with no end in sight is becoming an ever more divisive issue for Americans. A clear divide is developing between those who want to continue the present course and those who feel it's time to craft an exit strategy.

But with volunteers in extremely short supply, an even more emotional divide is occurring over the ways in which soldiers for this war are selected. Increasing numbers of Americans are recognizing the inherent unfairness of the all-volunteer force in a time of war. That emotional issue will become more heated as the war continues. And it is sure to resonate in the wars to come.

Source: Copyright © 2005 by The New York Times Co. Reprinted with permission. This column appeared on 27 June 2005.

Books by Bob Herbert: *Promises Betrayed: Waking Up from the American Dream* (New York: Times Books, 2005).

Further Readings: "Bob Herbert." [Online]. Discoverthenetworks.org: A Guide to the Political Left Website www.discoverthenetwork.org/individualPorfile.asp; "Columnist Biography: Bob Herbert" [Online]. New York Times Web site www.nytimes.com/ref/opinion.

Hickman, Fred (1956–)

Since late 2004, Fred Hickman has been with ESPN; prior to that time, he was sports anchor for the YES Network, which he joined in 2002. Still earlier, he was a senior anchor for "CNN/Sports Illustrated," having rejoined the network he had first served in 1980 as one of its original sports show hosts. He was raised in Springfield, Illinois, and attended Coe College in Cedar Rapids, Iowa, for two and a half years before leaving school in 1977 to take his first broadcast job, as a news anchor for Cedar Rapids radio station KLWW-AM. He moved to Springfield, Illinois, and a similar job at WFMB-AM. In 1979, he switched to television work as sports director and anchor for WICS-TV in Springfield. In June 1980, he was hired by CNN at age 23 as one of the original cohosts of "Sports Tonight." The first of these programs aired on 1 June 1980, with Hickman and Nick Charles hosting. After almost four years, Hickman left the network and from 1984 through 1986 was sports anchor for Detroit, Michigan, station WDIV-TV. He experienced difficult personal problems, including substance abuse and subsequent drug treatment but was rehired by CNN in 1986. He rejoined Nick Charles on "Sports Tonight" and in 1989, began as host of CNN's "This Week in the NBA" and the TBS show "NBA Preview." When Nick Charles began hosting a new show in 1998, Hickman cohosted "Sports Tonight" with Vince Cellini. He also did anchor duty for an NBA studio program on Wednesdays and covered the Goodwill Games in 1986, 1990 and 1994 and the Winter Olympics in 1992 and 1994. He left CNN to become the first sports anchor for YES Network when it was launched in 2002. Here, he hosted the pre- and post-game shows for the New York Yankees and New Jersey Nets and was host of a weekly show, "Yankees Magazine." In 2004, Hickman joined the staff of ESPN.

In 1993 and 1994, Hickman won CableACE awards for excellence in sports hosting; he also had been nominated for that award in 1991 and 1992. He has never been afraid to take a contrarian stand. In 2000, he was the only NBA

Most Valuable Player judge to select Allen Iverson over Shaquille O'Neal, and in 2001, when golf great Tiger Woods drew widespread criticism for complaining about losing money due to tour endorsements, Hickman took his part, pointing out how much Woods had done to invigorate the game. In 2003, he remarked that there is no such thing as a moral victory in sports. In July 2003, Hickman wrote for the YES Network's Web site about a heartwarming tee ball game played on the White House lawn by challenged youngsters, helped along by sports figures such as Darrell Green of the Washington Redskins and Ellis Burks of the Cleveland Indians. He "tipped his cap" to President George W. Bush for holding the event and recalled that in 1954, Bush himself had played Little League baseball in Texas. In a January 2004 Yes Network commentary on www.2.yesnetwork.com, Hickman wrote approvingly about the New York Yankees' Fantasy Camp in Tampa, Florida, where hero-worshiper fans can pay to spend a week staying in the team hotel, eating where the team eats during spring training, riding team buses, helping the team trainers and, pride of prides, having their own locker with their name on it.

Further Readings: "Fred Hickman." [Online, June 1999]. CNN/Sports Illustrated site http://sportsillustrated.cnn.com; "Fred Hickman." [Online]. Online Sports Web site www.onlinesports.com; "Fred Hickman." [Online, 2004]. YES Network Web site www.2.yesnetwork.com/announcers.

Holmes, Steven A. (?–)

Former *New York Times* deputy education editor and reporter Steven Holmes is now deputy national editor for domestic policy at the *Washington Post*. He joined the *Post* during the summer of 2005. He was born in Brooklyn, New York, and spent most of his formative years in Mt. Vernon, New York. He is a graduate of City College of New York and supported himself during his college years by driving a taxicab in the city. Holmes also attended the Michele Clark Memorial Program for Minority Journalists that Robert Maynard had founded prior to founding his better-known Maynard Institute. Holmes' first job in journalism was as a *Herald Statesman* police beat reporter in Yonkers, New York. Other early jobs were with United Press International, working out of Dallas, and with the *Constitution* in Atlanta. Next, he was a national correspondent for *Time Magazine*. Here, he did bureau work in Chicago, Los Angeles, Washington and London. He wrote about politics, finance, agriculture, the U.S. legal system and sports. One of his sports assignments was covering the Olympics in 1984. He joined the *New York Times* in the early 1990s, remaining with this paper until 2005. For much of this time, he worked in the paper's Washington bureau, where he wrote about matters of race and covered Congress and the State Department. He also reported on the campaigns of presidential hopefuls Patrick Buchanan and H. Ross Perot and both wrote and edited for the paper's 2001 Pulitzer Prize winning series "How Race is Lived in America." In 2000, Holmes published an unauthorized biography of Clinton-intimate Ron Brown, who had been President Bill Clinton's commerce secretary. The book titled *Ron Brown: An Uncommon Life*, was praised by some critics and criticized by others as too inclined to overlook Brown's faults. Holmes' book did not dwell on the conspiracy theories that sprang up after Brown's death in a plane crash in Bosnia-Croatia just after he had told the Clintons that he planned to enter a plea in the influence-peddling and illegal fundraising scandal that had already tarnished his reputation. An affair between Brown and a woman named Nolanda Hill had also just come to light, and Hill had implicated the secretary in taking drugs and accepting payoff money. Holmes accepted a new job as the *Washington Post*'s deputy national social policy editor in summer 2005 and has also continued to write, as well. Holmes has appeared on such television programs as "Washington Week in Review" on PBS and "Lead Story" on BET. In November 2005, he was a fellow in the Hoover Institution's William and Barbara Edwards Media Fellows Program.

In July 1991, Holmes wrote a story for the *New York Times* on the relationship between abortion and the subset of unborn babies that had been identified as disabled. His story pointed out the "eugenics mentality" sometimes directed at a disabled fetus and how it affected attitudes held by advocates for the disabled. One of his 1997 stories in the *Times* described the improved financial situation of racial minorities and how the Clinton administration was taking credit for this improvement. Holmes' story, however, also cited Census Bureau figures that showed no substantial economic improvement for the poorest fifth of U.S. families. On many occasions, Holmes has written stories with colleagues, as was the case in 2001 when he and Steven Greenhouse wrote about the troubles of Linda Chavez, who had just withdrawn her name from consideration to become U.S. secretary of labor. The conservative Chavez, a columnist and commentator, had been nominated by President-elect George W. Bush, but her candidacy ran aground when it was revealed that she had employed an illegal alien as her housekeeper. Another cowritten story for the *Times*, with David M. Halbfinger, appeared in 2005 and examined the makeup of the U.S. military, which the writers likened to people found at community colleges far more than either those attending four-year universities or living in ghetto/barrio neighborhoods. The most striking fact discussed in the story is that the affluent part of America is virtually absent from the military. Holmes and Halbfinger also noted the decline in members of Congress who had served in the military and what this situation implies about knowledgeable oversight of the armed services. Holmes again wrote on this topic in 2003 in a story that further examined how un-representative the makeup of the modern all-volunteer military had become as compared to the U.S. population in general. Another of his 2003 stories in the *Times* was about the marijuana-smoking admissions of three Democratic presidential candidates and how little the public seemed to care. In 2004, he wrote about Jenny House, a second cousin of President George W. Bush, who had founded an organization called Bush Relatives for Kerry, and he wrote a 2005 story regarding the death of Vice Adm. James B. Stockdale, who had been Ross Perot's vice-presidential running mate in 1992.

At the *Washington Post*, Holmes has continued his practice of often writing with a colleague. He and Hamil R. Harris wrote about tributes to Coretta Scott King in 2006, and with Richrad Morin, he has written about the findings of a survey conducted by the *Post*, the Henry J. Kiser Foundation and Harvard University to examine the climate for the black man in today's America. One striking finding was that most African-American men reported feeling that plenty of opportunity now exists for them but that due to residual acts of discrimination, they fear losing ground later. Also, they still perceive the court system as tougher on black men than on whites.

Books by Steven A. Holmes: *Ron Brown: An Uncommon Life* (New York: Chichester: John Wiley & Sons, 2000).

Further Readings: "Return of Draft Discussed by New York Times' Steven Holmes." [Online, 13 October 2003]. Hoover Institution Newsletter http://www.hoover.stanford.edu/pubaffairs/newsletter, "Steven A. Holmes." [Online]. University of Southern California Annenberg Institute for Justice and Journalism Web site www.justicejournalism.org.

Holt, Lester (8 March 1959–)

Blessed with a pleasant voice and movie star looks, Lester Holt has been lead anchor for daytime news and breaking news on MSNBC, is cohost of MSNBC's "Weekend Today" on Saturday and Sunday mornings, and has often filled in for host Matt Lauer on NBC's "Today" show. Holt was born in San Francisco, where his Air Force NCO father was stationed. He majored in government at California State University at Sacramento but dropped out of college to do radio reporting in San Francisco, where he was a disk jockey playing country and western music and was also a newsreader, mentored by the station's news director, Jerry Nachman. Two years later, at age 22, he moved to New York City and during 1981 and 1982, was a reporter for WCBS-TV. In 1982, he was transferred to KCBS-TV in Los Angeles to work as a reporter and weekend anchor for roughly two years, then in 1984, returned to New York's WNCB-TV in the same capacity. From 1986 to 2000, he worked at WBBM-TV in Chicago as evening anchor and reported from news locations around the world and in 1989, contributed to programming on the CBS magazine-format show "48 Hours." After 13 years in Chicago, he moved to MSNBC to cover the war in Afghanistan, the U.S. invasion of Iraq and the 2000 presidential election campaign. He coanchored "Newsfront" with Ashleigh Banfield on week nights and anchored "Lester Holt Live." In 2002, he began to substitute for the regular host of the "Today" show, where he appeared to mesh well with Katie Couric, and in June 2003, he replaced David Bloom, who had died while covering the Iraq war, as cohost of NBC's "Weekend Today," sharing the desk with a fellow rising star, the elegant Ms. Campbell Brown. The dapper, Saks Fifth Avenue-clad Holt is her match in elegance, and both hosts have the news reporting experience to contribute much more than regular features and well-tailored clothes.

In December 2002, Holt moderated an MSNBC show examining a controversial documentary about the founder of Islam, the Prophet Muhammad, that had been partially funded by the Public Broadcasting System. Critics saw the documentary as missionary work designed to bring Americans into the Muslim faith; their position was voiced by *New York Post* columnist and founder of the Middle East Forum, Daniel Pipes. Defenders of the show were represented by Hussein Ibish, representing the American-Arab Anti Discrimination Committee. Holt's well informed moderating demonstrated his ability to handle debate-style programming between people having radically different points of view. This ability was put to use only a few days thereafter when his "Today" show opponents were arguing the dangers and benefits of treating the effects of aging with human growth hormone therapy. One physician was running a successful Manhattan practice that administered these hormones to improve patients' energy, skin appearance and feeling of well being, while his opponent advised waiting until long-term studies were done on possible side effects.

In June 2003, Holt interviewed comedian and book author Al Franken about the comic's tiff with Fox's Bill O'Reilly. O'Reilly had been angered by his unflattering portrayal in Franken's book *Lies and the Lying Liars Who Tell Them: A Fair and Balanced Look at the Right* (New York: Dutton, 2003). The book's title, of course, made sport of the Fox network's "fair and balanced" slogan, and the book was as far to the left as Fox programming is to the right. A March 2004 Holt interview was with Vice President Dick Cheney. Holt asked polite but pointed questions about the administration's plans for exiting Iraq and about the military's failure to capture Osama bin Laden. The vice president predicted that bin Laden would be caught and interpreted the increased insurgent attacks in Iraq as a sign of their desperation.

During his long career as a broadcast reporter, Holt has reported from many a world trouble spot, including Iraq, Northern Ireland, Haiti, Somalia, and El Salvador; yet his most frightening story, essentially a stunt story, was done on the roof of the America's tallest building, the Sears Tower in Chicago, where he interviewed the tower's maintenance chief. His less dangerous current work has included cohosting, with Telemundo News Anchor Maria Celeste Arraras, the 2004 Brown-Black Presidential Forum. Telemundo is a Spanish-language television network owned by General Electric and managed by NBC. Holt was also a panelist in the 2004 presidential debate held in Wisconsin. The Emmy-winning Holt was the recipient in 1990 of the Robert F. Kennedy Journalism Award for his work on "48 Hours," and in recent years he has been a spokesman for better mentoring of beginning broadcasters.

Further Readings: "About Weekend Today." [Online, 11 December 2003]. MSNBC site http://msnbc.msn.com; Battaglio, Stephen. "Holt to Fill Slot at 'Weekend Today.'" [Online,

27 June 2003]. New York Daily News.com Web site www.nydailynews.com; Brady, James. "In StepWith...Lester Holt." [Online, 8 August 2004]. Parade Magazine site http://archive.parade.com; "Lester Holt, MSNBC Anchor." [Online, 2004]. MSNBC Web site www.msnbc.com/news; "Lester Holt, Panelist, Wisconsin Presidential Debate 2004." [Online, 15 February 2004]. Wisconsin Presidential Debate Web site www.wisconsindebate.com/panelists; Rosenthal, Phil. "90 Stories Up, Holt Reaches New Heights." [Online, 25 February 2004]. Chicago Sun-Times Web site www.suntimes.com.

Hughes, Alan J. (1967–)

Business journalist Alan J. Hughes is features editor of *Black Enterprise* magazine. He was born in New York City and got a bachelor's degree in journalism from Rutgers University, after which he was employed as local news editor for the *Hudson Dispatch* in Union City, New Jersey. He left newspaper journalism to write about the financial markets for Standard & Poor's for six years, then became an editor at *BusinessWeek Online*, for which he wrote and edited feature articles. In his present position, Hughes has multiple responsibilities. He is responsible for the magazine's feature stories; directs coverage of the BE 100, the magazine's listing of the nation's largest black-owned businesses; and edits the "how-to" department, which is devoted to the needs of small business owners and persons wishing to go into business for themselves. He plans and moderates a biannual meeting of the magazine's Board of Economists, who meet to discuss business and economic trends affecting African Americans, and he also works on planning for the yearly Black Enterprise Entrepreneurs Conference.

Many of his own articles in *Black Enterprise* are written in answer to readers' inquiries and appear under the standing title "Savvy Solutions." Such a story replied to a reader who was interested in self-publishing children's books; another reader wanted guidance on drafting a mission statement for his new company. Another entrepreneur-to-be asked about the state of the American economy and if summer 2003 was a good time to launch a new business; Hughes replied that there is no reliable way to tell about a "good" or "bad" time to start a business, and that other factors were more important. Some of Hughes' articles are not presented in Q&A format, but are essay-style presentations of his thoughts on business-related topics. In one, he discussed the "glass ceiling" for minorities, saying that it had developed cracks, but was still part of corporate America. Another such article presented statistics showing that black Americans are saving and planning for retirement more than in earlier times, and still another was an assessment of the future of dotcom companies in general.

Further Readings: "Alan J. Hughes." [Online]. Black Enterprise Web site www.blackenterprise.com.

Hughes, Catherine "Cathy" Liggins (22 April 1947–)

The remarkable Cathy Hughes is founder and chairperson of Radio One network, which controls 68 stations, and its new venture, TV One, a cable/satellite television network geared to the interests of African Americans. Her stations reach in excess of 18 million viewers daily and her staff numbers around 1,500. She runs this broadcast empire in conjunction with her son, Alfred Charles Liggins III. Hughes' spectacular success story started in an Omaha, Nebraska, housing project. Her father was the first black person to receive a degree in accounting from Creighton University and her mother was a trombonist and nurse. Cathy Hughes attended high school at the Duchesne Academy of the Sacred Heart in Omaha, where she was the first African-American student. She became pregnant at age 16, withdrew from school and married Alfred Liggins. She and Liggins soon divorced, and she succeeded in completing high school while raising Alfred III as a single mother. She studied business administration from 1966 to 1969 at Creighton University, where she worked on the campus radio station and at black-owned radio station KOWH in Omaha, then took more coursework at the University of Nebraska. Although she had not completed a college degree, she was hired in 1971 by broadcaster and Howard University Journalism dean Tony Brown to work as his assistant and to lecture at Howard. Now that she was living in Washington, D.C., more opportunities began to open up for her. Dean Brown placed her in charge of sales for WHUR-FM, the university's radio station, in 1973, and in 1975, she became the station's vice president and general manager. She is said to have been the first black woman to run a Washington radio station. In this position, she introduced a highly successful new night-time format known as "Quiet Storm" that featured romantic music played by dreamy-voiced disk jockeys and that was aimed at single African-American women.

In 1978, she left WHUR and took a job with another Washington station, WYCB-AM. She remarried, this time to television producer Dewey Hughes. After about a year with WYCB, she resigned due to creative differences, and in 1980, she and Hughes founded Radio One upon the purchase of beleaguered station WOL-AM. With $100,000 of their own and $450,000 in borrowed funds, finally secured after having been turned down by more than 30 banks, they began running their new station with an all news and talk format, trying to fill a market niche that had been neglected by other area broadcasters. The station was moved from its expensive Georgetown location to what had been a drug house in a hard-bitten section of Washington. She installed a glass-front control room so that passersby could see the station in action, and she established good relations with the neighborhood gangs. In 1981, she started her own daily talk program, "The Cathy Hughes Show," but for a while, insolvency seemed imminent. Dewey wanted to give up on the station and move to California;

Hughes, Catherine "Cathy" Liggins

Cathy was determined to make the station profitable. This disagreement led to their divorce, and she and her young son moved into the station building after she lost her house to creditors and had her car repossessed. She slept on the station floor in a sleeping bag, cooked on a plug-in hotplate and personally did as much of the station's work as possible. She bought out Dewey's interest in the company and negotiated with lenders to keep the station on the air. Her lenders insisted that she abandon the talk show format and instead play soul music; she countered with a compromise that included a morning talk show of her own. By 1986, the station was finally profitable, and not only did she return to the talk format, but also bought her second station, Washington's WMMJ-FM. Again her bankers interfered with her programming, demanding that she play middle-of-the-road music aimed at a mainly white audience. This course of action was a financial disaster, and nearly two years later, she returned to offering programming of her own choosing. Hughes gained popularity, and listeners, by crusading for the city's substantial black community. She took on the local utility companies, especially in regard to their draconian cut-off policies, crusaded against the *Washington Post* for what she deemed stereotypical treatment of blacks, and encouraged her listeners to trade more often with black-owned businesses. She Supported Mayor Marion Barry, even after his conviction for indulging in crack cocaine, and criticized the Maryland legislature for expelling black state Sen. Larry Young, who was charged with unethical behavior. Hughes hired him to do his own talk show.

She purchased station WWIN in 1992 from Ragan Henry of Philadelphia and in 1995, bought Washington's WKYS for a reported $40 million. From mid-1988 to the end of 1999, she bought 18 more stations, selecting stations that needed turning around in cities that had large black populations: Atlanta, Baltimore, Cleveland, Detroit, St. Louis and Richmond, Virginia. Radio One's profits continued to climb, allowing her to pay down her debt. Son Alfred began working at the station as an account manager in 1985, became general sales manager in 1987, general manager in 1988 and president in 1989. Alfred, a graduate of the Executive MBA Program at the Wharton School of Business, also proved to be acquisition-minded, and today the company owns 68 radio stations, making it quite an influential force in black America. Radio One bought the Bell Broadcast System in Detroit in 1997 and Blue Chip Broadcasting in Cincinnati in 2001 and today controls stations in about half the 20 biggest U.S. markets. In 2000, the company went public with a successful IPO that raised $172 million and made Cathy Hughes the first black woman to control a publicly traded media company. Hers is also the largest black-controlled radio company in the nation, and she and son Alfred now own roughly 70 percent of the firm's stock. She has, in fact, claim to even more firsts. When she bought WERQ-AM/FM in Baltimore for $9.5 million, she became the first U.S. broadcaster to own four radio stations in a single market. Hers was also the first black-owned radio company to dominate listenership in several major markets and was the first such company owned by a woman to control the leading station in a major U.S. market. In 1995, she gave up hosting her radio talk show due to time constraints. Near the end of 2004, Radio One bought out Reach Media Inc., for around $56 million and thereby took ownership of the popular "Tom Joyner Morning Show." A year earlier, Radio One, in conjunction with Comcast, launched TV One, a cable channel aimed at black viewers. In March 2003, Jonathan A. Rodgers, formerly president of the CBS-owned company Discovery Networks, became president of the new cable channel. Cathy Hughes returned to host her own talk show, "TV One on One." One 2005 show featured her interview with legendary music figure Quincy Jones.

Over the years, Hughes has been active with a number of organizations. She has served on the boards of the DC Boys/Girls Club and the United Black Fund and has chaired the Community Communication Corporation. She is a Lincoln University trustee; has served in this capacity for the Piney Woods Country Life School in Mississippi, a private boarding school that had been founded by her maternal grandfather; and is on the Federal Reserve Bank's Small Business Committee and the board of the Baltimore Development Corporation. In 2002, she joined the board of Broadcast Music Inc. Her many honors include four honorary degrees, the Turner Broadcasting System's Trumpet Award, the National Media Coalition's 1988 People's Champion Award, the Lifetime Achievement Award from the Washington Area Broadcasters Association, the Department of Commerce's Ron Brown Business of the Year Award, the Baltimore NAACP chapter's Parren J. Mitchell Award, the 1996 Thomas A. Dorsey Leadership Award, and in 2001, both the Advertising Club of Metropolitan Washington's Silver Medal Award and the National Association of Broadcasters Distinguished Service Award. She has been recognized with the Golden Mike Award of the Broadcasters' Foundation, as well, and in 2004, she was honored by the National Urban League with a Women of Power Award.

Further Readings: "Catherine Liggins Hughes." *The African-American Almanac*, 9th ed. Edited by Jeffrey Lehman. (Detroit, Mich.: Gale Group, 2003), pp. 870–71; "Cathy Hughes." [Online, 25 November 2004]. Black Entrepreneur's Hall of Fame site http://blackenrepreneurshalloffame.blogspot.com; "Cathy Hughes." *Current Biography Yearbook*. (New York: H.W. Wilson, 2000), pp. 303–06; "Ms. Catherine Liggins Hughes." [Online, 2005]. Howard University Web site www.howard.edu/commencement/2005; Norment, Lynn. "Cathy Hughes: Ms. Radio." *Ebony*, May 2000; Prince, Richard. "Godgers Wants Cathy Hughes for Role at Network." [Online, 24 March 2003]. Richard Prince's Journal-isms. Maynard Institute Web site www.maynardije.org.

Hunter, Karen (?–)

New York City talk-radio host, university professor and former New York *Daily News* columnist Karen Hunter has also carved out an unusual niche for herself as a collaborative book author. Hunter joined the sports staff of the *Daily News* in 1989 gradually broadening her interests, becoming a member of the paper's editorial board and writing a weekly op-ed column. She was part of the *Daily News* team that won a 1999 Pulitzer Prize for editorials that helped save the historic Apollo Theater from being demolished. Since 2001 she has been an assistant professor in the Hunter College film and media program, and before that had taught writing part-time at New York University and in the city's public schools. In 2003, she became host of the WWRL Morning Show, a radio talk show that mixes controversy and wit. She has cohosted the show with Rabbi Shea Hecht, who was replaced in 2005 by Steve Malzberg, for 23 years host of a WABC radio talk show. Malzberg, a conservative, was selected to provide a point-counterpoint with Hunter, who for the most part has liberal views. In 2005, *Talkers Magazine* named Hunter one of America's 100 most important radio talk show hosts.

Her columns sometimes surprise, as did a January 2004 example that disagreed with the New York public schools' new policy of granting maternity leave to unwed pregnant teenagers. Her position was that our society needs to bring back a higher level of shame to discourage having babies out of wedlock; she suggested night school or alternative schools instead. When the president's daughter, Jenna Bush, applied to teach in a mostly black charter school in Harlem, Hunter used her column to offer advice on how Bush might best connect with her new students. And when conservative demigod Rush Limbaugh remarked that Philadelphia Eagles quarterback Donovan McNabb got little criticism for lackluster games because he is black, Hunter called Limbaugh a racist and added that such remarks give African Americans a chance to hear what some whites say in private when the political correctness monitors are not running. The column reproduced below is her reaction to the 2004 campaign speech made by then-congressional candidate Barack Obama.

The unusual side of Hunter's writing career is her book work. In 1997, she collaborated with the rap performer who calls himself LL Cool J on the book *I Make My Own Rules*. Similar collaborations with other African-American personalities have followed in quick succession, the most recent being *On the Up and Up: a Survival Guide for Women Living with Men on the Down Low*, written with Brenda Stone Browder. The latter book is about black heterosexual men who also have homosexual sex on the side.

"Obama's Right—We Must Be United" by Karen Hunter

It was 41 years ago that Martin Luther King Jr. described his dream of an America where color and creed would have no bearing on the heights one could reach. He saw a country where content of character would determine success.

This week at the Democratic convention, Barack Obama gave a glimpse of what King's dream look like in reality. He captivated the delegates with his keynote speech.

Afterward, his bright political future was the topic of conversation on the convention floor, but it was the content of his speech that had me dreaming. Obama talked of his own vision for the nation—not "a liberal America and a conservative America" but the *United* States of America.

In saying that, he defined the American ideal. Unfortunately, however, we have allowed pundits and politicians to divide the country along label lines. We as a people have been painted into corners based on ideology that, if pressed, few of us could defend.

I changed my party affiliation this year to register as a Republican. Not so much because I believe in the Republican platform but because I believe in the American ideal that my vote, my views, should matter.

More than 90% of blacks are registered as Democrats, and in many ways that has nullified their power. It has made it easy for Republicans to ignore the black vote and has allowed Democrats to take it for granted. We should not even talk about a "black vote." The very notion is silly and underscores the myth that all blacks think alike.

In my circles, it's hard to find any two people who agree down the line on all the issues. I am for school vouchers, a Republican issue. I am also for affirmative action, a Democratic issue. I am pro-choice but do not necessarily believe two men should be married. I know that I am not alone. There are millions of Americans who can sway in either political direction on many issues that face us. That's the beauty of this country.

But forcing people to choose sides is ugly. Worse, urging people to hate those on the other side will be our undoing as a nation. Only through understanding those who hold different views will we get stronger.

The theme of the Democratic convention is "a stronger America." There has been a lot of talk of harmony, of unity. "We are one people, all of us pledging to the Stars and Stripes, all of us defending the United States of America," Obama said.

But not quite yet. Obama's goal is still a dream. But it is easily realized if we put aside partisanship and start viewing ourselves as one nation made up of different people with different views from different places. As Obama said, we are the United States of America. We'd better start acting like it.

Source: New York Daily News, L.P., reprinted with permission. The column originally appeared on 30 July 2004.

Books by Karen Hunter: With LL Cool J, *I Make My Own Rules* (New York: St. Martin's Press, 1997); with Queen Latifah, *Ladies First: Revelations of a Strong Woman* (New York: William Morrow, 1999); with Mason Betha, *Revelations: There's a Light after the Lime* (New York: Pocket Books, 2001); with Dawn Hunter, *Heads Up!* (Toronto: Lorimer, 2001); with Al Sharpton, *Al on America* (New York: Dafina Books, 2002); with Wendy Williams, *Wendy's Got the Heat* (New York: Atria Books, 2003); with Wendy Williams, *The Wendy Williams Experience* (New York: Dutton, 2004); with Brenda Stone Browder, *On the Up and Up: A Survival Guide for Women Living with Men on the Down Low* (New York: Dafina Books, 2005).

Further Readings: "Karen Hunter." [Online]. WWRL Web site www.wwr111600.com.

Hunter-Gault, Charlayne (27 February 1942–)

Many Americans who are familiar with Charlayne Hunter-Gault know her from her nearly 20 years as a correspondent for television's "MacNeil/Lehrer Report" and more recently, "The News Hour with Jim Lehrer." She left the program in June 1997 to move to Johannesburg, South Africa, to join her husband, Ron Gault, who had become managing director of J.P. Morgan there. Some older Americans will remember her for a different accomplishment: she , along with Hamilton Holmes, became civil rights icons when they integrated the University of Georgia in 1961. She was born in Due West,

South Carolina, to a Methodist Army chaplain father and a mother who worked at a real estate firm. During the periods when her father was stationed abroad, she was reared by her mother with the help of her grandmother, a woman of little formal education, but a regular reader of three newspapers: the *Atlanta Constitution*, the *Atlanta Journal* and the historically black *Atlanta Daily World*. Part of Hunter-Gault's youth was spent in Covington, Georgia. When her father was home, he held Charlayne to very high academic standards. By age 12, she had decided to become a journalist, and her childhood heroine was comic strip character Brenda Starr, the glamorous reporter. Her family moved to Atlanta in 1951; she went to high school there, worked for the school newspaper and wanted to continue her education at a good university journalism program. In Georgia, the only choice at that time was the University of Georgia, which had not yet been integrated when she finished high school in 1959. Guided by representatives of the NAACP, she entered the journalism program at Wayne State University in Detroit, Michigan, awaiting the result of an integration request filed with a federal court. The order was granted, and in January 1961, she and fellow African-American student Hamilton Holmes, who hoped to become a physician, became the first black students to enroll at Georgia's flagship university. Her time in college was challenging due to protests over her presence, but she persevered. After a brick was thrown through her dorm window, both she and Holmes were sent to Atlanta in the care of state patrolmen. The university suspended the two students, but they soon returned under a court order. Life was made unpleasant for her in many ways, such as the nightly pounding on the dorm floor above her room, and she spent most weekends in Atlanta. Nevertheless, she arranged a summer internship with the *Louisville Courier-Journal*—the first such offer to a black student made by that paper, and she graduated from the university with a B.A. in journalism in 1963. Not long before graduating, she married a white fellow student and Georgian, Walter Stovall. The couple later divorced.

Hunter's first jobs after graduation were in the print media. She got a foot in the *New Yorker*'s door as a secretary/trainee, after which she became a staff writer. She appears to have been the first African American to work there. From 1964 to 1967 she contributed copy to the magazine's "Talk of the Town" feature and also wrote some short stories. She secured a Russell Sage Fellowship in 1967, studied social science at Washington University of St. Louis and began writing for *Trans-Action* magazine. An assignment to report on protests in the nation's capital led to her first broadcast job, reporting and anchoring the news for WRC-TV in Washington. The following year, she returned to print-media work, this time with the *New York Times*. Here, she was a metropolitan reporter providing coverage of the city's black community and she founded and ran the paper's Harlem bureau, remaining in this job until 1978. Her personal stock went up at the *Times* in 1970, when she and colleague Joseph Lelyveld won the paper's Publishers Award for their story about a youthful heroin addict, a story that in hindsight, sounds similar to the "Jimmy" story that won a Pulitzer for reporter Janet Cook at the *Washington Post* but that got her fired and stripped of the prize when it came to light that Jimmy was not an actual person. The difference, of course, is that Hunter-Gault's 12-year-old addict was real, not a composite figure. She won two more Publishers awards in 1974 and 1976 and was recognized by the National Urban Coalition for her urban-affairs reportage and won Lincoln University's Unity Award for reporting about unemployed teens. Meanwhile, she had remarried, this time to an African-American man from Chicago, Ronald Gault, who was a vice president of the financial firm First Boston. During her *Times* years, she also became one of the directors of Columbia University's Michele Clark Fellowship program for minority students who wished to pursue a career in journalism.

In 1978, she left the *Times* to join PBS on the "MacNeil/Lehrer Report," where her face and voice became familiar to a great many U.S. viewers. She served as a substitute anchor and did on-the-ground reporting from many parts of the globe. When the program became the "MacNeil/Lehrer NewsHour" in 1983, Hunter-Gault began working as its national correspondent. During her almost 20 years with the "NewsHour," Hunter-Gault won two Emmys, the 1986 George Foster Peabody Award from her alma mater's Henry W. Grady School of Journalism for her series on apartheid in South Africa, a Journalist of the Year Award in 1986 from the National Association of Black Journalists, a Broadcast Personality of the Year award from *Good Housekeeping* magazine, the American Women in Radio and Television Award, the 1990 Sidney Hillman Award, the Woman of Achievement Award from the New York chapter of the American Society of University Women, the Tom Paine Award, Amnesty International's Media Spotlight Award and two awards given by the Corporation for Public Broadcasting for excellence in local programming. The University of Georgia honored Hunter-Gault and her co-integrator of that institution by naming the Holmes-Hunter Academic Building in their honor—Holmes had become a surgeon and died in 1995, and Hunter-Gault has been accorded more than 20 honorary degrees. She has contributed articles to such periodicals as *Essence*, the *New York Times Magazine*, the *New York Times Book Review*, *Saturday Review*, *Life* and *Vogue*. She has also published a memoir of her part in the civil rights movement, *In My Place*, and she was the subject of her former *New Yorker* colleague Calvin Trillin's book *An Education in Georgia: Charlayne Hunter, Hamilton Holmes, and the Integration of the University of Georgia* (Athens: University of Georgia Press, 1964).

In her "NewsHour" career, one of her favorite assignments was interviewing Nelson Mandela soon after his release from a South African prison after 27 years of confinement. She interviewed Mandela on more recent occasions as well, and she also recalls a poignant interview in Somalia with an Irish nurse trying to help sick and dying children there. Another such interview was with a black South African woman who had been beaten by security police, and other interviews she has mentioned as noteworthy were with Madeleine Albright, Hafez Al-Assad and Shimon Peres. Other noteworthy reports she filed include an interview with trumpeter Wynton Marsalis after he had won the first-ever Pulitzer Prize for jazz; an interview conducted in Cairo with Egypt's president, Hosni Mubarak; an interview with celebrated architect Philip Johnson, who had just turned 90; and a wonderful piece of reporting on America's first black sculptress, Edmonia Lewis, and her lost-but-now-recovered two-ton sculpture "The Death of Cleopatra." Before leaving "NewsHour," Hunter-Gault spoke with pride about the way the program had remained committed to substantive reporting during the years in which so much of television news had been transformed into news-light to give greater emphasis to coverage of entertainment. She urged younger people not to regard print media work as outdated, but to prepare for serious news coverage by studying history, economics and other basic subjects, and to realize the importance of learning other languages. As she prepared to leave for Africa to join her husband there, she noted the need for better U.S. media coverage of events in Africa, a continent about which most Americans are sadly ignorant. Her departure from the program came in summer 1997; at that time she became the South Africa correspondent for National Public Radio, holding that job until 1999, when she became Johannesburg bureau chief for Cable News Network. She has continued to report on the progress of South Africa's black-controlled government but has remarked that only two out of every 20 stories she files for CNN are broadcast in the United States. Afrikaans resistance still exists, and USAfrica Online reported that on 15 October 2000, Hunter-Gault and her husband were assaulted by a white man outside the Johannesburg restaurant where they had just dined. Two nearby police officers did nothing to stop the assault. She has gone from apartheid in Georgia to apartheid on the southern tip of Africa but is still doing important work to counter it. Recently, the AllAfrica Foundation established the Charlayne Hunter-Gault Journalism Fellowship program, through which persons working in the media of that continent can travel to Europe or the United States for research or training.

Books by Charlayne Hunter-Gault: *In My Place* (New York: Farrar Straus Girooux, 1992).

Further Readings: Atkins, Latrese Evette. "Huner-Gault, Charlayne." In *Black Women in America*, 2nd ed. Edited by Darlene Clark Hine (New York: Oxford University Press, 2005), pp. 86–7; Botsch, Carol Sears. "Charlayne Huner-Gault." [Online]. The Black Journalists Movement: How T\hey Got Their Start. Maynard Institute Web site www.maynardije.org; "Charlayne Hunter-Gault." [Online]. University of South Carolina-Aiken Web site www.usca.edu/aasc; "Charlayne Hunter-Gault Farewell Forum." [Online, 13 June 1997]. PBS Web site www.pbs.org/newshour/forum; Clark, Mary Marshall. "Charlayne Hunter-Gault Interviews." [Online]. Washington Press Club Foundation site http://npc.press.org; Holley, Mary R. "Charlayne Hunter-Gault." In *Notable Black American Women*. Edited by Jessie Carney Smith (Detroit, Mich.: Gale, 2003), pp. 535–36; "Hunter-Gault, Charlayne." In *African-American Writers. A Dictionary*. Edited by Shari Dorantes Hatch, Michael R. Strickland (Santa Barbara, Calif.: ABC-Clio, 2000), pp. 81–82. McClam, Erin. "Hunter-Gault Returns to University." [Online, 10 January 2001]. Washington Post Web site www.washingtonpost.com.

I

Ifill, Gwen (29 September 1955–)

Moderator and managing editor of public television's longest-running public affairs program, "Washington Week in Review," senior correspondent for "The News Hour With Jim Lehrer," and cohost of "Flashpoints with Bryant Gumbel and Gwen Ifill," the calm, businesslike Ifill became even better known to the American viewing audience in 2004 when she moderated the vice-presidential debate between incumbent Dick Cheney and challenger John Edwards. She was born in the Queens section of New York and grew up in Staten Island and Buffalo, New York, living in public housing. Her father was a Methodist minister, and her ancestry is Panamanian on his side and from Barbados on her mother's side. Ifill is a 1977 graduate of Simmons College in Boston, Massachusetts, where she majored in communications. Immediately thereafter, she took her first media job as a food writer at the *Boston Herald-American*. She could not cook, but that position was the only one open at the time. She moved on to write about school boards in that city during an era of unrest and rioting. In 1981, she moved to the *Baltimore Evening Sun*, where she worked as a reporter, and in 1984, she was hired away by the *Washington Post* and became a political reporter. Her next move was to the *New York Times*, for which she worked in that paper's Washington bureau from 1991 to 1994 as congressional correspondent, and from 1994 to 1999 as White House correspondent. She began her broadcast career in 1992 as a panelist and sometimes moderator for "Washington Week in Review," the popular public affairs show that had been launched in 1967 to focus on the news of the previous week. In October 1999, Ifill became the program's regular moderator, and in the same year, she also joined "The News Hour With Jim Lehrer" as a correspondent. In the interim, from September 1994 to 1999, she had worked for NBC News as the network's chief congressional correspondent and political reporter. For NBC, she contributed to the "NBC Nightly News with Tom Brokaw," "Meet the Press," "The Today Show" and MSBNC. Since joining PBS in 1999, she has not only moderated "Washington Week in Review," but is also the program's managing editor, which entails responsibility for both story and panel selection. The latter selections usually give preference to reporters rather than columnists and commentators. An innovation she has made is to occasionally leave the nation's capital and instead do the show on-site where news is happening. She has also strengthened the show's coverage of national elections. She moderates "Washington Week Online," fielding questions and discussing the past week's news. On this interactive outlet, Ifill is usually content to let her guests have their say and to reply only briefly, making it clear that she prefers to report, not take sides or predict. Most recently, she has added a new role at PBS pairing with another veteran broadcast journalist, Bryant Gumbel, to cohost the new issues-oriented program "Flashpoints with Bryant Gumbel and Gwen Ifill."

Moderating the 5 October 2004 vice-presidential debate in Cleveland, Ohio was a highlight of Ifill's long career, although it brought her not only high visibility, but complaints of liberal bias as well. The rules of the 90-minute debate, which were enforced by Ifill were that the questions chosen by the moderator were to be divided between domestic and foreign issues. The candidates could not ask questions of each other and had two minutes to respond to each of Ifill's questions, after which the opponent had 90 seconds for rebuttal. At Ifill's discretion, a given topic could be discussed further for one additional minute. Online appraisals of her performance as moderator were positive overall ranging from opinions on Freerepublic.com that she did a superb job, to "very even-handed," to a more grudging remark to the effect that she did pretty well for a person with socialist/liberal leanings. Conservative outlet Nationalreview.com, on the other hand, accused her of showing a pro-Kerry-Edwards bias in her selection of questions. Such disagreement is to be expected, and it is likely that, on balance, her moderating that night enhanced her reputation for objectivity more than the opposite. Critics writing for Dailyhowler.com have also accused her of showing favoritism to Condoleezza Rice as regards her role in the Iraq war, and the Media Research Center's site Mrc.org has complained that she has played down the Clinton-era scandals and that she saves the tough questions for Republicans. Elsewhere, Ifill has been quoted as favoring responsible, calm reportage, as opposed to the loud, one-sided hate-mongering that passes for journalistic commentary in some circles today. She has also remarked that she thinks the popularity of "shout shows" will eventually decline in favor of more civil, thoughtful news and opinion delivery. Certainly, she is a journalist of more substance than some television news personalities, whose chief claims to fame are their regular features, better than average hair and pearly smile. She appears to have been the third African-American journalist to moderate a debate during a presidential campaign, following Bernard Shaw, who performed this role in 1988 and again in 2000, and Carole Simpson, who did it in 1992.

The first black journalist to take any part in a presidential debate was Robert C. Maynard, who, in 1976, was a panelist during a Gerald Ford-Jimmy Carter debate. *Portland Oregonian* managing editor William A. Hilliard was a panelist in the 1980 Jimmy Carter-Ronald Reagan debate, and Norma Quarles filled that same role for the George Bush-Geraldine Ferraro vice-presidential debate in 1984. Ifill, however, was the first black journalist to moderate a vice-presidential debate. Certainly, Ifill's 15 years as a print journalist adds to her credibility as a broadcaster. She has remarked that at PBS, she has the best of both journalistic worlds: a combination of the depth and seriousness of print and the immediacy and impact of broadcast. In a 2000 interview with Robert Margolis for Salon.com, she said that one thing she especially likes about her job with the "News Hour" is that the show allows for examination of multiple positions on a given issue. Asked why such a large part of her shows' audiences are in advanced middle age or senior citizens, she responded that one reason is that older people whose children have left the home simply have more time for in-depth discussions of the issues. When asked about the paucity of young viewers, she made a point not often expressed: that today's younger Americans exhibit a disconnect in their definition of "public issues" whereby, compared to their elders, they tend to see public issues more in terms of public service and less in terms of politics. This argument would seem to have merit, in that today's college student, for example, is far more likely than the students of their parents' generation to volunteer time for good causes, while simultaneously eschewing partisan politics as dull and essentially useless. Ifill's replies to most questions posed by viewers tend to be conservatively cautious. She avoids being confrontational. When asked how CBS, NBC and ABC could justify giving less air time to the 2004 Democratic presidential convention than did Al Jazeera, she contented herself with deflecting the question, passed up a chance to criticize the commercial networks' bottom-line mentality and instead pointed out that PBS, at least, covered the convention every night starting at 8 PM. In reply to another question about the Democratic convention, she was more forthcoming, noting that the two real highlights of the convention were the appearances of Bill Clinton and Barack Obama followed by that of Howard Dean—anything but a show of favoritism to Kerry-Edwards, as many conservatives charged her with doing. Interestingly, liberals and conservatives alike lambasted her for her remarks critical of filmmaker Michael Moore during a 27 June 2004 appearance she made on "Meet the Press." Specifically, she was critical of Moore's film "Fahrenheit 9/11" for what she perceived as picturing Americans as being too stupid to think for themselves. Ifill has also pointed out that media consumers sometimes project their own biases into the media material they watch, read or hear, then "blame the messenger" by leveling charges of bias on journalists. Asked by another viewer why biracial Democrat Obama is always referred to on television as black or African American, she responded that he self-identifies that way, and PBS policy is to call people what they call themselves. To young viewers, she suggests that they should be skeptical of politicians but should avoid becoming cynical. To young journalists, she recommends asking plenty of questions to get their facts straight. Ifill is a member of the boards of the Harvard University Institute of Politics, The Johnson Foundation's Wingspread Conference Center and the Philip Merrill College of Journalism at the University of Maryland. She is the recipient of eight honorary degrees.

Further Readings: Graham. Tim. "Uneven Ifill." [Online, 6 October 2004]. The National Review Web site www.nationalreview.com; "Gwen Ifill." [Online]. PBS Web site www.pbs.org/weta/washingtonweek; Prince, Richard. "3rd Person of Color in Moderator's Role." [Online, 13 August 2004]. Richard Prince's Journal-isms." Maynard Institute Web site www.maynardije.org; Wickham, DeWayne. "Analysis: Gwen Ifill: On the Cutting Edge of History." [Online, 6 October 2004]. Black America Web site www.blackamericaweb.com.

Ivory, Bennie (c.1949–)

Seasoned newspaperman Bennie Ivory is executive editor and vice president of the Louisville, Kentucky, *Courier-Journal*. He hails from Hot Springs, Arkansas, where he attended the public schools. He began his career in his hometown directly after his 1969 high school graduation as a general assignment reporter for the Hot Springs *Sentinel-Record*, for which he later worked as a government reporter and sports editor. While working nights at the paper on a full-time basis, he commuted to Henderson State University in Arkadelphia, 70 miles from Hot Springs, finally graduating with a bachelor's degree in journalism. In 1979, he moved to Monroe, Louisiana, to become assistant city editor of the *News-Star-World* there; he was promoted to city editor in 1981. In June 1982, Ivory left Monroe to become one of the beginning staffers at *USA Today*, working as state editor. Later he was the paper's night national editor. He became managing editor of the *Daily News* in Jackson, Mississippi, in 1985, and in 1988, doubled as managing editor of both that paper and the *Clarion-Ledger*. In the early 1990s, Ivory orchestrated coverage of the reindictment of white supremacist Byron De La Beckwith, who was convicted in 1994 of the 1964 murder of civil rights protest leader Medgar Evers. In 1993, Ivory became executive editor of Florida Today in Melbourne. Two years later, he assumed the same position in Wilmington, Delaware, with the *News Journal*. He became executive editor and vice president for news of the *Courier-Journal* in 1997. Here, he faces the familiar challenge of maintaining journalistic integrity while operating under the profit imperatives of a large media company.

Ivory has been a Pulitzer Prize juror four times, including the year 2000, when he chaired the jury for beat reporting. He belongs to the National Association of Black Journalists, the Kentucky Press Association and the American Society of Newspaper Editors. He serves on the board of visitors of Florida A&M University's School of Journalism & Graphic Communication.

In February 2005, he delivered the Patterson Lecture at Lyon College in Batesville, Arkansas, speaking about the importance of the First Amendment and also about the damage to public trust in journalism done by recent fabrication and plagiarism scandals. In May of that year, he participated in a Poynter Institute program, "Creating a Watchdog Culture." His work with Gannett was recognized in 1994, during his time at *Florida Today*, when he was named the group's Editor of the Year; in 2003, he was second runner-up for that award. In 2004, both he and Susan Ihne, executive editor of the *St. Cloud Times* in Minnesota, won the Robert G. McGruder Award for Diversity Leadership given by the Freedom Forum, the Associated Press Managing Editors and the American Society of Newspaper Editors. The award had special meaning for Ivory in that he had known the late Robert McGruder personally. Ivory served as a judge for the awards in 2005.

At the helm of the *Courier-Journal*, Ivory has been a staunch advocate of freedom of information. The paper sued in 2001 seeking the names of contributors to Kentucky Sen. Mitch McConnell's conservative McConnell Center for Political Leadership at the University of Louisville. The senator accused the paper of being not only liberal, but out of touch and irrelevant. In May 2005, a state court of appeals found against the newspaper's FOI petition. In November 2003, Kentucky Governor-elect Ernie Fletcher, a Republican, singled out the *Courier-Journal* as the only news medium in the state that would be required to submit its questions to the governor's office in writing. Ivory responded that the paper would continue to take seriously its role as a public watchdog. An experiment in media convergence done under Ivory's watch was a collaborative effort with Louisville station WHAS-TV on a series of stories about pollution. A battle against entrenched conservatism occurred in May 2004, when the paper published photographs of prisoners who had been abused and tortured by U.S. military personnel at Abu Ghraib prison. The paper was accused of making these pictures public as a means of furthering its liberal agenda. Some critics went so far as to accuse the *Courier-Journal* of treason. Ivory responded that the paper's job was to publish the news, not cover up unpleasantness.

"It Has Always Been About Giving Opportunity" by Bennie Ivory

I would like to thank APME, the Freedom Forum and ASNE for this award.

I am humbled, surprised and honored at the same time.

I am surprised because I have never thought that anything that I have done was anything special. I have done the things that I have done simply because I thought they were things I ought to do.

As one who grew up in the Deep South and spent most of my career there, I found that this stuff just comes to you somewhat naturally.

When you live it, breathe it and experience it, you realize how important it is.

I am honored because I knew Bob McGruder. That makes it truly special.

Bob was a fine editor and a wonderful person.

For a lot of years, when I attended APME and ASNE, there were only a few of us there—Bob, me, Al Johnson, Norm Lockman, Al Fitzpatrick and Merv Aubespin.

And every year at convention time, Bob and I would steal away once during the week to a corner of the bar and have a few drinks and talk about what wasn't happening in our industry.

For me, it always has been about opportunity—giving people the opportunity to do great journalism and hiring and promoting qualified people into decision-making positions.

We all should feel compelled to provide those opportunities when we get in positions to do so.

Ed Manassah, my publisher in Louisville, gave me an opportunity seven years ago when he asked me to come here to be his editor. He might regret it now, but it's too late.

Curtis Riddle gave me an opportunity when he asked me to come to Wilmington, Del., to be his editor. The Wilmington experience was unique because it likely will be the only time I will work for a person of color in the industry. The Wilmington experience also was unique because Curtis, who is African American, was the publisher, I was the editor and I hired E.J. Mitchell as my managing editor. Norm Lockman was the associate editor of the editorial page. And Sam Martin, the advertising director, also was African American.

One of our readers in Wilmington wrote a letter to our corporate counterparts in Washington asking the question: "Are there any qualified white people you could send to Wilmington?"

Mike Coleman gave me my first opportunity to become a top editor when he asked me to be his editor at Florida Today in Brevard County.

And then there was John Johnson, the late John Johnson.

John was my editor for most of the eight years I spent in Jackson, Miss., as managing editor.

John was my editor, but he became my friend.

I once heard Charles Overby say that if he were to leave his family with anyone, it would be John Johnson.

I later learned what Charles meant.

John gave me the opportunity of a lifetime. He gave me an opportunity a lot of other people probably wouldn't have. He gave me great latitude to do my job. To stretch and to grow.

John had my back, and I had his back.

We went through a lot of good times together and a lot of tough times.

There certainly were more good times than bad times, but even the good times can come with challenges in Mississippi.

When we were in the midst of the reporting that ultimately led to the reopening of the Medgar Evers case, there were a lot of days when we were out there all alone. There was a deafening silence in the community. There were divisions in the community and in the newsroom.

But John never wavered. He stood tall right next to me the whole time.

John Johnson was special.

Again, I'd like to say thank you for this honor.

Source: The above remarks were made by Mr. Ivory upon accepting the 2004 Robert G. McGruder Award for Diversity Leadership at the October 2004 convention of the Associated Press Managing Editors. His remarks are reprinted here by permission of Mr. Ivory.

Further Readings: Ivory, Bennie. "My First Job." [Online]. Chips Quinn Scholars Web site www.chipsquinn.org/jobs/first; "Ivory Will Be Patterson Lecturer in February." [Online]. Lyon College Web site www.lyon.edu; "McGruder Award Winners Announced." [Online, 2 October 2004]. American Society of Newspaper Editors Web site www.asne.org; Sharp, Rebecca. "Editor Ivory Talks About First Amendment." [Online]. Lyon College Web site www.lyon.edu; Wolfe, Charles. "Fletcher Curbs Paper's Questions." [Online, 22 November 2003]. Cincinnati Enquirer Web site www.enquirer.com; Yetter, Deborah. "UofL Group Need Not Reveal Individual Donors, Court Says." [Online, 21 May 2005]. Louisville Courier-Journal Web site www.courier-journal.com.

J

Jackson, Derrick Z. (31 July 1955–)

Derrick Jackson has been a *Boston Globe* columnist since 1988. He was born in Milwaukee, Wisconsin, and is a 1976 mass communication graduate of the University of Wisconsin, Milwaukee. He began his career as a sportswriter for the historically black weekly the *Milwaukee Courier* and also contributed sports copy to the *Milwaukee Journal* while he was a high school student. From 1976 to 1978 he wrote sports stories for the *Kansas City Star* after which he was *Newsday*'s New England bureau chief. He was a Nieman Fellow at Harvard in 1983–1984 and in 1988 began his long run as a columnist for the *Boston Globe*. He has been awarded honorary degrees by Salem State College in Salem, Massachusetts, and the Episcopal Divinity School in Cambridge, Massachusetts.

Jackson, a liberal, is a determined critic of George W. Bush and the Iraq war. The administration's trumpeted tactics of "shock and awe," Jackson wrote, blew up in its face like a roadside bomb, but nevertheless the war's main planners and their generals were being heaped with praise and given medals while their troops suffered for their leaders' mistakes. In a column headlined "What 'Coalition'?" Jackson quipped that the "Unilateral States of America" had flushed the United Nations into the East River, and he called the "coalition" a fiction. As evidence, he noted that while they sent 250,000 troops to Iraq, Great Britain was next with 45,000 military personnel, and the third heaviest representation was Australia's 2,000. He has excoriated the administration's no-body-count policy as a means of giving the public "sanitized warfare" and has deplored the use of dogs to intimidate the prisoners, comparing that practice to earlier use of dogs by the Nazis and by "Bull" Connor in Birmingham, Alabama. The administration's response to stories of U.S. abuse of prisoners, Jackson summarized as "misinformation accomplished," and a column about the nation's reason for invading Iraq began with a double-entendre about oil as a commodity "to die for." In the 2004 presidential campaign, he was disappointed by the Democrats' timid acceptance of the war, calling it the "Kerry crumble," also noted that for all their talk of outreach, the Republicans were "circling Pluto" in hopes of locating some black voters. The February 2000 column reprinted below took to task George W. Bush, Ronald Reagan and Bob Jones University, where Bush spoke during the campaign.

In other matters, Jackson has criticized the growing polarization in pay between U.S. executives and their workers, calling it corporate welfare made possible by Republicans having bamboozled the public with images of rugged individualism. He has mourned the fact that the National Rifle Association is the nation's most powerful lobby, and of the selection of a conservative new pope he writes that with this choice, the church has stayed with yesteryear in order to avoid facing today. He deplores U.S. materialism, wastefulness and overeating and also regrets that so many highly successful black athletes do little to help disadvantaged youth while providing a glamorous but unrealistic role model for so many boys who lack the physical skills to succeed in professional sports.

Jackson has won five awards for political and sports commentary from the National Association of Black Journalists and three times has won the New England Division of the American Cancer Society's Sword of Hope award. He has received the Meyer Berger Award for writing about New York City from Columbia University and was a finalist in 2001 for the Pulitzer Prize for commentary.

"At Bob Jones U., A Disturbing Lesson about the Real George W" by Derrick Jackson

Last week, in a graduation ceremony mysteriously underplayed by the white press, George W. Bush earned his master's degree from the Ronald Reagan Institute of Race Policy and Management.

Reagan established the institute in 1980 by kicking off his presidential campaign at the Neshoba County Fair in Philadelphia, Miss. The Neshoba County Fair for decades had been the legendary gathering spot of segregationists and near the site of the grisly murders of three civil rights workers.

Reagan took the microphone and, to the roar of thousands of white fairgoers, said, "I believe in states' rights." Anyone who knows Southern race policy knows that saying "states' rights" is like waving a Confederate flag, telling racists they can do whatever they want to black folks.

Reagan was never hounded by the press as to how he could make such a statement and expect to be elected as president. Reagan's handlers slyly scheduled a speech two days later before the Urban League. At the Urban League speech, Reagan said:

"For too many people, conservative has come to mean antipoor, antiblack, and antidisadvantaged. Perhaps some of you question whether a conservative really feels sympathy and compassion for the victims of social and economic misfortune and of racial discrimination... If you think of me as the caricatured conservative, then I ask you to listen carefully and maybe you'll be surprised by our broad areas of agreement."

History shows that the real Reagan was the one who spoke at the Neshoba County Fair and not the one at the Urban League. His presidency quickly became the most antipoor, antiblack, and antidisadvantaged in the latter half of the 20th century.

Now, 20 years later, here comes George W. Bush. Stung by his defeat in the New Hampshire primary, Bush needed a trump card in the South Carolina Republican primary. This was a problem, since he and John McCain are running neck-and-redneck on issues dear to racists. Both have chickened out on saying it is time to stop flying the Confederate flag over the state capitol.

Bush may have found his ace. He kicked off his homestretch drive in South Carolina by speaking at Bob Jones University. Bob Jones represents one of Reagan's early signs of being antiblack. Reagan fought to revoke the Internal Revenue Service's authority to deny charitable tax exemptions to the school. The denial was over the school's ban on interracial dating.

The Supreme Court, in an 8–1 decision, rebuked Reagan, saying schools that practice racial segregation can indeed be denied tax exemptions. Reagan would later appoint the lone dissenter, William Rehnquist, to chief justice.

Bob Jones University still bans interracial dating. George W.'s brother Jeb, the Florida governor who is married to a Latina, could not have graduated. Supreme Court Justice Clarence Thomas, who has a white wife and who was appointed by George W.'s father, could not have graduated.

Bob Jones practices homophobia. Two years ago, when a gay, 60-year-old alum asked if he could come back to visit the school, the dean of students wrote back, "With grief we must tell you that as long as you are living as a homosexual, you, of course, would not be welcome on the campus and would be arrested for trespassing if you did. We take no delight in that action. Our greatest delight would be in your return to the Lord."

George W. took delight in validating this perverted version of Christianity, telling 6,000 students, almost all white, "I look forward to publicly defending our conservative philosophy." He said he would seek "compassionate results." But compassion could not have been foremost on Bush's mind, since it was only *after* the speech that he criticized the school's racial policies, not during it and not directly to the students.

His compassion is irrelevant when out of all the colleges in South Carolina, he chose the most racist and homophobic, a venue more discriminatory on paper than even the Neshoba County Fair. Speaking of papers, Bush's appearance was so outrageous newspaper and television reporters should hound him as to how he deserves the White House when he panders to such base thinking.

While many editorials have dutifully questioned the appearance, subsequent news coverage has made little mention of Bob Jones and certainly not enough to suggest this was a deep, permanent stain. Like Reagan and the Urban League, Bush is smart enough to sprinkle just enough pepper in his white sauce, such as photo-ops with black children, to keep the hounds at bay.

Reagan told the Urban League he was not a caricatured conservative. In the end, he became the caricature of modern racism. Today we have Bush, who coined the term "compassionate conservatism." By going to Bob Jones, Bush showed that he will be so compassionate to conservatives he will be every bit as antipoor, antiblack, and antidisadvantaged as Reagan was.

Having earned his masters in Reagan race policy, by speaking at Bob Jones University George W. Bush is well on his way to his Ph.D.: philosopher of demagoguery.

Source: The above column appeared on 9 February 2000 and is reprinted here by permission of *The Boston Globe*.

Further Readings: "About Derrick Z. Jackson." [Online]. Boston Globe Web site www.boston.com; Fitzgerald, Mark. "Post-Dispatch Columnist Apologizes for Lifting Info." *Editor & Publisher*, 3 July 1993, p. 10

Jamieson, Robert L. Jr. (?–)

Robert Jamieson Jr. works as a reporter and, since March 2001, as thrice-weekly columnist for the *Seattle Post-Intelligencer*. He is a graduate of Stanford University and worked for the *Sunnyvale Valley Journal* in Northern California, the *Oakland Tribune* and the *Wall Street Journal* prior to joining the *Post-Intelligencer* in 1991. He has covered city hall, higher education and general assignment beats for his paper, and in 2000, he received a Pulitzer Prize nomination for a story about a homeless man in Seattle who had been stabbed by three teenagers.

More often than not, Jamieson's columns deal with local or regional people and issues. In March 2001, he wrote about a Mardi Gras celebration in Seattle's Pioneer Square that turned into a brawl, partially with racial overtones, and in the following year wrote a human interest column about an actor afflicted with Lou Gehrig's disease. In November 2003, he offered a tribute to a former University of Washington wrestling coach who was dying of cancer. He has also written columns to celebrate triumph, as in the case of a Seattle honor student who had come to the states after escaping the Taliban in Afghanistan. In January 2005, when his wrath was aroused by golden parachute retirement packages for local school principals who had been made to resign for ineptitude or moral turpitude, the result was a well documented, biting column naming names and listing specifics. Another highly critical column leveled charges of hypocrisy at newly elected Washington Gov. Christine Gregoire, once a member of an exclusionary, all-white sorority, for talking the talk but not walking the walk of equal treatment for all. The column reprinted below takes the federal government to task for its aborted prosecution of Army chaplain James Yee, a Muslim Yee was accused of espionage, locked up for 76 days, then released without apology.

A May 2003 column drew a parallel between *New York Times* plagiarist Jayson Blair and former Tacoma police chief David Brame. Both men, Jamieson wrote, were examples of white, guilt-fueled political correctness gone awry. He has also written about political activist Bayard Rustin, whose contributions to the civil rights struggle would be better known today if not for antigay prejudice; and upon entertainer Bob Hope's death at age 100, Jamieson extolled Hope's gentle humor and the way he took that humor to wherever U.S. troops were fighting—in World War II, Korea, Vietnam, cold war Europe and the Persian Gulf.

"Persecution of Muslim Chaplain Was Petty and Malicious"
by Robert L. Jamieson Jr.

When we look back in history for an example of how petty and malicious the U.S. government can be, the persecution of Army Capt. James Yee will stand out like a skunk at the family picnic.

The government's case against Yee can be summed up in an acronym that military folks know quite well. FUBAR—"Flubbed" Up Beyond All Recognition.

Even after the military last month dropped its long-standing criminal charges against Yee—having accused him of possible espionage—officials couldn't leave well enough alone.

They pumped life into claims that Yee, a Muslim chaplain from Fort Lewis, was involved in adultery and pornographic computer activity.

It was as if they were saying, why not keep dumping on the guy?

Why not keep shooting bullets at his character to discredit him among Muslims?

Why not turn public opinion against him and prompt people to write letters and Op-Ed pieces that lambaste him?

"Yee did what government investigators said he did," a Seattle Post-Intelligencer reader fumed to me in an e-mail. "Seems to me that it's Yee, and not the government, that needs to apologize."

Yee should apologize for nothing, especially since Uncle Sam this week dropped the picayunish claims of adultery and pornography, clearing him.

One can only imagine what Yee's critics—and Army brass—are thinking now.

How quickly this case, which began with Yee as a public enemy, collapsed like a house of cards. Adding insult to injury was the way in which Army Gen. James Hill, commander of the U.S. Southern Commmand, verbalized the government's hasty retreat on Tuesday.

Hill said: "While I believe that Chaplain Yee's misconduct was wrong, I do not believe, given the extreme notoriety of his case in the news media, that further stigmatizing Chaplain Yee would serve a just and fair purpose."

The good general has made bovine scatology—tossing around b.s.—high art.

Parsing Hill's words, it appears the government suspected its treatment of Yee was unjust, unfair. Yee spent 76 days in custody. At one point, Yee's lawyers tell me, Yee was blindfolded, shackled like a dog.

In a letter to President Bush, Yee's lawyer said that while he was incarcerated, Yee's guards refused to tell him the time of day and direction to Mecca.

What is worse, Hill huffily blamed the media for keeping Yee's story in the spotlight, where it belonged. The general should have better used that energy saying the government was sorry.

But it seems much easier for the government to maintain its wayward iron grip to the end. No sooner was Yee freed than he was given strict orders. "You may not wear a military uniform while participating in any speaking engagement or providing public commentary," an Army memo warned.

The chilly memo to Yee said he "must adhere to strict laws and regulations governing public speaking and public commentary." And it reminded him that speech undermining "the effectiveness of loyalty, discipline or unit morale is not constitutionally protected." Uncle Sam basically wants Yee to zip his lips.

I wonder if the Army thinks its dismissal of charges can easily erase its scarification of the Yee family.

An e-mail I received last night answered that question.

"My wife and I are very happy that the Army has wiped the slate clean as far as James' record is concerned," Joseph Yee, James' father, told me.

He wasn't done. Joseph was angry the government refuses to come out and acknowledge its mistake. Like me, he is puzzled that the military last month dropped criminal charges against his son, citing "national security concerns" that could have arisen had the matter gone to court. The feds feared a public hearing might have exposed sensitive government secrets.

I have a hunch they were just being sensitive about airing dirty laundry, as in dubious prosecution tricks.

This week the government dropped the adultery and pornography charges based on "media attention" and what was described as "a matter of mercy and equity."

Mercy? Equity? No wonder Yee's father is in a funk.

"This is mercy because they will no longer prosecute him?" Joseph Yee said in the e-mail. "This is equity from the 76 days of confinement in a military brig and the hell that he and his family went through? Where is (James') career now and what is his future? Who leaked the original accusations of espionage and dragged this case for six months? Where is the vindication, the clearing of his name, and above all, an apology?"

Are you listening, Defense Secretary Donald Rumsfeld? President Bush?

Joseph's son deserves to be known for who he is—not for how the government tried to paint him.

The public should know this James Yee.

He is a proud graduate of West Point. He has two brothers, both of whom are also military men and officers. Together, the Yee family forms a living portrait of honor, duty and sacrifice.

He works hard. He serves our country.

He is well liked by neighbors in the Olympia area. In spite of his ordeal, he speaks well about the military. Still.

He is a loving husband of a wife who survived the crushing weight of this witch hunt. He is the father of a cute little girl. And a devout Muslim.

James Yee is also this: a victim of America.

And the cover-your-butt U.S. government that assailed him and abused its power is too wimpy—or embarrassed—to admit the terror of its ways.

Source: The above column originally appeared on 17 April 2005 and is reproduced here by permission of the *Seattle Post-Intelligencer*.

Jarrett, Vernon D.

Further Readings: "Chat with Robert L. Jamieson Jr." [Online, 2 April 2003]. Seattle Post-Intelligencer Web site http://seattlepi.nwsource.com.

Jarrett, Vernon D. (19 June 1918–23 May 2004)

One of the earliest African Americans to find success in both mainstream newspaper and broadcast work, Vernon Jarrett was a Chicago media fixture for nearly 60 years. He was born in Saulsbury, Tennessee, lived for a time in Paris, Tennessee, but spent most of his youth in Tuscaloosa, Alabama. The son of two schoolteachers, Jarrett earned the B.A. in history at historically black Knoxville College and later took coursework in journalism at Northwestern University broadcasting at the University of Kansas City and urban sociology at the University of Chicago. He served in the Navy, and after he was discharged in 1946, moved north to Chicago in what is remembered as the Great Migration, hoping to find a job at the celebrated black newspaper the *Chicago Defender*. He did so, and two years later took a new job with the Associated Negro Press, first covering sports, then news. In 1948, Jarrett and composer Oscar Brown produced America's first black daily radio news show, "Negro Newsfront," on Marshall Field's WJJD-AM in Chicago. In 1954, Jarrett left journalism briefly for a public relations job in Kansas City but soon returned to Chicago to write and broadcast in support of civil rights. In 1968, he produced and was a commentator for the show "For Blacks Only" on WLS-TV, Channel 7. Then in 1970, he became the first African American columnist at the *Chicago Tribune* espousing equal rights and combating racism in this position until 1983 when he became a columnist and later editorial board member at the *Chicago Sun-Times*. He remained there until he retired in 1995. He estimated that as a columnist for these two papers, he wrote perhaps 3,600 columns. Having produced about 1,600 shows at WLS-TV, he began producing another show, "Jarrett's Journal," for black-owned WVON-AM, also in Chicago. He was one of six owners of this talk-radio station. In addition, he appeared on such news programs as "60 Minutes," "Nightline," "The News Hour with Jim Lehrer," and "Meet the Press."

Later in life, Jarrett appeared on the PBS documentaries "Harry Truman" in 1997 and "Eleanor: The Life and Times of Eleanor Roosevelt" in 2000. He helped found the National Association of Black Journalists in 1975 and was its president from 1977 to 1979, and in 1977 founded ACT-SO, the Afro-Academic, Cultural and Scientific Olympics, a NAACP-affiliated program to direct black youth to careers outside sports and entertainment. He served on the board of Fisk University's Race Relations Institute and on the editorial board of *Crisis* magazine, voice of the NAACP. He was also on the board of the Chicago chapter of the National Academy of Television Arts & Sciences and was board chairman of Chicago's DuSable Museum of African-American History.

At one time or another, he taught history and journalism at Northwestern University and at City College of Chicago. For the Great Cities Institute of the University of Illinois in Chicago, he started the Freedom Readers, an attempt to encourage black youth to read more. In 2002, just two years before his death, he became president of the Chicago Association of Black Journalists. In his final years, he returned to the *Defender* as a columnist; he had long said that America's black press was the institution that gave oppressed blacks the necessary sense of self that made possible the drive for civil rights that finally began in the 1950s. He also inspired the creation of a summer writing institute at his alma mater, Knoxville College; the institute is named in his honor. At the time of his death from cancer, Jarrett was working on an autobiography and on a book of essays about black leaders, many of whom he had interviewed or had otherwise known during his long, distinguished career.

His awards were many. An *Ebony* magazine poll in 1970 identified him as one of the country's five most important black communicators. He was given the American Civil Liberties Union's James P. McGuire Award in 1988; and in 1993, he won the President's Award from the National Association of Black School Educators. He was a 1998 inductee into the National Literary Hall of Fame at the University of Chicago Gwendolyn Brooks Center, and he was the inaugural recipient of the James Weldon Johnson Award given by the NAACP. The National Association of Black Journalists in 2004 gave him its posthumous Legacy Award.

Further Readings: Curry, George E. "Remembering Vernon Jarrett." [Online, 27 May 2004]. Atlanta Daily world Web site www.zwire.com; Dawkins, Wayne. "Death of Pioneering Black Journalist Marks End of an Era." [Online, 25 May 2004]. BlackAmerica Web site www.blackamericaweb.com; Fitzgerald, Mark. "Vernon Jarrett: An Appreciation." [Online, 24 May 2004]. Editor & Publisher Web site www.mediainfo,com; "Jarrett: Journalists Must Know History." [Online, 16 January 2001]. Medill School of Journalism Web site www.medill.nwu.edu; Lamb, Yvonne Shinhoster. "Vernon Jarrett, 84; Journalist, Crusader." [Online, 25 May 2004]. Washington Post Web site www.washingtonpost.com; Morial, Marc. "OpEd: Vernon Jarrett, Dreamer and Doer." [Online, 31 May 2004]. Civil Rights Coalition for the twenty-first Century Web site www.civilrights.org; Norment, Lynn. "A Salute to NABJ's Presidents: Vernon Jarrett." [Online]. National Association of Black Journalists Web site www.nabj.org; "Obituary of Vernon Jarrett." [Online]. NABJ Web site www.nabj.org; Prince, Richard. "Firming Up Jarrett's Legacy." [Online, 26 May 2004]. In Richard Prince's Journal-isms, Maynard Institute Web site www.maynardije.org; Stein, M.L. *Blacks in Communications: Journalism, Public Relations and Advertising.* New York: Julian Messner, 1972, pp. 57–58.

Jefferson, Stebbins (1 February 1936–)

Since 1989, retired West Palm Beach schoolteacher Stebbins Jefferson has written a column for the *Palm Beach Post*. She was born in Arcadia, Florida, and earned a bachelor's in English from Florida A&M University in 1957 and a masters, also in English, from Stetson University in 1967. For 33 years she taught English and speech at Lake Worth High School and at Palm Beach Community College, where she served as chair of Humanities. In addition to writing her column, she served on the *Post*'s editorial board from 1992 until 1995. Mrs. Jefferson is an example of an accomplished newspaper columnist who did not come up through journalism by the usual route. She became a columnist by first writing occasional commentary pieces in answer to a request from a former student who had become a *Post* editor, then in 1989 began her regular column. Her maiden name was Freddie Stebbins, her married name, Jefferson. To have a line of demarcation between her teaching and her column writing, she chose to appear in the *Post* under the pen name Stebbins Jefferson.

Her columns often reveal a mind that wants to believe in the kind of America we like to think we are, but is having an increasingly difficult time keeping that faith, as evidenced in the column reproduced below. Our democracy, she reminds her readers, remains a work in progress. She regrets that in the wake of the attacks on 11 September 2001, Americans were so traumatized and so fearful of future attacks that they quietly relinquished some of their civil rights. She also pictures the George W. Bush administration's emphasis on moral values as having no more substance than the soft drink commercials that assured us their product was "the real thing." Although she seldom gets into the thick of partisan politics, Jefferson is very clear in her belief that the United States made war with haste with Iraq for reasons self-serving to those in power. Like so many other columnists, she laments that too few citizens bother to think, but, sheep-like, follow clever political slogans and are swayed by initiatives that have been given positive-sounding names, such as The Patriot Act. At this writing, she has begun to think that America's illusions about the Iraq war are growing thin, and she criticizes the widespread abuses practiced by military recruiters, citing local examples. A column about Tony Blair's June 2005 visit to the Untied States points out that the English prime minister's cooperation with President Bush in attacking Iraq was not repaid when Blair sought big increases in U.S. aid to Africa's poorest nations. Helping starving Africans, she wrote, does not appear high on the Bush administration's agenda.

More than once Jefferson has written about conservative radio provocateur Rush Limbaugh, who had to go on hiatus from his show to check into an expensive rehab center to break his dependence on painkillers—this after he had repeatedly argued for stiff sentences for drug addicts. Blessed is he, wrote Jefferson, who can pay for his medical treatment. She argues for spending more public dollars for rehabilitation and less concentration on jailing people who are addicted to drugs. A Christmas column argued for more emphasis on finding similarities among religions as opposed to pious certainly that only one religion is valid. She points out that when religion-minded people focus on differences, religion can become a weapon of mass destruction. A 1993 column written in her early years with the *Post* reflected on the twenty-fifth anniversary of the Kerner Commission Report on civil disorders, making the strong point that U.S. cities, once one of their greatest strengths, are now becoming one of their greatest weaknesses. Like any good teacher, she urges readers to know the value of history and not to assume that only the present matters; the occasion was a column she wrote about Black History Month, which had its origins as Black History Week, started in 1929 by Carter G. Woodson. Her columns are occasionally tributes, such as a June 2004 example written upon the death of entertainer Ray Charles. Similarly occasional are light-hearted observations, such as a column from June 2005 about the health benefits for older people of walking regularly. The column's humor came in assurances that she and her fellow walkers were not merely gossiping, but discussing serious subjects, such as possums and the kha-nyou, a guinea pig-like mammal just discovered in Laos.

"Purging Ethics from Voter Rolls?" by Stebbins Jefferson

After an elderly aunt saw Neil Armstrong walk on the moon and plant an American flag, she turned to us and said: "That's just one of those make-believe picture shows. Don't let what you think you see mess up your mind."

Though some relatives laughed, I didn't. I understood that, having fixed her faith in a world ideally handcrafted by an omnipotent, moral god and having ordered her life accordingly, she intended to keep that faith uncompromised. Now a senior citizen myself, I find myself struggling with the same kind of dilemma. I don't want to believe what I think I'm seeing in the news because to do so would threaten my faith in our democratic system.

According to the Florida Division of Elections, 33 of our 67 counties have not reinstated voters improperly removed from the voter rolls before the 2000 presidential election. You will recall that in the two years prior to that debacle, Secretary of State Katherine Harris hired an Atlanta-based company to purge Florida's voting rolls of felons, dead people and those with duplicate registrations. So zealous was this effort that in 1999 and 2000, more than 12,000 voters were identified as felons and another 7,500 were listed as duplicate voters.

Blatant errors were made. For example, many who had committed felonies in states that automatically restore all civil rights upon completion of prison sentences were improperly removed from state voter rolls. Only felonies committed in Florida should have been considered, since Florida is one of only a few states that do not immediately restore the right to vote when an inmate leaves prison. Instead, people who commit such crimes within Florida must petition the governor for restoration of voting rights. The procedure is so onerous as to discourage appeals. And few who cannot afford a lawyer are likely to succeed.

As could have been predicted in this suspiciously timed rush to judgment, people with names similar to convicted Florida felons, dead people and duplicate voters were purged. So gross were the errors on lists the state sent to counties that the NAACP and other civil rights groups sued the state in 2001. In September 2002, a settlement was reached, stipulating that "false positives" names improperly removed from county voter rolls would be restored.

By Sept. 30, 2003, Elections Division Director Ed Kast had instructed all county election supervisors to correct the initial purge lists. Yet as of Wednesday, only 33 counties were in compliance with that order. Palm Beach County, the national joke in the last election, is among the counties that have not reported corrections. Those counties that have reported their findings to the state restored 679 voters' eligibility. George W. Bush won Florida by 537 votes.

Another development that causes me to question whether I can keep faith in our government is the news out of Tallahassee that Gov. Bush signed into law on Tuesday a measure eliminating the requirement that absentee ballots be signed by a witness. This bipartisan legislation, sponsored by Republican Paula Dockery in the Senate and pushed through the House by Democrat Roger Wishner, seems to invite voter fraud.

I've tried to shake the feeling that there is mischief afoot, but I can't do so when I recall that on election night, when the networks at first declared Florida for Al Gore, our governor declared that assessment to be impossible because the absentee ballots had not been counted. He knew that a major effort had been made to send such ballots to Republicans in some parts of the state. As it turned out, the elections supervisors in Martin and Seminole counties had allowed Republican campaign workers to fill out applications for absentee ballots and done other favors that a judge later ruled to have been wrong.

Observing these realities, my late aunt would tell me to hold onto my belief that the fundamental right of every American citizen to vote is inviolate. We've invested too much in that premise to abandon it now. I would reply that I'm trying to keep that faith, but it's getting harder and harder to do so.

Source: Copyright 2004, the Palm Beach Post. This column which appeared on 29 May 2004, is reprinted here by permission of the Palm Beach Post.

Further Readings: "Stebbins Jefferson." [Online]. Palm Beach Post Web site www.palmbeachpost.com.

Johnson, John Harold (19 January 1918–8 August 2005)

Self-made entrepreneur, philanthropist and publisher of *Ebony* and other magazines for the African-American market, John Johnson died of heart failure at age 87 after a truly spectacular career. He was born in Arkansas City, Arkansas, and after his father died in a sawmill accident, moved with his mother and stepfather to Clerical as part of the Great Migration that took black southerners northward in hopes of better futures. Johnny was enrolled in high school where, due to a clerical error, he was entered as a sophomore instead of a freshman, skipping a grade. A diligent student, he did well in school, was editor of the school newspaper, business manager of the yearbook, member of the debating team and president of his class; two of his fellow students who also achieved fame were singer Nat King Cole and comedian Redd Foxx. Johnson won a scholarship to the University of Chicago, but it covered only tuition. In order to afford the other costs of college, he took a parttime job in 1936 working for Harry Pace, founder of the Supreme Liberty Life Insurance Company, who had heard Johnson speak at an Urban League meeting. Two years later, Johnson left school to work fulltime for Pace and for Earl Dickerson, a Chicago alderman who also worked for Pace's company; later, Johnson did further study at the Northwestern School of Commerce and edited the house magazine for Supreme Liberty Life. It was at this time of his life that he changed his name from Johnny Johnson to John Harold Johnson.

In 1941 and 1942, Johnson began work on his first magazine venture, a black-oriented version of *Reader's Digest* titled *Negro Digest*. He raised the initial capital for this risky launch by pawning his mother's furniture for $500, which he used for a direct-mail campaign directed at policyholders of Supreme Liberty Life. After a strong response, he published his first issue in November 1942, during World War II. The advertising-free monthly had a positive, patriotic tone, yet Johnson had to trick a distributor into trucking it to newsstands, first in Chicago, then in New York, Detroit and Philadelphia. Circulation grew remarkably and soared after the appearance of Eleanor Roosevelt's article

"If I Were a Negro." Johnson closed this magazine in 1951 when he brought out *Jet*, but reader complaints caused its reappearance in 1961. It was published under its original title until 1970, when it was rechristened *Black World*, appearing as such until 1976. *Black World*, under managing editor Hoyt Fuller, took on a somewhat militant tone and by 1976, circulation and profitability had declined considerably.

Meanwhile, Johnson had launched other titles that proved much more successful. *Ebony*, a black-readership monthly in the styles of *Life* and *Look*, premiered in November 1945 with Johnson as editor-in-chief and Ben Burns as editor. Burns was not as conservative in selecting content as was his boss, and the two men parted company in the mid-1950s, although they worked together again some years later on another new magazine. Johnson understood the profit potential of the positive, optimistic approach, and the magazine became a great success; circulation grew from 25,000 at inception to 1.9 million by the late 1990s. The magazine's title was selected by Johnson's wife, Eunice, who survives her husband and is secretary-treasurer of Johnson Publishing Company. *Ebony* carried "Advice for Living," a column written by Martin Luther King, Jr., in the 1950s and the photographs of Moneta Sleet, Jr., the first African-American photographer to win a Pulitzer Prize; and for many years *Ebony* has benefited from the writing and editing of executive editor and popular historian Lerone Bennett. Without national advertising, however, the magazine could not have succeeded. Reluctance of national advertisers to take out ads in minority-oriented media had long been the bane of both magazines and newspapers aimed at black audiences, and it took Johnson years of patient effort to break this barrier. He finally succeeded in doing so in 1946 by personally persuading Zenith president Eugene McDonald by appealing to McDonald's interest Arctic exploration. Not only did Zenith advertise in *Ebony*, but its president convinced other corporate CEOs to do likewise. Johnson was also able to persuade some national publishers to begin using African-American models in their advertisements. *Ebony* continued to prosper and grow and offered its readers a wide array of subject matter from politics to sports and the social scene, personalities, music and the other arts, fashion and cooking. *Ebony* has spawned three spin-off magazines: the children's monthly *Ebony Jr.*, in 1973, published until 1985; *EM:Ebony Man*, launched in 1985 to cater to the interests of upwardly mobile African-American men; and *Ebony South Africa* in 1995. Less successful than *Ebony*, but remaining in publication under three different titles until 1981, was *Tan Confessions*, which appeared in 1950. Its lightweight copy emulated that which was found in *True Story, True Romance* and other such periodicals sold to white America by another enterprising publisher, Bernarr McFadden. The magazine's title was shortened in 1952 to *Tan*, and in 1971, it was retitled *Black Stars* and converted into a periodical appealing to the celebrity culture. Circulation rose to at least 250,000, but the magazine's profit picture was not satisfactory, and Johnson laid the magazine to rest in 1981.

In November 1951, appeared Johnson's second most successful magazine: *Jet: The Weekly Negro News Magazine*. Like *Negro Digest* before it, *Jet* was a digest-size monthly; Ben Burns rejoined the company as the new magazine's executive editor. In 1971, it began appearing with a larger page size and a broadened range of content. *Jet* now has a circulation of around 950,000.

Although John Johnson is primarily remembered as a magazine publisher, his other business ventures were numerous. He bought three radio stations: WJPC-AM, Chicago's first black-owned station, in 1972; WLNR-FM in Lansing, Illinois, in 1982; and WLOU-AM, Louisville, Kentucky, also in 1982. He also started Ebony Fashion Fair, which tours the nation, sells through a mail-order catalogue and is headed by his widow, Eunice; Fashion Fair Cosmetics, Supreme Beauty Products, a hair care line for both men and women; and a book publishing subsidiary. In addition, he bought control of Supreme Life Insurance Company and was its chairman and CEO. The growing success of his enterprises was mirrored by the offices that housed Johnson's closely held company. He began publishing out of a single room in Earl Dickerson's law offices, which were in the Supreme Life building. Only a year later, Johnson moved to his own storefront building on South State Street, and in 1949, relocated to what had been a funeral parlor on South Michigan Avenue. In 1972, he built an opulent headquarters on Chicago's Loop, becoming the first black-owned business on that part of Michigan Avenue. The frequently toured building houses a collection of works by black artists as well as a black-interest library.

Johnson's honors have been legion. In 1951, the U.S. Junior Chamber of Commerce named him one of the year's 10 Outstanding Men, the first time an African American had made the list. He received the Wall Street Journal/Dow Jones Entrepreneurial Excellence Award in 1993 and both the NAACP's Springarn Medal and the National Newspaper Publishers' John Russwurm Award in 1966. In 1972, the Magazine Publishers Association selected him as its first African-American Publisher of the Year, and in 1987, the NABJ's Lifetime Achievement Award went to Johnson. In 1996, President Bill Clinton presented Johnson the Presidential Medal of Freedom for the way in which he had helped break harmful stereotypes of blacks, citing Johnson as the most influential black publisher in the nation's history. In 2001, he was inducted into the Arkansas Business Hall of Fame, an awards program sponsored by the Sam M. Walton College of Business at the University of Arkansas. By 1990, Johnson's net worth was estimated at $150 million, and he was courted by every president since Dwight D. Eisenhower. In 1957, he traveled with President Richard Nixon on a nine-country goodwill tour of Africa and two years later went with Nixon to Russia and Poland. He represented his country at President John F. Kennedy's invitation in 1961 at the Ivory Coast's independence ceremonies and performed the same role again under President Lyndon Johnson in 1963 in Kenya. In 1966, Lyndon Johnson appointed him to the National Selective Service Commission, and in 1970, President Nixon made him a member of the President's Commission for the twenty-fifth anniversary of the United Nations.

Johnson received a number of honorary degrees, including one from Howard University; he had made a $4 million gift to Howard's Communications School in 2003, after which the school was renamed the John H. Johnson School of Communications. Johnson also served on the board of the United Negro College Fund for at least 30 years and was a director of the Magazine Publishers Association. At the time of Johnson's death, the University of Arkansas at Pine Bluff was engaged in a five-year project that is to result in a John H. Johnson Museum and a John H. Johnson Delta Cultural and Entrepreneurial Complex at the school. His publishing company successor is his daughter, Linda Johnson Rice, a Northwestern University MBA groomed for years for the job. Johnson wrote one book, his autobiography, *Succeeding against the Odds*, which appeared in 1989 and was updated in 2004. The extent of Johnson's prominence was reflected in the luminaries who attended his funeral. His widow was escorted to her seat by former President Bill Clinton, and in attendance were the Revs. Al Sharpton and Jesse Jackson; political figures Barack Obama (D-Ill.), Chicago Mayor Richard Daley and ex-Senator Carol Moseley Braun; show business figures Travis Smiley, Dick Gregory and Don King; and fellow publishers Christie Hefner and Earl Graves.

Books by John Harold Johnson: *Succeeding against the Odds* (New York: Warner Books, 1989).

Further Readings: Bell, Gregory S. "Johnson, John." In *African American Lives*. Edited by Henry Louis Gates and Evelyn Brooks Higginbotham. New York: Oxford University Press, 2004, pp. 457–58; Falkof, Lucille. *John H. Johnson, "The Man from Ebony."* (Ada, Okla.: Garrett Educational Corp., 1992); Hamilton, Kerry-Ann. "Howard University Ranames Communications School for John H. Johnson." [Online, 29 September 2003]. Black College Wire Web site www.blackcollegewire.org; Pride, Karen E. "Final Tributes Paid to John H. Johnson as Thousands Attend Chicago Funeral Service." [Online, 15 August 2005]. Black Journalist Web site www.blackjournalist.com; Roberson, Patt Foster. "John H. Johnson." In Vol. 137, *Dictionary of Literary Biography: American Magazine Journalists, 1900–1960, Second Series*. Edited by Sam G. Riley. (Detroit, Mich.: Gale Research, 1994), pp. 132–41; Rowan, Carl T. "Words That Give Us Strength." *Reader's Digest*, 66 (April 1987): 49–58.

Johnson, Robert L. (8 April 1946–)

Ask anyone to name the wealthiest African-American connected with the media, and the answer will almost surely be Oprah Winfrey. In 2005, that answer would be wrong, however. Although Ms. Winfrey's personal wealth at that time was estimated at around $800 million, she still would have to save a while longer to catch up with Robert Johnson, who became the first African-American billionaire when he sold the company he had founded in 1980, Black Entertainment Television, to Viacom for $2.7 billion in 1999. His personal worth is estimated at $1.3 billion. Johnson was born in Hickory, Mississippi, the ninth of 10 children. His family moved to Freeport, Illinois, where he worked a paper route delivering the *Rockford Morning Star*, mowed lawns, did gardening, and was a county fair roustabout. While working at a battery factory, he discovered that he would like to work for himself if the opportunity arose. The only one among his siblings to attend college, he enrolled at the University of Illinois, where he pondered a career in teaching or perhaps the Foreign Service, graduating in 1968 with a history degree. He then went to Princeton, where he studied international affairs, and in 1972 he earned a masters in public administration.

Johnson began his career as a Capitol Hill aide, and after working as press secretary to D.C. delegate Walter E. Fauntroy, he left in 1976 to become a lobbyist for the cable industry after that career change had been suggested to him by a young lady he met at a party. He became the National Cable & Telecommunications Association's vice president for pay television, and lobbied the Congress and the FCC to ease the restrictions on the showing of movies on cable. It was in this job that Johnson came to understand the implications of segmented, targeted audiences and how cable television had the potential of doing electronically what John Johnson's magazines were doing in the magazine business. He recalls sharing a taxi with a stranger who wanted to launch a cable channel targeted at senior citizens and who wanted to meet with Florida Congressman Claude Pepper. In exchange for arranging a meeting with Pepper, Johnson was given the man's business plan, which he changed to target the black rather than the elderly audience.

In spring 1979, Johnson secured a $15,000 bank loan and approached cable executive John Malone, who then headed Tele-Communications Inc., the industry's third largest cable company. Johnson was black, Malone white; Johnson was politically liberal, Malone, conservative. The two men hit it off, however, and Malone called in his lawyer to immediately draw up an agreement by which Malone would buy a 20 percent stake in Johnson's new company for $180,000 and would lend the new entrepreneur an additional $320,000. Malone advised Johnson to keep costs low and to grow his revenues by continual expansion. As BET began to develop, Malone lent the business additional capital, and other funds were secured from Taft Broadcasting, HBO and Time Warner. Within five years, BET was profitable. Johnson credits Malone's prestige and credibility in the industry with having opened doors for BET that otherwise might have remained shut. Programming costs were kept low by creating little original material and instead using existing music videos, sitcom reruns of shows such as "The Parkers," "Benson" and "The Jeffersons" and movies that starred black actors or were otherwise of special interest to African Americans. BET first aired in 1980, offering only two hours of content weekly. The company grew steadily and remains the most successful cable provider for the African-American market. It has concentrated on entertainment programming and has done only a modest amount of less profitable public affairs programming, which has drawn criticism but generated big profits. On Sundays, the usual rap and hip-hop fare is interrupted by hours of gospel music and religious programs, such as "Let's Talk Church," with gospel singer Bobby Jones. BET has spun off three new music channels, BET Gospel, BET Hip-Hop and BET Jazz. In 1991, BET became the first African American–controlled company to be listed on the New York Stock Exchange. In 1998, however Johnson repurchased the publicly held shares and made the company private again. BET's parent company BET Holdings Inc., was based in Washington, D.C., and also had interests in clothing, hotels, casinos, restaurants, cosmetics, film production and magazine publishing via its part-ownership of Vanguard Media, publisher of *Honey*, *Heart & Soul* and *Impact*. Later in a 1999 joint venture with Microsoft, USA Networks, Liberty Digital and News Corporation, the interactive Web site BET.com was launched. The company then had around 500 employees and yearly sales of perhaps $170 million, and Johnson had retained 63 percent ownership. In 1999, Johnson sold BET to corporate giant Viacom for $2.7 billion, staying on as CEO and chairman. By that time, BET was on the air 24 hours a day and reached a reported 65 million homes; by 2004, that figure had increased to 78 million—in the United States, Canada and the Caribbean. Since the sale to Viacom, the company has cut back its already small amount of public affairs programming. In 2001, the Tavis Smiley talk show was discontinued as was "BET Tonight" and a youth-appeal program titled "Teen Summit." The morning news show "Lead Story" was cancelled in 2002 and was replaced with "BET Nightly News," which in turn was replaced with a series of day-long news updates by anchor Jackie Reid. The channel has continued to stress programming with youth appeal, in contrast to its rival channel TV One, which aims at the family market niche. In June 2005, Johnson announced that he would step down as CEO and chairman in January 2006 and that his replacement would be Debra L. Lee, the company's president and chief operating officer.

In 2003, Johnson achieved another first by becoming the only African American to own a major-league sports franchise when he bought the Charlotte Bobcats of the National Basketball Association. At the same time, he became owner of the WNBA team the Charlotte Sting. After selling BET to Viacom, Johnson founded RLJ Companies, a holding company for his various interests in the gaming and hospitality industries. He serves on the boards of Hilton Hotels, US Airways, General Mills, the American Film Institute, the National Cable Television Association and the United Negro College Fund. He is also on the boards of the Brookings Institution and the Cleveland-based Rock and Roll Hall of Fame. He was awarded the 1997 Hall of Fame Award by *Broadcasting & Cable Magazine* and has been listed by *Cablevision Magazine* as one of the 20 most influential people in cable television. He has also been accorded a distinguished alumni award by Princeton University.

Further Readings: Johnson, Robert. "How We Got Started." [Online]. Fortune magazine Web site www.fortune.com; Miller, Robert G. "Robert L. Johnson: A Business Titan Redefining Black Entrepreneurial Success." [Online]. The Black Collegian Web site www.black-collegian.com; Rawlinson, Raymond. "Can Robert Johnson Bring More Blacks Online?" [Online, 6 October 1999]. Salon.com http://archive.salon.com; "Robert Johnson Steps Down from BET."

[Online, 2 June 2005]. MSNBC Web site www.msnbc.msn.com. "Robert L. Johnson Sells BET." [Online]. African Genesis Web site www.afgen.com.

Johnson, Roy S. (1956–)

Having served three tours of duty at *Sports Illustrated*, the last of which ended in December 2005, Roy Johnson also wrote sports for eight years at the *New York Times* and was the founding editor-in-chief of *Savoy* magazine. He has, in addition, worked for *Fortune* and *Money* magazines and the *Atlanta Journal & Constitution*. In early 2006, he wrote a weekly online column for AOL Black Voices. Johnson hails from Tulsa, Oklahoma, where he attended Holland Hall Preparatory School. He went on to earn a B.A. in political science at Stanford University. His career began in 1978 at *Sports Illustrated*, where he was a reporter until 1981. He was hired away by the *New York Times*, where he was a sports writer until returning to *Sports Illustrated* in 1989 as a senior editor. After his return, he cowrote a major interview-based story for the magazine that described the sudden retirement of basketball legend Earvin "Magic" Johnson, who revealed that he had contracted the HIV virus. In 2000, Roy Johnson left *Sports Illustrated* for a second time to be the founding editor of a slick new magazine, *Savoy*, which was designed to appeal to sophisticated urban African Americans. The magazine was owned by Vanguarde Media, led by Keith Clinkscales. Unable to make a go of it, the magazine went into Chapter 11 bankruptcy in 2003, and what remained of the company was bought in 2004 by Hermene Hartman, publisher of *N'Digo*. *Savoy* was relaunched in February 2005, this time with Monroe Anderson as editor-in-chief. When the reputation of *Savoy* declined, Johnson again returned to *Sports Illustrated*, this time as assistant managing editor and weekly "Pass the Word" columnist for SI.com. His column appeared until December 2005, when his contract reportedly was bought out during a period of job cuts at Time Inc. properties. At age 49, he was the highest-ranking African-American journalist at the magazine. Since his second return to the magazine, he had worked as executive producer of television specials for his employer; had started a 90-minute Westwood One radio show, "Sports Illustrated Monday Night Live"; and, with managing editor Terry McDonnell, had coproduced a *Sports Illustrated* swimsuit model DVD. Soon after leaving the magazine, Johnson began writing his weekly column for AOL Black Voices. Along the way, he has coauthored two books, with major basketball figures Magic Johnson and Charles Barkley. The first appeared in 1989, the second in 1992. Johnson has benefited his prep school alma mater, the Holland Hall School, by founding the Roy S. Johnson Foundation to financially assist minority students who wish to study there. He is a member of the National Association of Black Journalists and is on the board of the

International Amateur Athletic Foundation. Johnson is also associated with the Bill Spiller/Homeboy Golf Classic.

In a column that appeared in August 2005 on Chicago Defender.com, Johnson recalled having met another Mr. Johnson—magazine publisher John H. Johnson. He credited John Johnson with having been one of the early successes that opened the door of opportunity to African-American journalists of the Roy Johnson generation. The older man was, he wrote, the bridge that linked Frederick Douglass and Ida B. Wells to Oprah Winfrey. It was ironic, Roy Johnson wrote, that the older publisher directed a brief diatribe at him because he had chosen to work for *Sports Illustrated* rather than lending his talents to the historically black media. It was soon after that meeting that Roy Johnson conceived the idea for the upscale black magazine *Savoy*. He added, however, that although *Savoy* was hailed as a new concept periodical, the cover of the first issue of the older Johnson's flagship magazine *Ebony* had pictured an affluent-looking black family with the headline "The New Black Middle Class." *Savoy*'s approach, then, wasn't entirely new.

In a May 2003 SI.com column, Johnson mentioned meeting with boxer Mike Tyson at a time when the fearsome fighter was just beginning his ring career and noted what a pleasant young man he was. He went on to describe how fame had not treated Tyson well and how dangerously out-of-control the man appeared to have become. In Johnson's opinion, Tyson should never be allowed to box again. Another 2003 column in which Johnson might have jumped to a premature conclusion opined that golfer Tiger Woods had indeed "lost his mojo." If Woods had indeed lost it, more recent tournaments show that it was only temporarily misplaced. A May 2005 Johnson column told the story of Reggie Fowler's attempt to become the first African-American owner of an NFL team. His efforts to buy the Minnesota Vikings came to naught due to insufficient millions. The column was cleverly couched in the form of an open letter to billionaire entertainer Oprah Winfrey, pointing out that women love pro football too—the brutality, the strategy and the players' tight pants. Johnson, tongue-in-cheek, suggested that Oprah should consider buying a team. In July 2005, Johnson tipped his hat to cyclist Lance Armstrong, crediting him with the second greatest winning streak in sports history—after the 56-game hitting streak of baseball legend Joe DiMaggio. Admitting that sports stars are, in their own muscular way, court jesters, Johnson wrote a delightful column in August 2005 about sports' 25 greatest "characters" from the previous 25 years. Among them were three tennis players: grumpy John McEnroe, Andre Agassi of the changed image and glamor girl Anna Kornikova. Other choices were basketball bad-boys Allen Iverson and Dennis Rodman, major appliance-sized football lineman William Perry and Joe Namath, who will be remembered not just for his football prowess, but also for his nude pose for *Ms.* magazine. In another column that appeared in that same month and year, Johnson came out against the use of American Indian mascot names, citing the Southeastern Oklahoma

State Savages as perhaps the worst offender of them all. A column of tribute published in October 2005 was Johnson's nod to lightweight boxer Leavander Johnson, who died from brain injuries five days after a September 2005 bout with Jesus Chavez in Las Vegas. And in November 2005, not long before he parted ways with *Sports Illustrated*, Johnson expressed the opinion that only three black head coaches in all of I-A college football was insufficient and reflected lingering racism. This message was repeated in one of his first Black Voices.com columns in early 2006; here, he discussed the NFL's Rooney Rule, which mandates that at least one minority candidate must be interviewed for every head coaching vacancy in the league. The lack of success most of these job candidates meet, wrote Johnson, shows that the Rooney Rule does not go far enough. And what, he added, of all those jobs in other fields where there is no Rooney Rule at all? As the 2006 Winter Olympics in Turin, Italy, ground to an end, Johnson blasted the U.S. contingent for their lack of team spirit, their immature behavior and their disappointing performance; he was especially hard on the overhyped skier Bode Miller. As to Shani Davis, the speed skater who was the first black athlete to win an individual gold medal at a Winter Olympics, Johnson noted that Davis had been the target of racial epithets and had been stereotyped as coming from a "gang-infested" neighborhood in Chicago. Must all poor black urban neighborhoods be described as "gang infested"? asked Johnson.

Books by Roy S. Johnson: With Charles Barkley, *Outrageous: The Fine Life and Flagrant Good Times of Basketball's Irresistible Force* (New York: Simon and Schuster, 1992); With Earvin Johnson, *Magic's Touch* (Reading, Mass.: Addison-Wesley, 1989).

Further Readings: "Biography." [Online]. Sports Illustrated.com site http://sportsillusrated.cnn.com/writers; Prince, Richard. [Online, 9 December 2005]. "Veteran Wants to See 'What's on the Open Market.'" Richard Prince's Journal-isms. Maynard Institue Web site www.maynardije.org.

Jones, Starlet Marie (24 March 1962–)

Star Jones is best known as one of the hosts of "The View," an ABC talk show for women, and formerly was a prosecuting attorney, a legal analyst for a variety of network television shows and the host of the syndicated show "Jones and Jury." She was born in the North Carolina town of Badin, where she lived with her grandmother until her mother finished college and moved with her two daughters to Trenton, New Jersey. Her mother worked as a human services administrator and married Trenton's chief of security. Star attended parochial schools and decided at age seven to be a lawyer. She worked during school years at a McDonalds and is a 1979 graduate of American University, where she majored in administration of justice. Between her junior and senior years, she was diagnosed with a tumor on her thymus gland and was told she had only months to live. She sought a second opinion, had surgery and recovered. In 1986, she earned a Juris Doctor at the University of Houston. After graduating from law school, she passed the New York Bar and worked in Brooklyn, New York, as a prosecutor in the homicide bureau of the district attorney's office. Flamboyant and charismatic, Jones was successful at prosecuting violent crimes, winning 31 of 33 felony cases; and in 1991, she was promoted to senior assistant district attorney. During the rape trial of William Kennedy Smith in 1991, Jones worked as a commentator for the program "Court TV," and in 1992, she took a new job as NBC's legal correspondent. She made frequent appearances on the "NBC Nightly News" and "The Today Show" during the rape trial of boxer Mike Tyson and during the trial that followed the caught-on-videotape 1992 beating of Rodney King in Los Angeles. In 1994, she became the host of her own show, "Jones and Jury," on which the studio audience functioned as an actual jury. Their rulings on the small-claims cases adjudicated on the show were legally binding. Jones attempted to break through the various mysteries surrounding the practice of law and its less than user-friendly jargon for the benefit of her viewers. In 1995, she joined "Inside Edition" as that show's senior correspondent and chief legal analyst. In this capacity, she covered both the criminal and civil trials of former football great O.J. Simpson and was successful in getting an interview with Simpson where other members of the press had failed to do so. Then in August 1997, Barbara Walters launched the daytime ABC talk show "The View." Jones was one of the hosts of the program, alongside Walters, who is executive producer, Elisabeth Hasselbeck, Joy Behar and Meredith Vieira. The highly conversational "infotainment" show ranges widely in content, covering family issues, selfesteem, the law, education, race and other areas of interest. Jones is known not just for her legal expertise, but also for her earthy, outspoken attitude and her high-style wardrobe. She is said to own around 500 pairs of shoes, which has caused some observers to refer to her as the American Imelda Marcos. Her love of shoes has also been good for business. She has become the national spokesperson for the nation's largest shoe retailer, Payless ShoeSource. She appears in that company's advertisements and in 2003, launched her own signature line of shoes, sold only at Payless. Her considerable media exposure and her full-figure size have also attracted the attention of satirists. Late-night television host Conan O'Brien has made many wisecracks about her weight, and sports radio talk show host Jim Rome refers to her as "Planet," alluding to her size. In spring 2005, for April Fool's day, the advocacy group People for the Ethical Treatment of Animals targeted Jones because of her fondness for wearing furs. In a parody advertisement featuring a portly cross-dresser who calls himself Flotilla DeBarge, this individual appeared coiffed and dressed as Jones and wore a white fur coat stained with blood. Similar PETA parodies have singled out entertainer Joan Rivers and *Vogue* magazine editor Anna Wintour. PETA has also included Jones several times on its annual list of the Worst-Dressed Americans. Jones attracted a good deal of attention, both positive and negative, early in 2002 when she remarked on

"The View" that she would not vote for any presidential candidate who was an atheist. Her position was that a president should feel a sense of responsibility to a higher power in order to do the job properly. In October 2003, Jones' penthouse home was featured in the magazine *Architectural Digest*, and she was sued by a landscaping company that claimed it was not given the agreed-upon credit for its work. Even more publicity erupted in November 2004 over her marriage to banker Al Reynolds. Reynolds had proposed with flamboyance of his own at the February 2004 NBA All-Star Game—on the Los Angeles Staples Center arena's Jumbotron, witnessed by 20,000 fans. The wedding at Saint Bartholomew's Church in New York reportedly cost more than $1 million and featured three matrons of honor, fourteen bridesmaids and junior bridesmaids, three best men, fifteen groomsmen and junior groomsmen, four ring bearers, four flower girls and six footmen. Jones appears to take such criticism in good grace, enjoying the fallout from her extravagant, highly publicized lifestyle.

In 1994, Jones appeared on a panel on racial insensitivity at the Atlanta UNITY convention; her fellow panelists were Jesse Jackson, columnist Donna Britt of *The Washington Post* and *Time* magazine's managing editor James R. Gaines. Since 2000, she has made many television guest appearances, including in "The Rosie O'Donnell Show," "The Tonight Show with Jay Leno," "Late Night with Conan O'Brien," "The Late Late Show with Craig Ferguson," "Live with Regis and Kelly," "Larry King Live," "Charlie Rose," "Celebrity Poker Showdown," "The Tony Danza Show," "The Daily Show with Jon Stewart," "Hollywood Squares," "Soul Food" and "Sex and the City." She has also appeared on several Emmy Award shows. Jones had a 2001 shopping show, "It's All about You with Star Jones," on cable's ShopNBC, and she has set up her own Web site, starjones.com, as well. Jones has published two books and created her own foundation, the Starlet Fund, to help provide support for women and girls in need. She was recognized in 2002 for her work to benefit children of low-income homes via the East Harlem School at Exodus House, on whose board she serves. She is also on the boards of the organizations God's Love We Deliver, Dress for Success, and Girls, Inc. Jones and her cohosts of "The View" were honored in 2001 with the Safe Horizon Champion Award for their efforts to combat violence directed at women. In all that she has done, Jones' signature appeal is that of a "down-to-earth diva," a curious combination to be sure.

Books by Startlet Marie Jones: With Daniel Paisner, *You Have to Stand for Something, or You'll Fall for Anything* (New York: Bantam Books, 1998); as Star Jones Reynolds, *Shine: A Physical, Emotional, and Spiritual Journey to Finding Love* (New York: HarperCollins, 2006).

Further Readings: "'Fur Is a Drag,' Says 'Star Jones' in PETA's New Parody Ad." [Online]. FurIsDead.com Web site www.furisdead.com; Gregory, Deborah. "Star Jones." *Essence* 25 (January 1995): 42; Nicholson, Dolores. "Star Jones." *Notable Black American Women, Book II*. Ed. by Jessie Carney Smith. (Detroit, Mich.: Gale Research, 1996), pp. 361–62; Pener, Degen. "Star Power for NBC." New York 25 (9 March 1992): 22; "Star Jones." [Online, 2004]. ABC site http://abc.go.com/theview/hosts/jones; Starling, Kelly. "A View of Star Jones." *Ebony*, December 1998.

Joyner, Thomas (1949–)

Founder and host of "The Tom Joyner Morning Show" syndicated by ABC Radio Network, BlackAmericaWeb.com and other ventures, Tom Joyner is the most widely syndicated man on U.S. morning radio. He was born in Tuskegee, Alabama, the son of a secretary mother and a father who was one of the Tuskegee Airmen. Joyner graduated from Tuskegee Institute with a bachelor's degree in Sociology. Immediately after graduating, he entered media work as a news announcer for the black-owned Montgomery, Alabama, station WRMA-AM, where he trained under Tracy Larkin. He made several subsequent moves to work as a news reader and disk jockey for WLOK-AM in Memphis, KWK-AM in St. Louis and KKDA-FM in Dallas. From there he relocated to Chicago, where he worked for stations WJPC-FM, WVON-AM, WBMX-FM and WGCI-FM. In the mid-1980s he was faced with a choice of keeping the afternoon slot at Chicago's WGCI or working the morning drivetime show for KKDA in Dallas. He decided to do both, commuting daily by air and earning the nickname "The Fly Jock." His highly successful program "The Tom Joyner Show" premiered in 1994, syndicated to 29 stations. In early 2006, it reached 120 markets and 7–8 million listeners. The show offers a mix of commentary, comedy and music and has featured such guests as President Bill Clinton, Tipper Gore, Oprah Winfrey, Stevie Wonder, Wesley Snipes, Evander Holyfield and Spike Lee. Regular features on the show have included political commentary by Tavis Smiley, "Little-Known Black History Facts," "Thursday Morning Mom" and a tribute-oriented contest called "Real Fathers, Real Men." Some of Joyner's assistant hosts have been Sybil Wilkes, J. Anthony Brown, Myra J. and Ms. Dupre. The four-hour show is decidedly upbeat. Joyner has remarked that his technique is to first get the audience comfortable and laughing, then insert the informative content to set them thinking. The formula seems to work and has given this show the largest morning audience in urban U.S. radio. In 1996, a voter registration drive organized by Joyner and Tavis Smiley is said to have registered around 250,000 black voters. Later, when Christie's International Auction House announced plans to hold an auction of artifacts from the slave trade in America, Joyner and Smiley swung into action, pointing out that the New York auction house had a policy that precluded auctioning items associated with the Holocaust. The slave trade auction was cancelled. The show has also brought pressure to bear on advertisers who were slighting the African-American media, notably Katz Media Group and CompUSA. Then in 1998, the busy host set up the Tom Joyner Foundation, dedicated to the purpose of raising funds to help students at historically black colleges and universities. The foundation occupies an unusual niche in that it seeks to help students remain in school when they otherwise might have to drop out for lack of money.

Each month the foundation selects a school and donates funds for this purpose. Recipients are selected based on need and on their level of academic achievement. Most of the nation's black institutions of higher learning have received help from the foundation, and, in addition to soliciting donations from his show's listeners, Joyner has succeeded in finding corporate backers who will provide matching funds. In 2001, Joyner produced an album titled the "Tom Joyner Allstars," donating the proceeds to his foundation. As of 2006, the foundation had raised more than $30 million for students on more than 80 campuses. One of Joyner's two sons, Thomas Jr., is the foundation's CEO. In early 2004, the foundation began a year of partnering with the Louisville, Kentucky-based Long John Silver's restaurant chain to sell "Tom Joyner Platters." A portion of the proceeds from this venture went to aid needy college students. A year later, the foundation partnered with the National Education Association to provide around $700,000 for helping minority teachers complete their certification and go on to teach minority children. The program has offered assistance in paying tuition, purchasing books and providing financial support while recipients prepared for state teacher license examinations. The assistance is given by way of scholarships handled by historically black colleges and universities. Participating schools were Clark Atlanta University, Bowie State University, Jackson State University, Johnson C. Smith University, Cheney State University, Tennessee State University and Harris Stowe State College.

In June 2001, Joyner launched BlackAmericaWeb.com, an interactive Internet site providing news, commentary and other information targeted at the black audience. His wish is to make the site as comprehensive as possible a source of material for African Americans. Joyner's other son, Oscar, became the site's vice chair. In July 2005, the site offered one of the first of its major podcasts: an interview with Terry McMillan, author of *How Stella Got Her Groove Back* (New York: Viking, 1996). A recent addition to the site the BlackAmericaWeb.com Relief Fund was set up after the devastation caused by Hurricane Katrina to solicit and handle donations that would provide support for Gulf Coast families displaced by the storm. The site, updated daily, has around 850,000 registered members as of late 2005.

Joyner created a parent company for his various enterprises in January 2003: REACH Media; its president and CEO is Joyner's son Oscar. Under its umbrella come The Tom Joyner radio show, BlackAmericaWeb.com and SkyShow TV, a new venture for developing television properties. Each year, Joyner also promotes and sponsors the annual Tom Joyner's Fantastic Voyage, a week-long cruise designed especially for people of color.

Given his success and his philanthropic efforts, it is little wonder Joyner has received many honors. In 1998, he was the first African American to be inducted into the Radio Hall of Fame. He has also been accepted into the halls of fame of the Texas and Illinois Broadcasters organizations, has been awarded four Best Urban Contemporary Air Personality awards from *Billboard* magazine and has won the Hubert Humphrey Award from the Leadership Conference on Civil Rights. In addition, he has received the National Association of Broadcasters Education Foundation's Good Samaritan Award and an Essence Award, was once named one of the 20 most politically influential Americans by *Newsday*, received the Mickey Leland Humanitarian Award from the Congressional Black Caucus and has been accorded the NAACP's President's Award. One really unusual recognition is that he won *Impact Magazine*'s Joe Loris Award for broadcast excellence so often that the magazine renamed it the Tom Joyner Award.

Joyner has cowritten three books, the most successful of which was the most recent, *I'm Just a DJ but—It Makes Sense to Me*, a look at his career that takes on topics as diverse as relationships, race, money and life in general.

Books by Thomas Joyner: With Valerie J. Robinson and John Solomon Sandridge, *Little Known Black History Facts, as Featured on the Tom Joyner Show* (Oak Brook, Ill.: McDonald's Corp., 1999); with Mary Flowers Boyce and Muriel L. Sims, *"Go with the Bit": The Tom Joyner Morning Show* (Chicago: Johnson Pub., 1999); with Mary Flowers Boyce, *I'm Just a DJ but—It Makes Sense to Me* (New York: Warner Books, 2005).

Further Readings: "Tom Joyner." *The African-American Almanac*, 9th ed. Edited by Jeffrey Lehman. (Detroit: Gale Group, 2003); "Tom Joyner." [Online, 16 January 2006]. Tuskegee University Web site www.tuskegee.edu; "Tom Joyner's BlackAmericaWeb.com Offers Exclusive Podcast." [Online, 19 July 2005]. Forbes magazine Web site www.forbes.com; "Tom Joyner Foundation Partners with National Education Association." [Online, 3 January 2005]. National Education Association Web site www.nea.org.

K

Kane, Eugene A. (15 May 1956–)

Three times a week the readers of the *Milwaukee Journal Sentinel* read the column of Eugene Kane, a native of Philadelphia who launched his column for this paper in 1985. Kane attended Temple University in his home city, graduating with a B.A. in journalism in 1980. He also holds a 1982 graduate certificate from the University of California at Berkeley's summer program for minority journalists. He reported briefly for the *Philadelphia Bulletin* in 1980 and since 1981 has been with the *Journal Sentinel*, first as a general assignment reporter, then covering the federal court and suburban affairs beats. In 1985, he began his column, also writing feature stories and entertainment reviews. Often his column is directed at issues especially affecting the black community, sometimes about topics not so directly tied to race. Kane has the ability to make some readers laugh and others swear.

In an unusually long April 2001 column, Kane wrote that President George W. Bush had thus far lived up to the unimpressive reputation he had when he first took office. A few days later, he expressed dismay at the president's having scrapped a treaty that attempted to limit the number of nuclear warheads around the world in favor of resurrecting President Ronald Reagan's dubious "Star Wars" missile defense shield program. Prior to the 2004 presidential election, he remarked that the candidates' positions on issues were so different that there should be no such thing as "undecided voters." His real message was that the remaining members of "the wavering classes" were simply people who had not been paying attention. When fellow columnist Armstrong Williams was outed as having taken government money to promote the administration's No Child Left Behind program, Kane quipped that whenever an American writer is labeled as a "black conservative," what you are really getting is a black Republican.

A liberal, Kane favors increasing the minimum wage, pointing out that at $5.15 an hour, a 40-hour work week would result in before-tax earnings of only $206 a week—hardly a living wage. He also has pointed out that the people voting on a Wisconsin bill that would increase the minimum wage in that state to $6.50 are so removed from economic reality as to have no idea how difficult life is when one earns so little.

Like most African-American columnists, Kane makes a special effort to celebrate the passing of black notables, as in his January 2005 tribute to Shirley Chisholm, the first black woman to serve in Congress and the first, in 1972, to run for president. An earlier Black History Month tribute column, in February 1999, addressed the career of athlete/lawyer/actor/singer Paul Robeson, who had died in 1976. Kane portrayed Robeson as a sort of Michael Jordan, Michael Jackson and Muhammad Ali rolled into one, inasmuch as he had broken so many racial barriers. When basketball great Michael Jordon attempted a comeback in 2001 at age 38, Kane made what proved an accurate prediction: that the only fellow Jordon could not beat at one-on-one was Father Time. In recent years, Kane has written fewer humorous columns in favor of more columns that have a serious bite. He does not shrink from offending even the fiercest critics of all, the NRA, as in an April 2001 column about yet another Milwaukee murder by handgun. He remarked that today the city has more people with guns than with cell phones.

"President Lives Up to His Original, Unimpressive Reputation" by Eugene Kane

Some of us have been anxiously waiting for President George W. Bush to reach the 100-day mark in his administration.

About 50 million Americans who didn't vote for him, to be exact.

The 100-day mark generally is considered a good time to consider the performance of any new occupant of the Oval Office.

At the very least, it's become the accepted time frame in which to deliver a preliminary presidential report card. What has to be of great concern to Bush supporters is that this is one guy who probably gets cold sweats at the idea of having to pass any kind of test.

Back in November, and parts of December, there was much consternation among those who saw their man, Al Gore, win the popular vote but still lose.

The U.S. Supreme Court stepped in to halt re-voting in Florida, effectively awarding the race to Bush. Since then, there have been bitter cries of voter disenfranchisement, irregularities and malfunctions in the voting process in the Sunshine State.

After several reviews—some validating Bush's close win in Florida—there's plenty of evidence to suggest something went wrong in the Sunshine State. That this state just happened to be the one with Bush's brother Jeb serving as governor just accentuates the suspicion.

Nevertheless, since the debacle of the 2000 presidential elections, most Americans who didn't vote for Bush decided to be fair and give the guy a chance. Mainly because there was no other alternative.

He's the president; all you can do is accept it.

So with 100 days under his belt, Bush has had ample time to convince the 50 million plus who didn't vote for him that he has the right stuff.

Speaking for just one out of that number: I am not impressed.

Yes, I can hear it now: "Oh, sure, you're the one who used to call him 'George Bush the Younger and the Dumber.'"

True, I've always considered Bush an intellectual lightweight but don't lay the "Bush is Dumb" rap on me. It's an opinion shared by a large number of political commentators and observers.

I'm just agreeing with the consensus.

His Ivy League degrees and dubious achievements in business never impressed me; what amazes me is how so many who should know better point to his mediocre record as some sign of stellar achievement.

He failed miserably as an oil-man, by most accounts. The only reason he used to own a professional baseball team was because of his family name. Same for his job as governor of Texas.

Look at Bush's resume and reasonable people must admit: the only thing he's pretty good at is picking his parents.

Now, the 100-day review.

According to an ABC-*Washington Post* poll, Bush receives good marks (63% approval) for the way he's handled himself in office. But a slim majority of Americans also believe his policies are tilted more toward wealthy Americans and corporations than the average working stiff.

When asked whether Bush "understands the problems of people like you," 51% said he did not, while 47% said he did.

(Ironically, this is the same category Bill Clinton used to score best; that "I feel your pain" stuff must have worked.)

In terms of efficiency, there's also a report comparing Bush's progress in filling top jobs in his administration to that of Clinton's.

The Washington Post said at the same point in his presidency, Clinton had confirmed 47 officials in 48 top positions. Bush has managed to get only 35 confirmed.

Some have pointed to the 35-day election controversy as the reason for Bush lagging behind. But Clinton's first 100 days were considered the height of inefficiency and downright incompetence by many of the same people now making excuses for George W.

Bush gets solid marks in the poll for the way he's handled foreign affairs, a 62% approval rating. But that probably owes more to the American people's tendency to rally around any president in time of international discord.

As a former governor, Bush has little foreign affairs experience to draw on (neither did Clinton), and it's clear he's content to let foreign experts like Colin Powell and Condoleezza Rice handle the heavy lifting.

That's probably for the best, because whenever he opens his mouth on foreign affairs, he's likely to make a serious gaffe. Just take a look at his recent interpretation of America's responsibility to defend Taiwan from Chinese aggression, which most foreign policy experts say was wrong.

In terms of presidential image, Bush has been content with staying out of sight during big stories. Many conservatives lauded Bush's decision not to appear at a homecoming for the American crewmen returned to the states after colliding with the Chinese jet.

They said it showed Bush didn't have the same need to hog the spotlight as Clinton.

My take: What do we have presidents for if not for these types of largely ceremonial appearances?

He's supposed to be the face of the nation in times of crisis and prosperity. What, is he going to skip the annual photo-op next Thanksgiving where the president pardons a turkey? And if he doesn't, what message will that send to the returning crewmen?

"You mean he didn't come to greet us, but he's willing to stand next to that stupid bird?"

As for personal style, Bush still seems halting and unfocused in his public appearances, like a guy straining mightily to remember all the stuff they piled into his brain behind the curtain.

He still mangles words ("Is our children learning?" is a personal favorite), which doesn't do an awful lot to dispel the "dumb" label.

According to several national publications, his most significant characteristic as president is hitting the sack by nine o'clock most nights.

He's considered a "corporate" model of a president, delegating much of his authority to his subordinates. That fits, because he's more of a president to business owners and corporate interests than he is for the working man.

Some of this may be harsh, but it's nothing compared to the vitriol and bitterness—even hatred—that was piled on the most popular president in modern times, Bill Clinton, during his presidency.

This is a country where even people who oppose the president are supposed to belong to the "loyal opposition." Well, I'm still paying taxes, so put me down as being as loyal as the next guy.

But after 100 days, I'm not going to act like Bush is knocking my socks off. With gas prices rising, more international turmoil bubbling and a sinking feeling about the stock market, it's time to give this guy a grade.

So far, it's a "C-Minus." Which is below average and nowhere near good enough for the leader of the free world.

Source: This column, which originally appeared on 29 April 2001, is reproduced with the permission of the *Milwaukee Journal Sentinel* and the Copyright Clearance Center.

Further Readings: "Eugene Kane." In Sam G. Riley, *The Best of the Rest: Non-Syndicated Columnists Select Their Best Work*. Westport, Conn.: Greenwood Press, 1993, pp. 117–120; "Eugene Kane, Milwaukee Journal Sentinel." [Online]. Society of Professional Journalists Web site www.spj.org.

Kennedy, Tonnya (c.1965–)

Tonnya Kennedy is managing editor of the *State* in Columbia, South Carolina. Her father was in the Air Force, and the family moved frequently during her youth—from Tennessee's Sewart Air Force Base where she was born to Beale in California to Little Rock, Arkansas, and in the 1970s when Tonnya was a preteen, to Ankara, Turkey. Unable to speak the language there, she spent much of her free time in the base library and also listened with her family to the English-language broadcasts of BBC and Voice of America. Living abroad and listening to those broadcasts gave her the idea that she might like to become a foreign correspondent. The family returned to the United States, to Holloman in New Mexico, after which her father retired and moved the family to Tennessee. Tonnya attended Vanderbilt University, where she earned a 1987 B.S., majoring in biology and minoring in chemistry. Thereafter, she went on to earn a 1991 M.S. in mass communication at Murray State University in Kentucky. Her professional career began in Tennessee at the *Nashville Banner*, where she was a business reporter from August 1987 until May 1989. She was a business writer in Newport News, Virginia and at the *Daily Press* from May 1989 until May 1990, when she returned to school to work on her masters. In August 1992, she went back to the *Nashville Banner*, covering business news until March 1993, when she was named the paper's assistant business editor. She was promoted to region editor in April 1994, was executive sports editor from May 1995 to April 1997, and managing editor from April 1997 to March 1998. In April 1998, she became assistant managing editor of the *Herald-Leader* in Lexington, Kentucky. In December 1999, she was named deputy managing editor of the *Virginian-Pilot* in Norfolk, Virginia; in this position she oversaw business news, features, sports and special sections, and coordinated the paper's writing teams. During this time, she helped direct coverage of the October 2000 Al Qaeda attack on the *USS Cole*; the March 2001 training tragedy in which 21 guardsmen died when their transport plane crashed near Unadilla, Georgia; and the World Trade Center attacks of 11 September 2001.

In April 2003, Kennedy became managing editor of the *State*, the Knight Ridder paper in South Carolina's capital city, Columbia. She replaced John Drescher, who left to become managing editor of the *News & Observer* in Raleigh, North Carolina.

Quoted by Richard Prince in his "Journal-isms" in March 2003, Kennedy listed several goals she hoped to meet at her new job—bonding with the community, becoming an effective watchdog for the public interest, finding the local relevance of national and world news, and acting as a writing coach at the paper. She belongs to the Society of Professional Journalists, the National Association of Black Journalists and the National Association of Minority Media Executives. In 2006, she was elected to the executive committee of the South Carolina Press Association. She has been a University of Missouri Davenport Fellow in business reporting and at Northwestern University, a Robert McCormick Fellow.

Further Readings: Prince, Richard. "Tonnya Kennedy Named ME in Columbia, S.C." [Online, 19 March 2003]. Richard Prince's Journal-isms. Maynard Institute Web site www.maynardije.org; "Tonnya Kennedy." [Online, 18 August 2003]. American Society of Newspaper Editors Web site www.asne.org.

Keyes, Allison (?–)

Experienced broadcast journalist Allison Keyes reports for the national desk of National Public Radio. Her stories appear on "Morning Edition," "All Things Considered" and "Weekend Edition Sunday." Keyes is a graduate of Illinois Wesleyan University, where she majored in English and journalism. Her radio career began in 1988 at WBEZ, a Chicago NPR affiliate station. There, she worked as a reporter, anchor and assistant news director. She spent several years working at WCBS Newsradio and thereafter worked for nearly a year at WNYC Radio, where she covered City Hall and was a show host. She has also worked as a reporter for *Black Enterprise Magazine* and has coauthored two biographical books about prominent African Americans and helped create the African American Heritage Perpetual Calendar, which is available for purchase through *Reader's Digest's* online store (www.rdstore.com) and which showcases events in black history and pertinent quotations. She has worked for NPR since 2002, when she became a reporter for "The Tavis Smiley Show." When "News & Notes with Ed Gordon" began in January 2005, she became a national reporter for that program, specializing in news affecting African Americans nationwide. She began her present job with the NPR national desk in October 2005. She has also done writing and producing for ABC's "World News Tonight" and "Good Morning America."

Keyes, Allison

In 1997, prior to joining NPR as a fulltime staffer, Keyes reported for "Weekend Edition" on the Million Woman March that took place in October of that year in Philadelphia. In December 2002, serving as a substitute host for Tavis Smiley, she reported on what she characterized as the Bush administration's "incomplete account" of weapons of mass destruction in Iraq. Other stories she did around that same time involved faith-based charities and federal funds, an exhibit in New York examining the image of Harriet Beecher Stowe's character Uncle Tom, controversial New Jersey poet laureate Amiri Baraka, the beating of a student at Morehouse College and the reversal of the conviction of five men for the rape and beating of a female jogger in New York's Central Park. An outstanding 2003 interview Keyes conducted was with jazz great Dave Brubeck, who spoke about the importance of jazz in American musical life. Many listeners were surprised to learn that Brubeck had been heading toward life as a cowboy before he began to perform on piano. In 2004, she reported on Chicago landmarks that no longer exist—the Vendome, the Mecca building, the Grand Terrrace, the Rum Boogie, the Regal, the Savoy—during a Tavis Smiley interview with Timuel Black, who had authored a book on the migration of African Americans to that city from the South during the World War I era. Another 2004 interview story Keyes did was with Joseph Shabalala, leader of the remarkable singing group "Ladysmith Black Mambazo" from South Africa, and yet another was on the subject of black philanthropy in the United States. During 2003 and 2004, she conducted multiple interviews with former U.S. Ambassador to the United Nations Andrew Young for "News & Notes," and in a 2005 story, she reported on President George W. Bush's efforts to prevent the further spread of gang activity in America. Some of her 2006 stories have been on a 100-year-old general store for sale in the village of Crogan, New York; the controversial film "Diary of a Tired Black Man," which addresses interracial dating and portrays many black women as too angry to be desirable dates; ineptitude on the part of FEMA, which apparently doled out $1.5 billion in Hurricane Katrina aid to people or companies that were not entitled to it; and the death at 87 of Lloyd Richards, the first African American to direct a play on Broadway ("Raisin in the Sun").

In 2002, Keyes' reporting on the World Trade Center attacks of September 2001 won the Newswoman's Club of New York Front Page Award for Breaking News. She also shared in the New York State Associated Press Broadcast Award for that same reporting. In 2001, she won the Radio News Award given by the National Association of Black Journalists for her story on the funeral of Patrick Dorismond, a young New York security guard shot by police. Keyes is a member of the NABJ.

Books by Allison Keyes: With Smallwood, David and Stan West, *Profiles of Great African Americans* (Lincolnwood, Ill.: Publications International, 1998); with Blakely, Gloria, *Great African Americans* (Lincolnwood, Ill.: Publications International, 2002).

Further Readings: "Allison Keyes." [Online, 31 July 2006]. National Public Radio Web site www.npr.org.

King, Colbert (Colby) I. (20 September 1939–)

After a long and distinguished career in finance, Colbert King became a *Washington Post* columnist in 1990 and in 2003, won the Pulitzer Prize for commentary. King was born in the district of Columbia in 1939 and graduated from Howard University in 1961, after which he spent two years as an Army lieutenant. From 1962 until 1970, he was a Foreign Service attaché with the U.S. Department of State. During 1970 and 1971, he was an assistant undersecretary of HEW, the Department of Housing, Education and Welfare. For the following year he was director of programs and policy for VISTA (Volunteers in Service to America), and from 1972–1976, he was staff director of the Commission on the District of Columbia. In 1974 he also worked in the reelection campaign of Maryland's Senator Charles Mathias. He was director of government relations for Potomac Electric Power Company from 1975 through 1977, then joined the Treasury Department as deputy assistant secretary for legislative affairs. His name became better known in 1979 when President Jimmy Carter nominated him as U.S. executive director of the World Bank; he filled that post from 1977 to 1979, after which he joined the Riggs National Bank as executive vice president and member of the bank's board. King was with the bank for ten years before entering journalism at the *Post*, writing his hard-hitting and highly readable column. King seems to take completely to heart the notion that journalism should comfort the afflicted and afflict the comfortable. The accomplished and well connected King found himself in the odd position of getting occasional advice from his son, Ron King of the *Philadelphia Inquirer*, who has been a journalist five years longer than his father. In his Saturday column, the elder King takes on issues of local, national and international scope while also serving as the paper's deputy editorial page editor. He reports enjoying editorial writing perhaps even more than doing his column. King appears to be a moderate, going after Democrats who need criticizing as quickly as he castigates Republicans. Reporting and commenting on television evangelist Pat Robertson's flirtation with the diamond business in Africa, he bit right into that man of the cloth and shook him the way a terrier shakes a rat. Another favorite target is any judge, especially in the District, who appears to be overly lenient with criminals. King finds our nation's fawning, look-the-other-way relationship with oil-rich Saudi Arabia hard to take and tries to make life a little more unpleasant for those civil servants who appear indifferent in performing their jobs. As did many other columnists, King criticized George W. Bush for lavishing $40 million on his inaugural celebrations in 2004, commenting that in Washington, right and wrong are made to step aside, and winning is all that really seems to matter. Although he doesn't make it a habit to dwell on the topic, he considers the invasion of Iraq a calamity, and he sees same-sex marriage as a mainly diversionary issue that takes people's minds off far bigger problems, such as our nation's absurdly high murder rate. He is especially saddened by the regularity of homicides in Washington, D.C., and the fact that a high percentage of those murders that are black-on-black. The column reprinted below is done in a style King seldom employs: the use of fictitious literary characters to make a point. In addition to his print media work, King is a weekly commentator on Washington's WTOP news radio and appears often on the television talk show "Inside Washington."

King was on the Africare board of directors from 1987 to 1989 and the board of the Arena Stage Theatre from 1986 to 1988. He was a fellow of Health, Education and Welfare in 1970 and 1971. He was accorded the Distinguished Service Award in 1980 by the U.S. Secretary of the Treasury and in 1987 was given the Distinguished Graduate Award in Business by the trustees of Howard University. In addition to the Pulitzer he won in 2003, King had been a finalist in that competition in 2000.

"Sen. Byrd: The View from Darrel's Barbershop" by Colbert I. King

Things finally started to calm down in Darrell's barbershop after Big Jerome, the trash talker, left the premises. The place had been in an uproar minutes earlier when Jerome, angry at being left out of the poor-mouthing contest between Sen. Robert Byrd and Treasury Secretary Paul O'Neill, cut loose with some of his own choice "I'm so poor..." lines.

The fellows were still wiping away tears of laughter. But Darrell hoped the shop would get back to normal so he and the other barbers could get on with their work. Before long, with composure regained, customers and barbers were lost in their reveries.

It didn't last long.

Fishbone, now seated in Darrell's chair, broke the silence. "Somebody help me," he pleaded.

"Look, I understand all that stuff Byrd and O'Neill were laying on each other about not having running water, telephones and electricity when they were young. And I get the bit about 'little wooden outhouses.'"

"But," said Fishbone, wrinkling his brow, "when Byrd took a shot at O'Neill for once being a big shot in a big-bucks corporation, O'Neill got all teary-eyed and said something about dedicating his life to getting rid of rules that limit human potential. And he started talking about rules that said, 'Colored don't enter here.' Can somebody tell me what that was all about?" wailed Fishbone.

The only sound was that of scissors snipping away.

Finally Fatmouth piped up. "Man, don'tcha know? It was in all the papers!"

"I don't take the paper," said Fishbone sheepishly.

"See there," thundered Fatmouth. "If you wanna keep a secret from certain folks," he said, "all you have to do is put it in a book." "Man, Fatmouth said indignantly," you should start reading the Post. (Yes, 'tis a shameless promotion, but my wife and two dogs also have to eat.)

"All right, you guys, chill," ordered number two barber Bobby T. "Fishbone," he said with exasperation, "O'Neill was cracking on Byrd for having been a member of the Ku Klux Klan."

"He was *what*?" asked Fishbone incredulously. "You mean that powerful ol' dude in the Senate was one of those Kluxers in sheets and pointed hoods who burned crosses and hated black folks?"

"If I'm lyin', I'm flyin'," said Bobby T.

Herman, who was sweeping up hair cuttings on the floor, tried to come to Byrd's rescue. "As I recall," said Herman, "they said it was a 'youthful indiscretion' or something like that."

"'Youthful indiscretion' my butt," injected Rodney, who, despite having already had his hair cut, couldn't leave the shop.

"Sounds just like when my Aunt Edith shot her boyfriend and said it was an accident," he said. "Aunt Marilyn was downstairs when it happened. She heard the gun when it went off."

"One 'boom' sounds like an accident." Aunt Marilyn announced.

"'Boom, boom, boom' sure ain't."

Just then, Mr. Jackson, a Washington old-timer and local historian known for his photographic memory, entered the shop for his weekly trim and chance to smoke his cigar, since Mrs. Jackson was having none of that in her house. He soon caught the drift of the discussion and waited patiently until Darrell turned to him for a definitive reading on the Byrd situation.

"What's the real deal, Mr. Jackson?" asked Darrell.

Settling into a well-worn chair in the middle of the shop where he usually held court, Mr. Jackson pulled out his stogie, lit it, took a few unhurried puffs and let the smoke drift to the ceiling. "The real story came out during the 1960 presidential primary in West Virginia, where Byrd was a key figure in the 'Stop Kennedy' campaign," Jackson said.

"Word got around that Byrd had been a Klan member, but he tried to say it was only briefly." Mr. Jackson, who'd anticipated a barbershop discussion of just this topic, pulled an old news clipping out of his pocket, an April 21, 1960, Washington Post story by David Wise of the Herald Tribune News Service. He read from it:

"The Ku Klux Klan developed primarily as a terrorist group aimed at the Southern Negro in Reconstruction times, but it is also virulently anti-Catholic."

John F. Kennedy, Mr. Jackson reminded his audience, was Catholic.

On the business about Byrd's brief Klan membership, Mr. Jackson again quoted the story: "The fact is that he was a Kleagle, or organizer, for the Klan during World War II and wrote as late as 1946 to Dr. Samuel Green of Atlanta, Imperial Grand Wizard of the Klan, recommending a friend as a Kleagle and urging promotion of the Klan throughout the nation."

Mr. Jackson said the story also reported that in 1946, Byrd wrote to Imperial Wizard Green: "The Klan is needed today as never before and I am anxious to see its rebirth here in West Virginia."

As for "youthful indiscretion," Mr. Jackson observed that in 1946, Robert Byrd was 29 years old. American Taliban John Walker Lindh, he pointed out, is 20.

Byrd knew what he was doing, said Mr. Jackson. In 1945, a year earlier, Byrd wrote to Mississippi's virulent segregationist Sen. Theodore Bilbo that he would never serve in an integrated Army. "Rather I should die a thousand times, and see Old Glory trampled in the dirt never to rise again, than to see this beloved land of ours become degraded by race mongrels, a throwback to the blackest specimen from the wilds," Byrd wrote. Confronted with the letter in 1999, Byrd said he didn't recall writing it, but he said, "I will not dispute the quote, though I consider it deplorable."

Mr. Jackson, ever the historian, said that in 1946, the same year Kleagle Robert Byrd was writing to his imperial wizard, six blacks were lynched in America, including two black couples at the Moore's Ford Bridge near Monroe, Ga., and a young black man who was burned alive with a blowtorch by a Louisiana mob. And a black Army veteran also had his eyes gouged out with the butt of a billy club by South Carolina police.

The resurgence of lynchings and violence against blacks in the South got so bad in '46 that President Truman was spurred to order a special federal investigation. That same year, Byrd was elected to the West Virginia legislature. Four years later, he went to Congress, where he's been ever since.

And that, said Mr. Jackson, may help explain why Sen. Byrd rode the city so hard when he became chairman of the Senate Appropriations subcommittee on the District of Columbia.

At a public hearing this week, said Mr. Jackson, Byrd lectured the Bush administration on the difficulties of rooting out terrorists. Mr. Jackson added softly, "He should know."

With that recitation, Mr. Jackson crossed his legs at the knee, folded his hands in his lap and said primly, "You gentlemen may take it from there."

A hush fell over the shop.

An angry voice was heard from the back of the shop.

"And since he's been in Washington, Byrd's been using my money and yours to build monuments to himself in West Virginia." It was Fast Frankie, who, until that moment, had not said a word.

Frankie has folks in the Charleston area and gets back to visit frequently. Frankie said Byrd has more pork in West Virginia than there is in all the packing houses in the world—all in his name.

"Don't think so?" he challenged. "There's the Robert C. Byrd Highway, the Robert C. Byrd Hilltop Office Complex, the Robert C. Byrd Federal Courthouse, the Robert C. Byrd Life Long Learning Center, the Robert C. Byrd Locks and Dams, the Robert C. Byrd Rural Health Center, the Robert

C. Byrd Academic and Technology Center, the Robert C. Byrd United Technical Center, the Robert C. Byrd High School, the Robert C. Byrd Health Sciences Center, the Robert C. Byrd Institute for Advanced Flexible Manufacturing ... "

It was getting dark outside, and everyone was eager to go home. But Darrell couldn't budge Fast Frankie. So he flipped the "closed" sign on the door, locked his barbershop and left Fast Frankie inside, comfortably seated in his chair, still going strong:

"... the Robert C. Byrd Green Bank Telescope, the Robert C. Byrd National Technology Transfer Center, the Robert C. Byrd Intermodal Transportation Center and Garage ...

Source: Copyright © 2002, *The Washington Post*. Reprinted with permission. This column appeared on 2 March 2002.

Further Readings: Abramsky, Sasha. "Pulitzer-Winning King Can't Get Used to the Prize." [Online, 15 April 2003]. Editor & Publisher Web site www.editorandpublisher.com; Shafer, Jack. "Riding with the King: The Best Washington Post Columnist You've Ever Heard of." [Online, 9 January 2003]. Slate http://slate.msn.com; "Colbert King." [Online, 27 June 2005]. Podium Prose Web site www.podiumprose.com.

King, Emery (1948–)

After a 19-year run as news reporter and anchor for Detroit's WDIV-TV, the debonnaire Emery King now produces documentaries and specials for the station through his own production company, Kingberry Productions, and is also director of communications for the Detroit Medical Center. He was born in Gary, Indiana. His early years in broadcasting were with Chicago station WBBM-TV and CBS News. Before coming to Detroit in 1986, King was for six years a White House correspondent for NBC News. He covered the Reagan administration, traveling the world to do so. Upon moving to Detroit and station WDIV, he reported on political news at all levels, covered presidential elections from 1988 to 2004 and worked as an anchor. He covered the Clinton impeachment story and reported on the attacks of 11 September 2001 from Washington. In September 2003, he did a one-on-one interview with Secretary of State Colin Powell to discuss the Iraq war, which Powell characterized as "not another Vietnam," and the Valerie Plame outing, which Powell suggested might have been done by someone who did not know she was a CIA undercover operative. King and Ruth Spencer were the station's evening news coanchors for 12 years until he was abruptly fired in March 2005. The parting was not amicable, and it was reported that management had him escorted from the building. His supporters were many and were vociferous in their condemnation of station management. Charges of racism were bandied about, and King reportedly remarked that his bosses had considered him arrogant. Whatever the causes of his having been fired, community support was so considerable that station management later approached him and brought him back to the station in a different capacity—producer of news documentaries and specials that would be exclusive to WDIV. *Detroit News* columnist Betty DeRamus, who wrote two columns in King's support, pointed out that Detroit citizens of all races were protesting his firing. She noted that given the giddy format favored today by so many television news stations, experience and seriousness were no longer desirable traits for broadcast news people. Other critics said his firing was due to the increasing commercialization of broadcast news. In his column posted on 21 March 2005 on www.gaylordtimes.com, Tim Skubick put King's departure into the perspective of other political correspondents in Michigan who had fallen prey to station owners' belief that viewers no longer cared about political news: Tom Green, Jim Herrrington, Joe Weaver, Matt McLogan, Tim Jones, Dennis Larson, Andy Such, and Walt Song. In mid-April, another Betty DeRamus column was about an appearance by King before the Detroit City Council, which had passed a resolution in protest of King's firing and had requested that station executives explain the reason for it. In late June 2005, a WDIV spokesman announced that King had entered into a new contract with the station whereby his Kingberry Productions, which King and his wife, Jacqueline Casselberry King, had launched in 1993, would produce documentaries and news specials and that King would host the station's twice-yearly televised town hall meetings. The production company had already turned out a number of documentaries that had appeared on WDIV and had been distributed by Filmmakers Library in New York City to universities, school districts and libraries. Those earlier productions included "The Rouge: the Factory and the Workers," about people who had immigrated to Detroit to do automobile assembly plant work; "The Freedom Train," about the National Negro Labor Council; "Cobb: A Detroit Legend," on the famous baseball player; and "Rosa Parks: Path to Freedom," about that civil rights icon. Other specials King had hosted and helped write were "Buffalo Soldiers Wrapped in Steel," "Idlewild: A Place in the Sun," "Paradise Lost, Paradise Found" and "Flashpoint: On the Road to Mackinac," the last of which was about race relations in the Detroit area. In July 2005, Illinois Gov. Jennifer Granholm installed King as the new chair of the Michigan Film Advisory Committee, which had been created in 2002 as an economic development agency. Roughly a month later, the Detroit Medical Center at Wayne State University announced that King would become its principal spokesperson and its communication director. The DMC declared King the nation's first Internet medical anchorman. Now interested individuals can access Emery King's Medical Video Library by computer to learn about health concerns and new medical procedures. Wayne State's Journalism Institute for Minorities used its 20-year celebration to salute the work of Emery King, and in late December 2005, Detroit Public Television aired a pilot "Emery King Show." King appears to be the living embodiment of the adage, "You can't keep a good man down."

King is on the boards of the Michigan Multiple Sclerosis Society and the Society of Yeager Scholars, which helps young people find scholarship support. He has been active in support of the American Red Cross and since 1996 has served as master of ceremonies or host of the annual American Red Cross Everyday Heroes event in Detroit. In April 2006, he spoke on "Bridging the

Racial Gap" before the Council of Michigan Foundations' Detroit Area Grantmakers meeting. In this talk, he likened race to an elephant in the room in that everyone sees it, but no one wants to talk about it. In May, he was the Lem Tucker keynote speaker at an annual event sponsored by Central Michigan University. His documentary "The Rouge" won a 1997 Iris Award, and in 2002, the Michigan chapter of the National Academy of Television Arts and Sciences gave him its Silver Circle award for his more than 30 years as a broadcaster. He also has won several Emmy awards and a Monte Carlo International Film Festival award.

Further Readings: Blake, Allyson. "King's Reign Begins: New Chair for Michigan Film Advisory Commission." [Online, 13 June 2006]. Screen Magazine Web site www.screenmag.tv/feature; DeRamus, Betty. "Detroiters Rally to Emerry King's Side, and Station May Be Listening." [Online, 18 March 2005]. Detroit News Web site www.detnews.com; DeRamus, Betty. "Emery King May Be Off TV, but He's Not Forgotten by his Loyal Fans." [Online, 15 April 2005]. Detroit News Web site www.detnews.com; Skubick, Tim. "King's Departure from TV a Blow to Democracy." [Online, 21 March 2005]. Gaylord Herald Times Web site www.gaylordheraldtimes.com; "Duggan Names King as DMC Communication Director." [Online, 4 August 2005]. Detroit Medical Center, Wayne State University Web site www.dmc.org; "Emery King to Produce, Host Specials at Local 4." [Online, 1 July 2005]. Click On Detroit Web site www.clcikondetroit.com; "Ex-Anchor will Do Documentaries, But Not News." [Online, 30 June 2005]. Maynard Institute Web site www.maynardije.org.

Kirk, Beverly (?–)

Kentucky-born Beverly Kirk has been with National Public Radio since 2003 and is currently the weeknight newscaster for "PBS/NPR Newsbrief," produced at NPR and heard on PBS stations. She was born in Burkesville, a small town in Kentucky's Cumberland County. Her father was a truck driver, her mother, a teacher's aide. Kirk was valedictorian of her graduating class at Cumberland High School, where she found a mentor in the school's librarian, who complimented Kirk's writing and suggested she consider a college program in journalism. She attended Western Kentucky University, double-majoring in broadcast journalism and history and working in news for the local public radio station, WKYU-FM. Her earliest interest was in doing the weather, then sports broadcasting, but university president Kern Alexander advised her to widen her sights and go into general news work. Kirk graduated summa cum laude, then in 1989, took her first regular job as early morning anchor for Bowling Green's station WBKO-TV, where she later anchored the midday news and hosted a sports show. Three years later, she moved to Lexington, Kentucky, to work as weekend anchor and to report on city government for station WLEX-TV. She was also the host of that station's program "Focus," a minority-oriented public affairs show that aired once a month. She eventually reduced her hours at the station and returned to school to earn a 1996 M.A. in international politics at the

University of Kentucky's Paterson School of Diplomacy and International Commerce. There, she has remarked, she learned the value of networking, and after finishing the program, she was hired in 1997 by NBC as a reporter. In that fast-moving assignment, she reported the January 1999 visit of the Pope to Mexico City; the January 1999 impeachment trial of President Bill Clinton, in which voting in the Senate was done mainly along party lines; and the 2000 Olympics held in Sydney, Australia. On 11 September 2001, Kirk was on her way to interview Michael Jordon, who was about to return to the basketball court with the Washington Wizards, when she heard the first report of a plane that had hit one of the World Trade Center towers in New York City. She quickly dropped the sports story and drove to Capitol Hill intending to conduct interviews about the growing tragedy. Seeing smoke rising from the direction of the Pentagon, she soon heard about that building having been struck by a plane and drove to the scene as quickly as she could. For the next several hours, Kirk and her crew reported from outside the Pentagon. Later, she covered various aspects of the Bush administration's war on terrorism as well as the October 2002 sniper attacks in the Washington area. From time to time, she did feature stories for the weekend "NBC Nightly News." Shaken by some of her experiences and weary from the travel demands of a network broadcast reporter, she left her high-profile NBC job. She returned to television work to freelance briefly as a reporter for Washington, D.C., station WTTG-TV; and in January 2002, she joined the newly created "PBS/NPR Newsbrief" as its coanchor alongside Sheilah Kast, formerly a correspondent for ABC and public television. The two women's assignment is to do headline news reports at the top of each prime time hour (8 PM to 1 AM), seven days a week. The reports are heard on roughly 70 PBS stations nationwide. On 10 November 2002, Kirk conducted one of her biggest interviews—with Secretary of State Colin Powell on Black Entertainment Television's show "Lead Story," a program she hosted for a brief period. In March 2004, she was a speaker at the Women's Center's leadership conference, held at the McLean Hilton.

Further Readings: "Beverly Kirk." [Online, 27 March 2006]. National Public Radio Web site www.npr.org; Bouvier, Marie. "Beverly Kirk: Big-Time Reporter, Small-Town Roots." [Online]. University of Kentucky Alumni Web site www.ukalumni.net; "PBS/NPR Newsbrief Announces Journalists Beverly Kirk and Sheilah Kast as Anchors." [Online, 27 March 2006]. National Public Radio Web site www.npr.org.

L

Lacy, Sam Harold (23 October 1903–8 May 2003)

A legend among sports writers, Sam Lacy worked for around 60 years in what has sometimes been called the parallel universe of the black press. He is remembered for his intimate knowledge of baseball, but even more so for his efforts to integrate both baseball and sports journalism. Although both his birth date and his place of birth have been called into question, he appears to have been born in 1903 in Mystic, Connecticut, and grew up in Washington, D.C., just blocks from Griffith Stadium, the home field of the old Washington Senators. As a boy, he chased balls at batting practice, ran errands for players and was a snack vendor at Senators games in exchange for tickets in the ballpark's "colored section." Journalist Ralph Wiley, who knew Lacy personally, says that Lacy's determination not only to cover sports but to see them integrated stemmed in part from a hurtful incident at a parade for the Senators in which his father, an enthusiastic fan of the team, was spat upon for waving a team pennant—simply because of his skin color. Lacy's father, who was African American, was a legal researcher and notary, his mother a Shinnecock Indian. Lacy attended Armstrong Technical High School, where he played baseball and football despite his modest size. After finishing high school in 1924, he briefly played semi-pro baseball, graduated with a degree in education from Howard University and held part-time jobs in print journalism and radio. His first regular job began in 1926 at the *Washington Tribune*, where he was a sportswriter and later sports editor. He left journalism in 1929 to again play baseball but returned to the *Tribune* in 1930, and remained there until 1938. As writer, sports editor and managing editor, he began pushing for integration of athletics, although one of his 1937 stories prevented a black athlete from competing. Syracuse University had identified its star player, Wilmeth Sidat-Singh, as Indian, but Lacy revealed that he was actually African American, which, in those tightly segregated times, caused the University of Maryland to threaten to cancel a big game if Sidat-Singh played. In that same year, Lacy lobbied the Senators' owner, Clark Griffith, to allow black players to compete. Griffith replied that the times were not yet right for the change and that he feared such an action would cause rioting by fans and dissention among team members, some of whom were Southerners. Griffith also pointed out that integrating baseball would likely mean the end of the Negro Leagues, which of course it eventually did. The *Washington Afro-American* bought out the *Tribune* in or around 1940 and, dissatisfied with the paper's new management, Lacy relocated to Chicago to work as the *Chicago Defender*'s assistant national editor, which represented a break in his sportswriting career. Even so, he continued to press for integration of baseball and very nearly got to make a presentation to major league commissioner Kenesaw Mountain Landis. Unhappy with his publisher, Lacy took a new sports job with the *Baltimore Afro-American* and began his decades-long tenure there as columnist and sports editor. Thanks to his urgings and those of other black sports journalists such as the *Pittsburgh Courier*'s Wendell Smith, the team owners of the major leagues in 1945 created the Major League Committee on Baseball Integration, which included Lacy, the New York Yankees' Larry McPhail and the Brooklyn Dodgers' Branch Rickey. Sports history attributes the fact that the committee never actually met to McPhail's reluctance, but the sport's great breakthrough came about when Rickey reviewed a number of leading black players and consulted with Lacy and Wendell Smith to decide which man might most smoothly break the color line in baseball. Lacy and Smith advised Rickey that although they did not consider Jackie Roosevelt Robinson the very best ballplayer of them all, he would be the best choice due to his modesty, even temperament, Army service and college degree. Robinson had finished at UCLA, where he lettered in four sports and excelled at each. On 23 October 1945, Lacy's forty-second birthday, Dodgers' general manager Rickey signed Jackie Robinson to a minor league contract with the organization's Montreal farm team. Robinson's uniform number, 42, was eventually retired by all 30 major league teams in honor of Robinson's achievements. For the next two years, Lacy spent much of his time covering Robinson, traveling the nation and enduring the slings and arrows of racial discrimination: inferior accommodations, refusal of service at restaurants, not being allowed to sit in the regular press box at games or use the same restroom as whites, snubs, curses and the like. Robinson made it to the majors in 1947, ushering in the era of integrated baseball and, in general, giving racial inclusiveness in the United States a huge boost. A year later, the U.S. military was integrated. Lacy continued to travel with Robinson when he could and the two became good friends. An oft-told story from a 1940s spring training exhibition in New Orleans was that officials would not allow Lacy to sit in the press box, but told him he could sit up on the press box roof. He was touched when Shirley Povich and a few other white sports writers joined him there, slyly saying that they wanted to "work on their tans."

In his column "A to Z," Lacy wrote about a wide variety of sports, including baseball, basketball, football, tennis, golf, automobile and horse racing, boxing, and track and field events. He covered the greats of each sport and became friends with such major black athletes as track stars Wilma Rudolph and Jesse Owens, boxer Joe Lewis, tennis standout Arthur Ashe, football star Willie Lanier, and many more. He also covered six Olympics. Perhaps of more lasting importance, he cataloged racial indignities and drummed away at the need for inclusion in athletics in a way that was patiently persuasive, not shrill. He argued for integration of spring training venues, for hiring more black coaches and officials, equality in housing for athletes, eliminating the designated-hitter rule as a means of dissuading pitchers from throwing at hitters and, more recently, for allowing women members at the Augusta National Golf Club. Lacy was known for his integrity, humility and pleasant, forthright nature; and he continued to cover black high school sports in Baltimore, which otherwise would have been largely ignored by the city's mainstream press. He is remembered as a mentor to many younger sports writers, who considered him a walking history lesson on sports. For years, he made it a practice to write many of these individuals letters of encouragement. One of his greatest honors came in 1997 when he received the J.G. Spink Award for baseball writing, and in 1998 he became the second African American to be inducted into the writers' section of the Baseball Hall of Fame. Lacy was the first African American to gain membership in the Baseball Writers Association and was a recipient of the Red Smith Award given by the Associated Press. In 1994, he was recognized by the Washington, D.C., chapter of the Society of Professional Journalists, Sigma Delta Chi. Lacy published his memoir *Fighting for Fairness* in 1998, and in 1999, Northeastern University gave him its Excellence in Sports Journalism Award. In 2002, the Maryland Press Club presented him its Lifetime Achievement Award for Journalism.

In early May 2003, Lacy entered a Baltimore hospital, complaining that he had lost his appetite. His problem was a disorder of the esophagus that made swallowing difficult. He wrote his last column longhand while in his hospital bed, giving it to his son to deliver to the paper. He died at 99 and for years had been unable to type due to severe arthritis in his hands, so handwriting his column, which he had re-titled "Viewpoint," was nothing new. His son has carried on Lacy's tradition on the *Baltimore Afro-American* with his own sports column titled "Another Viewpoint." Despite the infirmities of old age, Lacy had continued driving to the paper in Baltimore from his home in Washington and had never wanted to retire. He had become an iconic figure in the sports field and could have moved into the mainstream press decades ago had he wished, but he told people who asked that he had never regretted remaining with the historically black press.

Books by Sam Harold Lacy: With Moses J. Newson, *Fighting for Fairness: The Life Story of Hall of Fame Sportswriter Sam Lacy* (Centreville, Md.: Tidewater Publishers, 1998).

Further Readings: Aldridge, David. "More Than a Good Newspaperman." [Online, 2003]. ESPN Page 2 site http://espn.go.com; Ginsburg, David. "Pioneer Sportswriter San Lacy Dead at 99."

[Online, 9 May 2003]. USA Today Web site www.usatoday.com/sports; Johnson, Chuck. "Appreciation: Lacy Helped Bring Change." [Online, 11 May 2003]. USA Today Web site www.usatoday.com/sports; Litsky, Frank. "Sam Lacy, Who Fought Racism as Sportswriter, Dies at 99." [Online, 2003]. The New York Times Web site www.nytimes.com; Mayo, Jonathan. "Writers Lacy, Smith Played Big Role in Baseball Integration." [Online]. MLB Advanced Media Web site www.mlb.com; Nathan, Daniel A. "Lacy, Sam." In *African American Lives*. Ed. by Gates, Henry Louis Jr. and Evelyn Brooks Higginbotham. New York: Oxford University Press, 2004, pp. 507–508; Preston, Mike. "Lacy Was a Grand Champion for Biggest of Sports' Causes." [Online, 17 May 2003]. Baltimore Sun Web site www.baltimoresun.com; Prince, Richard. "Sam Lacy Services Scheduled Friday in Washington." [Online, 12 May 2003]. Richard Prince's Journal-isms. Maynard Institute Web site www.maynardije.org; Taylor, Phil. "Scribe's Influence in Integrating Baseball Is Immeasurable." [Online, 12 May 2003]. Sports Illustrated.com site http://sportsillustrated.cnn.com; Wickham, DeWayne. "Journalist's Induction into Hall Long Overdue." USA Today, 30 July 1988; Wiley, Ralph. "Swinging through Time with Sam." [Online, 2003]. ESPN Page 2 site http://espn.go.com; Will, George. "Commencement Address." [Online, 18 May 2003]. Boston University Web site www.bu.edu; Wynn, Ron. "Sam Lacy Was Authentic Sports Journalism Pioneer." [Online, 19 May 2003]. Nashvillecitypaper.com Web site www.nashvillecitypaper.com.

Lemon, Don (1 March 1970–)

Up-and-coming broadcast journalist Don Lemon coanchors the evening NBC5 News with Marion Brooks and also reports for the 10 PM news on weeknights. He was born in Baton Rouge, Louisiana, and he earned a bachelor's degree in broadcast journalism in 1994 at Brooklyn College. While in college, he was a Fox News trainee. He began his career after graduation as a general assignment and investigative reporter for St. Louis, Missouri, station WTVI-TV; and from September 1996 to August 1997, he was a reporter at WBRC-TV in Birmingham, Alabama. From June 1999 to June 2002, he was a general assignment reporter and weekend anchor for the NBC affiliate in Philadelphia, WCAU-TV. There, he reported on the World Trade Center attacks of 11 September 2001, the November 2001 crash of American Airlines flight 587 and the mailing of anthrax-filled letters to Senators Patrick Leahy and Tom Daschle, NBC anchorman Tom Brokaw and the newsroom of the *New York Post*, also in 2001. In July 2002, the dapper Lemon was hired by NBC News in New York. In that job, he was a correspondent for "NBC News" and "The Today Show" as well as a weekend anchor for MSNBC's "Weekend Today." Some of his biggest stories were the Washington Beltway sniper attacks and the October 2002 arrest of Lee Boyd Malvo and John Allen Muhammad, the February 2003 disintegration of the space shuttle Columbia that killed its crew of seven, and the 2003 appearance in Canada of SARS, or Severe Acute Respiratory Syndrome. In August 2003, he moved to Chicago to coanchor the evening news at NBC5 News, replacing Mark Suppelsa, who moved to Fox News. There, Lemon has reported on the effects of Hurricane Katrina, the ominous spread of AIDS on the African continent and various Chicago real estate issues. In 2005, he reported on Dr. Ed Diener, a University of Illinois at Urbana-Champaign faculty member whose work includes the measuring of happiness. Lemon's reporting from the field has been supplemented by blogging. As he traveled through Kenya, Rwanda, Tanzania and Malawi to report on the spread of HIV and AIDS, accompanied by a cameraman and a student intern, Lemon wrote a brief daily blog that also described slums, filthy living conditions, malaria, dengue fever, tuberculosis, and the lack of medicine to treat victims of disease. Poverty and need in the United States, brought into stark relief by Hurricane Katrina, were the subject of another Lemon blog, in which he told of worsening conditions at the Superdome, attempts to restore utilities, a 104-year-old man who rode out the storm and another Katrina victim who had survived hurricane winds while clinging to the roof of his house.

Lemon won an Emmy for his coverage of Chicago's real estate market and received the Edward R. Murrow Award for his reporting on the Beltway Snipers attacks and arrest.

Further Readings: "Don Lemon, Anchor; Reporter." [Online]. NBC5 Web site www.nbc5.com; "Don Lemon, '95." [Online]. Brooklyn College Web site www.brooklyn.cuny.edu.

Lewis, Dwight (1 March 1948–)

Dwight Lewis has been a community affairs columnist for Nashville's the *Tennessean* since July 1993 and has worked for that paper since 1971. He was born in Knoxville and spent part of his youth in Strawberry Plains, Tennessee. He majored in business administration, played baseball and edited the school newspaper at Tennessee State University. He began work at the *Tennessean* in 1971 as a part-time campus correspondent and two months later was hired fulltime as a general assignment reporter. During his years as a reporter, he covered the state's prison system and state politics, and in 1976 and 1977 was the paper's Washington correspondent. In 1981 and 1982 he studied at the University of Michigan on a National Endowment for the Humanities Fellowship and in 1986 was a participant in the Multicultural Management Program at the University of Missouri. He coauthored a book about athletics at Tennessee State University in 1983, appeared in the MGM/United Artists film "Marie" in 1985 and has served as a Pulitzer Prize juror twice, in 1994 and 1995. Lewis also worked as a part-time professor at Fisk University from 1996 to 2003 and was interim advisor to Tennessee State's campus newspaper in 1994.

Most of his columns are tied to the local scene in some way. During a week in June 2005 that saw more than the usual violence and mayhem, he asked his readers what could be wrong with Nashville teenagers to account for so many shootings. An interview with a local judge produced the answer: the combination of guns and drugs. Some of the city's youthful drug dealers, the judge added, were better armed than the police. In another column during that same month, Lewis wrote that Tennessee's Sen. Lamar Alexander belonged in the "hall of shame" for not joining 84 other senators who signed a lynching apology directed at the nation's African Americans. Lamar's reason for refusing to sign, Lewis added, was nothing more than the senator's desire to appease the far right. In still another column, Lewis quoted Jesse Jackson as having remarked that in 1954, the U.S. Supreme Court had ushered in 50 years of equal protection under the law, but that far-right conservatives have never given up on taking away those civil rights gains.

Another column argued against recent moves to strike thousands of people from coverage under TennCare, the state's health insurance program. Reform, he wrote, should not mean that the sick should suffer more. He also had scornful words for four members of the Tennessee General Assembly who had been indicted for influence peddling. In a different sort of column, he posed the question—What does love mean to you? Lewis answered his own question by quoting the words of a troubled Nashville nine-year-old who had written his teacher a remarkably poignant answer to that same question. The column that appears below imparts great human-interest value to the matter of voting, which many Americans ignore and many others take for granted.

Lewis won the 1994 award for commentary from the National Association of Black Journalists; and in 1995, he received the Jerry Thompson Communicator Award from the Nashville chapter of the National Conference of Christians and Jews as well as the Philanthropist Award for Mass Media Outreach given by the humanitarian organization Take Time in Nashville. In 2001, he received the Living Legends Award for community advocacy from the Nashville Alliance of Black School Educators and in 2002, an Omega Psi Phi Fraternity Citizen of the Year Award. In 2005, he was the recipient of a second Jerry Thompson Communicator Award as well as the Making Kids Count Award from the Tennessee Commission on Children and Youth. He is coauthor of one book and contributed a chapter to DeWayne Wickham's book *Thinking Black: Some of the Nation's Best Black Columnists Speak Their Minds* (New York: Crown Publishers, 1996).

"Just How Important It Is for Iraqis to Get a Chance to Vote Here" by Dwight Lewis

He was a poor sharecropper named Otis Moss Sr.

He had worked all his life to raise and care for his family, suffering indignities that generations before him had long endured.

While in his fifties, the day was nearing when he hoped to be able to cast his vote for the first time in his life. When election day rolled around, he got up before dawn, dressed in his best suit that he used for funerals and weddings, and prepared to walk to the polls to vote against a "racist" Georgia governor in favor of a more moderate one.

He walked six miles, and when he got to the polling place, he was told he was in the wrong place and was sent to another location. Surely disappointed, he is said to have walked another five or six miles then was sent on to a third voting place. When he arrived at the third location, it is said that

Moss was told, "Boy, you are a little late, the polls just closed."

Moss had walked all day, covering more than 18 miles. By the time he got back home, he was "exhausted and depleted," never experiencing the joy of voting. He told this story to anyone who would listen, and he lived in great anticipation of his next chance to vote.

"He never got that chance to choose," a relative would later tell me. "So, now I do. And every time I cast a ballot, I choose not only for myself but also for Otis Moss Sr., and for the countless others who wanted to, but couldn't."

"Years ago, Oprah Winfrey met ... Rev. Otis Moss Jr., who is the pastor of one of the largest African-American churches in Cleveland, and he shared the story ... with her. She in turn shared it with her audience a few months ago.

"Thank you for indulging me. I hope my story will help you understand my passion about the Iraqi election."

This story was sent in an e-mail Wednesday to Mayor Bill Purcell from Metro Parks Director Roy Wilson after a movement was started by businesses and churches demanding that city leaders move one of the Nashville polling sites, Coleman Community Center, in the upcoming Iraq elections. The group requesting the move told reporters Wednesday that they had addressed their concerns to Purcell's office and to the police department several times.

"Security is our main concern," the Rev. Joseph Breen of St. Edward Catholic Church, said.

The mayor's office announced Thursday that after working with the International Organization for Migration, approval had been given for consolidation of registration and voting for the Iraqi Out of Country program. The mayor's office said IOM had decided to move all voting and registration to the state fairgrounds.

Purcell said he had worked to bring all parties together, both locally and internationally, to make "these changes possible." He said in a press release that moving all registration and voting operations to the fairgrounds would reduce the time required for registration and voting, and eliminate the need for voters to board buses.

"This message is long, but please read it for better understanding of why the Iraqi election is so important to me," Wilson said in his e-mail to Purcell on Wednesday.

"As you know, I grew up in Montgomery, Ala. My first four years of elementary school were spent growing up in the Trenholm Court projects, which are situated in the shadows of First Baptist Church (Ralph Abernathy was the pastor).

"I participated with my family in the Selma-to-Montgomery march, was on the Edmund Pettis Bridge that awful Sunday before the march, watched my parents suffer (we didn't have a car at the time) during inclement weather by refusing to ride the city bus during the bus boycott and endured cruelties that make me shed tears even as I write this message but what I know for sure, is that I don't take the right to vote lightly.

"This is why I support the Iraqi election."

And that's why he was not one of those who opposed making Coleman Community Center available for the Iraqi vote to take place.

"I remember George Wallace standing in the door..." he told me, "Alabama is a very different place today than when I was growing up ... I know what my folks went through ..."

I hope all of us understand Metro Parks Director Roy Wilson a little better now. I hope all of us understand a little better now why he wants to make sure that the Iraqi expatriates get a chance to get their ballots later this week.

In a way, they will be casting one for Otis Moss Sr.

Source: Copyrighted, *The Tennessean*. The column is reprinted here by permission of Mr. Lewis and *The Tennessean*. It originally appeared on 24 January 2005.

Books by Dwight Lewis: With Susan Thomas, *A Will to Win* (Mt. Juliet, Tenn.: Cumberland Press, 1983).

Lewis, Edward T. (15 May 1940–)

Ed Lewis had intended to be a banker but made an abrupt career change in the 1960s to cofound *Essence*, which in time became the nation's premier magazine for African-American women. He is a native New Yorker, born in the Bronx, and he holds a bachelors in political science and international relations from the University of New Mexico. He was accepted into Georgetown University Law School but left after one year and entered the executive training program at New York's First National City Bank (now Citibank). He planned to become a loan officer but while attending a conference on African-American entrepreneurship sponsored by a Wall Street brokerage house, he heard a discussion about the need for a style magazine for black women and decided to pursue the idea. With four partners, Lewis founded Essence Communications Inc., in 1968, with himself initially listed as financial manager. The magazine's first issue appeared in May 1970; it consisted of 100 pages, 13 of which contained advertisements. The initial print run was 50,000. Growth in advertising revenues was not easy to achieve, and within four years, three of the founders had abandoned the venture, leaving Lewis and Clarence O. Smith as coowners. Since that time, *Essence* has grown into the biggest magazine of its kind, with a 2005 circulation of around 1,063,000, sold mainly by subscription. As a women's lifestyle magazine, it devotes much of its editorial space to home, beauty and fashion topics but adds substance with articles on health and fitness, consumer finance and social and political issues. *Essence* was the first successful high-fashion magazine for African-American women, and around half its subscribers have a college degree.

During the decades since the founding of *Essence*, coowners Lewis and Smith launched side ventures in book publishing—an agreement was signed in 1999 with Crown Publishers—plus television production, direct-mail marketing and lines of eyewear and other products. In October 2000, the company entered a joint venture agreement with Time Inc. as Essence Communications Partners. Lewis and Smith retained 51 percent of the stock. Apparently dissatisfied with the arrangement, Smith sold out to Lewis, and in March 2005, Time Inc. bought Lewis's interest in the company, which again was titled Essence Communications Inc. Lewis remained as chairman and founder. Currently, the company's president is Michelle Ebanks, formerly with Time Inc., the Institute of Econometric Research and Conde Nast Publications. Editorial director is longtime company executive Susan Taylor, and editor-in-chief is Angela Burt-Murray, who earlier had been executive editor of *Teen People* magazine. The magazine keeps reader interest not only by its contents, but also with the help of ancillary activities such as the Essence Model Search; the Essence Short-Fiction Contest; the annual Essence Music Festival, which began in 1995; its more recent Women Who Are Shaping the World Leadership Summit workshops, which were added in 2004; and its Web site, essence.com. The first Essence Designer Showhouse, a restored Harlem brownstone, was publicized in 2005. Lewis directs the many activities of the company from his New York City headquarters and also has offices in Chicago, Atlanta, Detroit and Los Angeles. In 1992, Lewis bought *Income Opportunities*, a monthly subtitled "The Original Small Business/Home Office Magazine." He launched an online version of the magazine in 1995, and the entrepreneurship-oriented periodical is now headed by managing publisher Donald P. Mazzella. Also in 1995, Lewis entered a joint venture to publish *Latina*, which bills itself as the nation's first and largest-circulation bilingual lifestyle magazine for Hispanic women. In September 2004, Lewis launched another new title: *Suede*, an ultra-hip fashion magazine intended for a multicultural audience. To edit the new magazine, he hired Canadian-born Suzanne Boyd, who had been editor at *Flare*, Canada's top fashion title. Results after four issues did not justify the high production costs involved, and Essence Communications suspended publication of *Suede*, which might or might not reappear. If it is relaunched, it is unlikely that Boyd will edit it, inasmuch as she has parted company with Time Inc.

Lewis' overall business success has been considerable. He has often spoken out on social issues, most recently on the problem of police brutality. He has provided scholarships in journalism, communication and political science at the University of New Mexico, which in turn bestowed upon him an honorary doctorate in 2003. He has lectured for several years at the Stanford Publishing Institute for mid-career professionals. He has served on various boards for education and the arts in New York and has received a number of recognitions. He has been honored by the American Advertising Federation as a role model, Ernst & Young as an entrepreneur, and the United Negro College Fund for his efforts to emphasize the importance of education. He became chairman of the Magazine Publishers of America in 1997, the first African American to hold this trade-group position. In 1998, he was accorded the Media-Bridge-Builder Award from the Tannenbaum Center for Interreligious Understanding, and in 2002, was given the Magazine Publishers Association's Henry Johnson Fisher Award for lifetime achievement.

Further Readings: "Ed Lewis." [Online]. Greater Talent Network Web site www.greatertalent.com/bios; "Edward Lewis." [Online]. Essence Magazine Web site www.essence.com/essence/bios; "Edward T. Lewis." In *The African American Almanac*, 9th ed. Edited by Jeffrey Lehman. (Detroit, Mich.: Gale Group, 2003), pp. 874–76; Prince, Richard. "Essence Spinoff Pulled Back for Rethinking." [Online, 23 February 2005]. Richard Prince's Journal-isms. Maynard Institute Web site www.maynardije.org.

Lockman, Norman Alton (11 July 1938–18 April 2005)

Norm Lockman will be remembered fondly for his liberal column in the Wilmington, Delaware, *News Journal*, which was distributed to other papers by Gannett News Service. Lockman was born in Kennett Square, Pennsylvania, began covering sports for the *Kennett News & Advertiser* when he was 16, and attended Penn State University from 1957 to 1959. He often remarked that his one consuming interest in college was working for the campus newspaper, the *Daily Collegian*. From 1961 to 1965 he served in the Air Force, reporting for and editing a military paper in California and attending the Department of Defense School of Journalism. He then returned to the sports section of the Kennett Square newspaper, working there for nine years and also writing his first column, which he titled "Beyond the Norm." In 1969 Lockman became the first African-American reporter at the Wilmington *News Journal*, working general assignment and the city hall beat, plus serving as Washington bureau chief during the Watergate scandal and remaining at the *News Journal* until taking a reporting job at the *Boston Globe* in 1975. Toward the end of his nine years at that paper, he shared the 1984 Pulitzer Prize for local investigative reporting with six *Globe* colleagues for their series on race relations in Boston. Thus anointed with the Pulitzer magic, he was lured back to the *News Journal* in 1984 as managing editor; he was one of the first black journalists to hold that position at a mainstream daily. In 1991 he became a member of the paper's editorial board, resuming his role as columnist and writing editorials on government, politics, education, the media and other topics that interested him. His column appeared in as many as 65 other papers.

In 2000, Lockman developed Lou Gehrig's disease, which eventually confined him to a wheelchair. As the disease worsened, he wrote his farewell column, which appeared on 4 December 2004. Lockman died in April of the following year. Curtis Riddle, his publisher at the *News Journal*, praised Lockman for how he liked to use his column and editorials to make people think. Gannett columnist DeWayne Wickham called him a gentlemanly curmudgeon who was a skeptic, but not a cynic and who believed that a columnist needs to do some actual reporting to be effective. Another longtime journalist, Wayne Dawkins, described him as lanky, statuesque, dignified and confident. Dawkins, in this commentary piece for BlackAmerica.com, related an anecdote about a delegation of black U.S. journalists visiting Cuba. While the group followed the prescribed route with their government guide, Lockman got off the bus and managed to get an exclusive interview with the president of Cuba's Supreme Court.

Although Lockman will be remembered mainly for his newspaper work, he also worked as an announcer for WCOJ in Coatesville, Pennsylvania, in 1965 and 1966, hosted a talk show on Wilmington's WILM, was a panelist in the mid-1970s on National Educational Television's "Black Perspective on the News," and was a weekly news panelist for WHYY-TV serving the Wilmington/Philadelphia market. He was also one of the founders of the Trotter Group of black media professionals.

Lockman's physical affliction had not diminished his political savvy in 2004, when he pointed out in a column that if John Kerry were to lose the presidential election, it might well be due to the huge mistake he made in agreeing with President Bush that our invasion of Iraq was the right thing to have done, despite the absence of weapons of mass destruction. Kerry, said Lockman, was taking a risk, betting that economic issues would carry the day for him. If the war should be viewed by the public as an even bigger issue, Lockman predicted,

Kerry would lose, which is exactly what happened. The calm, reasoned Lockman was no shrill Bush-basher, but he was ever ready to point out the administration's warts. He pointed, for example, to the earlier Bush-Gore debates in which Bush argued that nation-building was a bad idea for America. His preemptive strike in Iraq, Lockman wrote, was a major flip-flop—far more consequential than the flip-flopping of which the 2004 Bush campaign accused Kerry. Lockman also wondered about the wisdom of dismantling the Iraqi army, then very soon reinstating some of Saddam Hussein's former generals so that they in turn could re-hire ex-Iraqi soldiers. Appearing below is an August 2003 column critical of the Bush administration's lack of candor and of its handling of the war.

On less global matters, Lockman described beleaguered entertainer Michael Jackson as the Dorian Gray of popular entertainers and as a one-man lesson on how not to age gracefully. In the same column, he likened Jackson's legal pursuer, Santa Barbara, California, District Attorney Tom Sneddon, to Inspector Javert and his efforts to capture Jean Valjean in the story "Les Miserables" and commented on the venality of what he termed "vulture journalism." He was a member of the National Press Club, the National Association of Black Journalists and the Trotter Group of African-American columnists, of which he was a founding member.

"White House Talks Gibberish about Iraq" by Norman Lockman

In Guyana, a ripe mixture of African, Asian, European, Arawak and East Indian cultures expressed through English have produced some pithy slang. If you hear a Guyanian describe something as "cama lama and boogaloo," you may safely assume he is not paying a compliment.

It roughly means "bogus," but the nuances are richer. "Cama lama" is a derisive term for self-induced delusion, like belief in a phony monk. "Boogaloo" means ridiculous machinations performed to induce others to join the delusion.

So when I heard a Guyanian friend comment several weeks ago that he thought America had gone from shock and awe to cama lama and boogaloo in Iraq, I figured he was pretty astute. When the White House prefers to dwell on a list of 90 positive minor developments in Iraq while blaming escalating major terrorism on a few disgruntled petty thugs, the evidence of self-delusion is pretty convincing.

If disgruntled thugs—or anybody else—can blow up an oil pipeline to Turkey and a water main and bomb the Jordanian embassy and United Nations headquarters in downtown Baghdad, all within a few days, the positive developments begin to fade in the face of an uglier reality.

The dilemma faced by the White House and the Pentagon is that their good intentions are being stymied by a campaign of error aimed not only at American soldiers but anybody and anything related to the American postwar efforts, even if it causes more pain and suffering for ordinary Iraqi people, whom we claim to have liberated from such horrors.

What our leaders refuse to face is that our actions in Iraq, while decapitating a totalitarian regime, have left such instability that there is now more terrorism in Iraq, not less. Our inability to control Iraq has made it the prime destination for anti-American terrorists from all over the Arab world.

Terrorists linked to al-Qaida, Saudi jhadis and other fanatics have been pouring into Iraq undeterred for weeks because, although we have 150,000 troops in the country, coalition forces have been unable to secure the borders. The "victory" in Baghdad has created an opportunity for the bad guys that didn't exist before.

As the organized resistance strengthens, American troops have had to worry more about "force Protection," which has them either hunkered down or mounting raids on suspected bad guys. That plays into the hands of terrorists, who are then better able to strike at unprotected "soft" targets because our guys are distracted and spread too thin.

It is classic low-intensity warfare, which doesn't require command and control centers because terrorist cells are primed to strike targets of opportunity rather than implement a formal battle plan.

If the Iraqi people see that the American-led coalition cannot prevent free-lance murders from disrupting their lives, the reservoir of goodwill we expected will rapidly evaporate. Iraqis will turn to other sources for succor and it will almost certainly not be abstract principles of freedom and democracy, which are turning to ashes daily.

Meanwhile, the White House insists this is merely a little rough spot, that things are better than they were before, that it is only a matter of time until the good guys get things in hand, and in any case we are not to blame for sabotage against our efforts to implant the American dream. "We are on course and every day things get better," proclaims the White House.

If that isn't cama lama and boogaloo, then it must be its twin brother.

Source: Reprinted with permission of *The News Journal* of Wilmington, Delaware. It originally appeared on 22 August 2003.

Further Readings: Dawkins, Wayne. "Remembering Pioneering Newsman Norman Lockman, a 'Busybody' Who Excelled" [Online, 28 April 2005]. Blackamericanweb.com commentary Web site www.blackamericaeb.com; Oong, Tom. "Norman Lockman, 66; Part of Pulitzer-winning Effort." [Online, 20 April 2005]. Boston Globe Web site www.boston.com; Prince, Richard. "A Disabled Norman Lockman Retires His Column." [Online, 6 December 2004]. Maynard Institute Web site www.maynardije.org; Prince, Richard. "Columnist Norman Lockman Dies at 66" [Online, 18 April 2005]. Maynard Institute Web site www.maynardije.org; Wickham, DeWayne. "Lockman Was Old-School, No-Nonsense, No Celebrity." [Online, 24 April 2005]. Cincinnati Enquirer Web site www.news.enquirer.com.

Louis, Errol T. (c.1962–)

A new and well-informed column voice in the *New York Daily News* is that of Errol Louis, formerly an associate editor at the *New York Sun*. He was born in Harlem and grew up in New Rochelle. Now a resident of Brooklyn, Louis has an intimate familiarity with the city in which he covers local politics. He holds a 1984 bachelor's degree from Harvard, in Government; a 1989 Yale masters, in political science, and a 2005 Juris Doctor from Brooklyn University Law School. At Harvard, he wrote opinion matter for *The Harvard Crimson* in 1982 and was a Boston-based intern in 1983 for the *Wall Street Journal*. In 1984, he worked for the now-defunct black weekly the *City Sun*; freelanced for a time; and from 1993 to 1997, managed and was treasurer of the Central Brooklyn Credit Union, which he founded. Louis was also executive director of the Bogolan Merchants Association in Brooklyn's Fort Green section. He has written a column on commerce and community for *Our Time Press* since 1998 and from 1998 to 2001 was a visiting assistant professor of social science at the Pratt Institute in Brooklyn. From 2002 to 2004 he was columnist and associate editor for the *New York Sun*. Before taking the position at the *Sun*, he ran for Brooklyn City Council, finishing third in the 1997 race but gaining an insider's view of politics. He moved to his present job in June 2004. In a recent interview in *Recount: A Magazine of Contemporary Politics*, Louis said that he sees his column assignment as covering the local politics that tend to be ignored or downplayed in the *New York Times*. Certainly New York offers a wealth of stories for the columnist who knows where to look to find corrupt judges, officials on the take, flagrant nepotism, campaign abuses and the various other ways in which honesty suffers in big-city political life. Louis, a Democrat, sometimes broadens his scope to comment upon the national scene as well, as when he covered the national conventions during the 2004 presidential race, in the column reproduced below that reflects upon Martin Luther King's birthday.

Examples of Louis's eye for city problems include an August 2004 column taking the Lower Manhattan Development Corporation to task for its tendency to fund organizations having ties to the LMDC board, a May 2005 swipe at the city for locating its garbage collection stations in minority neighborhoods, and a June 2005 complaint about a city law enforcement problem—thousands of arrested and jailed persons not being arraigned within the legally prescribed 24-hour period. Louis also enjoys peering across the river into New Jersey at what he terms a parade of ethically challenged local politicians. The occasion of that remark was the August 2004 resignation of New Jersey Gov. Jim McGreevey. On the more positive side, Louis has written about the appointment of former *Wall Street Journal* reporter and later *New York Sun* contributing editor Raymond Joseph as the new Haitian government's ambassador to the United States.

In 1996, Louis was named by *New York Magazine* as one of 10 New Yorkers making a difference.

"Keep Up the Fight" by Errol Louis

As always, celebrations of Martin Luther King's birthday briefly open a window for fleeting, ritualistic speeches about the state of American race relations. After that, it's back to a yawning public silence on an issue that remains stubbornly wedged in our culture and politics, like an unexploded land mine in the middle of the sidewalk.

Mayor Bloomberg and a half-dozen or so of the politicians running against him are scheduled to appear Monday at an annual King Day event hosted by the Rev. Al Sharpton. All can be expected to mouth the required pieties, but it's safe to predict that most of the assembled pols will say little, if anything, about race relations during the remainder of the mayoral campaign—not even something as simple as a promise to help break down the city's deep racial segregation in housing and public education.

That reluctance may be understandable: Talking about race carries a risk of political backlash, lawsuits or plain old misunderstandings and hurt feelings. Few politicians need the headache.

But punting on race is a shame, and a betrayal of King's work with measurable effects. According to the standard measures statisticians use, such as the likelihood of living next door to a person of a different race, New York still ranks among the most segregated cities in America.

We also suffer from the scourge of predatory lending, the practice of charging outrageously high interest rates and fees for mortgage loans. Predatory lending was unmistakably targeted at black neighborhoods in central Brooklyn and southeast Queens throughout the 1990s.

But a political silence around issues of race left hundreds of victims unaware they had been targeted by race for the ripoff practices. State officials eventually developed tough laws and regulations to ban the practice, but only when community groups ran computer analyses showing how the ripoff loans were concentrated in areas with 80% or more black residents.

Since the politicians are running scared, it will be up to the rest of us—concerned citizens of every background—to make some sort of dialog happen, through cultural forums if political channels will not work.

One bright spot this King holiday is "Unforgivable Blackness," a documentary by Ken Burns on the career of Jack Johnson, set to air on PBS on Monday and Tuesday. Johnson, the first black heavyweight boxing champ, exercised a controversial, dominant influence over American sports and culture during his five-year reign in the early decades of the 20th century.

Unconnected to any political or cultural movement, Johnson was virtually unbeatable, pummeling white challengers mercilessly with a broad grin on his face. Outside the ring, he dressed to the nines, sporting flashy gold caps on his teeth, and he drove custom-made hot rods.

A hard-core individualist, Johnson openly consorted with white women, many of them prostitutes, at a time where such liaisons could lead to mob violence and murder. "So long as I do not interfere with any other man's wife, I shall claim the right to select the woman of my own choice," he said.

In 1910, when Johnson demolished a much-beloved former heavyweight champion, Jim Jeffries, race riots erupted across America, resulting in dozens of deaths. Congress passed a law forbidding the interstate transport of boxing films, to prevent white audiences from seeing Johnson happily knock out a seemingly endless string of "Great White Hopes."

What makes a documentary about the boxer's raucous life appropriate for the King holiday? "It's the question of race running on all cylinders, like the fast cars Johnson liked to drive," says Burns.

"African-American history is at the center of American history, a reminder of our great promise and our great failing. The story of Jack Johnson helps us start a conversation."

Source: © *New York Daily News*, L.P., reprinted with permission. This column originally appeared on 14 January 2005.

Further Readings: Beyer, Rebecca. "Lecture: Errol Louis." [Online]. New York University Journalism School Web site http://journalism.nyu.edu; Parsley, Aaron. "For Daily News Columnist Errol Louis, All Politics Is Local." [Online, 27 September 2004]. New York University Journalism School Web site http://journalism.nyu.edu.

Lowe, Herbert (1963–)

Herb Lowe, who was the fifteenth president of the National Association of Black Journalists, is a staff writer for *Newsday* in New York. He was born in Camden, New Jersey, and was raised by a single mother. He is a 1984 graduate of Marquette University, where he double-majored in journalism and political science and was president of the campus organization for black journalism students. Before joining the staff of *Newsday* in February 2000, Lowe worked as reporter and editor for a number of other newspapers and one magazine. He has worked at the *Milwaukee Community Journal*; the *Press* in Atlantic City, New Jersey; the *Record* of Hackensack, New Jersey; the *Virginian-Pilot* in Norfolk, Virginia; and the *Philadelphia Inquirer*, where he spent six years. He also has been employed by *Amateur Sports* magazine and has been an adjunct journalism faculty member at Norfolk State University in Virginia. At *Newsday*, Lowe has covered the Queens County courts since October 2001. He has reported on crime, politics, real estate development, people attempting to do good works in their communities and even the Miss America Pageant.

Lowe long has been active in groups that advocate for and represent minority journalists. He was a member of the Hampton Roads Black Media Professionals group in the Norfolk, Virginia area; the Garden State Association of Black Journalists in New Jersey, which he served as president; and the Philadelphia Association of Black Journalists, the organization that in the early 1970s had provided the model for creating the National Association of Black Journalists. Lowe is the fifth member of the PABJ to serve as president of the national organization, joining founding president Chuck Stone (1975–1977), Arthur Fennell (1995–1997), Vanessa Williams (1997–1999) and Will Sutton (1999–2001). Before his election as president and chair of the organization's 19-member board, Lowe had been national secretary in 1995 and again in 1997, and vice president—print in 1999. In 1996, he helped turn the *NABJ Journal* into a magazine, replacing its old newsletter format, and in 2000–2001, he was managing editor of the organization's booklet "Committed to the Cause" that celebrated the contributions of those who had served as NABJ president. He ran unsuccessfully for president in 2001 but won the 2003 election, beating out candidates Cheryl Smith, editor of the *Dallas Weekly* and Mike Woolfolk of WACH-TV in Columbia, S.C. When he assumed the NABJ presidency, the group had around 3,100 members; at the end of his term, it was roughly 4,700 strong. Lowe was placed on the board of UNITY: Journalists of Color Inc., in November 2003. That group represents around 10,000 African-American, Asian-American, Native American and Hispanic journalists. Its conference held in August 2004 in the nation's capital attracted 8,100 members and is said to have been the largest gathering of journalists ever held in the United States. In May 2004, Lowe was listed by *Ebony* magazine as one of its 100 Most Influential Black Americans. During his NABJ presidency, the organization's Hall of Fame was brought back to life, and nearly all the 50 local chapters were audited. Lowe traveled considerably, appearing at all eight regional conferences and attending events in around 30 cities. After NBC anchorman Brian Williams made comments downplaying the importance of newsroom diversity, Lowe and three other NABJ members visited NBC News president Neal Shapiro to argue for the opposite view. Less successful was a visit to Hampton University to protest charges that the administration there had intimidated student journalists; those charges were refuted by Tony Brown, dean of the communications school there. Also, a NABJ stylebook was published during his administration, the Web site was revamped to be more up to date, and the awards event was moved to Washington, D.C., as opposed to being operated as part of the group's annual convention. In comments from the 2006 Unity convention, published by the Knight Foundation on Knightfdn.org, Lowe remarked that while greater numbers of minorities are now in positions of authority in the news media, the furthering of diversity will depend on whether journalism is seen as a decent, honorable trade. Lowe's wife, Mira Lowe, is an associate editor at *Newsday*, where she is in charge of LI Life, a section of the Sunday paper, recruitment and hiring, the intern program and the paper's training program for minority trainees.

Further Readings: "Herbert Lowe Biography." [Online, 2004]. National Association of Black Journalists site http://members.nabj.org/prezbio; Jones, Jackie. "Herbert Lowe Jr." [Online,

Lowe, Herbert

1 February 2006]. National Association of Black Journalists Web site www.nabj.org; Olisemeka, Nkechi. "Lowe Sees Legacy as 'NABJ 365.'" [Online, 2005]. NABJ Convention Web site www.nabjconvention.org; Prince, Richard. "Herb Lowe Wins 3-Way Race for NABJ President." [Online, 8 August 2003]. Richard Prince's Journal-isms. Maynard Institute Web site www.maynardije.org.